SINGLE CASE
EXPERIMENTAL DESIGNS

THIRD EDITION

SINGLE CASE EXPERIMENTAL DESIGNS

Strategies for Studying Behavior Change

DAVID H. BARLOW

Boston University

MATTHEW K. NOCK

Harvard University

MICHEL HERSEN

Pacific University

Boston ∎ New York ∎ San Francisco

Mexico City ∎ Montreal ∎ Toronto ∎ London ∎ Madrid ∎ Munich ∎ Paris

Hong Kong ∎ Singapore ∎ Tokyo ∎ Cape Town ∎ Sydney

Senior Series Editor / Series Editor: Susan Hartman
Series Editorial Assistant: Courtney Mullen
Marketing Manager: Kate Mitchell
Production Editor: Patrick Cash-Peterson
Editorial Production Service: TexTech International
Composition Buyer: Linda Cox
Manufacturing Buyer: JoAnne Sweeney
Electronic Composition: TexTech International
Cover Administrator: Elena Sidorova   *10 05465 745*

For related titles and support materials, visit our online catalog at www.ablongman.com.

Between the time website information is gathered and then published, it is not unusual for some sites to have closed. Also, the transcription of URLs can result in typographical errors. The publisher would appreciate notification where these errors occur so that they may be corrected in subsequent editions.

ISBN-13: 978-0-205-47455-4
ISBN-10:   0-205-47455-1

Library of Congress Cataloging-in-Publication Data
Barlow, David H.
    Single case experimental designs : strategies for studying behavior for change / David Barlow, Matthew Nock, Michel Hersen.—3rd ed.
        p. cm.
    Includes bibliographical references and index.
    ISBN-13: 978-0-205-47455-4
    ISBN-10:   0-205-47455-1
    1. Psychology—Research. 2. Experimental design. 3. Single subject research.
I. Nock, Matthew. II. Hersen, Michel. III. Title.
    BF76.5.H47 2009
    150.72'4—dc22

                                                                2008000545

Printed in the United States of America

10 9 8 7 6 5 4 3 2 1   12   11   10   09   08

CONTENTS

CHAPTER 3

General Procedures in Single-Case Research   61

CHAPTER 4

Behavior Assessment   99

CHAPTER 5

Basic A-B-A Withdrawal Designs   135

CHAPTER 6

Extensions of the A-B-A Design, Uses in Drug Evaluation and Interaction Design Strategies 167

CHAPTER 9

Statistical Analyses for Single-Case Experimental Designs 271

CHAPTER 10

━━━━━━

Beyond the Individual: Direct, Systematic, and Clinical Replication Procedures   307

PREFACE

■ ■ ■ ■ ■

In the preface to the first edition of this book in 1976 we said:

> We do not expect this book to be the final statement on single-case designs. We learned at least as much as we already knew in analyzing the variety of innovative and creative applications of these designs to varying applied problems. The unquestionable appropriateness of these designs in applied settings should ensure additional design innovations in the future.

Now, over 30 years have passed and the original authors (Barlow and Hersen), writing their first book at that time, are approaching the end of their careers providing an unusual perspective on the development of these methodologies. Since the second edition was published in 1984, the original authors were diverted into large scale clinical trial efforts as well as administration, but both continued to publish using single case design methodology. But we did not fully anticipate the explosive growth of interest in single-case designs and how many methodological and strategical innovations would subsequently appear. During this time new, fresh applied scientists have emerged with creative and innovative applications, and the original authors were fortunate to recruit one of the best of them, Matthew Nock, as an author representing this generation. In choosing experiments to best illustrate the varying design options, we decided to retain the best examples of some original and classic work, but to integrate new and more contemporary examples, some of which contain important innovations and extensions of the classic studies. As a result of developments in the 20 plus years since the second edition, this book can be more accurately described as new than as revised.

Developments in the field have not been restricted to new or modified experimental designs. New thinking has emerged on the analyses of data from these designs, particularly with regard to use of statistical procedures. We were most fortunate in having Tim Houle, one of the recognized experts in the world in this area write a new chapter taking into account these developments in statistical analyses for single-case experimental designs. Furthermore, the area of techniques of measurement and assessment relevant to single-case designs remains a bedrock of this methodology. Pat Friman, the current Editor of the *Journal of Applied behavior Analysis*, has strengthened the book considerably with his lucid chapter. Nevertheless, the primary purpose of the book was, and remains, the provision of a sourcebook of single-case designs, with guidelines for their use in applied settings.

To, Cherryl Blanding, Christine Cha, Alana Curewitz, Tara Deliberto, and Mara Fleisher, we express our deep appreciation for their efforts in pulling this edition together. And to our Editor, Susan Hartman for her encouragement and patience, and our publisher, Allyn and Bacon who kept the second edition in print for over 20 years, a heartfelt "thank you" Finally, this work really is the creation of the community of scientists dedicated to creating methodologies to better explore ways to alleviate human suffering and enhance human potential. These intellectual colleagues and forebears are now too numerous to name.

Since this is likely to be the last edition with which the original authors will be associated, we leave it to the next generation of applied scientists to realize Gordon Allport's vision to integrate an idiographic approach more fully into the applied research enterprise. It is to this next generation that we dedicate our efforts.

David H. Barlow
Nantucket Island

Matthew K. Nock
Cambridge, Massachusetts

Michel Hersen
Portland, Oregon

Epigram

Conversation between Tolman and Allport

TOLMAN: "I know I should be more idiographic in my research, but I just don't know how to be."

ALLPORT: "Let's learn!"

CHAPTER 1

THE SINGLE CASE IN BASIC AND APPLIED RESEARCH: AN HISTORICAL PERSPECTIVE

1.1. INTRODUCTION

The individual is of paramount importance in the clinical science of human behavior change. Until recently, however, this science lacked an adequate methodology for studying behavior change in individuals. This gap in our methodology has retarded the development and evaluation of new procedures in the mental health professions as well as in educational fields.

Historically, the intensive study of the individual held a preeminent place in the fields of psychology and psychiatry. In spite of this background, an adequate experimental methodology for studying the individual was very slow to develop in applied research.* To find out why, it is useful to gain some perspective on the historical development of methodology in the broad area of psychological research.

The purpose of this chapter is to provide such a perspective, beginning with the origins of methodology in the basic sciences of physiology and experimental psychology in the middle of the 19th century. Because most of this early work was performed on individual organisms, reasons for the development of between-group comparison methodology in basic research (which did not occur until the beginning of the 20th century) are outlined. The rapid development of inferential statistics and sampling theory during the early 20th century enabled greater sophistication in research methodology. The manner in which this affected research methods in applied areas during the middle of the century is discussed.

In the meantime, applied research was off to a shaky start in the offices of early psychiatrists with a technique known as the case study method. The separate development of applied research is traced from those early beginnings through the grand collaborative group comparison studies proposed in the 1950s. Difficulties with this approach in applied research became apparent and

---

*In this book applied research refers to experimentation in the area of human behavior change relevant to the health-related professions and education and with an emphasis on mental health and disorders.

forced a search for alternatives. The rise and fall of the major alternatives—process research and naturalistic studies—is outlined near the end of the chapter. This disenchantment also set the stage for a renewal of interest in the scientific study of the individual. The multiple origins of single-case experimental designs in the laboratories of experimental psychology and the offices of clinicians complete the chapter. Descriptions of single-case designs and guidelines for their use as they are evolving in applied research comprise the remainder of this book.

1.2. BEGINNINGS IN EXPERIMENTAL PHYSIOLOGY AND PSYCHOLOGY

The scientific study of individual human behavior has roots deep in the history of psychology and physiology. When psychology and physiology became sciences, the initial experiments were performed on individual organisms, and the results of these pioneering endeavors remain relevant to the scientific world today. The science of physiology began in the 1830s, with Johannes Müller and Claude Bernard, but an important landmark for applied research was the work of Paul Broca in 1861. At this time, Broca was caring for a man who was hospitalized for an inability to speak intelligibly. Before the man died, Broca examined him carefully; subsequent to death, he performed an autopsy. The finding of a lesion in the third frontal convolution of the cerebral cortex convinced Broca, and eventually the rest of the scientific world, that this was the speech center of the brain. Broca's method was the clinical extension of the newly developed experimental methodology called *extirpation of parts*, introduced to physiology by Marshall Hall and Pierre Flouren in the 1850s. In this method, brain function was mapped out by systematically destroying parts of the brain in animals and noting the effects on behavior.

The importance of this research in the context of the present discussion lies in the demonstration that important findings with wide generality were gleaned from single organisms. This methodology was to have a major impact on the beginnings of experimental psychology.

Boring (1950) fixed the beginnings of experimental psychology in 1860, with the publication of Fechner's *Elemente der Psychophysik*. Fechner is most famous for developing measures of sensation through several psychophysical methods. With these methods, Fechner was able to determine sensory thresholds and just noticeable differences (JNDs) in various sense modalities. What is common to these methods is the repeated measurement of a response at different intensities or different locations of a given stimulus in an individual subject. For example, when stimulating skin with two points in a certain region to determine the minimal separation which the subject reliably recognizes as two stimulations, one may use the method of constant stimuli. In this method the two points repeatedly stimulate two areas of skin at five to seven fixed separations, in random order, ranging from a few millimeters apart to the relatively large separation of 10 mm.

During each stimulation, the subject reports whether he or she senses one point or two. After repeated trials, the point at which the subject "notices" two separate points can be determined. It is interesting to note that Fechner was one of the first to apply statistical methods to psychological problems. Fechner noticed that judgments of just noticeable differences in the sensory modalities varied somewhat from trial to trial. To quantify this variation, or "error" in judgment, he borrowed the normal law of error and demonstrated that these errors were normally distributed around a mean, which then became the "true" sensory threshold. This use of descriptive statistics anticipated the application of these procedures to groups of individuals at the turn of the century, when traits or capabilities were also found to be normally distributed around a mean. The emphasis on error, or the average response, raised issues regarding imprecision of measurement that were to be highlighted in between group comparison approaches (see below and chapter 2). It should be noted, however, that Fechner was concerned with variability *within* the subject, and he continued his remarkable work on series of individuals.

These traditions in methodology were continued by Wilhelm Wundt. Wundt's contributions, and those of his students and followers, most notably Titchener, had an important impact on the field of psychology, but it is the scientific methodology he and his students employed that most interests us.

To Wundt, the subject matter of psychology was immediate experience, such as how a subject experiences light and sound. Since these experiences were private events and could not be directly observed, Wundt created a new method called *introspection*. Mention of the procedure may strike a responsive chord in some modern-day clinicians, but in fact this methodology is quite different from the first introspection technique of free association and related strategies, often used in clinical settings to uncover repressed or unconscious material. Nor did introspection bear any relation to the armchair dreams or reflections that are so frequently a part of experience. Introspection, as Wundt employed it, was a highly specific and rigorous procedure that was used with individual subjects who were highly trained. This training involved learning to describe experiences in an objective manner, free from emotional or language restraints. For example, the experience of seeing a brightly colored object would be described in terms of shapes and hues without recourse to aesthetic appeal. To illustrate the objectivity of this system, introspection of emotional experiences where scientific calm and objectivity might be disrupted was not allowed. Introspection of this experience was to be done at a later date when the scientific attitude returned. This method, then, became retrospection, and the weaknesses of this approach were accepted by Wundt to preserve objectivity. Like Fechner's psychophysics, which is essentially an introspectionist methodology, the emphasis hinges on the study of a highly trained individual with the clear assumption, after some replication on other individuals, that findings would have generality to the population of individuals.

Wundt and his followers comprised a school of psychology known as the Structuralist School, and many topics important to psychology were first studied with this rather primitive but individually oriented form of scientific analysis. The major subject matter, however, continued to be sensation and perception. With Fechner's psychophysical methods, the groundwork for the study of sensation and perception was laid. Perhaps because of these beginnings, a strong tradition of studying individual organisms has ensued in the fields of sensation and perception and physiological psychology. This tradition has not extended to other areas of experimental psychology, such as learning, or to the more clinical areas of investigation that are broadly based on learning principles or theories. This course of events is surprising because the efforts to study principles of learning comprise one of the more famous examples of the scientific study of the single-case. This effort was made by Hermann Ebbinghaus, one of the towering figures in the development of psychology. With a belief in the scientific approach to psychology, and heavily influenced by Fechner's methods (Boring, 1950), Ebbinghaus established principles of human learning that remain basic to work in this area.

Basic to Ebbinghaus's experiments was the invention of a new instrument to measure learning and forgetting—the nonsense syllable. With a long list of nonsense syllables and himself as the subject, he investigated the effects of different variables (such as the amount of material to be remembered) on the efficiency of memory. Perhaps his best known discovery was the retention curve, which illustrated the process of forgetting over time. Chaplin and Kraweic (1960) noted that he "worked so carefully that the results of his experiments have never been seriously questioned" (p. 180). But what is most relevant and remarkable about his work is his emphasis on repeated measures of performance in one individual over time (see chapter 4). As Boring (1950) pointed out, Ebbinghaus made repetition the basis for the experimental measurement of memory. It would be some 70 years before a new approach, called the *experimental analysis of behavior*, was to employ repeated measurement in individuals to study complex animal and human behaviors.

One of the best known scientists in the fields of physiology and psychology during these early years was Pavlov (Pavlov, 1928). Although Pavlov considered himself a physiologist, his work on principles of association and learning was his greatest contribution, and, along with his basic methodology, is so well known that summaries are not required. What is often overlooked, however, is that Pavlov's basic findings were gleaned from single organisms and strengthened by replication on other organisms. In terms of scientific yield, the study of the individual organism reached an early peak with Pavlov, and Skinner would later cite this approach as an important link and a strong bond between himself and Pavlov (Skinner, 1966a).

1.3. ORIGINS OF THE GROUP COMPARISON APPROACH

Important research in experimental psychology and physiology using single cases did not stop with these efforts, but the beginning of the 20th century witnessed a new development which would have a marked effect on basic and, at a later date, applied research. This development was the discovery and measurement of individual differences. The study of individual differences can be traced to Adolphe Quetelet, a Belgian astronomer, who discovered that human traits (e.g., height) followed the normal curve (Stilson, 1966). Quetelet interpreted these findings to mean that nature strove to produce the "average" man but, due to various reasons, failed, resulting in errors or variances in traits that grouped around the average. As one moved further from this average, fewer examples of the trait were evident, following the well-known normal distribution. This approach, in turn, had its origins in Darwin's observations on individual variation within a species. Quetelet viewed these variations or errors as unfortunate because he viewed the average man, which he termed *l'homme moyen*, as a cherished goal rather than a descriptive fact of central tendency. If nature were "striving" to produce the average man, but failed due to various accidents, then the average, in this view, was obviously the ideal. Where nature failed, however, man could pick up the pieces, account for the errors, and estimate the average man through statistical techniques. The influence of this finding on psychological research was enormous, as it paved the way for the application of sophisticated statistical procedures to psychological problems. Quetelet would probably be distressed to learn, however, that his concept of the average individual would come under attack during the 20th century by those who observed that there is no average individual (e.g., Dunlap, 1932; Sidman, 1960).

This viewpoint notwithstanding, the study of individual differences and the statistical approach to psychology became prominent during the first half of the 20th century and changed the face of psychological research. With a push from the American functional school of psychology and a developing interest in the measurement and testing of intelligence, the foundation for comparing groups of individuals was laid.

Galton and Pearson expanded the study of individual differences at the beginning of the 20th century and developed many of the descriptive statistics still in use today, most notably the notion of correlation, which led to factor analysis, and significant advances in construction of intelligence tests first introduced by Binet in 1905. At about this time, Pearson, along with Galton and Weldon, founded the journal *Biometricka* with the purpose of advancing quantitative research in biology and psychology. Many of the newly devised statistical tests were first published there. Pearson was highly enthusiastic about the statistical approach and seemed to believe, at times, that inaccurate data could be made to yield accurate conclusions if the proper statistics were applied (Boring, 1950). Although this view was rejected by more conservative colleagues, it points up a confidence in the power of statistical procedures that reappears from time to time in the execution of psychological research (e.g., D. A. Shapiro & Shapiro, 1983; M. L. Smith & Glass, 1977; G. T. Wilson & Rachman, 1983).

One of the best known psychologists to adopt this approach was James McKeen Cattell. Cattell, along with Farrand, devised a number of simple mental tests that were administered to freshmen at Columbia University to determine the range of individual differences. Cattell also devised the order of merit method, whereby a number of judges would rank items or people on a given quality, and the average response of the judges constituted the rank of that item vis-à-vis other items. In this way, Cattell had ten scientists rate a number of eminent colleagues. The scientist with the highest score (on the average) achieved the top rank.

It may seem ironic at first glance that a concern with individual differences led to an emphasis on groups and averages, but differences among individuals, or intersubject variability, and the distribution of these differences necessitate a comparison among individuals and a concern for a description of a group or population as a whole. In this context, observations from a single organism are irrelevant. Darwin, after all, was concerned with survival of a species and not the survival of individual organisms.

The invention of many of the descriptive statistics and some crude statistical tests of comparison made it easier to compare performance in large groups of subjects. From 1900 to 1930, much of the research in experimental psychology, particularly learning, took advantage of these statistics to compare groups of subjects (usually rats) on various performance tests (e.g., see Birney & Teevan, 1961). Crude statistics that could attribute differences between groups to something other than chance began to appear, such as the critical ratio test (Walker & Lev, 1953). The idea that the variability or error among organisms could be accounted for or averaged out in large groups was a commonsense notion emanating from the new emphasis on variability among organisms. The fact that this research resulted in an average finding from the hypothetical average rat drew some isolated criticism. For instance, in 1932, while reviewing research in experimental psychology, Dunlap pointed out that there was no average rat, and Lewin (1933) noted that ". . . the only situations which should be grouped for statistical treatment are those which have for the individual rats or for the individual children the same psychological structure and only for such period of time as this structure exists" (p. 328).

The influence of inferential statistics

During the 1930s, the work of R. A. Fisher, which subsequently exerted considerable influence on psychological research, first appeared. Many sophisticated statistical procedures for comparing groups were developed by Fisher. It would be difficult to pick up psychological or psychiatric journals concerned with behavior change and not find research data analyzed by the ubiquitous analysis of variance. It is interesting, however, to consider the origin of these tests. Early in his career, Fisher, who was a mathematician interested in genetics, made an important decision. Faced with pursuing a career at a biometrics laboratory, he chose instead a relatively obscure agricultural station on the grounds that this position would offer him more opportunity for independent research. This personal decision at the very least changed the language of experimental design in psychological research, introducing agricultural terms to describe relevant designs and variables (e.g., split plot analysis of variance). While Fisher's statistical innovations were one of the more important developments of the century for psychology, the philosophy underlying the use of these procedures is clearly in line with Quetelet's notion of the importance of the average. As a good agronomist, Fisher was concerned with the yield from a given area of land under various soil treatments, plant varieties, or other agricultural variables. Much as in the study of individual differences, the fate of the individual plant is irrelevant in the context of the yield from the group of plants in that area. Agricultural variables are important to the farm and society if the yield is better *on the average* than a similar plot treated differently. The implications of this philosophy for applied research will be discussed in chapter 2.

The work of Fisher was not limited to the invention of sophisticated statistical tests. An equally important contribution was the consideration of the problem of induction or inference. Essentially, this issue concerns generality of findings. If some data are obtained from a group or a plot of land, this information is not very valuable if it is relevant only to that particular group or plot of land because similar data must be collected from each new plot. Fisher (1925) worked out the properties of statistical tests, which made it possible to estimate the relevance of data from one small group with certain characteristics to the universe of individuals with those characteristics. In other words, inference is made from the sample to the population. This work and the subsequent developments in the field of sampling theory made it possible to talk in terms of psychological principles with broad generality and applicability—a primary goal in any science. This type of estimation, however, was based on appropriate statistics, averages, and intersubject variability in the sample, which further reinforced the group comparison approach in basic research.

As the science of psychology grew out of its infancy, its methodology was largely determined by the lure of broad generality of findings made possible through the brilliant work of Fisher and his followers. Because of the emphasis on averages and intersubject variability required by this design in order to make general statements, the intensive study of the single organism, so popular in the early history of psychology, fell out of favor. By the 1950s, when investigators began to consider the possibility of doing serious research in applied settings, the group comparison approach was so entrenched that anyone studying single organisms was considered something of an oddity by no less an authority than Underwood (1957). The zeitgeist in psychological research was group comparison and statistical estimation. While an occasional paper was published during the 1950s defending the study of the single-case (S. J. Beck, 1953; Rosenzweig, 1951), or at least pointing out its place in psychological research (duMas, 1955), very little basic research was carried out on single-cases. A notable exception was the work of B. F. Skinner and his students and colleagues, who were busy developing an approach known as the experimental analysis of behavior, or operant conditioning. This work, however, did not have a large impact on methodology in other areas of psychology during the 1950s, and applied research was just beginning. Against this background, it is not surprising that applied researchers in the 1950s employed the group comparison approach, despite the fact that the origins of the study of clinically relevant phenomena were quite different from the origin of more basic research described above.

1.4. DEVELOPMENT OF APPLIED RESEARCH: THE CASE STUDY METHOD

As the sciences of physiology and psychology were developing during the late 19th and 20th centuries, people were suffering from emotional and behavioral problems and were receiving treatment. Occasionally, patients recovered, and therapists would carefully document their procedures and communicate them to colleagues. Hypotheses attributing success or failure to various assumed causes emanated from these cases, and these hypotheses gradually grew into theories of psychotherapy. Theories proliferated, and procedures based on observations of cases and inferences from these theories grew in number. As Paul (1969) noted, those theories or procedures that could be communicated clearly or that presented new and exciting principles tended to attract followers to the organization, and schools of psychotherapy were formed. At the heart of this process is the *case study* method of investigation (Bolger, 1965). This method (and its extensions) was, with few exceptions, the sole methodology of clinical investigation through the first half of the 20th century.

The case study method, of course, is the clinical base for the experimental study of single-cases and, as such, it retains an important function in present-day applied research (APA, 2002; Barlow, 1980; Barlow, Hayes, & Nelson, 1984; Hayes, Barlow, & Nelson-Gray, 1999; Kazdin, 2003) (see section 1.7). Unfortunately, during this period clinicians were unaware, for the most part, of the basic principles of applied research, such as definition of variables and manipulation of independent variables. Thus, it is noteworthy from an historical point of view that several case studies reported during this period came tantalizingly close to providing the basic scientific ingredients of experimental single-case research. The most famous of these, of course, is the J. B. Watson and Rayner (1920) study of an analogue of clinical phobia in a young boy, where a prototype of a *withdrawal* design was attempted (see chapter 5). These investigators unfortunately suffered the fate of many modern-day clinical researchers in that the subject moved away before the "reversal" was complete.

Anytime that a treatment produced demonstrable effects on an observable behavior disorder, the potential for scientific investigation was there. An excellent example, among many, was Breuer's classic description of the treatment of hysterical symptoms in Anna O. through psychoanalysis in 1895 (Breuer & Freud, 1957). In a series of treatment sessions, Breuer dealt with one symptom at a time through hypnosis and subsequent "talking through," where each symptom was traced back to its hypothetical causation in circumstances surrounding the death of her father. One at a time, these behaviors disappeared, but only when treatment was administered to each respective behavior. This process of treating one behavior at a time fulfills the basic requirement for a multiple baseline experimental design described in chapter 7, and the clearly observable success indicated that Breuer's treatment was effective. Of course, Breuer did not define his independent variables, in that there were several components to his treatment (e.g., hypnosis, interpretation); but, in the manner of a good scientist as well as a good clinician, Breuer admitted that he did not know which component or components of his treatment were responsible for success. He noted at least two possibilities, the suggestion inherent in the hypnosis, or the interpretation. He then described events discovered through his talking therapy as possibly having etiological significance and wondered about the reliability of the girl's report as he hypothesized various etiologies for the symptoms. However, he did not, at the time, firmly link successful treatment with the necessity of discovering the etiology of the behavior disorder. One wonders if the early development of clinical techniques, including psychoanalysis, would have been different if careful observers like Breuer had been cognizant of the experimental implications of their clinical work. Of course, this small leap from uncontrolled case study to scientific investigation of the single case did not occur to early clinicians because of a lack of awareness of basic scientific methods that would make this possible. The result was an accumulation of successful individuals' case studies, with clinicians from varying schools claiming that their techniques were indispensable to success. In many cases their claims were grossly exaggerated. Brill noted in 1909 of psychoanalysis that "The results obtained by the treatment are unquestionably very gratifying. They surpass those obtained by simpler methods in two chief respects; namely, in permanence and in the prophylactic value they have for the future" (Brill, 1909). Later, in 1935, Kessel and Hyman observed, "this patient was saved from an inferno and we are convinced that this could have been achieved by no other method" (Kessel & Hyman, 1933). From an early behavioral standpoint, Max (1935) noted that electrical aversion therapy produced "95 percent relief" from the compulsion of homosexuality. Of course, dramatic and sweeping claims of causality continue to be made from nothing more than an uncontrolled case study.

These kinds of statements did little to endear the case study method to serious applied researchers when they began to appear in the 1940s and 1950s. In fact, the case study method, if anything, deteriorated somewhat over the years in terms of the amount and nature of publicly observable data available in these reports. Frank (1961) noted the difficulty in even collecting data from a therapeutic hour in the 1930s due to lack of necessary equipment, reluctance to take detailed notes, and concern about confidentiality. The advent of the phonograph record at this time made it possible at least to collect raw data from those clinicians who would cooperate, but this method did not lead to any fruitful new ideas on research. With the advent of serious applied research in the 1950s, investigators tended to reject reports from uncontrolled case studies due to an inability to evaluate the effects of treatment. Given the extraordinary claims by clinicians after successful case studies, this attitude is understandable. However, from the viewpoint of single-case experimental designs, this rejection of the careful observation of behavior change in a case report had the effect of throwing out the baby with the bathwater.

Early reports of percentage of success in treated groups

A further development in applied research was the reporting of collections of case studies in terms of percentage of success. Many of these reports were cited by Eysenck (1952). However, reporting of results in this manner from these early studies probably did more harm than good to the scientifically based evaluation of clinical treatment. As Paul (1969) noted, independent and dependent variables were no better defined than in most case reports, and techniques tended to be fixed and "school" oriented. Because all procedures achieved some success, practitioners within these schools concentrated on the positive results, explained away the failures, and decided that the overall results confirmed that their procedures, as applied, were responsible for the success. Due to the strong and overriding theories central to each school, the successes obtained were attributed to theoretical constructs underlying the procedure. This precluded a careful analysis of elements in the procedure or the therapeutic intervention that may have been responsible for certain changes in a given case, these methods also had the effect of reinforcing the application of a global, ill-defined treatment from whatever theoretical orientation, to global definitions of behavior disorders, such as *neurosis*. This, in turn, led to statements such as "psychotherapy works with neurotics." Although applied researchers later rejected these efforts as unscientific, one carryover from this approach was the notion of the average response to treatment without regard to specific individual outcome; that is, if a global treatment is successful on the average with a group of "neurotics," then this treatment will probably be successful with any individual "neurotic" who requests treatment.

Intuitively, of course, descriptions of results from 50 cases provide a more convincing demonstration of the effectiveness of a given technique than separate descriptions of 50 individual cases. A modification of this approach utilizing updated strategies and procedures and with the focus on individual responses has been termed *clinical replication*. This strategy can make a substantial contribution to the applied research process (see chapter 10). The major difficulty with this approach, however, particularly as it was practiced in early years, is that the category in which these clients are classified most always becomes unmanageably heterogeneous. The individual with "neuroticism" described in Eysenck's (1952) paper may have less in common than any group of people one would choose randomly. When cases are described individually, a clinician stands a better chance of gleaning some important information, since specific problems and specific procedures are usually described in more detail. When one lumps cases together in broadly defined categories, individual case descriptions are lost and the ensuing report of percentage success becomes meaningless. This unavoidable heterogeneity in any group of patients is an important consideration that will be discussed in more detail in this chapter and in chapter 2.

The development of the group comparison approach in applied research

By the late 1940s, clinical psychology and, to a lesser extent, psychiatry began to produce the type of clinician who was also aware of basic research strategies. These scientists were quick to point out the drawbacks of both the case study and reports of percentages of success in groups in evaluating the effects of psychotherapy. They noted that any adequate test of psychotherapy would have to include a more precise definition of terms, particularly *outcome criteria* or *dependent variables* (e.g., Knight, 1941). Most of these applied researchers were trained as psychologists, and in psychology a new emphasis was placed on the "scientist-practitioner" model (Barlow et al., 1984; Hayes et al., 1999). Thus, the source of research methodology in the newly developing areas of applied research came from experimental psychology. By this time, the predominant methodology in experimental psychology was the between-subjects group design.

The group design also was a logical extension of the earlier clinical reports of percentage success in a large group of patients, because the most obvious criticism of this endeavor is the absence of a control group of untreated patients. The appearance of Eysenck's (1952) ground-breaking article comparing percentage success of psychotherapy in large groups to rates of "spontaneous" remission gleaned from discharge rates at state hospitals and insurance company records had two effects. *First*, it reinforced the growing conviction that the effects of psychotherapy could not be evaluated from case reports or "percentage success groups" and sparked a new flurry of interest in evaluating psychotherapy through the scientific method. *Second*, the emphasis on comparison between groups and quasi-control groups in Eysenck's review strengthened the notion that the logical way to evaluate psychotherapy was through the prevailing methodology in experimental psychology—the between-groups comparison designs.

This approach to applied research did not suddenly begin in the 1950s, although interest certainly increased at this time. Scattered examples of research with clinically relevant problems can be found in earlier decades. One interesting example is a study reported by Kantorovich (1928), who applied aversion therapy based on pairing emetics with the taste and smell of alcohol to one group of twenty alcoholics in Russia and compared results to a control group receiving hypnosis or medication. The success of this treatment (and the direct derivation from Pavlov's work) most likely ensured a prominent place for aversion therapy in Russian treatment programs for alcoholics. Some of the larger group comparison studies typical of the 1950s also began before Eysenck's celebrated paper. One of the best known is the Cambridge-Somerville youth study, which was reported in 1951 (Powers & Witmer, 1951) but was actually begun in 1937. Although this was an early study, it is quite representative of the large group comparison studies of the mid 20th century in that many of the difficulties in execution and analysis of results were repeated again and again as these studies accumulated.

The major difficulty, of course, was that these studies did not prove that psychotherapy worked. In the Cambridge-Somerville study, despite the advantages of a well-designed experiment, the discouraging finding was that "counseling" for delinquents or potential delinquents had no significant effect when compared to a well-matched control group.

When this finding was repeated in subsequent studies (e.g., Barron & Leary, 1955), the controversy over Eysenck's assertion on the ineffectiveness of psychotherapy became heated. Most clinicians rejected the findings outright because they were convinced that psychotherapy was useful, while scientists such as Eysenck hardened their convictions that psychotherapy was at best ineffective and at worst some kind of great hoax perpetrated on unsuspecting clients. This controversy, in turn, left serious applied researchers groping for answers to difficult methodological questions on how to even approach the issue of evaluating effectiveness in psychotherapy. As a result, major conferences on research in psychotherapy were called during this era to discuss these questions (e.g., Rubenstein & Parloff, 1959). It was not until Bergin reexamined these studies in a very important article (Bergin, 1966; see also Bergin & Lambert, 1978) that some of the discrepancies between clinical evidence from uncontrolled case studies and experimental evidence from between-subject group comparison designs were clarified. Bergin noted that some clients were improving in these studies, but others were getting worse. When subjected to statistical averaging of results, these effects with their large error terms canceled each other out, yielding an overall result of no effect when compared to the control group. Furthermore, Bergin pointed out that these therapeutic effects had been described in the original articles, but only as afterthoughts to the major statistical findings of no effect. Reviewers such as Eysenck, approaching the results from a methodological point of view, concentrated on the statistical findings. These studies did not, however, prove that psychotherapy was ineffective for a given individual. What these results demonstrated is that people, particularly clients with emotional or behavioral disorders, are quite different from each other. Thus attempts to apply an ill-defined and global treatment such as psychotherapy to a heterogeneous group of clients classified under a vague diagnostic category such as neurosis are incapable of answering the more basic question on the effectiveness of a specific treatment for a specific individual.

The conclusion that psychotherapy was ineffective was premature, based on this reanalysis, but the overriding conclusion from Bergin's review was that

"Is psychotherapy effective?" was the wrong question to ask in the first place, even when appropriate between-group experimental designs were employed. During the 1960s, scientists (e.g., Paul, 1967) began to realize that any test of a global treatment such as psychotherapy would not be fruitful and that clinical researchers must start defining the independent variables more precisely and must ask the question: "What specific treatment is effective with a specific type of client under what circumstances?"

1.5. LIMITATIONS OF EARLY GROUP COMPARISON APPROACHES

The clearer definition of variables and the call for experimental questions that were precise enough to be answered were major advances in applied research. The extensive review of psychotherapy research by Bergin and Strupp (1972), however, demonstrated that even under these more favorable conditions, the application of the group comparison design to applied problems posed difficulties, many of which have been overcome more recently. These difficulties, or objections, which tended to limit the usefulness of early group comparison approaches in applied research, can be classified under five headings: (1) ethical objections, (2) practical problems in collecting large numbers of patients homogeneous for the targeted disorder or problem, (3) averaging of results over the group, (4) generality of findings, and (5) intersubject variability.

Ethical objections and practical problems

An oft-cited issue, usually voiced by clinicians, is the ethical problem inherent in withholding treatment from a no-treatment control group. This notion, of course, is based on the assumption that the therapeutic intervention, in fact, works, in which case there would be little need to test it at all. This objection has become even more relevant in recent years with the clear establishment of empirically supported treatments (Barlow, 2001; Nathan & Gorman, 2002). Despite the seeming illogic of this ethical objection for treatment without proven effectiveness, in practice many clinicians and other professional personnel react with distaste to withholding some treatment, however inadequate, from a group of clients who are undergoing significant human suffering. This attitude is reinforced by scattered examples of experiments where control groups did endure substantial harm during the course of the research, particularly in some pharmacological experiments.

On a more practical level, the collection of large numbers of clients homogeneous for a particular behavior disorder proven to be a very difficult task. In basic research in experimental psychology most subjects are animals (or college sophomores), where matching of relevant behaviors or background variables such as personality characteristics is feasible. When dealing with severe behavior disorders, however, obtaining sufficient clients suitably matched to constitute the required groups in the study was an insurmountable obstacle in many cases. The reason for this included the lack of an agreed-upon system of nosology prior to 1980 in the case of psychological disorders. Also, the vision of large, often multi-site, clinical trials had not yet been realized, so neither the infrastructure, in the form of large, specialty research clinics, nor resources from government funding agencies were available.

This began to change in the 1980s, most notably with a study by the National Institute of Mental Health testing the effectiveness of cognitive behavioral and Interpersonal Psychotherapy treatment of depression (NIMH, 1980; Elkin et al., 1989).

Averaging of results

A third difficulty noted by many applied researchers is the obscuring of individual clinical outcome in group averages. This issue was cogently raised early on by Sidman (1960) and Chassan (1967, 1979) and repeatedly finds its way into the informal discussions with leading researchers conducted by Bergin and Strupp and published in their book, *Changing Frontiers in the Science of Psychotherapy* (1972). Bergin's (1966) review of large-outcome studies where some clients improved and others worsened highlighted this problem. As noted earlier, a move away from tests of global treatments of ill-defined variables with the implicit question "Is psychotherapy effective?" was a step in the right direction. But even when specific questions on effects of therapy in homogeneous groups are approached from the group comparison point of view, the problem of obscuring important findings remains because of the enormous complexities of any individual patient included in a given treatment group. The fact that patients are seldom truly "homogeneous" was described by Kiesler (1966) in his discussion of the patient uniformity myth. For example, 10 patients, homogeneous for obsessive-compulsive disorder, may bring entirely different histories, personality variables, and environmental situations to the treatment setting and will respond in varying ways to treatment. That is, some patients will improve and others will not. The average response, however, will not represent the performance of any individual in the group.

Generality of findings

Averaging and the complexity of individual patients also bring up some related problems. Because results from group studies do not reflect changes in individual patients, these findings are not readily translatable or generalizable to the practicing clinician since, as Chassan (1967) pointed out, the clinician cannot determine which particular patient characteristics are correlated with improvement. In ignorance of the responses of individual patients to treatment, the clinician does not know to what extent a given patient is similar to patients who improved or perhaps deteriorated within the context of an overall group improvement. Furthermore, as groups become more homogeneous, which most researchers agree is a necessary condition to answer specific questions about effects of therapy, one loses, the ability to make inferential statements to the population of patients with a particular disorder because the individual complexities in the population will not have been adequately sampled. Thus it becomes difficult to generalize findings at all beyond the specific group of patients in the experiment. These issues of averaging and generality of findings will be discussed in greater detail in chapter 2.

Intersubject variability

A final issue bothersome to clinicians and applied researchers is variability. Between-subject group comparison designs traditionally considering only variability between subjects as a method of dealing with the enormous differences among individuals in a group. Progress in early studies was usually assessed only once (in a posttest). This large intersubject variability was, in part, responsible for the "weak" effect obtained in these studies, where some clients showed considerable improvement and others deteriorated, and the average improvement was statistically significant but clinically weak. Ignored in these studies was within-subject variability or the clinical course of a specific patient during treatment, which is of great practical interest to clinicians. This issue will also be discussed more fully in chapter 2. Of course, many of these early disadvantages have been overcome or investigations have proposed thoughtful integration of the strengths of these methodologies (e.g., Nugent, 1996).

1.6. EARLY ALTERNATIVE APPROACHES TO APPLIED RESEARCH

Many of these practical and methodological difficulties seemed overwhelming to clinicians and applied researchers. Some investigators wondered if serious, meaningful research on evaluation of psychotherapy was even possible (e.g., Hyman & Berger, 1966), and the gap between clinician and scientist widened. One difficulty here was the restriction placed on the type of methodology and experimental design applicable to applied research. For many scientists, a group comparison design was the only methodology capable of yielding important information in psychotherapy studies. In view of the dearth of alternatives available and against the background of case study and "percentage success" efforts, these high standards were understandable and correct. Since there were no clearly acceptable scientific alternatives, however, applied researchers failed to distinguish between those situations where group comparison designs were practical, desirable, and necessary (see section 2.9) and situations where the development of alternative methodology was required. During the 1950s and 1960s, several alternatives were tested.

Many applied researchers reacted to the difficulties of the group comparison approach with a "flight into process" where components of the therapeutic process, such as relationship variables, were carefully studied (Hoch & Zubin, 1964). A second approach, favored by many clinicians, was the "naturalistic study," which was very close to actual clinical practice but had dubious scientific underpinnings. As Kiesler (1971) noted at the time, these approaches are quite closely related because both are based on *correlational* methods, where dependent variables are correlated with therapist or patient variables either within therapy or at some point after therapy. This is distinguished from the *experimental* approach, where independent variables are systematically manipulated.

Naturalistic studies

The advantage of the naturalistic study for most clinicians was that it did little to disrupt the typical activities engaged in by clinicians in day-to-day practice. Unlike with the experimental group comparison design, clinicians were not restricted by precise definitions of an independent variable (treatment, time limitation, or random assignment of patients to groups). Kiesler (1971) noted that naturalistic studies involve ". . . live, unaltered, minimally controlled, unmanipulated 'natural' psychotherapy sequences—so-called experiments of nature" (p. 54). This approach had great appeal to clinicians, for it dealt directly with their activities and, in doing so, promised to consider the complexities inherent in treatment. Typically, measures of multiple therapist and patient behaviors are taken, so that all relevant variables (based on a given clinician's conceptualization of which variables are relevant) may be examined for interrelationships with every other variable.

This approach would evolve in later years into "qualitative" research with its emphasis on systematic observation of naturally occurring processes for purpose of hypothesis generation. Perhaps the best known example of this type of study is the project at the Menninger Foundation (Kernberg, 1973). Begun in 1954, this was truly a mammoth undertaking involving 38 investigators, 10 consultants, three different project leaders, and 18 years of planning and data collection. Forty-two patients were studied in this project. This group was broadly defined, although overtly psychotic patients were excluded. Assignment of patient to therapist and to differing modes of psychoanalytic treatment was not random but based on clinical judgments of which therapist or mode of treatment was most suitable for the patient. In other words, the procedures were those normally in effect in a clinical setting. In addition, other treatments, such as pharmacological or organic interventions, were administered to certain patients as needed. Against this background, the investigators measured multiple patient characteristics (such as various components of ego strength) and correlated these variables, measured periodically throughout treatment by referring to detailed records of treatment sessions, with multiple therapeutic activities and modes of treatment. As one would expect, the results were enormously complex and contain many seemingly contradictory findings. At least one observer (Malan, 1973) noted that the most important finding is that purely supportive treatment is ineffective with borderline psychotics, but working through of the transference relationship under hospitalization with this group is effective. Notwithstanding the global definition of treatment and the broad and vague diagnostic categories (borderline psychotic) also present in early group comparison studies, this report was generally hailed as an extremely important breakthrough in psychotherapy research. Methodologists, even then, however, were not so sure. While admitting the benefits of a clearer definition of psychoanalytic terms emanating from the project, May (1973) wondered about the power and significance of the conclusions. Most of this criticism concerns the purported strength of the naturalistic study—that is, the lack of control over factors in the naturalistic setting. If subjects are assigned to treatments based on certain characteristics, were these characteristics responsible for improvement rather than the treatment? What is the contribution of additional treatments received by certain patients? Did nurses and other therapists possibly react differently to patients in one group or another? What was the contribution of "spontaneous remission"?

In its pure state, the naturalistic study does not advance much beyond the uncontrolled case study in the power to isolate the effectiveness of a given treatment, as severe critics of the procedure pointed out (e.g., Bergin & Strupp, 1972), but this process is an improvement over case studies or reports of "percentage success" in groups, because measures of relevant variables are constructed and administered, sometimes repeatedly. However, to increase confidence in any correlational findings from naturalistic studies, it would seem necessary to undermine the stated strengths of the study—that is, the "unaltered, minimally controlled, unmanipulated" condition prevailing in the typical naturalistic project—by randomly assigning patients, limiting access to additional confounding modes of treatment, and observing deviation of therapists from prescribed treatment forms. But if this were done, the study would no longer be naturalistic.

A further problem was obvious from the example of the Menninger project. The practical difficulties in executing this type of study seem very little less than those inherent in the large group comparison approach. The one exception is that the naturalistic study, in retaining close ties to the actual functioning of the clinic, requires less structuring or manipulating of large numbers of patients and therapists. The fact that this project took 18 years to complete makes one consider the significant administrative problem inherent in maintaining a research effort for this length of time. This factor is most likely responsible for the admission from one prominent member of the Menninger team, Robert S. Wallerstein, that he would not undertake such a project again (Bergin & Strupp, 1972). Most seem to have heeded his advice because few, if any, naturalistic studies have appeared in recent years.

Correlational studies, of course, do not have to be quite so "naturalistic" as the Menninger study (Kazdin, 2003; Kendall, Butcher, & Holmbeck, 1999).

Kiesler (1971) reviewed a number of early studies without experimental manipulation that contain adequate definitions of variables and experimental attempts to rule out obvious confounding factors. Under such conditions, and if practically feasible, it was recognized that correlational studies could expose heretofore unrecognized relationships among variables in the psychotherapeutic process. Over the years, these basic approaches would evolve into sophisticated modeling techniques, which continue to gain enormous influences (Brown et al., 2005, see below). But the fact remained that correlational studies by their nature were incapable of determining causal relationships on the effects of treatment. As Kiesler pointed out, the most common error in these studies was the tendency to conclude that a relationship between two variables indicates that one variable is causing the other. For instance, the conclusion in the Menninger study that working through transference relationships is an effective treatment for borderline psychotics (assuming other confounding factors were controlled or randomized) is open to several different interpretations. One might alternatively conclude that certain behaviors subsumed under the classification *borderline psychotic* caused the therapist to behave in such a way that transference variables changed or that a third variable, such as increased therapeutic attention during this more directive approach, was responsible for changes.

Process research

The second alternative to between-group comparison research popular during these early years was the process approach so often referred to in the early APA conferences on psychotherapy research (e.g., Strupp & Luborsky, 1962). Hoch and Zubin's (1964) popular phrase "flight into process" was an accurate description of the reaction of many clinical investigators to the practical and methodological difficulties of the large group studies. Typically, process research concerned itself with what goes on *during* therapy between an individual patient and therapist instead of the final outcome of any therapeutic effort. In the late 1950s and early 1960s, a large number of studies appeared on such topics as relation of therapist behavior to certain patient behaviors in a given interview situation (e.g., Rogers, Gendlin, Kiesler, & Truax, 1967). As such, process research held much appeal for clinicians and scientists alike. Clinicians were pleased by the focus on the individual and the resulting ability to study actual clinical processes. In some studies repeated measures during therapy gave clinicians an idea of the patient's course during treatment. Scientists were intrigued by the potential of defining variables more precisely within one interview without concerning themselves with the complexities involved before or after the point of study. The increased interest in process research, however, led to an unfortunate distinction between process and outcome studies (see Kiesler, 1966). This distinction was well stated by Luborsky (1959), who noted that process research was concerned with how changes took place in a given interchange between patient and therapist, whereas outcome research was concerned with what change took place as a result of treatment. As Paul (1969) and Kiesler (1966) pointed out, the dichotomization of process and outcome led to an unnecessary polarity in the manner in which measures of behavior change were taken. Process research collected data on patient changes at one or more points during the course of therapy, usually without regard for outcome, while outcome research was concerned only with pre-post measures outside of the therapeutic situation. Kiesler noted that this was unnecessary because measures of change within treatment can be continued throughout treatment until an "outcome" point is reached. He also quoted Chassan (1962) on the desirability of determining what transpired between the beginning and end of therapy in addition to outcome. Thus the major concern of the process researchers, perhaps as a result of this imposed distinction, continued to be changes in patient behavior at points within the therapeutic endeavor. The discovery of meaningful clinical changes as a result of these processes was left to the prevailing experimental strategy of the group comparison approach. This reluctance to relate process variables to outcome and the resulting inability of this approach to evaluate the effects of psychotherapy led to a decline of "pure" process research. Matarazzo noted that in the 1960s the number of people interested in process studies of psychotherapy had declined and their students were nowhere to be seen (Bergin & Strupp, 1972). Because process and outcome were dichotomized in this manner, the notion eventually evolved that changes during treatment were not relevant or legitimate to the important question of outcome. Largely overlooked at this time was the work of M. B. Shapiro (e.g., 1961) at the Maudsley Hospital in London, begun in the 1950s. Shapiro was repeatedly administering measures of change to individual cases during therapy and also continuing these measures to an end point, thereby relating "process" changes to "outcome" and closing the artificial gap which Kiesler was to describe so cogently some years later.

1.7. THE SCIENTIST-PRACTITIONER SPLIT

The state of affairs of clinical practice and research in the 1960s satisfied few people. Clinical procedures were largely judged as unproven (Bergin & Strupp, 1972; Eysenck, 1965), and the prevailing naturalistic research was unacceptable to most scientists concerned with precise definition of variables and cause-effect relationships. On the other hand, the elegantly designed and scientifically rigorous group comparison design was seen as impractical and incapable of dealing with the complexities and idiosyncrasies of individuals by most clinicians. Somewhere in between was process research, which dealt mostly with individuals but was correlational rather than experimental. In addition, the method was viewed as incapable of evaluating the clinical effects of treatment because the focus was on changes within treatment rather than on outcome.

These developments were a major contribution to the well-known scientist-practitioner split that began to be recognized around that time (e.g., Joint

Commission on Mental Illness and Health, 1961). The notion of an applied science of behavior change growing out of the optimism of the 1950s did not meet expectations, and many clinician-scientists stated flatly that applied research had no effect on their clinical practice. Prominent among them was Matarazzo, who noted, "Even after 15 years, few of my research findings affect my practice. Psychological science *per se* doesn't guide me one bit. I still read avidly but this is of little direct practical help. My clinical experience is the only thing that has helped me in my practice to date. . . ." (Bergin & Strupp, 1972, p. 340). This opinion was echoed by one of the most productive and best-known researchers of the 1950s, Carl Rogers, who as early as the 1958 APA conference on psychotherapy noted that research had no impact on his clinical practice and by 1969 advocated abandoning formal research in psychotherapy altogether (Bergin & Strupp, 1972). Because this view prevailed among prominent clinicians who were well acquainted with research methodology, it followed that clinicians without research training or expertise were largely unaffected by the promise or substance of scientific evaluation of behavior change procedures. L. H. Cohen (1976, 1979) confirmed this state of affairs at that time when he summarized a series of surveys indicating that 40% of mental health professionals think that no research exists that is relevant to practice, and the remainder believe that less than 20% of research articles have any applicability to professional settings. Despite stunning advance in knowledge, the state of affairs is largely unchanged over the last several decades (Hayes et al., 1999; Barlow, 2004).

1.8. A RETURN TO THE INDIVIDUAL

Bergin and Strupp were harsh in their comments on group comparison design and failed to specify those situations where between-group methodology may be practical and desirable, nor did they anticipate the growth of large scale clinical trials beginning in the 1980s with all of their methodological advances (see chapter 2). However, their conclusions on alternative directions, outlined in a paper appropriately titled "New Directions in Psychotherapy Research" (Bergin & Strupp, 1970), had significant implications for the conduct of applied research. Essentially, Bergin and Strupp advised against investing further effort in process and outcome studies and proposed the experimental single-case approach for the purpose of isolating mechanisms of change in the therapeutic process. Isolation of these mechanisms of change would then be followed by construction of new procedures based on a combination of variables whose effectiveness was demonstrated in single-case experiments. As the authors noted, "As a general paradigm of inquiry, the individual experimental case study and the experimental analogue approaches appear to be the primary strategies which will move us forward in our understanding of the mechanisms of change at this point" (Bergin & Strupp, 1970, p. 19). The hope was also expressed that this approach would tend to bring research and practice closer together.

With the recommendations emerging from Bergin and Strupp's comprehensive analysis, the philosophy underlying applied research methodology had come full circle in a little over 100 years. The disillusionment with large-scale between-group comparisons observed by Bergin and Strupp and their subsequent advocacy of the intensive study of the individual is an historical repetition of a similar position taken in the middle of the last century. At that time, the noted physiologist, Claude Bernard, in *An Introduction to the Study of Experimental Medicine* (1957), attempted to dissuade colleagues who believed that physiological processes were too complex for experimental inquiry within a single organism. In support of this argument, he noted that the site of processes of change is in the individual organism, and group averages and variance might be misleading. In one of the more famous anecdotes in science, Bernard castigated a colleague interested in studying the properties of urine in 1865. This colleague had proposed collecting specimens from urinals in a centrally located train station to determine properties of the average European urine. Bernard pointed out that this would yield little information about the urine of any one individual. Following Bernard's persuasive reasoning, the intensive scientific study of the individual in physiology flourished.

But methodology in physiology and experimental psychology is not directly applicable to the complexities present in applied research. Although the splendid isolation of Pavlov's laboratories allowed discovery of important psychological processes without recourse to sophisticated experimental design, it is unlikely that the same results would have obtained with a household pet in its natural environment. Yet these are precisely the conditions under which most applied researchers must work.

The plea of applied researchers for appropriate methodology grounded in the scientific method to investigate complex problems in individuals is never more evident than in the writings of Gordon Allport. Allport argued most eloquently that the science of psychology should attend to the uniqueness of the individual (e.g., Allport, 1961, 1962). In terms commonly used in the 1950s, Allport became the champion of the idiographic (individual) approach, which he considered superior to the homothetic (general or group) approach.

> Why should we not start with individual behavior as a source of hunches (as we have in the past) and then seek our generalization (also as we have in the past) but finally come back to the individual not for the mechanical application of laws (as we do now) but for a fuller and more accurate assessment then we are now able to give? I suspect that the reason our present assessments are now so often feeble and sometimes even ridiculous, is because we do not take this final step. We stop with our wobbly laws of generality and seldom confront them with the concrete person. (Allport, 1962, p. 407)

Due to the lack of a practical, applied methodology with which to study the individual, however, most of Allport's own research was homothetic. The increase in the intensive study of the individual in applied research led to a search for appropriate methodology, and several individuals or groups began developing ideas during the 1950s and 1960s.

The role of the case study

One result of the search for appropriate methodology was a reexamination of the role of the uncontrolled case study so strongly rejected by scientists in the 1950s. Recognizing its inherent limitations as an evaluation tool, many clinical investigators at that time (e.g., Barlow, 1980; Kazdin, 1981; Lazarus & Davison, 1971) suggested that the case study could make important contributions to an experimental effort. One of the more important functions of the case study is the generation of new hypotheses, which later may be subjected to more rigorous experimental scrutiny. As Dukes (1965) observed, the case study can occasionally be used to shed some light on extremely rare phenomena or cast doubt on well-established theoretical assumptions. Carefully analyzing threats to internal validity when drawing causal inferences from case studies, Kazdin (1981) concluded that under certain very specific conditions, data from case studies can approach data from single-case experimental manipulations. Case studies may also make other important contributions to science (Hayes et al., 1999; Kazdin, 2003; see also chapter 10). Nevertheless, it was recognized then that the case study generally is not capable of isolating therapeutic mechanisms of change (Hersen & Barlow, 1976; Kazdin, 1981), and the inability of many scientists and clinicians to discriminate the critical difference between the uncontrolled case studies and the experimental study of an individual retarded the implementation of single-case experimental designs (see chapter 5).

The representative case

During this period, other theorists and methodologists were attempting to formulate viable approaches to the experimental study of single cases. Shontz (1965) proposed the study of the representative case as an alternative to traditional approaches in experimental personality research. Essentially, Shontz was concerned with validating previously established personality constructs or measurement instruments on individuals who appear to possess the necessary behavior appropriate for the research problem. Shontz's favorite example was a study of the contribution of psychodynamic factors to epilepsy described by Bowdlear (1955). After reviewing the literature on the presumed psychodynamics in epilepsy, Bowdlear chose a patient who closely approximated the diagnostic and descriptive characteristics of epilepsy presented in the literature (i.e., the representative case). Through a series of questions, Bowdlear then correlated seizures with a certain psychodynamic concept in this patient—acting out dependency. Since this case was "representative," Bowdlear assumed some generalization to other similar cases.

Shontz's contribution was not methodological, because the experiments he cites were largely correlational and in the tradition of process research. Shontz also failed to recognize the value of the single-case study in isolating effective therapeutic variables or building new procedures, as suggested later by Bergin and Strupp (1972). Rather, he proposed the use of a single-case in a deductive manner to test previously established hypotheses and measurement instruments in an individual who is known to be so stable in certain personality characteristics that he or she is "representative" of these characteristics. Conceptually, Shontz moved beyond Allport, however, in noting that this approach was not truly idiographic in that he was not proposing to investigate a subject as a self-contained universe with its own laws. To overcome this objectionable aspect of single-case research, he proposed replication on subjects who differed in some significant way from the first subject. If the general hypothesis were repeatedly confirmed, this would begin to establish a generally applicable law of behavior. If the hypothesis were sometimes confirmed and sometimes rejected, he noted that ". . . the investigator will be in a position either to modify his thinking or to state more clearly the conditions under which the hypothesis does and does not provide a useful model of psychological events" (Shontz, 1965, p. 258). With this statement, Shontz anticipated the applied application of the methodology of direct and systematic replication in basic research (see chapter 10) suggested by Sidman (1960).

Shapiro's methodology in the clinic

One of the most important contributions to the search for a methodology came from the pioneering work of M. B. Shapiro in London. As early as 1951, Shapiro was advocating a scientific approach to the study of individual phenomena, an advocacy that continued through the 1960s (e.g., M. B. Shapiro, 1961, 1966, 1970).

Unlike Allport, however, Shapiro went beyond the point of noting the advantages of applied research with single-cases and began the difficult task of constructing an adequate methodology. One important contribution by Shapiro was the utilization of carefully constructed measures of clinically relevant responses administered repeatedly over time in an individual. Typically, Shapiro would examine fluctuations in these measures and hypothesize on the controlling effects of therapeutic or environmental influences. As such, Shapiro was one of the first to formally investigate questions more relevant to psychopathology than behavior change or psychotherapy *per se* using the individual case. Questions concerning classification and the identification of factors maintaining the disorder and even speculations regarding etiology were all addressed by Shapiro. Many of these studies were correlational in nature, or what Shapiro refers to as simple or complex descriptive studies (1966). As such, these efforts bear a striking resemblance to process studies mentioned above, in that the effect of a therapeutic or potential-maintaining variable was correlated with a target response. Shapiro attempted to go beyond this correlational approach, however, by defining and manipulating independent variables within single-cases. One good example in the area of behavior change is the systematic alteration of two therapeutic approaches in a case of paranoid delusions (M. B. Shapiro & Ravenette, 1959). In a prototype of what was later to be called the A-B-A design, the authors measured paranoid delusions by asking the patient to rate the "intensity" of a number of paranoid ideas on a scale of 1 to 5. The sum of the score across 18 different delusions then represented the patient's paranoid "score." Treatments consisted of "control" discussion concerning guilt feelings about situations in the patient's life, unrelated to any paranoid ideation, and rational discussion aimed at exposing the falseness of the patient's paranoid beliefs. The experimental sequence consisted of 4 days of "guilt" discussion followed by 8 days of rational discussion and a return to 4 days of "guilt" discussion. The authors observed an overall decline in paranoid scores during this experiment, which they rightly noted as correlational and thus potentially due to a variety of causes. Close examination of the data revealed, however, that on weekends when no discussions were held, the patient worsened during the guilt control phase and improved during the rational discussion phase. These fluctuations around the regression line were statistically significant. This effect, of course, is weak and of dubious importance because overall improvement in paranoid scores was not functionally related to treatment. Furthermore, several guidelines for a true experimental analysis of the treatment were violated. Examples of experimental error include the absence of baseline measurement to determine the pretreatment course of the paranoid beliefs and the simultaneous withdrawal of one treatment and introduction of a second treatment (see chapter 3). The importance of the case and other early work from M. B. Shapiro, however, is not the knowledge gained from any one experiment, but the beginnings of the development of a scientifically based methodology for evaluating effects of treatment within a single-case. To the extent that Shapiro's correlational studies were similar to process research, he broke the semantic barrier which held that process criteria were unrelated to outcome. He demonstrated clearly that repeated measures within an individual could be extended to a logical end point and that this end point *was* the outcome of treatment. His more important contribution from our point of view, however, was the demonstration that independent variables in applied research could be defined and systematically manipulated within a single-case, thereby fulfilling the requirements of a "true" experimental approach to the evaluation of therapeutic technique (Underwood, 1957). In addition, his demonstration of the applicability of the study of the individual case to the discovery of issues relevant to psychopathology was extremely important.

Quasi-experimental designs

During that era, in the area of research dealing with broad-based educational or social change, most often termed evaluation research, Campbell and Stanley (1963) and Cook and Campbell (1979) proposed a series of important methodological innovations that they termed quasi-experimental designs. Education research, of course, is more often concerned with broad-based effects of programs rather than individual behavioral change. But these designs, many of which are applicable to either groups or individuals, are also directly relevant in our context. The two designs most appropriate for analysis of change in the individual were termed the *time series design* and the *equivalent time series design*. From the perspective of applied clinical research, the time series design is similar to M. B. Shapiro's effort to extend process observation throughout the course of a given treatment to a logical end point or outcome. This design goes beyond observations within treatment, however, to include observations from repeated measures in a period preceding and following a given intervention. Thus one can observe changes from a baseline as a result of a given intervention. While the inclusion of a baseline is a distinct methodological improvement, this design is basically correlational in nature and is unable to isolate effects of therapeutic mechanisms or establish cause-effect relationships. Basically, this design is the A-B design described in chapter 5. The equivalent time series design, however, involves experimental manipulation of independent variables through alteration of treatments, as in the M. B. Shapiro and Ravenette study (1959), or introduction and withdrawal of one treatment in an A-B-A fashion. Approaching the study of the individual from a different perspective than Shapiro, Campbell and Stanley arrived at similar conclusions on the possibility of manipulation of independent variables and establishment of cause-effect relationships in the study of a single case.

What was perhaps the more important contribution of these methodologists, was the description of various limitations of these designs in their ability to rule out alternative plausible hypotheses (internal validity) or the extent to which one can generalize conclusions obtained from the designs (external validity) (see chapter 2).

Chassan and intensive designs

It remained for Chassan (1967, 1979) to pull together many of the methodological advances in single-case research to that point in a book that made clear distinctions between the advantages and disadvantages of what he termed extensive (group) design and intensive (single-case) design. Drawing on long experience in applied research, Chassan outlined the desirability and applicability of single-case designs evolving out of applied research in the 1950s and early 1960s. While most of his own experience in single-case design concerned the evaluation of pharmacologic agents for behavior disorders, Chassan also illustrated the uses of single-case designs in psychotherapy research, particularly psychoanalysis. As a statistician rather than a practicing clinician, he emphasized the various statistical procedures capable of establishing relationships between therapeutic intervention and dependent variables within the single-case. He concentrated on the correlation type of design using trend analysis but made occasional use of a prototype of the A-B-A design (e.g., Bellak & Chassan, 1964), which, in this case, extended the work of M. B. Shapiro to evaluation of drug effects but, in retrospect, contained some of the same methodological faults. Nevertheless, the sophisticated theorizing in the book on thorny issues in single-case research, such as generality of findings from a single-case, provided the most comprehensive treatment of these issues to this time. Many of Chassan's ideas on this subject will appear repeatedly in later sections of this book.

1.9. THE EXPERIMENTAL ANALYSIS OF BEHAVIOR

While innovative applied researchers such as Chassan and M. B. Shapiro made methodological advances in the experimental study of the single-case, their advances did not have a major impact on the conduct of applied research outside of their own settings. As late as 1965, Shapiro noted in an invited address to the Eastern Psychological Association that a large majority of research in prominent clinical psychology journals involved between-group comparisons with little and, in some cases, no reference to the individual approach that he advocated. He hoped that his address might presage the beginning of a new emphasis on this method. In retrospect, there are several possible reasons for the lack of impact. *First,* as Leitenberg (1973) was later to point out, many of the measures used by M. B. Shapiro in applied research were indirect and subjective (e.g., questionnaires), precluding the observation of direct behavioral effects that gained importance with the rise of behavior therapy in the 1970s (see chapter 4). *Second,* Shapiro and Chassan, in studies of psychotherapy, did not produce the strong, clinically relevant changes that would impress clinicians, perhaps due to inadequate or weak independent variables or treatments, such as instructions within interview procedures. Finally, the advent of the work of Shapiro and Chassan was associated with the general disillusionment during this period concerning the possibilities of research in psychotherapy. Nevertheless, Chassan and Shapiro demonstrated that meaningful applied research was possible and even desirable in the area of psychotherapy. These investigators, along with several of Shapiro's students (e.g., Davidson & Costello, 1969; Inglis, 1966; Yates, 1970), had an important influence on the development and acceptance of more sophisticated methodology, which was beginning to appear in the 1960s.

It is significant that it was the rediscovery of the study of the single-case in basic research, coupled with a new approach to problems in the applied area, that marked the beginnings of a new emphasis on the experimental study of the single-case in applied research. One indication of the broad influence of this combination of events was the emergence of a journal in 1968 (*Journal of Applied Behavior Analysis*) devoted to single-case methodology in applied research and the appearance of this experimental approach in increasing numbers in the major psychological and psychiatric journals. The methodology in basic research was termed the *experimental analysis of behavior;* the new approach to applied problems became known as *behavior modification* or *behavior therapy.*

The relevance of the experimental analysis of behavior to applied research is the development of sophisticated methodology enabling intensive study of individual subjects. In rejecting a between-subject approach as the only useful scientific methodology, Skinner (1938, 1953) reflected the thoughts of the early physiologists such as Claude Bernard and emphasized repeated objective measurement in a single subject over a long period of time under highly controlled conditions. As Skinner noted (1966b), ". . . instead of studying a thousand rats for one hour each, or a hundred rats for ten hours each, the investigator is likely to study one rat for a thousand hours" (p. 21), a procedure that clearly recognizes the individuality of an organism. Thus, Skinner and his colleagues in the animal laboratories developed and refined the single-case methodology that became the foundation of a new applied science. Culminating in the definitive methodological treatise by Sidman (1960), entitled *Tactics of Scientific Research*, the assumption and conditions of a true experimental analysis of behavior were outlined. Examples of fine-grain analyses of behavior and the use of withdrawal, reversal, and multi-element experimental designs in the experimental laboratories began to appear in more applied journals in the 1960s, as researchers adapted these strategies to the investigation of applied problems.

It is unlikely, however, that this approach would have had a significant impact on applied clinical research without the growing popularity of behavior therapy. The fact that M. B. Shapiro and Chassan were employing rudimentary prototypes of withdrawal designs (independent of influences from the laboratories of operant conditioning) without marked effect on applied research would seem to support this contention. In fact, even earlier, F. C. Thorne (1947) described clearly the principle of single-case research, including A-B-A withdrawal designs, and recommended that clinical research proceed in this manner, without apparent effect (Hayes et al., 1999). The growth of the behavior therapy approach to applied problems, however, provided a vehicle for the introduction of the methodology on a scale that attracted attention from investigators in applied areas. Behavior therapy, as the application of the principles of cognitive and behavioral science to the clinic, also emphasized direct measurement of clinically relevant target behaviors and experimental evaluation of independent variables or "treatments." Since many of these "principles of learning" utilized in behavior therapy originally emanated from operant conditioning, it was a small step for behavior therapists to also borrow the operant methodology to validate the effectiveness of these same principles in applied settings. The initial success of this approach (e.g., Ullmann & Krasner, 1965) led to similar evaluations of additional behavior therapy techniques that did not derive directly from the operant laboratories (e.g., Agras et al., 1971; Barlow, Leitenberg, & Agras, 1969). During this period, methodology originally intended for the animal laboratory was adapted more fully to the investigation of applied problems and "applied behavior analysis" became an important supplementary and, in some cases, alternative methodological approach to between-subjects experimental designs.

The early pleas to return to the individual as the cornerstone of an applied science of behavior have been largely heeded. The decade of the 1970s witnessed the crumbling of barriers that precluded publication of single-case research in any leading journal devoted to the study of behavioral problems. Since that time, a proliferation of important books, or featured series in journals has appeared devoted, for example, to strategies for evaluating data from single-case designs (Kratochwill & Levin, 1992) to the application of these methods in social work (Jayaratne & Levy, 1979; Tripodi, 1994), counseling (Lundervold & Bellwood, 2000), pediatrics (Tervo, Estrm, Brockman & Symons, 2003), special education (Kennedy, 2004, in press; Stile, 1993), or to the philosophy underlying this approach to applied research (J. M. Johnston & Pennypacker, 1993). Other excellent books or series have appeared concentrating specifically on descriptions of design alternatives (e.g., Jones, 1993, polling method), and major handbooks on research are not complete without a description of this approach (e.g., Hersen, 2005; Roberts & Ilardi, 2003). Templates for developing clinical practice guidelines or best practice algorithms prominently feature the contribution of single case experimental designs in identifying effective practices (APA, 2002; Chambless et al., 1996; 1998).

More importantly, the field has not stood still. From their more recent origins in evaluating the application of operant principles to behavior disorders, single-case designs are now fully incorporated into the armamentarium of applied researchers generally interested in behavior change beyond the subject matter of the core mental health professions or education. Professions such as rehabilitation medicine are also turning to this approach as appropriate to the subject matter at hand (e.g., Schindele, 1981), and the field is progressing. New design alternatives and quantitative methods of analyzing data appeared recently, and strategies involved in more traditional approaches have been clarified and refined as outlined in subsequent chapters. On the other hand, publication utilizing this methodology has declined somewhat by the mid 1990s in traditional behavioral journals, perhaps reflecting more publication of these strategies across multiple journals, less opportunity for training in this methodology, or other factors.

Recently the National Institute of Drug Abuse (NIDA) commissioned a report conceptualizing three stages of intervention development (Kazdin, 2001; Rounsaville, Carroll & Onken, 2001). Stage 1 consists of the initial steps in treatment development, including feasibility and pilot testing, and also incorporates a specification of the details of the intervention and the developing the necessary tools to go forward, such as therapy manuals and measures of therapist adherence and competence while delivering the new treatment. Once a treatment has been fully articulated with promising pilot data, stage 2 would then proceed with evaluation of the efficacy of the intervention that had shown some promise in stage 1. In stage 3, the focus shifts to generality and transportability of treatments for which efficacy had been demonstrated in stage 2. This stage of evaluation is commonly called the "effectiveness" or "clinical utility" research (APA,

2002). The major questions in this stage have to do with generality of treatment efficacy across different practitioners, different settings, and different clients, as well as issues involved in training, dissemination, and cost-effectiveness.

At each stage, single-case experimental designs can play a pivotal role. Obviously, they are particularly well suited to initial pilot testing because one can establish important functional relationships between an intervention and the problem or disorder under consideration utilizing far fewer subjects. Several replicated single-case experiments consisting of thee subjects each might be sufficient to show the promise of treatment. In stage 2, the principal methodology for efficacy testing has been the randomized control trial, and these trials have become more sophisticated and methodologically sound in recent years (APA, 2002; Moher, Schulz, & Altman, 2001). Nevertheless, as articulated by the Division of Clinical Psychology , a series of replicated single-case experiments may provide equally important information on the efficacy of interventions, while at the same time highlighting possible mechanisms of action of the intervention through close-grained analyses of timing of the onset of behavior change, as outlined in some detail in subsequent chapters. Large multi-site clinical trials and more focused single-case approaches also complement each other in stage 3 research. In fact, clinical replication series, discussed in detail in chapter 10, retain a focus on the individual. At the same time, due to the methodological similarity to ongoing clinical practice, the clinical replication series can be instituted across large groups of clinicians in what are being called practice research networks. These networks, one of which has recently been formed in Pennsylvania (Borkevec, Echemendia, Ragusea, & Ruiz, 2001) may involve hundreds of clinicians, each utilizing innovative treatments under study with appropriate clients in their own setting, thus generating data very quickly on generality of findings across different practitioners, clients, and settings. Once again, there are good precedents for these strategies that will be discussed in more detail in chapter 10.

We believe that these recent methodological developments and the demonstrated effectiveness of this methodology provide an important contribution to a true science of human behavior with a focus on the paramount importance of the individual. A description of this methodology is the purpose of this book.

CHAPTER 2

GENERAL ISSUES IN A SINGLE-CASE APPROACH

2.1. INTRODUCTION

Two issues basic to any science are variability and generality of findings. These issues are handled somewhat differently from one area of science to another, depending on the subject matter. The first section of this chapter concerns variability.

In applied research, where individual behavior is the primary concern, it is our contention that the search for sources of variability in individuals must occur if we are to develop a truly effective clinical science of human behavior change. After a brief discussion of basic assumptions concerning sources of variability in behavior, specific techniques and procedures for dealing with behavioral variability in individuals are outlined. Chief among these are repeated measurement procedures that allow careful monitoring of day-to-day variability in individual behavior, and rapidly changing, improvised experimental designs that facilitate an immediate search for sources of variability in an individual. Several examples of the use of this procedure to track down sources of intersubject or intrasubject variability are presented.

The second section of this chapter deals with generality of findings. Historically, this has been a thorny issue in applied research. The seeming limitations in establishing wide generality from results in a single-case are obvious, yet establishment of generality from results in large groups has also proved elusive. After a discussion of important types of generality of findings, the shortcomings of attempting to generalize from group results in applied research are discussed. Traditionally, the major problems have been an inability to draw a truly random sample from human behavior disorders and the difficulty of generalizing from groups to an individual. Applied researchers attempted to solve the problem by making groups as homogeneous as possible so that results would be applicable to an individual who showed the characteristics of the homogeneous group. A complementary method of establishing generality of findings is the replication of single-case experiments. The relative merits of establishing generality of findings from homogeneous groups and replication of single-case experiments are discussed at the end of this section.

Finally, some research questions that cannot be answered through experimentation on single-cases are listed, and strategies for combining some strengths of single-case and between-subject research approaches are suggested.

2.2. VARIABILITY

The notion that behavior is a function of a multiplicity of factors finds wide agreement among scientists and professional investigators. Most scientists also agree that as one moves up the phylogenetic scale, the sources of variability in behavior become greater. In response to this, many scientists choose to work with lower life forms in the hope that laws of behavior will emerge more readily and be generalizable to the infinitely more complex area of human behavior. Applied researchers do not have this luxury. The task of the investigator in the area of human behavior disorders is to discover functional relations among treatments and specific behavior disorders over and above the welter of environmental and biological variables impinging on the patient at any given time. Given these complexities, it is small wonder that most treatments, when tested, produce small effects (Meehl, 1978).

Variability in basic research

One of the pioneers in considering the thorny problem of variability was Murray Sidman (Sidman, 1960). Sidman pointed out that even in basic research, behavioral variability is enormous. In attempting to deal with this problem, many experimental psychologists assumed that variability was intrinsic to the organism rather than imposed by experimental or environmental factors. If variability were an intrinsic component of behavior, then procedures had to be found to deal with this issue before meaningful research could be conducted. The solution involved experimental designs and confidence level statistics that would elucidate functional relations among independent and dependent variables over and above the intrinsic variability. Sidman (1960) noted early on that this is not the case in some other sciences, such as physics. Physics assumes that variability is imposed by error of measurement or other identifiable factors. Experimental efforts are then directed to discovering and eliminating as many sources of variability as possible so that functional relations can be determined with more precision. Sidman proposed that basic researchers in psychology also adopt this strategy. Rather than assuming that variability is intrinsic to the organism, one should make every effort to discover sources of behavioral variability among organisms such that laws of behavior could be studied with the precision and specificity found in physics. This precision, of course, would require close attention to the behavior of the individual organism. If one rat behaves differently from three other rats in an experimental condition, the proper tactic is to find out why. If the experimenter succeeds, the factors that produce that variability can be eliminated and a "cleaner" test of the effects of the original independent variable can be made. Sidman recognized that behavioral variability may never be entirely eliminated, but that isolation of as many sources of variability as possible would enable an investigator to estimate how much variability actually is intrinsic.

Variability in applied research

Applied researchers, by and large, have not been concerned with this argument. Every practitioner is aware of multiple social or biological factors that are imposed on-his or her data. If asked, many investigators might also assume some intrinsic variability in clients attributable to capriciousness in nature; but most are more concerned with the effect of uncontrollable but potentially observable events in the environment. For example, the sudden appearance of a significant relative or the loss of a job during treatment of depression may affect the course of depression to a far greater degree than the particular intervention procedure. Menstruation may cause marked changes in behavioral measures of anxiety. Even more disturbing are the multiple unidentifiable sources of variability that cause broad fluctuation in a patient's clinical course. Most applied researchers assume this variability is imposed rather than intrinsic, but they may not know where to begin to factor out the sources.

The solution, as in basic research, has been to accept broad variability as an unavoidable evil, to employ experimental design and statistics that hopefully control variability, and to look for functional relations that supersede the "error." As Sidman observed when discussing these tactics in basic research:

> The rationale for statistical immobilization of unwanted variables is based on the assumed random nature of such variables. In a large group of subjects, the reasoning goes, the uncontrolled factor will change the behavior of some subjects in one direction and will affect the remaining subjects in the opposite way. When the data are averaged over all the subjects, the effects of the uncontrolled variables are presumed to add algebraically to zero. The composite data are then regarded as though they were representative of one ideal subject who had never been exposed to the uncontrolled variables at all (1960, p. 162).

Although one may question this strategy in basic research, as Sidman did, the amount of control an experimenter has over the behavioral history and current environmental variables impinging on the laboratory animal makes this strategy at least feasible. In applied research, when control over behavioral histories or even current environmental events is limited or nonexistent, there is far less probability of discovering a treatment that is effective over and above these uncontrolled variables. This, of course, was the major cause of the inability of early group comparison studies to demonstrate that the treatment under consideration was effective. As noted in chapter 1, some clients were improving while others were worsening, despite the presence of the treatment. Presumably, this variability was not intrinsic but due to current life circumstances of the clients.

Clinical vs. statistical significance

Traditional experimental designs and data analytic procedures gleaned from the laboratories of experimental psychology have an added disadvantage in applied research. The purpose of research in any basic science is to discover functional relations among dependent and independent variables. Once discovered, these functional relationships become principles that add to our knowledge of behavior. In applied research, however, the discovery of functional relations is not sufficient. The purpose of applied research is to effect *meaningful* clinical or socially relevant behavioral changes. For example, if depression were reliably measurable on a 0–100 scale, with 100 representing severe depression, a treatment that improved *each patient* in a group of depressives from 80 to 75 would be statistically significant if all depressives in the control group remained at 80. This statistical significance, however, would be of little use to the practicing clinician because a score of 75 could still be in the suicidal range. An improvement of 40 or 50 points might be necessary before the clinician would consider the change clinically important. In the first edition of this book, we referred to the issue as *statistical versus clinical significance* (Barlow & Hersen, 1973), and this issue has been raised repeatedly over the decades (e.g., Garfield & Bergin, 1978; Kendall 1999, Sheldrick, Kendall, & Heimberg, 2001). In this simplified example, statisticians might observe that this issue is easily correctable by setting a different criterion level for "effectiveness," and, indeed, a number of workable strategies for ascertaining clinical significance have been proposed (Jacobson, Roberts Nerns & McGlinchey, 1999; Kazdin, 1999; Kendall, 1999). In the jungle of applied research, however, when any effect superseding the enormous "error" or variance in a group of heterogeneous clients is remarkable, the clinician and even the researcher will often overlook this issue and consider a treatment that is statistically significant to also be clinically effective.

As Chassan (1960, 1979) pointed out several decades ago, statistical significance can underestimate clinical effectiveness as well as overestimate it. This unfortunate circumstance occurs when a treatment is quite effective with a few members of the experimental group while the remaining members do not improve or deteriorate somewhat. Statistically, then, the experimental group does not differ from the control group, whose members are relatively unchanged. When broad divergence such as this occurs among clients in response to an intervention, statistical treatments will average out the clinical effects along with changes due to unwanted sources of variability. In fact, this type of intersubject variability is the rule rather than the exception. Bergin (1966) clearly illustrated the years that were lost to applied research because clinical investigators overlooked the marked effectiveness of these treatments on *some* clients (see also Kazdin 2003; Kennel, 1999). The issue of clinical versus statistical significance is, of course, not restricted to between-group comparisons, but is something applied researchers must consider whenever statistical tests are applied to clinical data (see chapter 9).

Nevertheless, the advantages of attempting to eliminate the enormous intersubject variability in applied research through statistical methods have intuitive appeal for both researchers and clinicians who want quick answers to pressing clinical or social questions. In fact, to the clinician who might observe one severely depressive patient inexplicably get better while another equally depressed patient commits suicide, this variability may well seem to be intrinsic to the nature of the disorder rather than imposed by definable social or biological factors.

Highlighting variability in the individual

In any case, whether variability in applied research is intrinsic to some degree or not, the alternative to the treatment of intersubject variability by statistical means is to highlight variability and begin the arduous task of determining sources of variability in the individual. To the applied researcher, this task is staggering. In realistic terms he or she must look at each individual who differs from other clients in terms of response to treatment and attempt to determine why. Because the complexities of human environments, both external and internal, are enormous, the possible causes of these differences number in the millions.

With the complexities involved in this search, one may legitimately question where to begin. Because intersubject variability begins with one client differing in response from some other clients, a logical starting point is the individual. If one is to concentrate on individual variability, however, the manner in which one observes this variability must also change. If one depressed patient deteriorates during treatment while others improve or remain stable, it is difficult to speculate on reasons for this deterioration if the only data available are observations before and after treatment. It would be much to the advantage of the clinical researcher to have followed this one patient's course *during* treatment so that the beginning of deterioration could be pinpointed. In this hypothetical case the patient may have begun to improve until a point midway in treatment, when deterioration began. Perhaps a disruption in family life occurred or the patient missed a treatment session, while other patients whose improvement continued did not experience these events. It would then be possible to speculate on these or other factors that were correlated with such change. In single-case research the investigator could adjust to the variability with immediate alteration in experimental design to test out hypothesized sources of these changes.[*]

Repeated measures

The basis of this search for sources of variability is repeated measurement of the dependent variable or problem behavior. If this tactic has a familiar ring to

---

[*]For an excellent discussion of the concept of variability and the relationship of measurement to variability, see J. M. Johnston and Pennypacker (1993).

practitioners, it is no accident, for this is precisely the strategy every practitioner uses daily albeit, not always in a systematic fashion. It is no secret to clinicians or other behavior change agents in applied settings that behavioral improvement from an initial observation to some end point sandwiches marked variability in the behavior between these points. A major activity of clinicians is observing this variability and making appropriate changes in treatment strategies or environmental circumstances, where possible, to eliminate these fluctuations from a general improving trend. Because measures in the clinic seldom go beyond gross observation, and treatment consists of a combination of factors, it is difficult for clinicians to pinpoint potential sources of variability, but they speculate; with increased clinical experience, effective clinicians may guess rightly more often than wrongly (Hayes et al., 1999; Stricker & Trierweiler, 1995). In some cases, weekly observation may go on for years. As Chassan (1967) pointed out a number of years ago:

> The existence of variability as a basic phenomenon in the study of individual psychopathology implies that a single observation of a patient state, in general, can offer only a minimum of information about the patient state. While such information is literally better than no information, it provides no more data than does any other statistical sample of one (1967, p. 182)

The relation of this strategy to process research, described in chapter 1, is obvious. But the search for sources of individual variability cannot be restricted to repeated measures of one small segment of a client's course somewhere between the beginning and the end of treatment, as in process research. With the multitude of events impinging on the organism, significant behavior fluctuation may occur at any time—from the beginning of an intervention until well after completion of treatment. The necessity of repeated, frequent measures to begin the search for sources of individual variability is apparent. Procedures for repeated measures of a variety of behavior problems are described in chapter 4.

Rapidly changing designs

If one is committed to determining sources of variability in individuals, repeated measurement alone is insufficient. In a typical case, no one event is clearly associated with behavioral fluctuation, and repeated observation will permit only a temporal correlation of several events with the behavioral fluctuation. In the clinic this temporal correlation provides differing degrees of evidence on an intuitive level concerning causality. For instance, if a person with claustrophobia became trapped in an elevator on the way to the therapist's office and suddenly worsened, the clinician could make a reasonable inference that this event caused the fluctuation. Usually, of course, sources of variability are not so clear, and the applied researcher must guess from among several correlated events. However, it would add little to science if an investigator merely reported at the end of an experiment that fluctuation in behaviors were observed and were correlated with several events. The task confronting the applied researcher at this point is to devise experimental designs to isolate the cause of the change or the lack of change. One advantage of single-case experimental designs is that the investigator can begin an immediate search for the cause of an experimental behavior trend by altering the experimental design on the spot. This feature, when properly employed, can provide immediate information on hypothesized sources of variability. In Skinner's words:

> A prior design in which variables are distributed, for example, in a Latin square, may be a severe handicap. When effects on behavior can be immediately observed, it is more efficient to explore relevant variables by manipulating them in an improvised and rapidly changing design. Similar practices have been responsible for the greater part of modern science (Honig, 1966, p. 21).

This feature of single-case designs has also been termed *response guided experimentation* (Edgington, 1983, 1984).

2.3. EXPERIMENTAL ANALYSIS OF SOURCES OF VARIABILITY THROUGH IMPROVISED DESIGNS

In single-case designs there are at least three patterns of variability highlighted by repeated measurement. In the first pattern, a subject may not respond to a treatment previously demonstrated as effective with other subjects. In a second pattern, a subject may improve when no treatment is in effect, as in a baseline phase. This "spontaneous" improvement is often considered to be the result of "placebo" effects. These two patterns of intersubject variability are quite common in applied research. In a third pattern, the variability is intrasubject in that marked cyclical patterns emerge in the measures that supersede the effect of any independent variable. Using improvised and rapidly changing designs, it is possible to follow Skinner's suggestion and begin an immediate search for sources of this variability. Examples of these efforts are provided next.

Subject fails to improve

One recent experiment by McCord and colleagues (2001) nicely illustrates the use of an "improvised and rapidly changing design" to determine how an intervention that was effective with one client could be easily modified to be successful with another client with whom it was initially only partially effective. The purpose of this investigation was to assess and treat problem behaviors (e.g., self-injurious behavior [SIB], aggression) evoked by the presence of loud noise. The basis for this study was that prior work suggests that up to 40% of those with a diagnosis of autism exhibit symptoms of sensitivity to loud sounds (Rimland & Edelson, 1995) and it has been proposed that some people with developmental disabilities may engage in problem behaviors because doing so leads to their escape from (or the termination of) the aversive noise. After determining that the introduction of loud noises was associated with an increased rate of problem behavior for two adult clients, Debbie and Sarah, the authors measured the frequency of problem behaviors during a baseline phase then introduced their intervention. The intervention involved the use of an extinction plus stimulus fading procedure during which problem behaviors did not lead to termination of the noise (i.e., extinction) and low levels of noise were presented and increased slightly only after three 1-minute sessions during which no problem behavior was present (i.e., stimulus fading). If problem behavior occurred, the noise volume was decreased slightly to the previous level and the criterion for increasing the noise was now doubled (i.e., six sessions of no problem behavior). In the treatment of Debbie, this procedure led to a complete reduction in problem behavior (see Figure 2.1).

In attempting to replicate this finding in a second client (see Figure 2.2), some variation in problem behavior was noted. The stimulus fading procedure reduced Sarah's problem behavior from its baseline level, but it continued to occur to some degree. At this point, the investigators adjusted the intervention to add a differential reinforcement of other behavior (DRO) contingency. In this condition, Sarah received an edible reinforcer (i.e., half a cheese puff) following each six-second interval during which she did not engage in any problem behaviors. The investigators used an A-B-A-B-A-B design to test the effectiveness of this added component, which led to a complete reduction in problem behavior for this client.

Merely observing the "outcome" of the 2 subjects at the end of a fixed point in time would have produced the type of intersubject variability so common in outcome studies of therapeutic techniques. That is, one subject would have improved with the initial stimulus fading procedure whereas one subject would have remained unchanged. If this pattern continued over additional subjects, the result would be the typical weak effect (Bergin & Strupp, 1972) with large intersubject variability. Highlighting the variability through repeated measurement in the individual and improvising a new experimental design as soon as a variation in response was noted allowed an immediate change in the design and resulted in immediate clinical benefit to the patient, providing a practical illustration of the merging of scientist and practitioner roles in the applied researcher.

Subject improves "spontaneously"

A second source of variability quite common in single-case research is the presence of "spontaneous" improvement in the absence of the therapeutic variable to be tested. In such instances, significant change is observed in the dependent variable before the intervention or manipulation is applied. This can take several different forms. For instance, within the context of an ABAB design, the behavior of interest may show significant and sustained improvement during the first A phase, before the intervention even begins. Within a multiple-baseline or changing criterion

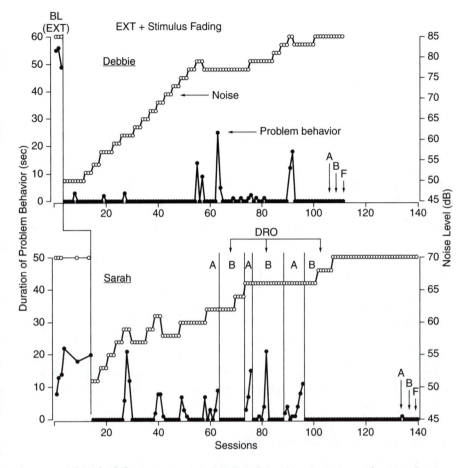

FIGURES 2.1 & 2.2 Results of Debbie's and Sarah's treatment evaluation. Sessions marked A and B near the end of treatment indicate two generalization probes in the natural environment; F indicates a follow-up probe. (Figure 4, p. 457 from: McCord, B. E., Iwata, B. A., Galensky, T. L., Ellingson, S. A., & Thomson, R. J. (2001). Functional analysis and treatment of problem behavior evoked by noise. *Journal of Applied Behavior Analysis*, **34** (4).)

design (discussed in greater detail in chapters 6 and 7) in which the intervention is administered across different phases, behaviors of interest may improve earlier than expected and before the intervention is directed at those behaviors. It also is possible that significant change can occur midway through a single phase. For instance, Nock and colleagues (Nock, Goldman, Wang, & Albano, 2004) reported data from a case in which they successfully reduced the frequency of panic attacks in a 10-year-old boy in which an abrupt improvement occurred within the intervention phase. Data collected entirely during the treatment phase (see Figure 2.3)

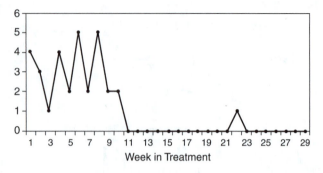

FIGURE 2.3   Frequency of panic attacks each week over Michael's treatment course. (Figure 1, p. 779, from: Nock, M. K., Goldman, J. L., Wang, Y., & Albano, A.M. (2004). From science to practice: The flexible use of evidence-based treatments in clinical settings. *Journal of the American Academy of Child and Adolescent-Psychiatry*, **43** (6) 777–780.)

showed that panic attacks remained present and fairly variable in frequency until the eleventh week of treatment, at which time they decreased to zero and remained at that level (aside from a single panic attack several weeks later). Although significant improvement occurred during the course of treatment, because the focus of this report was on demonstrating the flexible use of efficacious treatments rather than experimentally studying the cause of clinical change, this "spontaneous" improvement was left unexplained. In cases such as these, it is possible that improvement was due to some unidentified aspect of the assessment or intervention, and focused follow-up studies are needed to determine exactly why such change occurred.

Subject displays cyclical variability

A third pattern of variability, highlighted by repeated measurement in individual cases, is observed when behavior varies in a cyclical pattern. The behavior may follow a regular pattern (i.e., weekly) or may be irregular. A common temporal pattern, of course, is the behavioral or emotional fluctuation noted during menstruation. Of more concern to the clinician is the marked fluctuation occurring in most behavioral disorders over a period of time. In most instances the fluctuation cannot be readily correlated with specific, observable environmental or psychological events, due to the extent of the behavioral or emotional fluctuation and the number of potential variables that may be affecting the behavior. As noted in the beginning of this chapter, experimental clinicians can often make educated guesses, but the technique of repeated measurement can illustrate relationships that might not be readily observable.

A good example of this method is found in an early case of severe, daily asthmatic attacks reported by Metcalfe (1956). In the course of assessment, Metcalfe had the patient record in diary form asthmatic attacks as well as all activities during the day, such as games, shopping expeditions, meetings with her mother, and other social visits. These daily recordings revealed that asthmatic attacks most often followed meetings with the patient's mother, particularly if these meetings occurred in the home of the mother. After this relationship was demonstrated, the patient experienced a change in her life circumstances which resulted in moving some distance away from her mother. During the ensuing 20 months, only nine attacks were recorded despite the fact that these attacks had occurred daily for a period of two years prior to intervention. What is more remarkable is that eight of the attacks followed her now infrequent visits to her mother.

Once again, the procedure of repeated measurement highlighted individual fluctuation, allowing a search for correlated events that bore potential causal relationships to the behavior disorder. It should be noted that no experimental analysis was undertaken in this case to isolate the mother as the cause of asthmatic attacks. However, the dramatic reduction of high-frequency attacks after decreased contact with the mother provided reasonably strong evidence about the contributory effects of visits to the mother, in an A-B fashion. What is more convincing, however, is the reoccurrence of the attacks at widely spaced intervals after visits to the mother during the 20-month follow-up. This series of naturally occurring events approximates a contrived A-B-A-B . . . design and effectively isolates the mother's role in the patient's asthmatic attacks (see chapter 5).

Searching for "hidden" sources of variability

In the preceding case functional relations become obvious without experimental investigation, due to the overriding effects of one variable on the behavior in question and a series of fortuitous events (from an experimental point of view) during follow-up. Seldom in applied research is one variable so predominant. The more usual case is one where marked fluctuations in behavior occur that cannot be correlated with any one variable. In these cases, close examination of repeated measures of the target behavior and correlated internal or external events does not produce an obvious relationship. Most likely, many events may be correlated at one time or another with deterioration or improvement in a client. At this point, it becomes necessary to employ sophisticated experimental designs if one is to search for the source of variability. The experienced applied researcher must first choose the most likely variables for investigation from among the many impinging on the client at any one time. In the case described above, not only visits to the mother but visits to other relatives, as well as stressful situations at work, might all have contributed to the variance. The task of the clinical investigator is to tease out the relevant variables by manipulating one variable, such as visits to mother, while holding other variables constant. Once the contribution of visits to mother to behavioral fluctuation has been determined, the investigator must go on to the next variable, and so on.

In many cases, behavior is a function of an interaction of events. These events may be naturally occurring environmental variables or perhaps a combination of treatment variables which, when combined, affect behavior differently from each variable in isolation. For example, when testing out a variety of treatments for anorexia nervosa (Agras, Barlow, Chapin, Abel, & Leitenberg, 1974), it was discovered that the size of meals served to the patients seemed related to caloric intake. An improvised design at this point in the experiment demonstrated that size of meals was related to caloric intake only if feedback and reinforcement were present. This discovery led to inclusion of this procedure in an early recommended treatment package for anorexia nervosa. Experimental designs to determine the effects of combinations of variables will be discussed in section 6.6 of chapter 6.

2.4. BEHAVIOR TRENDS AND INTRASUBJECT AVERAGING

When testing the effects of specific interventions on behavior disorders, the investigator is less interested in small day-to-day fluctuations that are a part of so much behavior. In these cases the investigator must make a judgment on how much behavioral variability to ignore when looking for functional relations among overall trends in behavior and treatment in question. To the investigator interested in determining all sources of variability in individual behavior, this is a very difficult choice. For applied researchers, the choice is often determined by the practical considerations of discovering a therapeutic variable that "works" for a specific behavior problem in an individual. The necessity of determining the effects of a given treatment may constrain the applied researcher from improvising designs in mid-experiment to search for a source of each and every fluctuation that appears.

In correlational designs, where one simply introduces a variable and observes the "trend," statistics have been devised to determine the significance of the trend over and above the behavioral fluctuation (Campbell & Stanley, 1966; Cook & Campbell, 1979; see also chapter 9). In experimental designs such as A-B-A-B, where one is looking for cause-effect relationships, investigators will occasionally resort to averaging two or more data points within phases. This intrasubject averaging, which is sometimes called *blocking*, will usually make trends in behavior more visible, so that the clinician can judge the magnitude and clinical relevance of the effect. This procedure is dangerous, however, if the investigator is under some illusion that the variability has somehow disappeared or is unimportant to an understanding of the controlling effects of the behavior in question. This method is simply a procedure to make large and clinically significant changes resulting from introduction and withdrawal of treatment more apparent. To illustrate the procedure, the original data on caloric intake in a subject with anorexia nervosa will be presented for comparison with published data (Agras et al., 1974). The data as published are presented in Figure 2.4. After the baseline phase, material reinforcers such as cigarettes were administered contingent on weight gain in a phase labeled *reinforcement*. In the next phase, informational *feedback* was added to reinforcement. Feedback consisted of presenting the subject

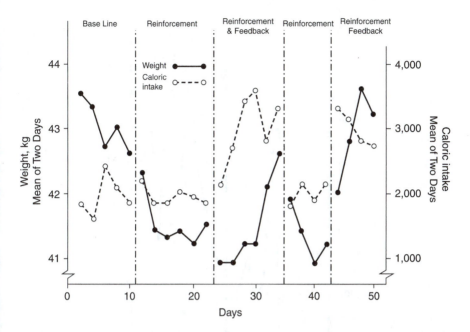

FIGURE 2.4 Data from an experiment examining the effect of feedback on the eating behavior of a patient with anorexia nervosa (Patient 4). (Figure 3, p. 283, from: Agras, W. S., Barlow, D. H., Chapin, H. N., Abel, G. G., and Leitenberg, H. [1974]. Behavior modification of anorexia nervosa. *Archives of General Psychiatry*, *30*, 279–286. Copyright 1974 by American Medical Association. Reproduced by permission.)

with daily weight counts of caloric intake after each meal and counts of number of mouthfuls eaten. The data indicate that caloric intake was relatively stable during the reinforcement phase but increased sharply when feedback was added to reinforcement. Six data points are presented in each of the reinforcement and reinforcement-feedback phases. Each data point represents the mean of two days. With this method of data presentation, caloric intake during reinforcement looks quite stable.

In fact, there was a good deal of day-to-day variability in caloric intake during this phase. If one examines the day-to-day data, caloric intake ranged from 1,450 to 3,150 over the 12-day phase (see Figure 2.5). Since the variability assumed a pattern of roughly one day of high caloric intake followed by a day of low intake, the average of two days presents a stable pattern. When feedback was added during the next 12-day phase, the day-to-day variability remained, but the range was displaced upward, from 2,150 to 3,800 calories per day. Once again, this pattern of variability was approximately one day of high caloric intake followed by a low value. In fact, this pattern obtained throughout the experiment.

In this experiment, feedback was clearly a potent therapeutic procedure over and above the variability, whether one examines the data day-by-day or in

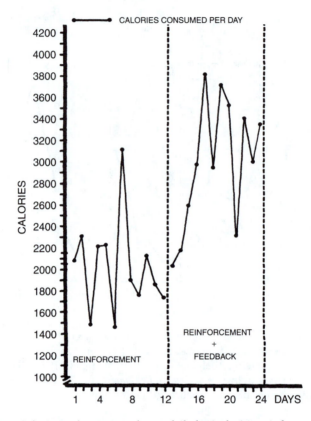

FIGURE 2.5   Caloric intake presented on a daily basis during reinforcement and reinforcement and feedback phases for the patient whose data is presented in Figure 2.4. (Replotted from Figure 3, p. 283, from: Agras, W. S., Barlow, D. H., Chapin, H. N., Abel, G. G., and Leitenberg, H. 1974). Behavior modification of anorexia nervosa. *Archives of General Psychiatry*, **30**, 279–286. Copyright 1974 by American Medical Association. Reproduced by permission.)

blocks of 2 days. The averaged data, however, present a clear picture of the effect of the variable over time. Because the major purpose of the experiment was to demonstrate the effects of various therapeutic variables with anorexics, we chose to present the data in this way. It was not our intention, however, to ignore the daily variability. The fairly regular pattern of change suggests several environmental or metabolic factors that may account for these changes. If one were interested in more basic research on eating patterns in individuals with anorexia, one would have to explore possible sources of this variability in a finer analysis than we chose to undertake here.

It is possible, of course, that feedback might not have produced the clear and clinically relevant increase noted in these data. If feedback resulted in a small increase in caloric intake that was clearly visible only when data were averaged, one would have to resort to statistical tests to determine if the increase could be attributed to the therapeutic variable over and above the day-to-day variability (see chapter 9). Once again, however, one may question the clinical relevance of the therapeutic procedure if the improvement in behavior is so small that the investigator must use statistics to determine if change actually occurred. If this situation obtained, the preferred strategy might be to improvise on the experimental design and augment the therapeutic procedure such that more relevant and substantial changes were produced. The issue of clinical versus statistical significance, which was discussed in some detail above, is a recurring one in single-case research. In the last analysis, however, this is always reduced to judgments by therapists, educators, and so on, on the magnitude of change that is relevant to the setting. In most cases, these magnitudes are greater than changes that are merely statistically significant.

The above example notwithstanding, the conservative and preferred approach of data presentation in single-case research is to present all of the data so that other investigators may examine the intrasubject variability firsthand and draw their own conclusions on the relevance of this variability to the problem.

Large intrasubject variability is a common feature during repeated measurements of target behaviors in a single-case, particularly in the beginning of an experiment, when the subject may be accommodating to intrusive measures. How much variability the researcher is willing to tolerate before introducing an independent variable (therapeutic procedure) is largely a question of judgment on the part of the investigator. Similar procedural problems arise when introduction of the independent variable itself results in increased variability. Here the experimenter must consider alteration in length of phases to determine if variability will decrease over time (as it often does), clarifying the effects of the independent variable. These procedural questions will be discussed in some detail in chapter 3.

2.5. RELATION OF VARIABILITY TO GENERALITY OF FINDINGS

The search for sources of variability within individuals and the use of improvised and fast-changing experimental designs appear to be contrary to one of the most cherished goals of any science—the establishment of generality of findings. Studying the idiosyncrasies of one subject would seem, on the surface, to confirm Underwood's (1957) observation that intensive study of individuals will lead to discovery of laws that are applicable only to that individual. In fact, the identification of sources of variability in this manner leads to increases in generality of findings.

If one assumes that behavior is lawful, then identifying sources of variability in one subject should give us important leads in sources of variability in other similar subjects undergoing the same treatments. As Sidman (1960) pointed out,

> Tracking down sources of variability is then a primary technique for establishing generality. Generality and variability are basically antithetical concepts. If there are

major undiscovered sources of variability in a given set of data, any attempt to achieve subject or principle generality is likely to fail. Every time we discover and achieve control of a factor that contributes to variability, we increase the likelihood that our data will be reproducible with new subjects and in different situations. Experience has taught us that precision of control leads to more extensive generalization of data. (p. 152)

And again,

It is unrealistic to expect that a given variable will have the same effects upon all subjects under all conditions. As we identify and control a greater number of the conditions that determine the effects of a given experimental operation, in effect we decrease the variability that may be expected as a consequence of the operation. It then becomes possible to produce the same results in a greater number of subjects. Such generality could never be achieved if we simply accepted intersubject variability and gave equal status to all deviant subjects in an investigation. (p. 190)

In other words, the more we learn about the effects of a treatment on different individuals, in different settings, and so on, the easier it will be to determine if that treatment will be effective with the next individual walking into the office. But if we ignore differences among individuals and simply average them into a group mean, it will be more difficult to estimate the effects on the next individual, or "generalize" the results. In applied research, when intersubject and intrasubject variability are enormous, and putative sources of the variability are difficult to control, the establishment of generality is a difficult task indeed. But the establishment of a science of human behavior change depends heavily on procedures to establish generality of findings. This important issue will be discussed in the next section.

2.6. GENERALITY OF FINDINGS

Types of generality

Generalization means many things. In applied research, generalization usually refers to the process in which behavioral or attitudinal changes in the treatment setting "generalize" to other aspects of the client's life. In educational research this can mean generalization of behavioral changes from the classroom to the home. Generalization of this type can be determined by observing behavioral changes outside of the treatment setting.

There are at least three additional types of generality in behavior change research, however, that are more relevant to the present discussion. The first is generality of findings across subjects or clients; that is, if a treatment effects certain behavior changes in one subject, will the same treatment also work in other subjects with similar characteristics? As we shall see below, this is a large question because subjects can be "similar" in many different ways. For instance, subjects may be similar in that they have the same diagnostic labels or behavioral disorders (e.g., schizophrenia or phobia). In addition, subjects may be of similar age (e.g., between 14 and 16) or come from similar socioeconomic backgrounds.

Generality across behavior change agents is a second type. For instance, will a therapeutic technique that is effective when applied by one behavior change agent also be effective when applied to the same problem by different agents? A common example is the classroom. If a young, African American, female teacher with a positive attitude successfully uses reinforcement principles to control disruptive behavior in her classroom, will an older Caucasian male teacher who is more stern also be able to apply successfully the same principles to similar problems in his class? Will an experienced therapist be able to treat a middle-aged individual with claustrophobia more effectively than a naive therapist who uses exactly the same procedure?

A third type of generality concerns the variety of settings in which clients are found. The question here is will a given treatment or intervention applied by the same or similar therapist, to similar clients, work as well in one setting as another? For example, would reinforcement principles that work in the classroom also work in a summer camp setting, or would anger management training focused on work settings for an individual with post traumatic stress disorder, generalize to the home?

These questions are very important to clinicians who are concerned with which treatments are most effective with a given client in a given setting. Typically, clinicians have looked to the applied researcher to answer these questions.

Problems in generalizing from a single-case

The most obvious limitation in studying a single-case is that one does not know if the results from this case would be relevant to other cases. Even if one isolates the active therapeutic variable in a given client through a rigorous single-case experimental design, critics note that there is little basis for inferring that this therapeutic procedure would be equally effective when applied to clients with similar behavior disorders (client generality) or that different therapists using this technique would achieve the same results (therapist generality). Finally, one does not know if the technique would work in a different setting (setting generality). This issue, more than any other, has retarded the development of single-case methodology in applied research and has caused many authorities on research to deny the utility of studying a single-case for any other purpose than the generation of hypotheses. On the other hand some limitations exist in generalizing from large group designs that are often overlooked. The purpose of this section is to outline the major issues, assumptions, and goals of generality of findings as related to behavior change in an individual and to describe the advantages and disadvantages of the various procedures to establishing generality of findings.

2.7. SOME LIMITATIONS OF GROUP DESIGNS IN ESTABLISHING GENERALITY OF FINDINGS

In chapter 1, section 1.5, several limitations of group designs in applied research were outlined. One of the limitations referred to difficulties in generalizing results from a group to an individual. In this category, two problems stand out. The first is inferring that results from a relatively homogeneous group are representative of a given population. The second is generalizing from the average response of a heterogeneous group to a particular individual. These two problems will be discussed in turn.

Random sampling and inference in applied research

After the brilliant work of R. A. Fisher, early applied researchers were most concerned with drawing a truly random sample of a given population, so that results would be generalizable to this population. For instance, if one wished to draw some conclusion on the effects of a given treatment for schizophrenia, one would have to draw a random sample of all people with schizophrenia.

In reference to the three types of generality mentioned above, this means that the clients under study (e.g., individuals with schizophrenia) must be a random sample of all such individuals, not only for behavioral components of the disorder, such as positive and negative symptoms, but also for other patient characteristics such as age, sex, and socioeconomic status. These conditions must be fulfilled before one can infer that a treatment that demonstrates a statistically significant effect would also be effective for other individuals with schizophrenia outside of the study. As Edgington (1967) pointed out, "In the absence of random samples hypothesis testing is still possible, but the significance statements are restricted to the effect of the experimental treatments on the subjects actually used in the experiment, generalization to other individuals being based on logical nonstatistical considerations" (p. 195). If one wishes to make statements about effectiveness of a treatment across therapists or settings, random samples of therapists and settings must also be included in the study.

Random sampling of characteristics in the animal laboratories of experimental psychology is feasible, at least across subjects, since most relevant characteristics such as genetic and environmental determinants of individual behavior can be controlled. In clinical or educational research, however, it is extremely difficult to sample adequately the population of a particular syndrome. One reason for this is the prototypical status of diagnostic categories (APA, 2000). In order to sample the population of people with schizophrenia one must be able to pinpoint the various behavioral characteristics that make up this diagnosis and ensure that any sample adequately represents these behaviors. But in one setting, the clients might be characterized by mostly positive symptoms (hallucinations, delusions, etc.) while in another, negative symptoms (behavioral withdrawal) may be more evident with relatively little overlap.

A second problem that arises when one is attempting an adequate sample of a population is the availability of clients who have the needed behavior or characteristics to fill out the sample (see chapter 1, section 1.5). In laboratory animal research this is not a problem because subjects with specified characteristics or genetic backgrounds can be ordered or produced in the laboratories. In applied research, however, one must study what is available (termed a sample of convenience), and this may result in a heavy weighting on certain client characteristics and inadequate sampling of other characteristics. Results of a treatment applied to this sample cannot be generalized to the population. For example, techniques to control disruptive behavior in the classroom will be less than generalizable if they are tested in a class where students are from predominantly middle-class suburbs and inner-city students are underrepresented.

It should be noted that all examples above refer to generality of findings across clients with similar behavior and background characteristics. Most studies at least consider the importance of generality of findings along this dimension, although few have been successful. What is perhaps more important is the failure of most studies to consider the generality problem in the other two dimensions—namely, setting generality and behavior change agent (therapist) generality. In regard to setting generality, as far back as 1956, Brunswick suggested that, "In fact, proper sampling of situations and problems may be in the end more important than proper sampling of subjects considering the fact that individuals are probably on the whole much more alike than are situations among one another" (p. 39). Because of these problems, many sophisticated investigators specializing in research methodology have accepted the impracticability of random sampling in this context and have sought other methods for establishing generality (e.g., Edgington, 1995).

The failure to be able to make statistically inferential statements, even about populations of clients based on most clinical research studies, does not mean that no statements about generality can be made. As Edgington (1995) pointed out early on, one can make statements at least on generality of findings to similar clients based on logical non-statistical considerations. Edgington referred to this as *logical generalization*, and this issue, along with generality to settings and therapists, will be discussed below in relation to the establishment of generality of findings from a single case.

Problems in generalizing from the group to the individual

The above discussion might be construed as a plea for more adequate sampling procedures involving larger numbers of clients seen in many different settings by a variety of therapists—in other words, the notion of the "grand collaborative study," which emerged from the conferences on research in psychotherapy in the 1960s (e.g., Bergin & Strupp, 1972; Strupp & Luborsky, 1962). In fact, this has been the predominant trend of the last several decades across the health care spectrum, as investigators and policymakers strive for representation of findings. Thus, in recent years, the Government has spent hundreds of millions of dollars on large multi-site collaborative randomized clinical trials. In some studies, two or three different sites may be involved; in others, twenty or more sites are included, with hundreds and sometimes thousands of patients enrolled in these (e.g., Barlow, Gorman, Shear & Woods, 2000; Clever et al., 2006). The goal here, of course, is to make broad general statements about the likely response of patients across a variety of settings treated by a large number of different therapists. If (clinically) significant effects emerge, policy makers and the public at large are more sanguine about the relevance of these findings. Nevertheless, one of the pitfalls of a truly random sample in applied research is that the more adequate the sample, in that all relevant population characteristics are represented, the less relevance will this finding have for a specific individual. The major issue here is that the better the sample, the more heterogeneous the group. The average response of this group, then, will be less likely to represent a given individual in the group. Thus, if one were establishing a random sample of individuals with severe depression, one should include clients of various ages, and racial, and socioeconomic backgrounds. In addition, clients with various combinations of the prototypical behavior and thinking or perceptual disorder associated with severe depression must be included. It would be desirable to include some patients with severe agitation, others demonstrating psychomotor retardation, still others with varying degrees and types of depressive delusions, and those with somatic correlates such as terminal sleep disturbance. As this sample becomes truly more random and representative, the group becomes more heterogeneous. The specific effects of a given treatment on an individual with a certain combination of problems become lost in the group average. For instance, a certain treatment might alleviate severe agitation and terminal sleep disturbance but have a deleterious effect on psychomotor retardation and depressive delusions. If one were to analyze the results, one could infer that the treatment, on the average, is better than no treatment for the population of patients with severe depression. For the individual clinician, this finding is not very helpful and could actually be dangerous if the clinician's patient had psychomotor retardation and depressive delusions.

Most studies, however, do not pretend to draw a truly random sample of patients with a given diagnosis or behavior disorder. Most studies choose clients or patients on the basis of availability after deciding on inclusion and exclusion criteria and then randomly assign these subjects into two or more groups that are matched on relevant characteristics. Typically, the treatment is administered to one group while the other group receives variations of the treatment alternative treatments, or perhaps, no-treatment, although this is less likely in present years. This arrangement, which has characterized much clinical and educational research, suffers for two reasons; (1) To the extent that the "available" clients are not a random sample, one cannot generalize to the population; and (2) to the extent that the group is heterogeneous on any of a number of characteristics, one cannot make statements about the individual. The only statement that can be made concerns the average response of a group with that particular makeup which, unfortunately, is unlikely to be duplicated again. As Bergin noted as early as 1966, it was even difficult to say anything important about individuals within the group based on the average response because his analysis demonstrated that some were improving and some deteriorating (see Strupp & Hadley, 1979). The result, as Chassan (1967, 1979) eloquently pointed out, was that the behavior change agent did not know which treatment or aspect of treatment was effective that was statistically better than no treatment, but that actually might make a particular patient worse.

Improving generality of findings to the individual through homogeneous groups: logical generalization

What Bergin and Strupp (1972) and others (e.g., Kiesler, 1971; Paul, 1967) in those early years recognized was that if anything important was going to be said about the individual, after experimenting with a group, then the group would have to be homogeneous for relevant client characteristics. For example, in a study of a group of patients with panic disorder with agoraphobia (PDA), they should all be in one age group with a relatively homogeneous amount of fear and approximately equivalent background (personality) variables. Naturally, clients in the control group must also be homogeneous for these characteristics.

Although this approach sacrifices random sampling and the ability to make inferential statements about the population of patients with panic disorder with agoraphobia, one can begin to say something about other individuals with agoraphobia with the same or similar characteristics as those in the study through the process of logical generalization (Edgington, 1967, 1980a.). That is, if a study shows that a given treatment is successful with a homogeneous group of 20- to 30-year-old females with panic disorder with agoraphobia with certain personality characteristics, then a clinician can be relatively confident that a 25-year-old female suffering from panic disorder with agoraphobia with those personality characteristics will respond well to that same treatment. The process of logical generalization depends on similarities between the patients in the homogeneous group and the individual in question in the clinician's office. Which features of a case are important for extending logical generalization and which features can be ignored (e.g., hair color) will depend on the judgment of the clinician and the state of knowledge at the time. But if one can generalize in logical fashion from a patient whose results or characteristics are well specified as part of a homogeneous group, then one can also logically generalize from a single individual whose response and biographical characteristics are specified. In fact, the rationale has enabled applied researchers to generalize the results of single-case experiments for years (Dukes, 1965; Hayes et al., 1999; Kazdin, 2003; Shontz, 1965). To increase the base for generalization from a single-case experiment, one simply repeats the same experiment several times on similar patients, thereby providing the clinician with results from a number of patients.

2.8. HOMOGENEOUS GROUPS VERSUS REPLICATION OF A SINGLE-CASE EXPERIMENT

Because the issue of generalization from single-case experiments in applied research is a major source of controversy (Hayes et al., 1999; Kazdin, 2003), the sections to follow will describe our views of the relative merits of replication studies versus generalization from homogeneous groups.

As a basis for comparison, it is useful to compare the single-case approach with Paul's (1967, 1969) still incisive analysis of the power of various experimental designs using groups of clients. Within the context of the power of these various designs to establish cause-effect relationships, Paul reviewed the several procedures commonly used in applied research. These procedures range from case studies with and without measurement, from which cause effect relationships can seldom if ever be extracted, through series of cases typically reporting percentage of success with no control group. Finally, Paul cited the two major between-group experimental designs capable of establishing functional relationships between treatments and the average response of clients in the group. The first is what Paul referred to as the nonfactorial design with no-treatment control, in other words the comparison of an experimental (treatment) group with a no-treatment control group. The second design is the powerful factorial design, which not only establishes cause effect relations between treatments and clients but also specifies what type of clients under what conditions improve with a given treatment; in other words, client-treatment interactions. The single-case replication strategy paralleling the nonfactorial design with no-treatment control is *direct replication*. The replication strategy paralleling the factorial design is called *systematic replication*.

Direct replication and treatment/no-treatment control group design

When Paul's article was written (1967), applied research employing single-case designs, usually of the A-B-A variety, was just beginning to appear (e.g., Ullmann & Krasner, 1965). Paul quickly recognized the validity or power of this design, noting that "The level of product for this design approaches that of the nonfactorial group design with no-treatment controls" (p. 117). When Paul spoke of level of product here he was referring, in Campbell and Stanley's (1963) terms, to internal validity, that is, the power of the design to isolate the independent variable (treatment) as responsible for experimental effects—and to external validity or the ability to generalize findings across relevant domains such as client, therapist, and setting. We would agree with Paul's notions that the level of product of a single-case experimental design only "approaches" that of treatment/no-treatment group designs, but for somewhat different reasons. It is our contention that the single-case A-B-A design approaches rather than equals the nonfactorial group design with notreatment controls only because the number of clients is considerably less in a single-case design ($N = 1$) than in a group design, where eight, ten, or more clients are not uncommon. It is our further contention that, in terms of external validity or generality of findings, a series of single-case designs in similar clients in which the original experiment is directly replicated three or four times can produce robust results that may equal or surpass those produced by the experimental group/no-treatment control group design. Some of the reasons for this assertion are outlined next.

Results generated from an experimental group/no-treatment control group study as well as a direct replication series of single-case experimental designs yield some information on generality of findings across clients but cannot address the question of generality across different therapists or settings. Typically, the group study employs one therapist in one setting who applies a given treatment to a group of clients. Measures are taken on a pre-post basis. Premeasures and postmeasures are also taken from a matched group of clients in the control group who do not receive the intervening treatment. For example, ten depressive patients homogeneous on behavioral and emotional aspects of their depression, as well as personality characteristics, would be compared to a matched group of patients who did not receive treatment. Logical generalization to other patients (but not to other therapists or settings) would depend on the degree of homogeneity among the depressives in both groups. As noted above, the less homogeneous the depression in the experiment, the greater the difficulty for the practicing clinician in determining if that treatment is effective for his or her particular patient. A solution to this problem would be to specify in some detail the characteristics of each patient in the treatment group and present individual data on each patient. The clinician could then observe those patients that are most like his or her particular client and determine if these experimental patients improved more than the average response in the control group. For example, after describing in detail the case history and presenting symptomatology of ten depressives, one could administer a pretest measuring severity of depression to the ten depressives and a matched control group of ten depressives. After treatment of the ten depressives in the experimental group, the post test would be administered. When results are presented, the improvement (or lack of improvement) of each patient in the treatment group could be presented either graphically or in numerical form along with the means and standard deviations for the control group. After the usual procedure to determine statistical significance, the clinician could examine the *amount* of improvement of each patient in the experimental group to determine (1) if the improvement were *clinically* relevant, and (2) if the improvement exceeded any drift toward improvement in the control group. To the extent that some patients in the treatment group were similar to the clinician's patient, the clinician could begin to determine, through logical generalization, whether the treatment might be effective with his or her patient.

However, a series of single-case designs where the original experiment is replicated on a number of patients also enables one to determine generality of findings across patients (but not across therapists or settings). For example, in the same hypothetical group of depressives, the treatment could be administered in an A-B-A-B design, where A represents baseline measurement and B represents the treatment. The comparison here is still between treatment and no treatment. As results accumulate across patients, generality of findings is established, and the results are readily translatable to the practicing clinician, since he or she can quickly determine which patient with which characteristics improved and which patient did not improve. To the extent that therapist and treatment are alike across patients, this is the clinical prototype of a direct replication series (Sidman, 1960), and it represents the most common replication tactic in the experimental single-case approach to date.

Given these results, other attributes of the single-case design provide added strength in generalizing results to other clients. The first attribute is flexibility (noted in section 2.3). If a particular procedure works well in one case but works less well or fails when attempts are made to replicate this in a second or third case, slight alterations in the procedure can be made immediately. In many cases, reasons for the inability to replicate the findings can be ascertained immediately, assuming that procedural deficiencies were, in fact, responsible for the lack of generality. An example of this result was outlined in section 2.3, describing intersubject variability. In this example, one patient improved with treatment, but a second did not. Use of an improvised experimental design at this point allowed identification of the reason for failure. This finding should increase generality of findings by enabling immediate application of the altered procedure to another patient with a similar response pattern. This is an example of Sidman's (1960) assertion that "tracking down sources of variability is then a primary technique of establishing generality" (see also Kazdin, 2003; Leitenberg, 1973; Skinner, 1966b). If alterations in the procedure do not produce clinical improvement, either differences in background, *personality* characteristics, or differences within the behavior disorder itself can be noted, suggesting further hypotheses on procedural changes that can be tested on this type of client at a later date.

Finally, using the client as his or her own control in successive replications provides an added degree of strength in generalizing the effect of treatment across differing clients. In group or single-case designs employing no-treatment controls or attention-placebo controls, it is possible and even quite likely that certain environmental events in a no-treatment control group or phase will produce considerable improvements (e.g., placebo effects). In a nonfactorial group design, where treated clients show more improvement than clients in a no-treatment control, one can conclude that the treatment is effective and then proceed in generalizing results to other clients in clinical situations. However, the *degree* of the contribution of nonspecific environmental factors to the improvement of *each individual* client is difficult to judge. In a single-case design (for example, the A-B-A-B or true withdrawal design), the influence of environmental factors on each individual client can be estimated by observing the degree of deterioration when treatment is withdrawn. If environmental or other factors are operating during treatment, improvement will continue during the withdrawal phase, perhaps at a slower rate, necessitating further experimental inquiry. Even in a nonfactorial group design with powerful effects, the contribution of this factor to *individual* clients is difficult to ascertain.

Systematic and clinical replication and factorial designs

Direct replication series and nonfactorial designs with no-treatment controls come to grips with only one aspect of generality of findings—generality across clients. These designs are not capable of simultaneously answering questions on generality of findings across therapists, settings, or clients that differ in some substantial degree from the original homogeneous group. For example, one might ask, if the treatment works for 25-year-old females with agoraphobia with certain personality characteristics. will it also work for a 40-year-old female with agoraphobia with different personality characteristics?

In the therapist domain, the obvious question concerns the effectiveness of treatment as related to that particular therapist. If the therapist in the hypothetical study were an older, more experienced therapist, would the treatment work as well with a young therapist? Finally, even if several therapists in one setting were successful, could therapists in another setting and geographical area attain similar results?

To answer all of these questions would require literally hundreds of experimental group/no-treatment control group studies where each of the factors relevant to generalization was varied one at a time (e.g., type of therapist, type of client). Even if this were feasible, however, the results could not always be attributed to the factor in question as replication after replication ensued, because other sources of variance due to faulty random assignment of clients to the group could appear.

In reviewing the status and goals of psychotherapy research, many clinical investigators (e.g., Kazdin, 2003; Paul, 1967) proposed the application of one of the most sophisticated experimental designs in the armamentarium of the psychological researcher—the factorial design—as an answer to the above problem. In this design, relevant factors in all three areas of generality of concern to the clinician can be examined. The power of this design is in the specificity of the conclusion.

For example, the effects of two antidepressant pharmacological agents and a placebo might be evaluated in two different settings (the inpatient ward of a general hospital and an outpatient community mental health center) on two groups of depressives (one group with moderate to severe depression and a second group with mild depression). A therapist in the psychiatric ward setting would administer each treatment to one half of each group of depressives—the moderate-to-severe group and the mild group. All depressives would be matched as closely as possible on background variables such as age, sex, and personality characteristics. The same therapist could then travel to the community mental health center and carry out the same procedure. Thus we have a $2 \times 2 \times 2$ factorial design. Possible conclusions from this study are numerous, but results might be so specific as to indicate that antidepressants do work but only with moderate to severe depressives and only if hospitalized in a psychiatric ward. It would not be possible to draw conclusions on the importance of a particular type of therapist because this factor was not systematically varied. Of course, the usual shortcomings of group designs are also present here because results would be presented in terms of group averages and intersubject variability. However, to the extent that subjects in each experimental cell were homogeneous and to the extent that improvement was large and clinically important rather than merely statistically significant, then results would certainly be a valuable contribution. The clinical practitioner would be able to examine the characteristics of those subjects in the improved group and conclude that under similar conditions (i.e., an inpatient psychiatric unit) his or her moderate to severe depressive patient would be likely to improve, assuming, of course, that this patient resembled those in the study. Here again, the process of logical generalization rather than statistical inference from a sample to a population is the active mechanism.

Thus, while the factorial design can be effective in specifying generality of findings across all important domains in applied research (within the limits discussed above), one major problem remains: These studies are expensive and time consuming, usually requiring government funding across multiple sites. In addition, the arguments raised in the last section on inflexibility of the group design are also applicable here. If one patient does not improve or reacts in an unusual way to the therapeutic procedure, administration of the procedure must continue for the specified number of sessions. The unsuccessful or aberrant results are then, of course, averaged into the group results from that experimental cell, thus precluding an immediate analysis of the intersubject variability, which will lead to increased generality.

Systematic and clinical replication procedures involve exploring the effects of different settings, therapists, or clients on a procedure previously demonstrated as successful in a direct replication series. In other words, to borrow the example from the factorial design, a single-case design may demonstrate that a treatment for severe depression works on an inpatient unit. Several direct replications then establish generality among homogeneous patients. The next task is to replicate the procedure once again, in different settings with different therapists or with patients with different background characteristics. Thus the goals of systematic and clinical replication in terms of generality of findings are similar to those of the factorial study.

At first glance, it does not appear as if replication techniques within single case methodology would prove any more practical in answering questions concerning generality of findings across therapists, settings, and types of behavior disorder. While direct replication can begin to provide answers to questions on generality of findings across similar clients, the large questions of setting and therapist generality would also seem to require significant collaboration among diverse investigators, long-range planning, and a large investment of money and time. To some extent this is true. But the promise of recently established practice research networks (Borkenic NIDA) greatly increases the likelihood of meaningful collections of data in this manner. In view of the fact that systematic and clinical replication has the same advantages of logical generalization as direct replication the information yielded by the procedure has direct applicability to the clinic. Examples from these ongoing systematic replication and clinical series and procedures and guidelines for replication will be described in chapter 10.

2.9. BLURRING THE DISTINCTION BETWEEN DESIGN OPTIONS

The purpose of this book in general and this chapter in particular is to illustrate the underlying rationale for single-case experimental designs. To achieve this goal, the strategies and underlying rationale of more traditional between-group designs have been placed in sharp relief relative to single-case designs, to highlight the differences. As noted above, this need not be the case (e.g., Nugent, 1996; Hayes et al., 1999). As described throughout this chapter, group designs could be carried out with close attention to individual change and repeated measures across time. Furthermore, these strategies could be integrated.

If one were comparing treatment and no-treatment, for example, 10 depressed patients could be individually described and repeated measures could be taken of their progress. Amount of change could then be reported in clinically relevant terms. These data could be contrasted with the same reporting of individual data for a no-treatment group. Of course, statistical inferences could be made concerning group differences, based on group averages and intersubject variability within groups, but one would still have the individual data to fall back on. This would be important for purposes of logical generalization, which forms the only rational basis for generalizing results from one group of individual subjects to another individual subject. In our experience as editors of major journals, data from group studies are being reported increasingly in this manner, as investigators alter their underlying rationale for generality of findings from inferential to logical. With individuals carefully described and closely tracked during treatment, the investigator is in a position to speculate on sources of intersubject variability. That is, if one subject improves dramatically while another improves only marginally or perhaps deteriorates during treatment, the investigator can immediately analyze, at least in a *post hoc* fashion, differences between these clients. The investigator would be greatly assisted in making these judgments by repeated measurement within these group studies because the investigator could determine if a specific client was making good progress and then faltered, or simply did not respond at all from the beginning of treatment. Events correlated with a sudden change in the direction of progress could be noted for future reference. All that the investigator would be lacking would be the flexibility inherent in single-case design which would allow a quick change in experimental strategy or an experimental strategy based on the responses of the individual client to immediately track down the sources of this intersubject variability. Of course, many other factors must be considered when choosing appropriate designs, particularly practical considerations such as time, expense, and availability of subjects.

Once again we would suggest that if one is going to generalize from group studies to the variety of individuals entering a practitioner's office, then it is essential that data from individual clients be described so that the process of logical generalization can be applied in its most powerful form. In view of the inapplicability of making statistical inferences to hypothetical populations, based on random sampling, logical generalization is the *only* method available to us, and we must maximize its strength with thorough description of individuals in the study.

With these cautions in place, and with a full understanding of the rationale and strengths of single-case designs, the investigator can then make a reasoned choice on design options. For example, for comparing two treatments with no-treatment, where each treatment should be effective but the relative effectiveness is unknown, one might choose an alternating-treatments design (see chapter 8) or a more traditional between-group comparison design with close attention to individual change. The strengths and advantages of alternating-treatments designs are fully discussed in chapter 8, but if one has a large number of subjects available and a fixed treatment protocol that for one reason or another cannot be altered during treatment, regardless of progress, then one may wish to use a between-group strategy with appropriate attention to individual data. Subsequent experimental strategies could be employed using single-case experimental designs during follow-up to deal with minimal responders or those who do not respond at all or perhaps deteriorate. But sources of intersubject variability *must* be tracked down eventually if we are to advance our science and ensure the generality of our results. Treatment in between-group designs could also be applied in a relatively "pure" form, much as it would be in a clinical setting. Occasionally we will refer to these options in the context of describing the various single-case design options throughout this book.

A further blurring of the distinction occurs when single-case designs are applied to groups of subjects. Section 5.6 and Figure 5.17 describe the application of an A-B-A withdrawal design to a large group of subjects. Similarly, a multiple baseline design applied to a large group is discussed in section 7.2. Data are described in terms of group averages in both experiments. These experimental designs, then, approach the tradition of within-subject designs (Edwards, 1968), where the same group of subjects experiences repeated experimental conditions. Appropriate statistical analyses have long been available for these design options (e.g., Kazdin, 2003).

Despite the blurring of experimental traditions that is increasingly taking place, the overriding strength of single-case designs and their replications lies in the use of procedures that are appropriate to studying the subject matter at hand—the individual. It is to a description of these procedures that we now turn.

■ ■ ■ ■ ■

CHAPTER 3

GENERAL PROCEDURES IN SINGLE-CASE RESEARCH

3.1. INTRODUCTION

Some of the many advantages associated with the use of single-case experimental designs were summarized in chapter 2, along with general issues for the researcher or clinician to consider in using such designs. This chapter presents a more concrete and detailed analysis of the general procedures that should be followed in conducting single-case experimental research. Although the procedures used in single-case research have been outlined previously (e.g., Barlow & Hersen, 1973; Kazdin, 1982) (Franklin, Allison, & Gorman, 1997; Kazdin, 2003; Nock, Michel, & Photos, 2007; Photos, Michel, & Nock, 2008), a more comprehensive analysis, from both a theoretical and an applied framework, is needed for at least two reasons.

First, single-case experimental designs continue to be used by only a minority of researchers and clinicians and so the general procedures guiding the use of such designs may not be well-known to most. A review of the literature on psychological treatment research since the 1960s shows that the use of single-case experimental designs increased substantially over the 1960s and 1970s and reports of such designs often appeared in leading psychological and psychiatric journals such as the *Archives of General Psychiatry* (e.g., Agras et al., 1974; Barlow & Hersen, 1973) and the *Journal of Consulting and Clinical Psychology* (e.g., Hayes, 1981; Kazdin, 1978). However, this is no longer the case and sightings of single-case experimental designs are quite rare in these journals over the past several decades.

Second, although single-case experimental designs typically are used properly and effectively in most studies, there remain instances in which researchers make needless errors in the design, implementation, and inferences drawn from single-case studies. Thus, while the procedures reported in this chapter are not entirely new, there is a strong need to consider them anew and to review the various design considerations that are central to single-case research.

This chapter presents the theoretical rationale and practical considerations related to the use of repeated measurement, choosing an appropriate baseline, changing only one independent variable at a time, the use of reversals and withdrawals, the length of experimental phases, and the techniques for evaluating effects of "irreversible" procedures. For heuristic purposes, both correct and incorrect applications in each area will be examined and illustrations of actual and hypothetical cases will be provided. This chapter ends with a discussion of strategies that can be used to assess response maintenance following successful treatment.

3.2. REPEATED MEASUREMENT

In the typical treatment outcome study, whether testing psychological treatment, pharmacotherapy, or both, participants are randomly assigned to treatment conditions (e.g., experimental and control) and dependent measures are obtained at pre-treatment, post-treatment, and in some studies during treatment follow-up (e.g., Ellis et al., 2007). Occasionally, more rigorous designs are used in which dependent measures also are obtained at the midpoint of treatment (e.g., March et al., 2004) or once every three to six months over the course of longer-term treatment (e.g., Brown et al., 2005). Such designs provide the researcher with information about the overall magnitude of change in the dependent measures associated with treatment assignment, and when data are collected during the course of treatment about the gross temporal trends in such change.

However, whether espousing a behavioral, client-centered, existential, or psychoanalytic position, the experienced clinician is undoubtedly cognizant of the fact that changes unfortunately *do not* follow a smooth linear function from the beginning of treatment to its ultimate conclusion. Focusing only on the average amount of change across all individuals from before to after treatment, or even considering change at several pre-selected points, misses an opportunity to go beyond knowing *that* people changed in treatment to learn *how*, *why*, and *when* such change occurred. All of these questions can be addressed more adequately with the use of repeated measurement.

Practical implications and limitations

Numerous practical implications and limitations must be considered when using repeated measurement techniques. First, the methods involved in obtaining such measurements (whether they be motoric, physiological, or attitudinal) must be *specific, observable*, and *replicable* (Kazdin, 2001; Nock & Kurtz, 2005). Specificity refers to the precision of the defined target behavior, such that boundary rules should be clearly established so that it is clear when a behavior has and has not occurred. Observability refers to the extent to which a target behavior can readily measured by multiple observers (i.e., not simply based on self-report of internal events). Replicability refers to the extent to which the observation methods can be duplicated on multiple occasions so as to systematically measure changes in behavior. When measurement techniques require the use of human observers, independent reliability checks must be established (see chapter 4 for more details about assessment methods).

Second, and related to the above, repeated measurements must be performed under exacting and standardized conditions with respect to the measurement devices used, personnel involved, time(s) of day measurements are recorded, instructions to the subject, and specific environmental conditions (e.g., location) where the measurement sessions occur. Deviations from any of these conditions can lead to spurious effects in the data and might result in erroneous conclusions. It is especially important that measurement methods are not altered at the time of changes in experimental conditions (i.e., during the change from baseline to intervention phases). If changes in measurement occur simultaneously with changes in experimental conditions, resulting differences in the data can not be conclusively attributed to the experimental manipulation, inasmuch as a correlative change may have taken place. Under such circumstances, the experimenter must conduct another phase change and be sure to keep the measurement methods constant. Only in this way can the experimenter draw strong inferences about the relation between the independent variable (i.e., the intervention) and the dependent measure of interest (i.e., behavior change).

The importance of maintaining standard measurement conditions bears some illustration. Reyes and colleagues (2006) examined deviant arousal among adult male sex offenders with developmental disabilities. Their methods for assessing deviant arousal were very carefully and consistently applied. Ten participants were individually assessed on multiple occasions, using the same procedures each time (i.e., the same procedures were followed across both participants and assessment occasions). During each assessment, the participant entered a room 2 meters × 2.5 meters in size that contained a recliner covered with an absorbent pad and with a penile plethysmograph gauge on the seat, a television screen from which to view video clips, a metal tray that covered the participant's lap during the assessment, and a camera aimed at the shoulders and head of the participant when seated. Before each session the technician followed exactly the same procedure with each participant in terms of providing instructions to the participant about the experimental procedures, asking standard assessment questions and taking necessary measurements, and calibrating the measurement equipment. During the actual assessment, the participant viewed a series of standard video clips that were exactly 2.5 minutes long and contained people of different ages engaging in a range of activities while wearing a bathing suit (e.g., children and adults eating fruit, reading a magazine, and dipping their feet in a pool). Measurements of penile circumference were taken during the viewing of the clips, and afterwards standard procedures were followed for removing the equipment and ending the assessment occasion. This is but one example of the care and consistency that should be followed while conducting assessments for a careful experiment. Variation from these procedures can introduce variability in the data that can limit the examiner's ability to make inferences about the relation between the independent and dependent variables.

In addition to a change in procedures, there are instances when a change in the experimenter can seriously affect the participant's responses over time. Indeed, this was demonstrated empirically by Agras, Leitenberg, Barlow, and Thomson (1969), in an alternating treatment design (see chapter 8). However, if not explicitly planned, such change can mar the results obtained. For example, when employing the Behavioral Assertiveness Test (Eisler, Miller, & Hersen, 1973) repeatedly over time as a behavioral measure of assertiveness, it is clear that the use of different confederates to promote responding might result in unexpected interaction with the experimental condition (e.g., feedback or instructions) being manipulated. Even when using more objective measurement techniques, such as the mechanical strain gauge for recording penile circumference change (e.g., Reyes et al., 2006), extreme care should be exercised with respect to instructions given and to the role of the examiner (e.g., male versus female research assistant) involved in the measurement session (cf. Wincze, 1982; Wincze & Lange, 1981).

Several other important issues should be considered when using repeated measurement techniques in clinical research. For example, frequency of measurements obtained per unit of time should be given careful attention. The experimenter obviously must ensure that a sufficient number of measurements are recorded so that a representative sample is obtained. On the other hand, the experimenter must exercise caution to avoid taking too many measurements in a given period of time, as fatigue on the part of the subject may result. This is of paramount importance when taking measurements that require an active response on the subject's part (e.g., repeated modeling of responses during the course of a session in assertive training, or number of erections to sexual stimuli over a specific time period).

A unique problem related to measurement traditionally faced by investigators working in institutional settings involved the major environmental changes that take place at night and on weekends. The astute observer who has worked in these settings is quite familiar with the distinction that is made between the "day" and "night" hospital and the "work week" and the "weekend" hospital. Unless the investigator is in a position to exert control over the environment (e.g., Ayllon and Azrin, 1968) careful attention should be paid to such differences. One possible solution is to restrict assessment to only occur during similar periods or conditions (e.g., only take measurements during the day). An alternative would be to plot data separately for day and night measurements. This slight modification in data analysis could yield important information in the data and may reveal significant effects of the intervention that could be obscured by aggregating data across all conditions.

Another consideration in the use of repeated measurement is whether to incorporate the participant's self-report of the behavior of interest. For some outcomes, such as the occurrence of thoughts or feelings (e.g., suicide ideation, experience of fear or anxiety), the subjective experience of the participant may be what is most important. However, several potential problems exist when the experimenter relies in part, or in whole, on self-report data. First, it is possible that the repeated assessment of the participant's report is not capturing true change in the outcome, but instead that the participant's report is influenced by "experimental demand" (Orne, 1962) or social desirability (Crowne & Marlowe, 1960). Second, although the correlation of self-report (attitudinal) measures with motoric and physiological indices of behavior can support the validity of self-report, measurements of the same construct using these different methods often do not correspond (Barlow, Mavissakalian, & Schofield, 1980) (Hofmann, Newman, Ehlers, & Roth, 1995).

A final important issue to consider when collecting data using repeated measurement is how to analyze and interpret the extreme daily variability in the target behavior that can be captured using repeated measurements. In other words, although the observation of more fine-grained changes in behavior over time is a benefit of repeated measurement, it can provide an unwieldy amount of data and it can be especially difficult to interpret frequent and non-linear changes in performance over time. For instance, such problems in measurement can occur in the case of cyclic variation, an excellent example being the effect of the female's estrus cycle on behavior. Issues related to cyclic variation in terms of extended measurement sessions will be discussed more specifically in section 3.6 of this chapter.

3.3. CHOOSING A BASELINE

Virtually all single-case experimental designs (the exception being the B-A-B design) begin with a *baseline*, which refers to the initial period of observation during which repeated measurement is used to determine the natural frequency of the target behavior(s) under study. The baseline is most frequently designated as the "A" phase of study, although others have referred to it as "$O_1O_2O_3O_4$," highlighting the multiple observations (O) that occur during this phase in the absence of any intervention (X) (e.g., Campbell & Stanley, 1966) (Shadish, Cook, & Campbell, 2001).

Baseline measurement serves two primary functions: *descriptive* and *predictive*. The baseline provides a description of the natural occurrence of the target behavior, thus offering a standard by which the subsequent efficacy of an experimental intervention can be evaluated. In addition, the baseline period functions as a predictor for the level of the target behavior attained in the future (Risley & Wolf, 1972) (Kazdin, 2003). A number of statistical techniques for analyzing time series data have appeared in the literature (Edgington, 1982; Gorman & Allison, 1997; Wallace & Elder, 1980); the use of these methods will be discussed in chapter 9.

Baseline stability

Given the two functions of baseline measurement, it is important that the target behavior shows reliability or stability before the experimental (B) condition is initiated. But practically speaking, for how long should the baseline continue and what level of stability is actually required? Unfortunately, there is no simple response or formula that can be applied to these questions.

As a general rule, Kazdin (1982; 2003) suggests stability should be defined by the absence of variability and the absence of a trend (or slope) in the data. Similarly, in the context of basic animal research, where the behavioral history of the organism can be determined and controlled, Sidman (1960) has recommended that, for stability, rates of behavior should be within a 5 percent range of variability. Indeed, "basic science" research is in a position to create baseline data through a variety of interval and ratio scheduling effects. However, even in animal research, where scheduling effects are programmed to ensure stability of baseline conditions there are instances where unexpected variations take place as a consequence of extrinsic variables. When such variability is presumed to be *extrinsic* rather than *intrinsic*, Sidman (1960) has encouraged the researcher to first examine the source of variability through the method of experimental analysis. Then extrinsic sources of variation can be systematically eliminated and controlled.

Sidman acknowledged, however, that the applied clinical researcher, by virtue of his or her subject matter, when control over the behavioral history is nearly impossible, is at a distinct disadvantage. He noted that "The behavioral engineer must continuously take variability as he finds it, and deal with it as an unavoidable fact of life" (Sidman, 1960, p. 192). He also acknowledged that "The behavioral engineer seldom has the facilities or the time that would be required to eliminate variability he encounters in a given problem" (p. 193). When variability in baseline measurements is extensive in applied clinical research, it might be useful to apply statistical techniques for purposes of comparing one phase to the next. This would certainly appear to be the case when such variability exceeds a 50 percent level. The use of statistics under these circumstances would then meet the kind of criticism that has been leveled at the applied clinical researcher who uses single-case methodology. For example, Bandura (1969) argued that there is no difficulty in interpreting performance changes when differences between phases are large (e.g., the absence of overlapping distributions) and when such differences can be replicated across subjects (see chapter 10). However, he underscored the difficulties in reaching valid conclusions when there is "considerable variability during baseline conditions" (p. 243).

In deciding on the length of baseline assessment, one also must consider practical and ethical limitations to extending initial measurement beyond certain limits. The first involves a problem of logistics. For the experimenter working in an institutional setting (unless in an extended-care facility), the subject under study will have to be discharged within a designated period of time, whether upon self-demand, familial pressure, or exhaustion of insurance company compensation—all arguing in favor of a shorter baseline period. Second, even in a facility giving extended care to its patients, there is an obvious ethical question as to how long the applied clinical researcher can withhold a treatment application.

This assumes even greater magnitude when the target behavior under study results in serious discomfort either to the subject or to others in the environment (e.g., J. M. Johnston, 1972, p. 1036). Finally, even under circumstances under which an extended baseline may be possible, one must consider the fact that unexpected effects on behavior may be found as a result of extended measurement through self-recording procedures (Hollon & Bemis, 1981). Such effects have been found when subjects were asked to record their behaviors under repeated measurement conditions. For example, McFall (1970) found that when he asked smokers to monitor their rate of smoking, increases in their actual smoking behavior occurred. By contrast, smokers asked to monitor rate of resistance to smoking did not show parallel changes in their behavior. The problem of self-recorded and self-reported data will be discussed in more detail in chapter 4.

Examples of baselines

With only a few exceptions (e.g., Barlow & Hersen, 1973; 1984; Hersen, 1982;) the different types of baselines commonly encountered in applied clinical research have not been examined or presented in logical sequence in the experimental literature. Therefore, this section provides and familiarizes the reader with examples of baseline patterns. We provide descriptions and illustrations of these different baselines using hypothetical examples derived from common patterns reported in the literature. Along the way, we outline methods for dealing with each pattern and discuss some specific rules the experimenter should follow.

In the prior section we mentioned that in order to satisfy the descriptive and predictive functions, the baseline must show stability, ideally showing the absence of variability or trend. It should be noted that "A minimum of three separate observation points, plotted on the graph, during this baseline phase are required to establish a trend in the data" (Barlow & Hersen, 1973, p. 320). Thus three successively increasing or decreasing points would constitute establishment of either an upward or downward trend in the data. Obviously, in two sets of data in which the same trend is exhibited, differences in the slope of the line will indicate the extent or power of the trend. By contrast, a pattern in which only minor variation is seen would indicate the presence of a stable baseline pattern.

An example of a *stable baseline* pattern is depicted in Figure 3.1. Mean number of facial tics averaged over three daily 15-minute videotaped sessions are presented for a 6-day period. Visual inspection of these data reveals no apparent upward or downward trend. Indeed, data points are essentially parallel to the abscissa (X-axis), while variability on the ordinate (Y-axis) remains at a minimum. This kind of baseline pattern, which shows a constant rate of behavior, represents the most desirable trend as it permits an unequivocal departure for analyzing the subsequent efficacy of a treatment intervention. Following this stable pattern of behavior, the beneficial, absent, or detrimental nature of the intervention applied in the next phase would be quite clear.

In a second type of baseline, the target behavior does not occur at a level frequency, but instead appears to be worsening over time (also known as a *deteriorating baseline;* Barlow & Hersen, 1973). An example of such a pattern using our hypothetical data on facial tics is presented in Figure 3.2. Examination of this figure shows a steadily increasing linear function, with the number of tics observed augmenting over days. Although the data show a trend (or slope), the deteriorating baseline is an acceptable pattern inasmuch as the subsequent application of a successful treatment intervention should lead to a reversed trend in the data (i.e., a decreasing linear function over days). However, should the treatment

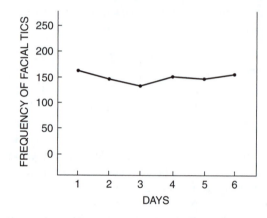

FIGURE 3.1 The stable baseline. Hypothetical data for mean number of facial tics averaged over three daily 15-minute videotaped sessions.

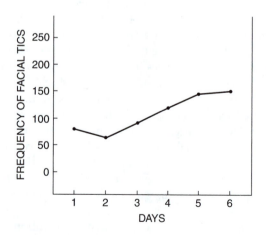

FIGURE 3.2 The increasing baseline (target behavior deteriorating). Hypothetical data for mean number of facial tics averaged over three daily 15-minute videotaped sessions.

be ineffective, no change in the slope of the curve would be observed. If on the other hand, the treatment application leads to further deterioration (i.e., if the treatment is actually detrimental to the patient) (see Dishion, McCord, & Poulin, 1999; Weiss et al., 2005) it would be most difficult to assess its effects using the deteriorating baseline. In other words, a differential analysis as to whether a trend in the data was simply a continuation of the baseline pattern or whether application of a detrimental treatment specifically led to its continuation could not be made. Only if there appeared to be a pronounced change in slope following introduction of a detrimental treatment could some kind of valid conclusion be reached on the basis of visual inspection. Even then, the withdrawal and reintroduction of the treatment would be required to establish its controlling effects. But from both clinical and ethical considerations, this procedure would be clearly unwarranted.

A third type of baseline, and one that perhaps presents the most difficulty for the experimenter, is one that reflects steady improvement in the subject's condition during the course of initial observation. An example of this kind of pattern appears in Figure 3.3. Inspection of this figure shows a linear decrease in tic frequency over a six-day period. The major problem posed by this pattern, from a research standpoint, is that application of a treatment strategy while improvement is already taking place will not allow for an adequate assessment of the intervention. A related problem is that if improvement is maintained following initiation of the intervention, the experimenter would be unable to attribute such continued improvement to the intervention unless a marked change in the slope of the curve were to occur. Moreover, removal of the treatment and its subsequent reinstatement would be required to show any controlling effects.

An alternative, and perhaps more desirable, strategy for dealing with the baselines in which there is an upward or downward trend involves the continuation of baseline measurement with the expectation that a plateau will be reached at some point. If this occurs, the effects of treatment can then be easily evaluated. It is also

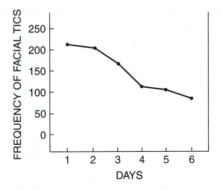

FIGURE 3.3   The decreasing baseline (target behavior improving). Hypothetical data for mean number of facial tics averaged over three daily 15-minute videotaped sessions.

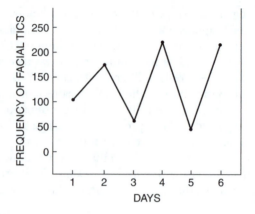

FIGURE 3.4 The variable baseline. Hypothetical data for mean number of facial tics averaged over three 15-minute videotaped sessions.

possible that improvement seen during baseline assessment is merely a function of some extrinsic variable (Sidman, 1960) of which the experimenter is currently unaware. Following Sidman's recommendations, it then behooves the experimenter, assuming that time limitations and clinical and ethical considerations permit, to evaluate empirically, through experimental analysis, the possible source of covariation (e.g., "placebo" effects). The results of this kind of analysis could indeed lead to hypothesis generation about the sources of variability, which then might be subjected to further verification through the experimental analysis method.

A fourth type of baseline is one in which there is extreme variability. Unfortunately, this kind of baseline pattern is frequently obtained during the course of applied clinical research and various strategies for dealing with it are required. An example of the variable baseline is presented in Figure 3.4. An examination of these data indicate a tic frequency of about 24 to 255 tics per day, with no discernible upward or downward trend clearly in evidence. However, a distinct pattern of alternating low and high trends is present.

One possibility (previously discarded in dealing with extreme initial variability) is to simply extend the baseline observation until some semblance of stability is attained, an example of which appears in Figure 3.5. A second strategy involves the use of inferential statistics when comparing baseline and treatment phases, particularly where there is considerable overlap between succeeding distributions. However, if overlap is that extensive, the statistical model will be equally ineffective in finding differences, as appropriate probability levels will not be reached. Further details regarding graphic presentation and statistical analyses of data will appear in chapter 9. A final strategy for dealing with the variable baseline is to systematically assess the sources of variability. However, as pointed out by Sidman (1960), the amount of work and time involved in such an analysis is better suited to the "basic scientist" than the applied clinical researcher. There are times when the clinical researcher will have to learn to live with such variability or to select measures that fluctuate to a lesser degree.

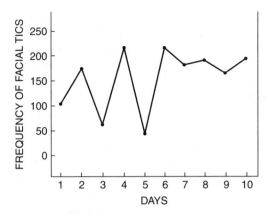

FIGURE 3.5   The variable-stable baseline. Hypothetical data for mean number of facial tics averaged over three daily 15-minute videotaped sessions.

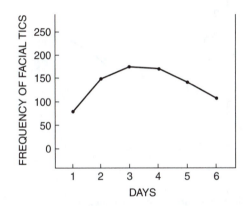

FIGURE 3.6   The increasing-decreasing baseline. Hypothetical data for mean number of facial tics averaged over three daily 15-minute videotaped sessions.

A fifth type of baseline pattern is one in which there is an initial period of deterioration that is followed by a trend toward improvement (see Figure 3.6). This type of baseline (increasing-decreasing) poses a number of problems for the experimenter. First, when time and conditions permit, an empirical examination of the covariants leading to reversed trends would be of great value. Second, although the trend toward improvement is continued in the latter half of the baseline period the application of a treatment will lead to the same difficulties in interpretation that are present in the improving baseline discussed above. Therefore, the most useful course of action involves continuation of measurement procedures until a stable and steady pattern emerges.

A sixth type of baseline that is very similar to the increasing-decreasing pattern is its reciprocal, the decreasing-increasing type of baseline (see Figure 3.7). This kind of pattern often reflects the placebo effects of initially being part of an experiment or being monitored (either self or observed). Although placebo effects are always of interest to the clinical researcher, when he or she is faced with time pressures, the preferred course of action is to continue measurement procedures until a steady pattern in the data is clear. If extended baseline measurement is not feasible, introduction of the treatment following the worsening of the target behavior under study is an acceptable procedure. This is especially true if the controlling effects of the procedure are subsequently demonstrated via its withdrawal and reinstatement.

A seventh and final type of baseline, the unstable baseline, also introduces problems for the experimenter. A hypothetical example of this type of baseline, obtained under extended measurement conditions, appears in Figure 3.8. Examination of these data reveals not only extreme variability but also the absence of a particular pattern. The problems found in the variable baseline are further compounded here by the lack of any trend in the data. This heightens the

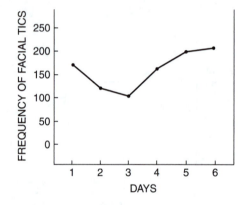

FIGURE 3.7 The decreasing-increasing baseline. Hypothetical data for mean number of facial tics averaged over three daily 15-minute videotaped sessions.

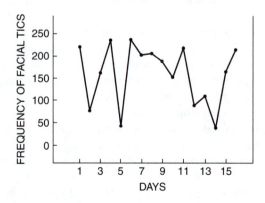

FIGURE 3.8 The unstable baseline. Hypothetical data for mean number of facial tics averaged over three daily 15-minute videotaped sessions.

difficulty in evaluating these data through experimental analysis. Even the procedure of blocking data usually fails to eliminate all instability on the basis of visual analysis. There is no completely satisfactory strategy for dealing with the variable baseline and the experimenter encountering such a pattern should employ the strategies for dealing with the variable baseline outlined above.

3.4. CHANGING ONE VARIABLE AT A TIME

A cardinal rule of single-case experimental research is to change only *one* variable at a time when proceeding from one phase to the next. Barlow and Hersen (1973) pointed out that when two variables are simultaneously manipulated, the experimental analysis does not permit conclusions as to which of the two components (or how much of each) contributed to improvements in the target behavior. It should be underscored that the one-variable rule holds, regardless of the particular phase being evaluated. These strictures are most important when examining the interactive effects of treatment variables (Barlow & Hersen, 1973; Elkin et al., 1973; Leitenberg, Agras, Thomson, & Wright, 1968). A more complete discussion of interaction designs appears in chapter 6, section 6.5.

Correct and incorrect applications

An error committed frequently in single-case experimental research involves the simultaneous manipulation of two variables so as to assess their presumed interactive effects. A review of the literature suggests that this type of error is often made in the latter phases of experimentation. In order to clarify the issues involved, selected examples of correct and incorrect applications will be presented.

For illustrative purposes, let us assume that baseline measurement in a study consists of the number of social responses (operationally defined) emitted by a patient with chronic schizophrenia during a specific observation period. Let us further assume that subsequent introduction of a single treatment variable involves the application of contingent (token) reinforcement following each social response that is observed on the ward. At this point in our hypothetical example, only one variable (token reinforcement) has been added across the two experimental phases (i.e., baseline to the first treatment phase). In accordance with design principles followed in the A-B-A-B design, the third phase would consist of a return to baseline conditions, again changing (removing) only one variable across the second and third phases. Finally, in the fourth phase, token reinforcement would be reinstated (addition of one variable from Phase 3 to 4). Thus, we have a procedurally correct example of the A-B-A-B design (see chapter 5) in which only one variable is altered at a time from phase to phase.

In the following example we present an inaccurate application of single-case methodology. Using our previously described measurement situation, let us assume that baseline assessment is now followed by a treatment combination comprised of token reinforcement and social reinforcement. At this point, the experiment is labeled A-BC. Phase 3 is a return to baseline conditions (A), while

Phase 4 consists of social reinforcement alone (C). Here we have an example of an A-BC-A-C design, with A = baseline, BC = token and social reinforcement, A = baseline, and C = social reinforcement. In this experiment the researcher is completely unable to tease apart the relative effects of token and social reinforcement. From the A-BC-A portion of this experiment, it is feasible only to assess the *combined* BC effect over baseline (A), assuming that the appropriate trends in the data appear. Evaluation of the individual effects of the two variables (social and token reinforcement) comprising the treatment package is not possible. Moreover, application of the C condition (social reinforcement alone) following the second baseline also does not permit firm conclusions, either with respect to the effects of social reinforcement alone or in contrast to the combined treatment of token and social reinforcement. The experimenter is not in a position to examine the interactive effects of the BC and C phases, as they are not adjacent to one another.

If our experimenter were interested in accurately evaluating the interactive effects of token and social reinforcement, the following extended design would be considered appropriate: A-B-A-B-BC-B-BC. Using this experimental strategy, the interactive effects of social and token reinforcement could be examined systematically by comparing differences in trends between the adjacent B (token reinforcement) and BC (token and social reinforcement) phases. The subsequent return to B and reintroduction of the combined BC would allow for analysis of the additive and controlling effects of social reinforcement, assuming expected trends in the data occur.

A classic, published example of the correct manipulation of variables across phases appears in Figure 3.9. In this study, Leitenberg et al. (1968) examined the separate and combined effects of feedback and praise on the mean number of seconds a knife-phobic patient allowed himself to be exposed to a knife. An examination of the seven phases of study reveals the following progression of variables: (1) feedback, (2) feedback and praise, (3) feedback, (4) no feedback and no praise, (5) feedback, (6) feedback and praise, and (7) feedback. A comparison of adjacent phases shows that only one variable was manipulated (added or subtracted) at a time across phases. In a similar design, Elkin et al. (1973) assessed additive and subtractive effects of therapeutic variables in a case of anorexia nervosa. The following progression of variables was used in a six-phase experiment: (1) 3,000 calories—*baseline*, (2) 3,000 calories—*feedback*, (3) 3,000 calories—*feedback and reinforcement*, (4) 4,500 calories—*feedback and reinforcement*, (5) 3,000 calories—*feedback and reinforcement*, (6) 4,500 calories—*feedback and reinforcement*. Again, changes from one phase to the next (italicized) never involved more than the manipulation of a single variable.

Exceptions to the rule

Legitimate exceptions to the rule of maintaining a consistent stepwise progression (additive or subtractive) across phases have appeared in a number of single-case experimental studies. As one example, Ramp et al. (1971) examined the effects of presenting instructions and delayed time-out in a nine-year-old male elementary school student with disciplinary problems. Two target behaviors (intervals out of

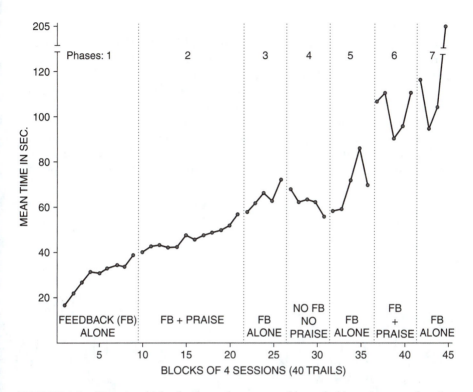

FIGURE 3.9   Time in which a knife was kept exposed by a phobic patient as a function of feedback, feedback *plus* praise, and no feedback or praise conditions. (Figure 2. p. 136, from Leitenberg, H., Agras, W. S., Thomson, L., & Wright, D. E. (1968), Feedback in behavior modification: An experimental analysis in two phobic cases. *Journal of Applied Behavior Analysis*, **1,** 131–137. Copyright 1968 by Society for the Experimental Analysis of Behavior, Inc. Reproduced by permission.)

seat without permission and intervals talking without permission) were selected for study in four separate phases. During baseline (A), the number of 10-second time intervals in which the subject was out of seat or talking was recorded for 15-minute sessions. In the next phase (B) instructions were presented that involved the teacher informing the subject that he must received permission (i.e., by raising his hand) to be out of his seat and to talk. The third phase (C) consisted of a delayed time-out procedure in which a red light was mounted on the subject's desk and illuminated for a 1–3-second period immediately following an instance of out-of-seat or talking behavior. The number of illuminations recorded was cumulated each day, with each classroom violation resulting in a 5-minute detention period in a specially constructed time-out booth while other children participated in gym and recess activities. The fourth phase was a return to baseline assessment (A). The results of this study appear in Figure 3.10. Inspection of the figure shows that the baseline (A) and instructions (B) phases do not differ significantly for either of the two target behaviors under study. Thus, although the independent variables differ across these phases, the resulting dependent measures are essentially alike. However, institution of the delayed time-out contingency (C) yielded a marked decrease in classroom violations. Subsequent removal of the time-out contingency in the fourth phase (A) led to a renewed increase in classroom violations.

Inspection of these data demonstrates that behavior was similar across phases A and B. In other words, providing instructions did not appear to be an effective intervention. If one then collapses data across these two phases (i.e., A-B becomes A), an A-C-A design emerges, with some evidence demonstrated for the controlling effects of delayed time-out. In this case the A-C-A design follows the experimental analysis used in the case of the A-B-A design (see chapter 5).

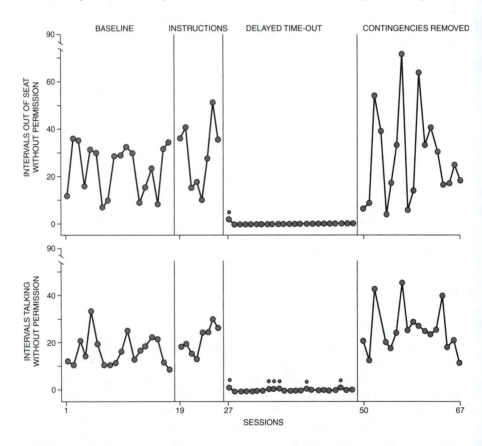

FIGURE 3.10 Each point represents one session and indicates the number of intervals in which the subject was out of his seat (top) or talking without permission (bottom). A total of 90 such intervals was possible within a 15-minute session. Asterisks over points indicate sessions that resulted in time being spent in the booth. (Figure 1, p. 237, from: Ramp, E., Ulrich, R., & Dulaney, S. (1971). Delayed timeout as a procedure for reducing disruptive classroom behavior: A case study. *Journal of Applied Behavior Analysis*, **4**, 235–239. Copyright 1971 by Society for the Experimental Analysis of Behavior, Inc. Reproduced by permission.)

However, further confirmation of the controlling effects would require a return to the C condition (delayed time-out). This new design would then be labeled as follows: A = B-C-A-C. It should be noted that without the functional equivalence of the first two phases (A = B) this would essentially be an incorrect experimental procedure. The equal sign between A and B represents their functional equivalence insofar as dependent measures are concerned.

The functional equivalence of different adjacent experimental phases warrants further illustration. Another excellent example is provided in a study by Wilder and colleagues (Wilder, Chen, Atwell, Pritchard, & Weinstein, 2006), who examined methods for decreasing tantrums among preschoolers during transitions from one activity to another. Tantrums were carefully operationalized (e.g., saying "No!" or "I don't want to!" at a volume above normal conversational tone, or forceful contact between the child's hand and parent's body) and observed across all phases. Baseline (A) consisted of the parent instructing the child to transition from one activity to another using verbal, gestural, and physical prompts as needed. The first treatment variable tested (B) was the provision of advanced notice of a transition (e.g., "the video will be turned off"). If a tantrum occurred during the ensuing transition, the child received access to the pretransition activity (e.g., the video). The second treatment variable tested (C) was differential reinforcement of other (DRO; i.e., non-tantrum) behavior with extinction. During this phase, the child was enthusiastically praised for not engaging in tantrum behavior (e.g., "Thank you for not screaming or whining, Amy!") and the occurrence of a tantrum did not lead to access to the pretransition activity.

As shown in Figure 3.11, Amy engaged in tantrums during 100% of sessions during the baseline phase, during the advanced notice phase, and during the return to baseline phase (A=B=A). However, tantrums decreased substantially upon initiation of the DRO with extinction phase (C), then increased again to 100% during the third return to baseline (A), and decreased substantially again

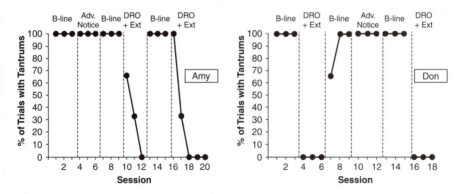

FIGURE 3.11   The percentages of trials with tantrums across baseline and treatment phases of the treatment evaluation for Amy (bottom left) and Don (bottom right). (Figure 1, p. 106, from Wilder, D. A., Chen, L., Alwell, J., Pritchand J., & Weinstein, P. (2006). Brief functional analysis and treatment of tantrums associated with transitions in preschool children. *Journal of Applied Behavior Analysis*, **39** (1), 103–107.)

during the second DRO with extinction phase. Thus, the overall design could be labeled as follows: A=B=A-C-A-C, and demonstrates that the treatment variable manipulated in the B phase was not effective, whereas the treatment variable manipulated in the C phase clearly was. The investigators tested each of these phases in a second child, a 40-month-old boy named Don. In this instance they rearranged the phases into a A-C-A=B=A-C design, which confirmed the earlier results regarding the effectiveness of the treatment variables.

Another important exception to the basic rule occurs when the experimenter is interested in testing the impact of a "treatment package" that contains two or more components (e.g., instructions, feedback, and reinforcement). In this case, more than one variable is manipulated at a time across adjacent experimental phases. An example of this type of design appeared in a series of analogue studies reported by Eisler, Hersen, and Agras (1973). In one of their studies the combined effects of videotape feedback and focused instructions were examined in an A-BC-A-BC design, with A = baseline and BC = videotape feedback and focused instructions. As shown in Figure 3.12, analysis of these data follows the A-B-A-B design pattern, with the exception that the B phase is represented by a compound

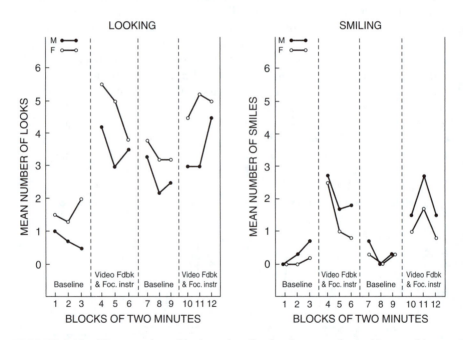

FIGURE 3.12   Mean number of looks and smiles for three couples in 10-second intervals plotted in blocks of 2 minutes for the Videotape Feedback Plus Focused Instructions Design. (Figure 3, p. 556, from: Eisler, R. M., Hersen, M., & Agras, W. S. (1973). Effects of videotape and instructional feedback on nonverbal marital interaction: An analog study. *Behavior Therapy*, **4**, 551–558. Copyright 1973 by Association for the Advancement of Behavior Therapy. Reproduced by permission.)

treatment variable (BC). Of course, although improvements over baseline appear for both target behaviors (looking and smiling) during videotape feedback and focused instructions conditions, this type of design does not allow one to draw any inferences about the relative contribution of each treatment component.

A related exception to the one-variable rule occurs when one examines the effect of administering a treatment package, and in doing so attempts to determine whether the full package is necessary or single components will be just as effective. One example of this is a study by Barlow, Leitenberg, and Agras (1969) that examined the controlling effects of the noxious scene in covert sensitization in a case of pedophilia. A four-phase A-BC-B-BC experimental design was used (Barlow & Hersen, 1973) in which: A = baseline, BC = covert sensitization treatment (verbal description of variant sexual activity and introduction of the nauseous scene), B = verbal description of deviant sexual activity but no introduction to the nauseous scene, and BC = covert sensitization (verbal description of sexual activity and introduction of the nauseous scene). For purposes of illustration, the data appear in Figure 3.13. As is evident from this design, initial differences between baseline (A) and acquisition (BC) only suggest efficacy of the total treatment package. When the nauseous scene is removed during extinction (B), the resulting increase

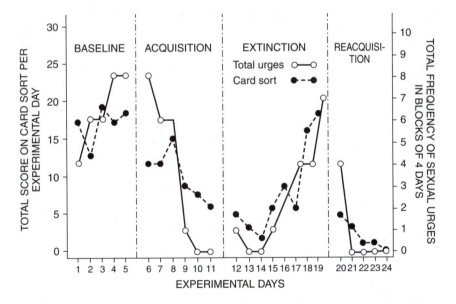

FIGURE 3.13 Total score on card sort per experimental day and total frequency of pedophilic sexual urges in blocks of 4 days surrounding each experimental day. (Lower scores indicate less sexual arousal.). (Figure 1, p. 599, from: Barlow, D. H., Leitenberg, H., & Agras, W. S. (1969). Experimental control of sexual deviation through manipulation of the noxious scene in covert sensitization. *Journal of Abnormal Psychology*, **74**, 596–601. Copyright 1969 by the American Psychological Association. Reproduced by permission.)

in deviant urges and card sort scores similarly *suggests* the controlling effects of the nauseous scene. In reacquisition (BC), where the nauseous scene is reinstated, renewed decreases in the data confirm its controlling effects. Therefore, despite an initial exception to changing one variable at a time across adjacent phases, a stepwise subtractive and additive progression is maintained in the last two phases, with valid conclusions derived from the ensuing experimental analysis. This strategy is similar conceptually to component analyses (or dismantling studies) using between group research designs (e.g., Foa et al., 2005; Jacobson et al., 1996); however, the use of a single-case experimental design here allows for a more flexible and efficient examination of treatment components.

Issues in drug evaluation

The design issues described here for testing psychological treatments (Barlow, 2004) are identical when analyzing the effects of drug treatments. Indeed, here too one should only change a single variable across adjacent experimental phases, with the same exceptions noted above. It is notable that experimenters with both a strong behavior modification bias (e.g., Liberman, Davis, Moon, & Moore, 1973) and those adhering to the psychoanalytic tradition (e.g., Bellak & Chassan, 1964) have used remarkably similar design strategies when investigating drug effects on behavior, either alone or in combination with psychological treatments.

Keeping in mind that one-variable rule, the following sequence of experimental phases has appeared in a number of studies: (1) no drug, (2) placebo, (3) active drug, (4) placebo, and (5) active drug. This kind of design, in which a stepwise application of variables appears, permits conclusions with respect to possible placebo effects (no-drug to placebo phase) and those with respect to the controlling influences of active drugs (placebo, active drug, placebo, active drug). Within the experimental analysis framework, Liberman et al. (1973) have labeled this sequence the A-A$_1$-B-A$_1$-B design. More specifically, they examined the effects of stelazine on a number of asocial responses emitted by a withdrawn patient diagnosed with schizophrenia. The particular sequence used was as follows: (A) no drug, (A$_1$) placebo, (B) stelazine, (A$_1$) placebo, and (B) stelazine. Once again following the one variable rule, Liberman et al. (1973) also showed how the combined effects of drugs and behavioral manipulations can be evaluated. Maintaining a constant level of medication (600 mg of chlorpromazine per day), the controlling effects of time-out on delusional behavior (operationally defined) were examined as follows: baseline plus 600 mg of chlorpromazine (AB), time-out plus 600 mg of chlorpromazine (CB), and removal of time-out plus 600 mg of chlorpromazine (AB). In this study (AB-CB-AB) the only variable manipulated across phases was the time-out contingency.

Similarly, within the psychoanalytic framework, Bellak and Chassan (1964) assessed the effects of chlordiazepoxide on variables (primary process, anxiety, confusion, hostility, "sexual flooding," depersonalization, ability to communicate) rated by a clinician during the course of 10 weekly interviews. A double-blind procedure was used in which neither the patient nor the clinician was informed about changes in placebo and active medication conditions. In this study, an A-A$_1$-B-A$_1$-B design was employed with the following sequential pattern: (A) no drug, (A$_1$) placebo, (B) chlordiazepoxide, (A$_1$) placebo, and (B) chlordiazepoxide.

Another example of the use of a single-case experimental evaluation of drug effects on behavior is a recent study by Kelley and colleagues (Kelley, Fisher, Lomas, & Sanders, 2006) that used double-blind administration of stimulant medication (i.e., Adderall®) versus placebo pill to determine the influence of stimulant medication on compliant and destructive behaviors (holding constant the antecedents and consequences for these behaviors). Using a B-A-B-A-B-A-B-A-B design, the authors demonstrated that the presence of stimulant medication was clearly associated with a lower frequency of destructive behaviors and a higher frequency of compliance behaviors throughout the study.

Another potential advantage of the single-case experimental design (over group comparisons) in testing the effects of drugs on behavior is the ability to experimentally examine multiple drugs within one study, or multiple doses of the same drug, within the same participants with great flexibility (e.g., Luiselli, Blew, Keane, Thibadeau, & Holzman, 2000). There are several other important issues related to the investigation of drug effects in single-case experimental designs that merit careful analysis. They include the length of phases, carryover effects, and the double-blind evaluation of results. These will be discussed in some detail in section 3.6 of this chapter and in chapter 7.

3.5. REVERSAL AND WITHDRAWAL

In their early survey of the methodological aspects of applied behavior analysis published in the first issue of the *Journal of Applied Behavior Analysis*, Baer et al. (1968) described two types of experimental designs that can be used to show the controlling effects of treatment on behavior: *reversal* and *multiple-baseline* design strategies. The reversal design is discussed in the following sections (and in more detail in chapter 5), whereas multiple-baseline designs are described in more detail later in this book (chapter 7).

A "reversal" refers to the removal (or "withdrawal") of the treatment variable that has been applied after baseline measurement has concluded. In practice, the reversal involves a withdrawal of the B phase (in the A-B-A design) after behavioral change has been successfully demonstrated. If the treatment administered in the B phase exerts control over the target behavior, a decreased or increased trend (depending on which direction indicates deterioration) in the data should follow its withdrawal.

Some terminological confusion has characterized the use of these designs, as clinical researchers frequently have referred to both their procedures and resulting data as "reversals." This represents confusion between the independent variable and the dependent variable, as from either a semantic, logical, or scientific standpoint, it is untenable that both a cause and an effect should be given an identical label. A careful analysis reveals that a reversal involves a *specific technical operation*, and that its result (changes in the target behavior[s]) is simply examined in terms of rates of the data (increased, decreased, or no change) in relation to patterns seen in the previous experimental phase. To summarize, a reversal is an active procedure; the obtained data may or may not reflect a particular trend.

The reversal design

A still finer distinction regarding reversals was made by Leitenberg (1973) in his examination of experimental single-case design strategies. He contended that the reversal design (e.g., A-B-A-B design) is inappropriately labeled, and that the term *withdrawal* (i.e., withdrawal of treatment in the second A phase) is a more accurate description of the actual technical operation. Indeed, a distinction between a withdrawal and a reversal was made, and Leitenberg showed how the latter refers to a specific kind of experimental strategy. It should be underscored that, although ". . . this distinction . . . is typically not made in the behavior modification literature" (Leitenberg, 1973), the point is well taken and should be considered by applied clinical researchers.

To illustrate and clarify this distinction, an excellent example of the reversal design, selected from the child behavior modification literature, will be presented. Allen, Hart, Buell, Harris, and Wolf (1964) were concerned with the contingent effects of reinforcement on the play behavior of a 4 $\frac{1}{2}$-year-old girl who evidenced social withdrawal from peers in a preschool nursery setting. Two target behaviors were selected for study: (1) percentage of interaction with adults, and (2) percentage of interaction with children. Observations were recorded daily during 2-hour morning sessions. As can be seen in Figure 3.14, baseline data show that about 15 percent of the child's time was spent interacting with children, whereas approximately 45 percent of the time was spent in interactions with adults. The remaining 40 percent involved "isolate" play. Inasmuch as the authors hypothesized that teacher attention fostered interactions with adults, in the second phase of experimentation an effort was made to demonstrate that the same teacher attention, when presented contingently in the form of praise following the child's interaction with other children, would lead to an increase in such interactions. Conversely, isolate play and approaches toward adults were ignored. Inspection of Figure 3.14 reveals that contingent reinforcement (praise) increased the percentage of interaction with children and led to a concomitant decrease in interactions with adults. In the third phase a "true" *reversal* of contingencies was put into effect. That is to say, contingent reinforcement (praise) was now administered when the child approached adults, but interaction with other children was ignored. Examination of Phase 3 data reflects the *reversal in contingencies*. Percentage of time spent with children decreased substantially while percentage of time spent with adults showed a marked increase. Phase 2 contingencies were then reinstated in Phase 4, and the remaining points on the graph are concerned with follow-up measures.

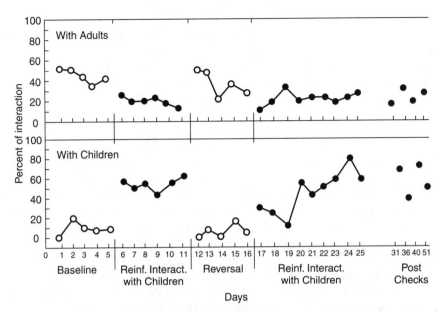

FIGURE 3.14   Daily percentages of time spent in social interaction with adults and with children during approximately 2 hours of each morning session. (Figure 2, p. 515, from: Allan, K. E., Hart, B. M., Buell, J. S., Harris, F. R., & Wolf, M. M. (1964). Effects of social reinforcement on isolate behavior of a nursery school child. *Child Development, 35,* 511–518. Copyright 1964. Reproduced by permission of The Society for Research in Child Development, Inc.)

Reversal and withdrawal designs compared

A major difference between the reversal and withdrawal designs is that in the third phase of the reversal design, following initiation of the treatment procedure, the same procedure is now applied to an alternative but incompatible behavior. By contrast, in the withdrawal design, the A phase following initiation of the treatment simply involves its removal and a return to baseline conditions. Leitenberg (1973) argued that "Actually, the reversal design although it can be quite dramatic is somewhat more cumbersome . . ." (pp. 90–91) than the more frequently employed withdrawal design. Moreover, the withdrawal design is much better suited for investigations that do not emanate from the operant (reinforcement) framework (e.g., the investigation of drugs and examination of non-behavioral therapies).

Withdrawal of treatment

Decisions about when to implement the withdrawal of the first treatment phase (i.e., transition from B back to A) should be based on several factors. Among these are time limitations imposed by the treatment setting, staff cooperation when working in institutions, and ethical considerations when removal of treatment can possibly lead to some harm to the subject (e.g., self-injurious behavior) or others in the environment (e.g., physical aggression toward others). Assuming that these important environmental considerations can be dealt with adequately and judiciously, a variety of parametric issues also must be taken into account before instituting withdrawal of the treatment variable. One of these issues involves the overall length of adjacent treatment phases, which will be examined in section 3.6 of this chapter.

This section considers the implementation of treatment withdrawal in relation to data trends during the first two phases (A and B). We will illustrate both correct and incorrect applications using hypothetical data. Let us consider an example in which A refers to baseline measurement of the frequency of social responses emitted by a withdrawn patient with schizophrenia. The subsequent treatment phase (B) involves contingent reinforcement in the form of verbal praise (e.g., "Hi! Great job making eye contact and saying 'hello'!"), while the third phase (A) represents the withdrawal of treatment and a return to original baseline conditions. For purposes of illustration, we will assume stability of "initial" baseline conditions for each of the following examples.

In our first example (see Figure 3.15) data during contingent reinforcement show a clear upward trend. Therefore, institution of withdrawal procedures at the conclusion of this phase will allow for analysis of the controlling effects of reinforcement, particularly if the return to baseline results in a downward trend in the data. Equally acceptable is a baseline pattern (second A phase) in which there is an immediate loss of treatment effectiveness, which is then maintained at a low-level stable rate (this pattern is the same as the initial baseline phase).

In our second example (see Figure 3.16) data during contingent reinforcement show the immediate effects of treatment and are maintained throughout the phase. After these initial effects, there is no evidence of an increased rate of responding. However, the withdrawal of contingent reinforcement at the

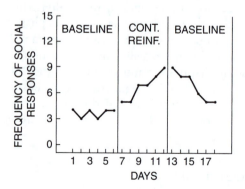

FIGURE 3.15 Increasing treatment phase followed by decreasing baseline. Hypothetical data for frequency of social responses in a schizophrenic patient per 2-hour period of observation.

conclusion of the phase does permit analysis of its controlling effects. Data in the second baseline show no overlap with contingent reinforcement, as there is a return to the stable but low rate of responding seen in the first baseline (as in Figure 3.16). Equally acceptable would be a downward trend in the data as depicted in the second baseline in Figure 3.15.

In our third example of a correct withdrawal procedure, examination of Figure 3.17 indicates that contingent reinforcement resulted in an immediate increase in rate, followed by a linear decrease, and then a renewed increase in rate, which then stabilized. Although it would be advisable to analyze contributing factors to the decrease and subsequent increase (Sidman, 1960), institution of the withdrawal procedure at the conclusion of the contingent reinforcement

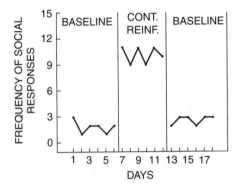

FIGURE 3.16   High-level treatment phase followed by low-level baseline. Hypothetical data for frequency of social responses in a schizophrenic patient per 2-hour period of observation.

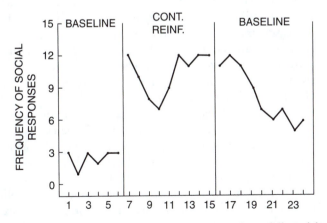

FIGURE 3.17   Decreasing-increasing-stable treatment phase followed by decreasing baseline. Hypothetical data for frequency of social responses in a schizophrenic patient per 2-hour period of observation.

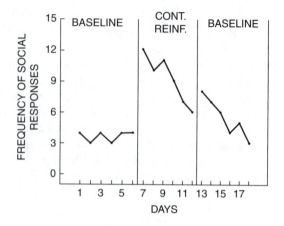

FIGURE 3.18   High-level decreasing treatment phase followed by decreasing baseline. Hypothetical data for frequency of social responses in a schizophrenic patient per 2-hour period of observation.

phase allows for an analysis of its controlling effects, particularly as a decreased rate was observed in the second baseline.

An example of the incorrect application of treatment withdrawal appears in Figure 3.18. Inspection of the figure reveals that after a stable pattern is obtained in baseline, introduction of contingent reinforcement leads to an immediate and dramatic improvement, which is then followed by a marked decreasing linear function. This trend is in evidence despite the fact that the last data point in contingent reinforcement is clearly above the highest point achieved in baseline. Removal of treatment and a return to baseline conditions on Day 13 similarly result in a decreasing trend in the data. Therefore, no conclusions as to the controlling effects of contingent reinforcement are possible, as it is not clear whether the decreasing trend in the second baseline is a function of the treatment's withdrawal or mere continuation of the trend begun during treatment. Even if withdrawal of treatment were to lead to the stable low-level pattern seen in the first baseline period, the same problems in interpretation would be posed.

When the aforementioned trend appears during the course of experimental treatment, it is recommended that the phase be continued until a more consistent pattern emerges. However, if this strategy is pursued, the equivalent length of adjacent phases is altered (see section 3.6). A second strategy, although admittedly somewhat weak, is to reintroduce treatment in Phase 4 (thus, we have an A-B-A-B design), with the expectation that a reversed trend in the data will reflect improvement. There would then be some evidence for the treatment's controlling effects.

A similar problem ensues when treatment is withdrawn in the example that appears in Figure 3.19. In spite of an initial upward trend in the data when contingent reinforcement is first introduced (B), the decreasing trend in the latter half of the phase, which is then followed by a similar decline during the second

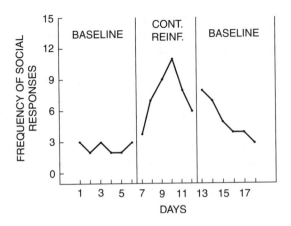

FIGURE 3.19   Increasing-decreasing treatment phase followed by decreasing behavior. Hypothetical data for frequency of social responses in a schizophrenic patient per 2-hour period of observation.

baseline (A), prevents an analysis of the treatment's controlling effects. Therefore, the same recommendations made in the case of Figure 3.18 apply here.

Limitations and problems

As mentioned earlier, the clinical researcher faces some unique problems when pursuing experimental analysis by withdrawing a particular treatment technique. These problems can be amplified in situations in which the researcher cannot control all sources of influence, such as with respect to staff cooperation or in terms of other important environmental contingencies (e.g., when dealing with individual problems in the classroom situation, responses of other children throughout the varying stages of experimentation may spuriously affect the results). Although these concerns have been articulated in the behavioral literature for decades (e.g., Baer et al., 1968; Kazdin, 1982; Franklin, Allison, & Gorman, 1997), a brief summary of the issues at stake may be useful.

A frequent criticism leveled at single-case experimental designs is that removal of the treatment will lead to the subject's irreversible deterioration (at least in terms of the behavior under study). However, as Leitenberg (1973) pointed out many years ago, this is a weak argument with no supporting evidence to be found in the experimental literature. If the technique shows initial beneficial effects and it exerts control over the targeted behavior being examined, then, when reinstated, its controlling effects will be established. To the contrary, Krasner (1971) reported that return to initially low levels of baseline performance often fails to occur in extended applications of the A-B-A design where multiple withdrawals and reinstatements of the treatment technique are instituted (e.g., A-B-A-B-A-B-A-B). Indeed, the possible carryover effects across phases and concomitant environmental events leading to improved conditions limit the researcher's ability to repeatedly demonstrate a causal relation between treatment and behavioral performance over long periods of time.

Another problem sometimes encountered by the single-case methodologist is one of staff resistance. Usually, the researcher working in an applied setting (e.g., hospital, school) is consulting with staff members from a particular unit or classroom on difficult problems. In efforts to remediate the problem, the experimenter encourages staff to apply treatment strategies that are likely to achieve beneficial results. When staff members are subsequently asked to temporarily withdraw treatment procedures, some may openly rebel. "What teacher, seeing Johnny for the first time quietly seated for most of the day, would like to experience another week or two of bedlam just to satisfy the perverted whim of a psychologist?" (J. M. Johnston, 1972, p. 1035). In other cases the staff member or parent (when establishing parental retraining programs) may be unable to revert to his or her original manner of functioning (i.e., his or her way of previously responding to certain classes of behavior). Under these circumstances, the use of withdrawal designs may not be the most appropriate choice, and the use of alternative experimental strategies such as multiple baseline or alternating-treatment designs are better suited (see chapters 7 and 8).

Overall, the researcher using a withdrawal design must ensure that (1) there is full staff or parental cooperation before beginning the experiment; (2) the withdrawal of treatment will lead to minimal environmental disruptions (i.e., no injury to the participant or others in the environment); (3) the withdrawal period will be relatively brief; (4) outside environmental influences will be minimized throughout baseline, treatment, and withdrawal phases; and (5) final reinstatement of treatment to its logical conclusion will be accomplished as soon as it is technically feasible.

3.6. LENGTH OF PHASES

Although there has been some intermittent discussion in the literature with regard to the length of phases when carrying out single-case experimental research (Barlow & Hersen, 1973; Borckardt & Nash, 2002; Kazdin, 1982), there has not yet been a complete resolution of the problems faced and the decisions to be made by the researcher. In this section, we consider the major issues involved including individual and relative length of phases, carryover effects and cyclic variations. These considerations will be examined as they apply to both psychological and pharmacological treatments.

Individual and relative length

When considering the individual length of phases independently of other factors (e.g., time limitations, ethical considerations, relative length of phases), most experimenters agree that baseline and experimental conditions should be continued until stability in the data is apparent (Kazdin, 1982; 2001). J. M. Johnston (1972) has examined these issues with regard to the study of punishment and has stated:

> It is necessary that each phase be sufficiently long to demonstrate stability (lack of trend and a constant range of variability) and to dispel any doubts of the reader that the data shown are sensitive to and representative of what was happening under the described condition (p. 1036).

He notes further:

> That if there is indication of an increasing or decreasing trend in the data or widely variable rates from day to day (even with no trend) then the present condition should be maintained until the instability disappears or is shown to be representative of the current conditions (p. 1036).

These recommendations reflect the ideal and apply best when each experimental phase is considered individually and independently of adjacent phases. If one were to fully carry out these recommendations, the possibility exists that widely disparate lengths in phases would result. The strategic difficulties inherent in unequal phases have been noted elsewhere by Barlow and Hersen (1973). Indeed, they cited the advantages of obtaining a relatively equal number of data points for each phase.

An illustration of the importance of their suggestions may be useful to make the points. The following is a hypothetical example in which the effects of time-out on frequency of hitting other children during a free-play situation were assessed in a three-year-old boy. Examination of Figure 3.20 shows a stable

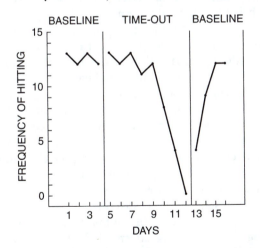

FIGURE 3.20   Extension of the treatment phase in an attempt to show its effects. Hypothetical data in which the effects of time-out on daily frequency of hitting other children (based on a 2-hour free-play situation) in a 3-year-old male child are examined.

baseline pattern, with a high frequency of hitting behavior exhibited. Treatment (time-out) is initiated on day 5, and no change is apparent until day 8 when a slight decline in frequency occurs. If the experimenter were to terminate treatment at this point, it is obvious that few statements about its efficacy could be made. Instead the treatment is continued for an additional 4 days (9-12), and an appreciable decrease in hitting is obtained. However, by extending (doubling) the length of the treatment phase, the experimenter cannot be certain whether additional treatment in itself leads to changes, whether some correlated variable (e.g., increased teacher attention to incompatible positive behaviors emitted by the child) results in changes, or whether the mere passage of time (maturational changes) accounts for the decelerated trend. Of course, the withdrawal of treatment on days 13–16 (second baseline) leads to a marked increased in hitting behavior, suggesting the controlling effects of the time-out contingency. The careful investigator would reinstate timeout procedures, to dispel any doubts as to its possible controlling effects over the target behavior of hitting. Additionally, once the treatment (time-out) phase has been extended to 8 days, it would be appropriate to maintain equivalence in subsequent baseline and treatment phases by also collecting approximately 8 days of data on each condition. Then, questions as to whether treatment effects are due to maturational or other controllable influences will be satisfactorily answered.

The relative equivalence of phase lengths is most desirable when possible in order to rule out the possibility that the results can be explained by phase length. If exceptions are to be made, they are most often in extending the initial baseline phase to achieve stability in measurement, or lengthening the last phase (e.g., second B phase in the A-B-A-B design) to insure maintenance of treatment effects. In fact, with respect to this latter point, investigators should make an effort to follow their experimental treatments with a full clinical application of the most successful techniques available.

An example of the ideal length of alternating behavior and treatment phases appears in Miller's (1973) analysis of the use of Retention Control Training (RCT) in a "secondary enuretic" child (see Figure 3.21). Two target behaviors, number of enuretic episodes and mean frequency of daily urination, were selected for study in an A-B-A-B experimental design. During baseline, the child recorded the natural frequency of target behaviors and received counseling from the experimenter on general issues relating to home and school. Following baseline, the first week of RCT involved teaching the child to postpone urination for a 10-minute period after experiencing each urge. Delay of urination was increased to 20 and 30 minutes in the next 2 weeks. During Weeks 7-9 RCT was withdrawn, but was reinstated in Weeks 10–14.

As shown in Figure 3.21, each of the first three phases was 3 weeks long, with data showing the controlling effects of RCT on both target behaviors. Reinstatement of RCT in the final phase led to renewed control, and the treatment was extended to 5 weeks to ensure maintenance of gains.

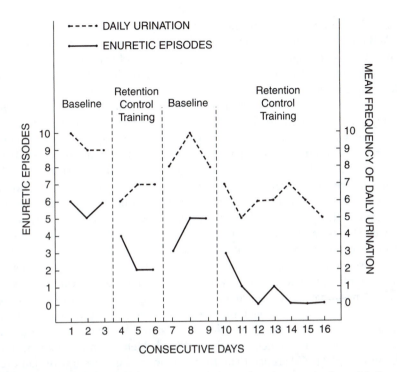

FIGURE 3.21   Number of enuretic episodes per week and mean number of daily urinations per week for Subject 1. (Figure 1, p. 291, from: Miller, P. M. (1973). An experimental analysis of retention control training in the treatment of nocturnal enuresis in two institutionalized adolescents. *Behavior Therapy, 4,* 288–294. Copyright 1973 by Association for the Advancement of Behavior Therapy. Reproduced by permission.)

Of course, data patterns often do not follow this ideal sequence, and experimenters frequently must make accommodations for ethical, procedural, or parametric reasons. Moreover, when working in an unexplored area where the issues are of social significance, deviations from some of our proposed rules during the earlier stages of investigation are acceptable. However, once technical procedures and major parametric concerns have been dealt with satisfactorily, a more vigorous pursuit of scientific rigor would be expected. In short, as in any scientific endeavor, as knowledge accrues, the level of experimental sophistication should reflect its concurrent growth.

Carryover effects

One parametric issue related to the comparative lengths of adjacent baseline and treatment phases is one of carryover effects, which refer to the lingering impact of the effects of one treatment phase on subsequent phases. One form of carryover effects often seen in behavioral studies occurs in the second baseline phase of the A-B-A-B type design and is characterized by an inability to retrieve original levels of baseline responding. Another form of carryover effects is one in which the behavior under study undergoes more rapid change the second time the treatment variable is introduced.

The influence of carryover effects has been acknowledged for many years and they are most often attributed to a variety of factors including changes in instructions across experimental conditions (Kazdin, 1973), the establishment of new conditioned reinforcers (Bijou et al., 1969), the maintenance of new behavior through naturally occurring environmental contingencies (Krasner, 1971), and the differences in stimulus conditions across phases (Kazdin & Bootzin, 1972). Clinically, carryover effects are not at all a problem as they are associated with lasting effects of the treatment administered. However, experimentally, carryover effects can severely limit the inferences one can draw about the controlling effects of the treatment procedures administered.

Those who have argued for the use of group comparison approaches often contend that the presence of carryover effects in single-case research is one of its major shortcomings as an experimental strategy. Both in terms of drug evaluation and with respect to behavioral research, short periods of experimentation (application of the treatment variable) have been recommended to counteract these difficulties. For instance, examining the problem from the operant framework, Bijou et al. (1969) argued that "In studies involving stimuli with reinforcing properties, relatively short experimental periods are advocated, since long ones might allow enough time for the establishment of new conditioned reinforcers" (p. 202). Carryover effects are also an important consideration in alternating treatment designs but are more easily handled through counterbalancing procedures (see chapter 8).

The examination of the effects of drug treatment on behavior was discussed in section 3.4 above, with particular attention given to the potential usefulness of the A-A_1-B-A_1-B design, in which A represents baseline, A_1 represents a placebo, and B the presumed active drug under investigation. Carryover effects can be potentially problematic in such designs, especially when withdrawing the active drug treatment (B phase) and returning to the placebo condition (second A_1). In such cases, of course, the extent of carryover effects would depend on the half-life of the drug under investigation, with greater carryover effects expected for those drugs that remain in the body for longer periods of time. In such studies, it is a good idea for the experimenter to demonstrate, via blood and urine laboratory studies, that controlling effects of the drug are truly being demonstrated. That is to say, correlations (statistical and graphic data patterns) between behavioral changes and drug levels in body tissues should be demonstrated across experimental phases.

Despite the carryover difficulties encountered with longer-acting drugs like tranquilizers and antidepressants, the possibility of conducting *extended studies* in long-term facilities should be explored, assuming that high ethical and experimental standards prevail. In addition, study of the *short-term* efficacy of shorter acting anxiolytics and amphetamines on selected target behaviors is quite feasible.

Cyclic variation

A very important, but very often neglected, consideration in single-case experimental research is that of cyclic variation, which refers to systematic, recurrent patterns or fluctuations in a target behavior that are not the direct result of the treatment variable (see chapter 2, sections 2.2 and 2.3, for a more general discussion of variability). The importance of cyclic variation was given early attention by Sidman (1960) with respect to basic animal research and Johnston & Pennypacker (1981) in a more applied context; however, this issue has received relatively little attention since these early papers. A notable exception is an excellent paper by Beasley, Allison, and Gorman (1997) that reviews the potential sources of cyclic variation (e.g., biological rhythms, cyclically chained responses), methods for detecting cyclic variation (such as through the use of some of the time-series analyses described in chapter 9 of this book), and proposes design strategies for limiting the influence of such variation (e.g., measuring and statistically controlling for constructs that might contribute to cyclic variations).

Regardless of whether one is examining behavioral or drug treatments the implications of cyclic variation for single-case methodology are enormous. Indeed, the psychiatric literature is replete with examples of how biological (e.g., menstrual, sleep, hormonal fluctuation), institutional (e.g., staff changes, inpatient unit schedules), and other cyclical patterns can influence human behavior. In conducting single-case experimental studies, it is important to demonstrate to the best of one's ability that the obtained results cannot be explained by cyclical variation, but that they are due to the influence of the treatment variable.

An illustration may help clarify the issue. Let's assume that we returned to the use of an A-A_1-B-A_1-B design to evaluate the effectiveness of a new drug treatment on the number of physical complaints made by a young woman in a psychiatric hospital, with each phase lasting three days in duration. Let's further assume that the baseline and first placebo phases (A-A_1) coincide with the premenstrual and early part of the subject's menstrual cycle. Initiation of the active drug (B) would then be confounded with cessation of the subject's menstrual phase. If the data showed a decrease in somatic complaints during the B phase, it is *entirely possible* that such change is primarily due to correlated factors (i.e., the menstrual cycle). In this particular example, the data from the last two phases (A_1 and B) might help determine the controlling effects of the intervention; however, interpretation of the data would be complicated unless the experimenter was aware of the role played by cyclic variation (i.e., the subject's menstrual cycle).

Although the use of short and equal phase lengths has been argued for above, the extension of phase lengths across some or all phases can be a useful way to rule out the potential influence of cyclic variation. Perhaps the best way to control for such variation, though, is to consider all possible sources a priori and include procedures to measure their occurrence (e.g., menstrual cycle, hormonal levels, staff changes). The use of extended measurement phases and measurement of a broader range of constructs under these circumstances in addition to direct and systematic replications (see chapter 10) across subjects is absolutely necessary in order to derive meaningful conclusions from the data.

3.7. EVALUATION OF IRREVERSIBLE PROCEDURES

Some procedures are irreversible and cannot be withdrawn once they have been applied (e.g., surgical lesions, therapeutic instructions). As such, the use of reversal and withdrawal designs is generally precluded when examining such irreversible procedures in single-case research. In psychology, the problem of irreversibility of behavior has attracted some attention and has been viewed by some as a major limitation of single-case experimental designs (e.g., Bandura, 1969). Indeed, many psychological treatment procedures result in new learning that will not reverse when the procedure is withdrawn. Thus, a withdrawal or reversal design will be unable to isolate that procedure as effective. In response to this, some have advocated withdrawing the procedure early in the treatment phase to effect a reversal. This strategy is based on the hypothesis that behavioral improvements may begin as a result of the therapeutic technique but are maintained at a later point by factors in the environment that the investigators cannot remove (see Kazdin, 1973; Leitenberg, 1973, also see chapter 5). The most extreme cases of irreversibility may involve a study of the effects of surgical lesions on behavior, or psychosurgery. Here the effect is clearly irreversible. This problem is easily solved, however, by using a multiple baseline design. In fact, the multiple baseline strategy is ideally suited for studying such variables, in that withdrawals of treatment are not required to show the controlling effects of particular techniques (Barlow & Hersen, 1973; Kazdin, 1982, 2003; Nock, Michel et al., 2007; Photos et al., 2008). A complete discussion of issues related to the varieties of multiple baseline designs currently being employed by applied researchers appears in chapter 7.

In this section, however, the limited use and evaluation of therapeutic instructions in withdrawal designs will be examined and illustrated. Let us consider the problems involved in "withdrawing" therapeutic instructions. In contrast to a typical reinforcement procedure, which can be introduced, removed, and reintroduced at will, an instructional set, after it has been given, technically cannot be withdrawn. Certainly, it can be stopped or changed, but it is not possible to remove it in the same sense as one does in the case of reinforcement. Therefore, in light of these issues, when examining the interacting effects of instructions and other therapeutic variables (e.g., social reinforcement), instructions are typically maintained constant across treatment phases while the treatment variable is introduced, withdrawn, and reintroduced in sequence (Hersen, Gullick, Matherne, & Harbert, 1972).

Exceptions

Several exceptions to the above have appeared in the psychological treatment literature and provide evidence of the usefulness of single-case experimental designs for demonstrating the controlling effects of instructional interventions. For instance, In one of a series of analogue studies, Eisler, Hersen and Agras investigated the effects of focused instructions ("We would like you to pay attention as to how much you are looking at each other") on two nonverbal behaviors (looking and smiling) during the course of 24 minutes of free interaction in three married couples. An A-B-A-B design was used, with A consisting of 6 minutes of interaction videotaped between a husband and wife in a small television studio. The B phase also involved 6 minutes of videotaped interaction, but focused instructions on looking were administered three times at 2-minute intervals over a two-way intercom system by the experimenter from the adjoining control room. During the second A phase, instructions were discontinued, while in the second B they were renewed, thus completing 24 minutes of taped interaction.

Retrospective ratings of looking and smiling for husbands and wives (mean data for the three couples were used, as trends were similar in all cases) appear in Figure 3.22. For both spouses, the baseline (A) duration of looking was moderate in frequency. The provision of focused instructions (B) resulted in a substantial increase followed by a slightly decreasing trend. This downward trend was maintained throughout the second baseline (second A); however, reintroduction of the instructions (second B) led to an upward trend in looking. Thus, there was some evidence for the controlling effects of introducing, discontinuing, and reintroducing the instructional set. Notably, data for a second but "untreated" target behavior—smiling—showed almost no parallel effects.

In a separate study, Bornstein and colleagues (Bornstein, Sturm, Retzlaff, Kirby, & Chong, 1981) examined the effects of providing verbal instructions to a 9-year-old boy, Tim, on his encopresis and chronic constipation. The dependent measures in this study were the number of soilings and number of appropriate bowel movements each week. The treatment was a paradoxical verbal instruction in which the clinician informed Tim that he should go to the bathroom and sit on the toilet once per hour for 5 minutes and "act as if you have to make a bowel movement but do not allow that to occur" (p. 168). The hypothesis in this case was that Tim's anxiety about making appropriate bowel movements, which he was able to do from age 3 until age 5, would be reduced by this intervention. The experimenters used an A-B-A-B design, with the instruction given once per week during the treatment (B) phases, but not during the baseline (A) phases.

As presented in Figure 3.23, Tim soiled his clothes 6–7 times per week and had only 0–1 appropriate bowel movements during the first 3-week baseline. The presentation of paradoxical instructions in the first treatment phase led to a

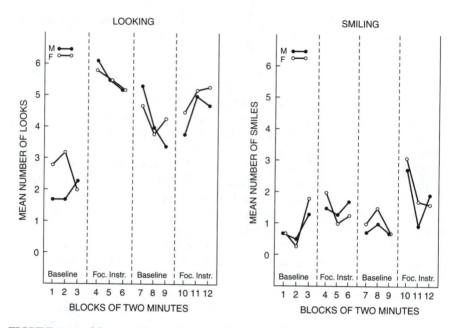

FIGURE 3.22 Mean number of looks and smiles for three couples in 10-second intervals plotted in blocks of 2 minutes for the Focused Instructions Alone Design. (Figure 4, p. 556, from: Eisler, R. M., Hersen, M., & Agras, W. S. (1973). Effects of videotape and instructional feedback on nonverbal marital interactions: An analog study. *Behavior Therapy*, **4**, 551–558. Copyright 1973 by Association for the Advancement of Behavior Therapy. Reproduced by permission.)

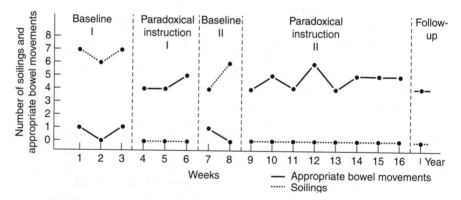

FIGURE 3.23 Number of soilings and appropriate bowel movements occurring across experimental conditions. (Figure 1, p. 169, from: Bornstein, P. H., Sturm, C. A., Retzlaff, P. D., Kirby, K. L., & Chong, H. (1981). Paradoxical instruction in the treatment of encopresis and chronic constipation: An experimental analysis. *Journal of Behavior Therapy and Experimental Psychiatry*, **12** (2), 167–170.)

complete absence of soiling incidents and 4–5 appropriate bowel movements during this 3-week period. When the instructions were removed at the start of the second baseline, Tim's soiling increased to 4–6 incidents per week and his appropriate bowel movements reverted to their baseline level. Readministration of the instructions during the second treatment phase demonstrated a clear return of successful bowel movements and absence of soiling. These instructions were faded over time and results remained at one year follow-up. Although the controlling effect of the instructions was clearly demonstrated, it is important to note that the mechanism through which the instructions had their effect remains an open question. As the experimenters correctly note, the treatment may have worked via "paradoxical intention," through a decrease in anxiety due to repeated exposure to the bathroom or toilet, or through some other mechanism, such as a higher likelihood of being in the bathroom when incontinence occurred. Nevertheless, although the mechanism is not known, these results demonstrate the usefulness of single-case designs for examining the effectiveness of instructional interventions, and the ability to show response maintenance following an initial ABAB sequence.

3.8. ASSESSING RESPONSE MAINTENANCE

The vast majority of attention and resources in psychological treatment research, and in the evaluation of drug treatments, has been devoted to determining the functional relations between treatment administration and behavior change. In other words, the emphasis has long been on showing response acquisition. However, researchers have become increasingly aware of the importance of evaluating and ensuring response maintenance following successful treatment. This is, of course, not an issue only for single-case experimental designs, but an important one for group comparison research as well.

Specifically with respect to single-case experimental designs, Rusch and Kazdin (1981) have described a methodology for assessing response maintenance. The techniques they have outlined are applicable to multiple baseline designs (see chapter 7) but also in some instances to the basic and more complicated withdrawal designs (see chapters 5 and 6).

As noted by Rusch and Kazdin (1981):

> In acquisition studies investigators are interested in demonstrating, unequivocally, that a functional relationship exists between treatment and behavioral change. In maintenance studies, on the other hand, investigators depend on the ability of the subject to discern and respond to changes in the environment when the environment is altered; the latter group relies upon subject's failure to discriminate between those very same stimuli or, possibly, upon the subject's failure to discriminate among functionally similar stimulus [sic] . . . (pp. 131–132)

Rusch and Kazdin referred to three types of response maintenance evaluation strategies: (1) sequential-withdrawal, (2) partial-withdrawal, and

(3) partial-sequential withdrawal. In each instance, however, a compound treatment (i.e., one comprised of several elements or strategies) was being evaluated. Let us consider the three response maintenance evaluation strategies in turn.

In *sequential-withdrawal*, one element of treatment is withdrawn subsequent to response acquisition (e.g., reinforcement). In the next phase a second element of the treatment (e.g., feedback) may be withdrawn, and then a third (e.g., prompting). This allows the investigator to determine which, if any, of the treatment elements is required to ensure response maintenance postacquisition. Examples of this strategy appear in Sowers, Rusch, Connis, and Cummings (1980) in a multiple baseline design and in O'Brien, Bugle, and Azrin (1972) in a withdrawal design.

The *partial-withdrawal* strategy requires use of a multiple baseline design. Here a component of treatment from one of the baselines or the entire treatment for one of the baselines is removed (see Russo & Koegel, 1977). This, of course, allows a comparison between untreated and treated baselines following response acquisition. Thus, if removal of a part or all of treatment leads to decreased performance, it would be clear that response maintenance following acquisition requires direct and specific programming. Treatment could then be readministered or altered altogether. It should be noted, however, that, "The possibility exists that the information obtained from partially withdrawing treatment or withdrawing a component of treatment may not represent the characteristic data pattern for all subjects, behaviors, or situations included in the design" (Rusch & Kazdin, 1981, p. 136).

Finally, in the *partial-sequential withdrawal strategy*, a component of treatment from one of the baselines or the entire treatment for one of the baselines is removed. To this point, the approach followed is identical to the procedures used in the *partial-withdrawal* strategy. But, this is followed in turn by subsequent removal of treatment in succeeding baselines. Irrespective of whether treatment loss appears across the baselines, Rusch and Kazdin (1981) argued that, "By combining the partial- and sequential-withdrawal design strategies, investigators can predict, with increasing probability, the extent to which they are controlling the treatment environment as the progression of withdrawals is extended to other behaviors, subjects, or settings" (p. 136).

■ ■ ■ ■ ■

CHAPTER 4

BEHAVIOR ASSESSMENT

PATRICK C. FRIMAN, Ph.D.

*Girls and Boys Town and The University of Nebraska School of Medicine**

Behavior assessment is a professional enterprise devoted to the identification of meaningful response units and their controlling variables for the united purposes of understanding and changing behavior (Hartmann, 1984; Hayes, Nelson, Jarrett, 1986; Kazdin, 1982). Single-case experiments are powerful scientific methods available for accomplishing these united purposes. There are, however, many other methods used to accomplish these purposes, and single-case experiments merely provide the most rigorous sort. Thus, although this book is devoted to single-case experiments and this chapter to behavioral assessment, behavioral assessment is actually a much larger conceptual category.

Although behavior assessment and single-case experiments converge in several ways, they diverge in others, one of the most prominent of which involves direct observation of behavior. Virtually all of the data analyzed with single-case experiments in the social sciences are obtained via some form of direct behavioral observation, yet direct observation is not always used in behavioral assessment, because either not all of the behavior assessed is observable or not all of the observations used in the assessment focus directly upon behavior. This divergence is due in no small part to the difficulty in defining the word "behavior." For such a universally used and seemingly understood word, there is surprisingly little consensus on what it actually means. As an indication of the difficulty, an influential text on behavior assessment of child behavior disorders that had used the words "behavior assessment" in the title of the first two editions, dropped the word "behavior" from the title in the third edition (Mash & Terdal, 1997). Even among behavior analysts, a group with an extraordinary amount of agreement on the subject matter of their science, disagreement often occurs over the word behavior. For example, in a recent exchange of papers,

*Correspondence to: Patrick C. Friman, Ph.D., ABPP, Clinical Services, Youthcare Building, Boys Town, NE 68010, 402-498-3353 (office), 402-498-3375 (fax), frimanp@boystown.org

there was a debate on whether behavior was a count or mass noun (i.e., whether it could be pluralized; Friman, 2004). Recognizing that consensus is unlikely, this chapter will emphasize a very simple definition of behavior. Specifically, behavior is defined here simply as what humans do; it involves activity. Some of the activity is public and some is private. Because of the emphasis on objectivity in behavioral assessment and single-case experiments, the chapter will assign priority to behavior that is observable by another person, at least in principle. Less priority will be assigned to activity that is not observable by another person and even less priority will be assigned to what people have (e.g., depression) and are (e.g., depressed). It can be helpful to think of behavior assessment as an enterprise that places priority on verbs (e.g., crying, sleeping avoiding) over nouns (e.g., depression).

As one example of the controversy that could stem from the definition of behavior and the emphasis on direct observation found here, consider the example of thinking. Thinking is something people do and thus is a behavior according to the definition provided here, but it is not possible to observe the thinking of other persons (barring instances of "thinking out loud"). Representations of thinking can be made available in a variety of observable mediums (e.g., in writing or speaking) but it is these representations of thinking that are observable, not the thinking itself. The thinking of another is inferred, not observed. It is possible to make accurate guesses about the composition of another person's thoughts and predictions about behavior related to those thoughts, however. For example, skilled poker players guess the unspoken thoughts and predict the card play of their companion players at a better than chance level, especially when the companion players are unskilled. Master chess players regularly and accurately guess the stratagems that occupy the thoughts of their less skilled opponents. Forensic interviewers can be trained to detect whether a person is lying. More technically, there is a growing literature in cognitive behavior science that employs overt behaviors to make inferences about cognitive processes (e.g., Greenwald et al., 2002). The poker players, chess masters, interviewers, and behavioral scientists, however, do not actually observe the thoughts of other persons. They observe overt behaviors exhibited by those persons and infer their thoughts.

The definition of behavior and emphasis on observation found here also excludes widely considered conditions in clinical psychology such as anxiety or depression. These conditions are not behaviors, they are constructs or categories that are composed or populated by behaviors that are, in principle, observable, but the conditions themselves are not. For example, it is possible to observe the trembling, shallow breathing, and avoidance that are often included in anxiety or the crying, excessive sleeping, and diminished eating that are often included in depression, but anxiety and depression themselves are inferred not observed. Thus, while acknowledging that constructs such as anxiety and private events such as thinking are important, top billing in this chapter will be accorded to behaviors that are observable in principle. Hypothetical constructs and private events, inferences about which are predicated upon observable behaviors, will be assigned only supporting roles (Friman, Hayes, & Wilson, 1998; Friman, Wilson, Hayes, 1998; Ryle, 1949). This book is devoted to single-case experiments for the social sciences and, in that context, the designs are used to measure behavior occurring over time. The hundreds of thousands of data points analyzed in published papers using single-case experiments almost all focused on behavior that was observable by another person, at least in principle. There may be a few that did not, but too few to mention, and this chapter was written in a way that is mostly consistent with that research tradition.

Another important issue involves whether behaviors that are assessed should be seen as a sample or a sign. The purpose of assessing behavior in the context of single-case experiments is a search for its determinative commerce with the environment in which it occurs. In that context, the behavior is usually assessed as a sample of a larger class of topographically or functionally similar behavior, not a sign of something else (e.g., anxiety, depression), but this is not to say that behavior cannot or should not be seen as a sign. As indicated above, behavior is seen easily and productively as a sign of private events such as thinking or psychological conditions such as anxiety. But in single-case experiments, instances of behavior are generally examined as samples of larger classes of functionally or topographically similar behavior, differing mostly in quantitative not qualitative terms (e.g., fingernail biting seen as a sample of hand–mouth behavior). Typically, they are not assessed as a sign of something qualitatively different (e.g., fingernail biting seen as sign of anxiety). Nonetheless, over the almost four decades of development of behavior assessment, its literature has become suffused with instances of behavior interpreted as a sign of something other than itself, often something qualitatively and conceptually different (e.g., Haynes & O'Brien, 2000; Nelson & Hayes, 1986). Thus, although behavior viewed as observable activity and as a sample rather than a sign is most consistent with single-case experimental tradition as well as the science of behavior analysis and the philosophy of that science (behaviorism), all of which were originating influences leading to the development of behavior assessment, the field has expanded to incorporate other views. In an attempt to provide a balanced description of the field, this chapter will describe a few aspects of assessment that are consistent with these other views. For much more thorough descriptions of behavior seen as a sign of something, however, (e.g., something a person is or has), please refer to books and chapters on traditional psychological assessment (e.g., Cohen & Swerdlik, 2002; Millon & Davis, 1996; Sattler, 2002).

In sum, this chapter is devoted to the assessment of behavior and it will emphasize, where possible, direct observation, repeated measures, a present locus, a focus on individuals, and an ideographic rather than nomothetic orientation. The chapter will discuss the selection of behaviors to assess, various aspects and examples of measurement methods, settings for observations, definition of behaviors to be observed, selecting and training observers, reliability and validity of observations, and the assessment of function.

4.1. SELECTION OF BEHAVIOR TO ASSESS

Consistent with purposes just stated, the selection of behavior to assess in single case experiments involves behaviors as defined here more than it does psychological conditions. The behavior chosen is often part of the class of behaviors that defines a condition, however. For example, if the individual whose behavior is being assessed is afflicted with attention deficit hyperactivity disorder (ADHD), a sample of the behaviors that compose ADHD (e.g., blurting, fidgeting, darting) would be the object(s) of the assessment and not the ADHD itself. If a person is afflicted with depression, a sample of behaviors that compose the condition (e.g., excessive sleeping, insufficient eating, hypoactivity) would be the object of the assessment, not the depression itself. Generally, behaviors are targeted for a single-case experiment because they are socially, clinically, organizationally, or personally significant and are potentially changeable.

Social significance

Establishing the social significance of target behaviors can be done in a variety of ways ranging from merely soliciting the opinion of persons affected by the behaviors of concern to empirically rigorous methods, the best example of which involves social validation. Merely obtaining individual opinion about the importance of a behavior needs little elaboration (although it will be discussed in more depth below) but social validation is a technical process. At the heart of the process is judgment about the importance of a behavior by a representative sample of the social communities that are most affected by, or knowledgeable about it. An instructive example involves incontinence in young children. It is possible to toilet train children before the age of one year and in some agrarian cultures it is common practice to do so (e.g., Smeets, Lancioni, Ball, & Oliva, 1985). Sampling the opinions of parents or health care providers in those cultures would likely show that incontinence in children that age would be acceptable as a target for behavior assessment and intervention. Conversely, sampled opinion in the United States would likely reflect considerable controversy over considering incontinence as a target in such young children. Although a small movement to toilet train infants has emerged recently (e.g., Bauer, 2001; Bouke, 2002), targeting incontinence before the age of one year is still much more likely to be socially criticized than validated in this country (e.g., Berk & Friman, 1990; Friman & Berk, 1990; Rosemond, 2005; Tarbox, Williams, & Friman, 2004).

Even when it is self-evident that behaviors are socially significant, choosing targets from among them to assess can be difficult. In clinical psychology, the assessor typically wants to target the behaviors that exert the greatest impact on a client's life. For example, there are three general types of behavior that oppositional children present in clinical settings. In decreasing order of importance they are: (1) behavior dangerous to self or others; (2) defiance; and (3) routine disruption (e.g., Greene, 2001). Whereas all three are important, dangerous behavior should routinely be the initial object of assessment. As another example, in major depression three cardinal symptoms are often present: (1) diminished appetite and eating; (2) increased somnolence and sleeping; and (3) decreased activity levels. All three are important but if caloric intake falls to unhealthful levels, appetite and eating should be the initial focus of assessment.

Since about 1977 (the approximate advent of the social validity line of research—Kazdin, 1977; Wolf, 1978), empirical methods for selection of socially significant target behaviors have been accumulating, and the most commonly used are social comparisons and surveys of social opinion. As just one example of social comparisons, a study on peer perceptions of thumb-sucking in first-grade children used photographs to obtain assessment information. Two children, a seven-year-old boy and girl, were photographed twice each, once while sucking their thumb and once while not sucking. All aspects of the photos were held constant with the exception of sucking (e.g., setting, clothing, pose, etc.). The photographs were then shown to classes of first-grade children who were asked to rate the children along a number of social dimensions, such as how attractive or smart the posed children were and how desirable they would be as seatmates, classmates, schoolmates, neighbors and friends. The showings occurred at two different time points two weeks apart. In the first showing the picture of the girl sucking and the boy not sucking were used and in the second the picture of the boy sucking and the girl not sucking were used. Ratings were obtained at both times. Analysis of the difference in ratings showed a significant reduction in ratings on all 10 questions for the thumb-sucking pose. In general, the children rated the children in the thumb-sucking pose as unacceptable for any type of relationship (e.g., seatmate) and as unintelligent and unattractive (Friman, McPherson, Warzak, & Evans, 1993). These results added a social dimension to the literature on the unhealthful sequelae of thumb-sucking in school-aged children that had previously been dominated by medical concerns (Friman, 1988). In this example of social comparison, the participant children were used as their own controls, with one photographed pose representing thumb-sucking and the other the normative alternative.

In other social validity research, comparisons are drawn between the behavior of target individuals and levels of that behavior sampled from larger groups, to provide norms to be achieved through intervention. For example, in the development of the Teaching Family Model for treatment of delinquent and predelinquent behavior exhibited by children in residential care, Montrose Wolf and colleagues obtained a variety of normative levels of a broad range of social skills and then, using baseline levels of those skills exhibited in delinquent children as a starting point, they trained the children to exhibit the skills at normative levels (e.g., greeting and conversation skills, table manners; Phillips, Phillips, Fixsen, & Wolf, 1974; see Minkin et al., 1976 for an empirical example involving conversational skill training for preadolescent girls).

Clinical significance

A subset of social significance is clinical significance and, because behavior assessment is such a widely used method in clinical practice and research, clinical significance is arguably the most widely used criteria for whether behavior should be the object of behavior assessment. A clinically significant behavior is one that deviates from established normative levels (e.g., social, developmental, educational), appears to be chronic (e.g., has been exhibited over extended time periods), and results in some form of impairment (e.g., social, medical). Although there are a variety of sources to consult about whether a behavior is appropriately deemed clinically significant, the most authoritative and widely used is the Diagnostic and Statistical Manual for the American Psychiatric Association (DSM IV-TR; APA, 2000). Clinical significance is discussed more thoroughly elsewhere in this book (chapters 1 and 10).

Organizational significance

Another subset of social significance involves the role that individual or group behavior plays in the health and well being (i.e., success) of organizations. For more than thirty years the field of organizational behavior management has been a steadily growing subfield of behavior science and its focus is upon behavior that affects organizations. As an example of its growing vitality as a scientific domain, a recent citation analysis indicated its primary journal, *Journal of Organizational Behavior Management*, has the third highest impact factor in all of applied psychology (Hantula, 2005). Examples of organizational behaviors to be assessed range from those exhibited by individuals, such as gossiping or spreading rumor (Houmanfar & Johnson, 2003) to those involving major components of the organization, such as appointment keeping rates in hospitals (Friman, Finney, Rapoff, & Christophersen, 1985), safety behaviors in retirement communities (Cox, Cox, & Cox, 2000), or even the work habits of the United States Congress (Critchfield, Haley, Sabo, Cobert, & Macropoulis, 2003).

Personal significance

Another criteria, albeit one that may not rise to the level of social, clinical, or organizational significance, involves the extent to which select behaviors matter to individuals who are interested in changing some aspect of their own lives. For example, diet-conscious persons may want to know the composition of their diet so that they can adjust it to fit health related goals even though they do not have a health problem related to diet. Other persons may want to improve their performance of a skilled activity, decrease their exhibition of behavior that is important primarily to themselves (e.g., modify accent, rate of speech, vocabulary, posture, eye contact, interactive style, etc.), or change their lives in some way. There are many other examples.

In more general terms, there are at least four considerations in the selection of behaviors for an assessment. The first involves whether the behavior of interest is important to a client or their representatives (e.g., family, parent, teacher, employer, etc.). The second involves whether the behavior represents some level of risk for the client (e.g., because it is physically, legally, socially, or professionally dangerous). The third involves the extent to which the behavior interferes with or impairs functioning in everyday life (e.g., fear of flying, excess sleeping, distractibility, etc.). This criterion has become so central to clinical significance that it has become part of the multi-axis diagnostic system, in the form of the Global Assessment of Functioning (GAF) scale that makes up axis V (APA, 2000). GAF ratings are now a required part of clinical reporting for most third party reimbursement health care organizations. The fourth involves deviance reflected by an obvious departure from performances where expectations are based on widely accepted norms (e.g., excessive sleep, incontinence in later childhood, hair-pulling resulting in alopecia). Note that these criteria for selection of target behaviors have been described in a variety of previous influential papers (e.g., Hawkins, 1986; Kazdin, 1982), including one focused on behavior assessment in a previous edition of this book (Hartmann, 1984). More technically, there is a growing literature in cognitive behavior science that employs overt behaviors to make inferences about cognitive processes (e.g., Greenwald et al., 2002).

4.2. MEASUREMENT OF BEHAVIOR

Primary measures: behavioral dimensions of proximal, directly observed behavior

As described previously, the primary emphasis here will be on behavior defined as a material event that is observable in principle and, thus, has fundamental qualities or properties that have quantifiable or measurable dimensions. Material objects lend themselves readily to the conventional measurement dimensions of length, width, height, and weight. If a dynamic aspect of the object is also of interest, a temporal dimension can easily be included (e.g., duration of existence). Use of conventional dimensions to measure an object allows consistent values to be obtained across measurements, even when they occur under a variety of conditions, including use of different persons to obtain measurements (this point bears on the reliability of measurement, a topic to be discussed in a subsequent section). The consistent values are made available by the use of standardized units that compose the quantifiable properties of objects (e.g., inches for length, width or height, pounds for weight, and minutes for time). Although not intuitively obvious, it is also the case that behavior has dimensions and can be measured with them. Yet not all of the conventional dimensions apply. For example, although behavior may have a type of length (i.e., duration) it does not have height, weight, or width. So what then are the dimensions of behavior?

What are the measurable aspects of its form? This chapter will describe the dimensional domains that most readily yield standardized measurement units, temporality and repeatability (cf., Johnston & Pennypacker, 1993). Measurement of abstract categories (e.g., psychological conditions such as anxiety or intelligence) will not be included because they are not in principle observable, have no form, and cannot be measured with conventional dimensional units.

Temporality dimensions

Latency.   A frequently used time-based dimension involves the time elapsed from the onset of an event and the emission of a response, often referred to as response latency. Latency measures have been used in many different lines of behavioral science investigations, a representative one of which involves reaction time. Reaction time measurements were central to two early branches of psychology, one involving the inference of mental processes and the other involving determination of individual differences (Corsini & Auerbach, 1996). Latency measures were also pivotal in experiments on classical conditioning (Pavlov, 1927) and are used in a wide range of contemporary studies.

Duration.   The length of time a response continues, or duration of response, is also a cardinal dimension of behavior and a venerable dependent measure in behavioral science. A representative behavior often assessed with duration measures is crying. The experience of infant crying can slow a new parent's perception of time and lead to the impression that the crying lasts for hours. Although it is indeed possible for infants to cry for hours, actual occurrences of such extended crying (excepting periodic fussing and whimpering) are the exception rather than the rule as duration-based behavior assessments show (Lester & Boukydis, 1985). Duration measures are also frequently used in sleep research. Sleep is cyclical and stages within cycles are established operationally using characteristic EEG readings. Rapid oscillations characterize the rapid eye movement stage (REM) and decreasing oscillations characterize stages I through IV in descending order. Duration measures are taken within and across stages in order to provide normative perspectives on sleep and also to assess sleep problems. As one example of a duration-based finding, time in stage IV sleep has been shown to supply more benefits, in terms of health and well being, than time in stages I-III (Kryger, Roth, & Dement, 1994). Duration measures are also used in research on health behavior. For example, one aspect of effective health-based self examinations (e.g., skin, breast, testicle) involves the duration of the exam. In a representative study, supplying a brief health education message prior to the conduct of testicular self examinations significantly increased the amount of time spent on self exams (Friman, Finney, Glasscock, Weigel, & Christophersen, 1986). There are numerous other examples of duration-based measures used in behavior assessment and research (e.g., time on task, length of tantrum, television viewing, breath holding, etc.).

Repeatability dimensions

Countablitity. Repeatability involves repetition through time. Its quantification property, countability, used alone or in combination with temporality, is virtually ubiquitous in behavior assessment literature. Simply stated, countability merely involves counting instances of behavior or responses. True, no two behaviors are identical, but it is possible for behaviors to belong to the same operational or functional class and be counted as members of those classes if they meet class inclusion criteria. Operational criteria usually involve clearly specifiable and observable topographical features. For example, responses that involve the placement of a thumb or finger between two enclosed lips could be counted as instances of finger sucking. Functional criteria usually involve clearly specifiable and observable effects of a behavior on some feature of the environment in which it occurs. For example, although bar presses by lab animals in experimental chambers are usually conducted with upper extremities (e.g., paws), all presses, regardless of how they occur, can be counted in the functional class (e.g., sitting on the bar would be counted the same as pressing it with a paw). Despite the simplicity and universality of countability as a property of behavior, experiments using only counts are actually rare. Counts are almost always incorporated with a temporal dimension.

Frequency. The most widely used dimension in all of behavioral science is frequency, also known as rate (but for a potential point of confusion, please see Johnston & Pennypacker [1993] p. 98) which merely involves count divided by units of time yielding a count of behavior (e.g., 12 instances of hand washing) per unit of time (e.g., in one hour). Frequency is the dominant dimension used in Skinnerian behavioral science (Skinner, 1938) and was considered to be the only useful dimension by some prominent behavior scientists (Lindsley, 1991).

Interresponse Time. Another time-based, countable feature of behavior is interresponse time (IRT), which refers to the interval between responses. IRT is responsive to environmental events in that changes in such events influence the frequency of responses that border the interval. Perhaps the finding that illuminates the potential value of IRT best involves how it was used to account for a historically anomalous finding from behavioral research. Specifically, various investigators observed that under some conditions contingent electric shock, an unconditional aversive stimulus, actually led to increases in response rate, sometimes referred to as shock maintained behavior. Two experiments using IRTs as dependent measures showed that using shock to punish long IRTs reduced their length and increased response rate (Galbicka & Branch, 1981; Galbicka & Platt, 1984). This occurred because the logical (and functional) obverse of IRT is response rate, and decreases in IRT are accompanied by increases in rate. Focusing solely on the increases apparently led to the spurious conclusion that shock can function as a reinforcer. In more practical settings, using time between responses as a measure of behavior can supply important applied implications about that behavior. For example, children with nocturnal enuresis rarely become continent spontaneously, rather, their continence is achieved gradually and time between accidents, or IRT, is sometimes used as a primary measure (Friman, 1995; Friman & Jones, 1998).

Interval Recording. Because true dimensional properties of behavior are often difficult to obtain outside of laboratory settings, proximal dimensional measures are often used, especially in applied behavioral research. These measures typically sample behavior directly observed within a temporal frame and then extrapolate from the samples to general levels of the behavior. The most widely used sampling method involves interval recording. With interval recording instances of a targeted behavior are observed within an established block of time ranging from a few minutes to several hours. The block of time is divided into short intervals (e.g., 10 minutes divided into sixty 10-second intervals). Individuals (or groups) of interest are observed for the entire block of time and the target behavior is recorded as having occurred or not occurred during the intervals. The measure of interest is the percentage of intervals in which the behavior occurs and not the count or duration of the behavior within the intervals.

An example of very short intervals involves the recording of motor tics (e.g., abrupt jerking movements of the head or shoulder, facial twitching, rapid eye blinking) in adults with tic disorders (Miltenberger, Fuqua, & McKinley, 1985). In this study, the investigators video taped the participants, then viewed the tapes and recorded the presence or absence of tics every 6 seconds. The length of the observational periods ranged from 10 to 30 minutes and percentage of intervals within the periods composed the dependent measure. Another example of short intervals involves recording out-of-seat behavior in a disruptive preschool student. The investigator video taped the student in a classroom setting for 10-minute observational periods and, while watching the tapes, recorded the occurrence or non occurrence of seat departure during 10-second intervals (Friman, 1990b). The primary dependent measure for the study was the percentage of intervals within the period that the boy was recorded as being out of his seat. Some examples of longer intervals are found in a series of studies on treatment of thumb-sucking in children. A two-hour period when thumb-sucking was deemed by parents as most likely to occur at home was used as the observational period. This period was subdivided into four 30-minute intervals. Parents functioning as observers then recorded whether thumb-sucking occurred within any of the intervals. Intervals were counted equally regardless of whether sucking occurred throughout an entire interval or only briefly within. The primary measure in the research was the percentage of intervals within the observational block during which thumb-sucking was recorded (e.g., Friman, 1990a; Friman, Barone, & Christophersen, 1986; Friman & Leibowitz, 1990).

There are variations of interval recording. In virtually all instances the observer faces the person(s) of interest in order to observe the target behaviors directly and records instances on a designated sheet of paper. Intervals are typically signaled using a time-based recording that makes a detectable sound at the end of each interval. If the target behavior is subtle or if several behaviors are to be recorded at once, a brief recording period is appended to each interval during which behavior is recorded. This period is not part of the measurement interval. Another variation involves a greater degree of sampling. Instead of using only one block of time during the observational day, observational intervals are spread throughout the day. Thus, the observer may use 10-second intervals, but they may be dispersed during morning, afternoon, and evening times. For example, in a study assessing patient and staff behavior on a pediatric intensive care unit, intervals were one minute in length and all behaviors targeted in the study that occurred within the interval were recorded. These full interval observations occurred every two hours between 9 A.M. and 5 P.M. (Cataldo, Bessman, Paker, Pearson, & Rogers, 1979).

For a variety of reasons, interval recording is one of the most widely used measurement strategies in applied behavioral research. For example, interval recording is highly flexible and can be used with virtually any behavior regardless, of countability, frequency, or duration. Quite simply, all behavior extends through time and dividing units of time into intervals and recording whether a behavior of interest occurs within them is a method that can be employed to measure all behavior as defined here. There is also authoritative research showing a close correlation between behavior sampled with the interval method and behavior measured using more exact method (Powell, Martindale, & Culp, 1975).

Secondary Measures: Distal, Indirect, and/or Supplementary Measures. Not all human behavior, even if it is observable in principle, is readily observable in practice. Behavior can be difficult to observe because it has an exceptionally low rate, short duration, or is covertly emitted. As indicated earlier, some human behavior is also private (e.g., thinking) and, although it often has a high rate and long duration, another person simply cannot observe it. When behavior is difficult or impossible to observe directly, supplemental, or indirect, observations can lead to credible accounts of it. For example, encountering broken branches, overturned boulders, freshly dug dirt, and warm black scat would quickly suggest the proximity of bears, formerly engaged in feeding-related behavior, to a seasoned hiker. The topography of these "signs" can suggest such dimensional properties as duration of feeding and size or number of bears. Minor rippling in an otherwise smooth pond, coupled with clouds of hovering insects, might suggest the presence of feeding fish to an ichthyologist. No dinosaur has ever been observed directly, yet a great deal is known about their behavior. The behavior of several elements of the subatomic physical universe is well understood even though the elements themselves have not been observed. Similarly private, covert, or simply difficult to observe behavior of persons can also be assessed through indirect or supplementary measures. The provision of this section is not intended to diminish the importance, the sin qua non status as it were, of direct observation; rather it is intended to discuss some methods that can supply information that cannot be obtained directly or to supplement information that was.

Products of behavior

A widely used indirect measure, similar to the example involving bears, fish, and dinosaurs above, involves the effects that behavior produces on the environment, and possibilities are limited only by the magnitude and accessibility of those effects. Note that the products of behavior are viewed as signs of the behavior that produced them rather than samples of it. But the practice of viewing the products of behavior as a sign of a particular kind of behaving is substantially different than the practice of viewing behavior as a sign of private events or psychological conditions as discussed in the introduction, for at least two reasons. First, the products are functionally related to the behavior that produced them and their relationship can be demonstrated empirically. Second, the behaviors of which the products are a sign are observable, in principle, by other persons. An example of a behavior that is often assessed indirectly, by obtaining products of it, involves trichotillomania, or chronic hair pulling. The pulling is often practiced covertly and thus direct observation using any of the methods described above could dramatically underestimate pulling, as indicated in a case reported by Altman, Grahs, and Friman (1982).

The subject, a three-year-old girl of normal intelligence, presented in clinic with extraordinary alopecia (abnormal hair loss) involving almost half of her scalp. Medical causes for the alopecia were ruled out, and her parents reported it was most likely caused by pulling but they had rarely seen her actually pull hair. Instead, they found large numbers of loose hairs in her bed each morning and assumed she pulled them out during the night. An assessment employing only direct observation of pulling itself would very likely have yielded little useful data. Although photographic equipment using the infra-red light spectrum and a time lapse image capturing system could conceivable have recorded active pulling, use of such methods was not feasible in this case. Instead, Altman et al. used the size of the alopecia and the number of hairs collected each morning as indirect measures for the pulling. During baseline conditions, the number of hairs obtained remained relatively constant and the size of the alopecia steadily grew. During treatment conditions, the number of hairs reduced to zero levels and the alopecia steadily reduced in size, and in follow-up photographs clinical experts were unable to detect it. In this case, alopecia and loose hairs were the presumed products of hair-pulling and used as indirect measures in the assessment of it. In a similar study, the weight (established by a Chan Electrobalance Scale), rather than number of hairs pulled, along with photographs of alopecia were used as the indirect measure of behavior (Byrd, Richards, Hove, & Friman, 2002).

As another example, anxious individuals often engage in repetitive self stimulatory behaviors ("nervous" habits). Some are readily observable (e.g., fingernail chewing) and some are harder to detect (e.g., teeth clenching). In a study on "nervous" intra oral biting in an adolescent boy, direct observations of biting, although possible in principle, were not feasible. The biting, however, usually led to bleeding and thus to assess biting, the boy was instructed to swab the interior of his mouth with gauze pads at regular intervals, place the pads in a plastic container, and supply them to investigators. The presence or absence of blood on the pads (and medical examination of the interior of his mouth) was used as an indirect measure of biting (Jones, Swearer, & Friman, 1997).

As another example, nocturnal enuresis is a common condition affecting as many as 25% of boys and 15% of girls at the age of six years. Although these children regularly urinate in their beds, the actual act of urination is rarely observed. Instead, the products of the urination, soiled beds, are universally used in the assessment of enuresis (Friman, 1995; Friman & Jones, 1998). In fact, as described earlier, cures for enuresis are usually achieved gradually and the amount of urine released during each accident is therefore a much more sensitive measure of change than the number of nights with accidents. A recent assessment innovation involving measurement of the size of the urine spot has allowed for progress to be followed more precisely (Ruckstuhl & Friman, 2002). Similar product-based measures are used to assess other forms of incontinence such as encopresis or fecal soiling (Friman, 2003; Friman & Jones, 1998). In fact, product measures are used to assess a broad range of habitual behaviors such as nail and cuticle damage for nail-biting, tooth abrasion for bruxism, skin trauma for picking or cutting, dental malocclusion for thumb-sucking, tooth enamel damage for purging, decreasing weight for chronic reluctance to eat, and escalating indices of liver function problems for chronic alcohol intake. Product measures are also often used to assess the behavior of organizations. For example, a critical assessment dimension of any commercial entity involves cumulative sales receipts. As another example, a critical assessment dimension of any therapeutic agency is the number of clients served. There are numerous other examples.

Behavior rating scales

One of the most vigorous areas of endeavor in clinical psychology and, indeed, in virtually all of social science, is the development of measurement scales. The field of behavior assessment is no exception. The number of scales available to assess some aspect of behavior would probably register in the thousands if ad hoc scales used for dissertation research were included in the database. This chapter will merely discuss two types of scales, one that can be used as a primary measure in single-case experiments and one that typically cannot, or at least, typically is not. The first is used to collect direct and relatively proximal observations. This type of scale can be used for repeated measures of the sort analyzed in single-case experiments. Data from scales of this type are typically interpreted as a sample of a larger category of topographically or functionally-related behavior rather than a sign of a condition. The second type of scale is used to collect indirect and direct observations that are usually distal. Data from scales of this type are almost never used for repeated measures of the sort analyzed in single-case experiments. Additionally, data from them are usually interpreted as a sign, usually of a nomothetically constructed condition.

Scales Used as Direct Measures.   There are behavior rating scales that are, in fact, designed to measure behavior directly within a time series. Typically these instruments list behaviors of interest and each is checked on observational days. The number of behaviors checked thus becomes the dependent measure. In some assessments the behaviors in the scale are those that compose a larger behavior that has been broken down into constituent steps, or "task analyzed." For example, in training programs for persons with developmental disabilities, tasks to be taught are deconstructed into smaller steps that then compose the scale. An illustrative example involves bed-making. Bed-making programs can involve as many as 20–40 steps beginning with tucking one corner of a bottom sheet and ending with the last tuck of the bedspread under the edge of a pillow. Another example involves setting the table for dinner. Step one might involve wiping the table clean with a wet cloth and the terminal step might involve placement of the last necessary utensil near a plate. Programs are usually conducted on a daily basis, and the dependent measure in evaluations of them involves the number of steps completed. Virtually any skill can be task-analyzed and, thus, the number of scales that are potentially available corresponds closely with the number of skills that could be taught.

There are also rating scales that are used to track multiple behaviors over time, and these can also be used as a primary measure in single-case experiments. For example, a series of studies on externalizing behavior problems in youth in residential care used an ad hoc measure, the Daily Incident Report (DIR), a list of 65 coded behaviors that could be collected daily. The data from the DIR were used to assess behavior problems, evaluate treatment outcome for individual youth, and program outcome for groups (Friman, 1999; Friman et al., 2000). One of the most widely used instruments for tracking multiple behaviors, at least in the behavior assessment of children, is the Parent Daily Report (PDR). The PDR is a 31-item list of behavior problems that a child could conceivably exhibit in the course of one day (Chamberlain, 1980; Chamberlain & Reid, 1987). As problems are observed, parents or caregivers check them on the PDR list and one list is completed for each day of the assessment with no limit on the number of days that could be included. The PDR has been used in many published studies on child behavior problems, many of which used single-case experiments. For example, the PDR was used in a study showing that improvements in parent/caregiver social interactions produced corresponding improvements in the daily rate of behavior problems exhibited by six highly disruptive adolescent boys (Friman, Jones, Smith, Daly, & Larzelere, 1997). As another example, the PDR was used in a study showing that adding a youth to a group foster home increased the rate of behavior problems exhibited by youth in the home by one per youth per day (Moore, Osgood, Larzelere, & Chamberlain, 1994).

Scales Used as Supplemental Measures.   Despite the productive use of scales used as direct measures, most scales used in single-case experiments are supplemental to other, more direct measures. The most widely used supplemental scales are typically nomothetic instruments with well-established psychometrics that meet conventional standards. Although they are used to collect (direct and indirect) behavior observations, the observations are typically quantified and cumulative scores are conventionally used to support the existence of a psychological condition, or something that cannot be directly observed. For example, the most widely used behavior rating scale for children is the Child Behavior Checklist (CBCL; Achenbach, 1991). The CBCL includes 120 items that are in principle observable, however, in scoring the CBCL, the ratings are distributed into 9 scales, each of which denotes a psychological condition that is not observable (e.g., depression). Therefore, the CBCL and other scales of this type are not appropriate for the time series measures that are used in single-case experiments.

Nonetheless, such scales can be used to supplement a single-case experimental account of behavior. For example, in single-case experimental evaluation of a behavioral intervention, direct measures of the problem behavior are taken regularly (e.g., daily) during baseline and treatment conditions. High levels of the problem during baseline and low levels during treatment are used as evidence that the treatment was successful. In addition, clinical investigators sometimes administer behavior scales before and after treatment and use improved scores to argue for broad-based successful effects of treatment and maintained scores to argue against symptom substitution, or any other iatrogenic effects of treatment (e.g., Levine, Mazonson, & Bakow, 1980; also see Friman, 1995; 2002; 2003). There are hundreds, perhaps even thousands, of behavior rating scales to choose from. There are also numerous resource guides describing the available instruments, ranging from those designed for behavioral and clinical applications (e.g., Cohen & Swerdlik, 2002; Millon & Davis, 1996; Sattler, 2002) to those for use within organizations (e.g., Schermerhor, 2004).

Self-reports

Self-reports have occupied a venerable role in traditional psychological assessments for decades, but in a behavior assessment context, especially when the focus of the assessment involves single-case experimental analysis, their use is viewed with some skepticism, at least from a scientific perspective. Generally, self-reports involve paper and pencil questionnaires on which persons are asked to record their feelings about or likelihood of responses to a variety of events or the extent to which they engage in a wide range of public and private behavior (e.g., thinking, feeling, overtly acting). One of the reasons for skepticism is that the object of self-reports is frequently in the cognitive or emotional domain and involves behaviors or conditions that either cannot be observed directly or are very difficult to observe by others. Therefore the obtained data are impossible to verify. More generally, the utility of self-report inventories for behavior assessments varies tremendously. They are subject to a broad range of limitations, especially as the reports pertain to something qualitatively different (e.g., depression) from the actual behaviors reported on (e.g., activity levels, thoughts, feelings) by the person supplying the report. They are subject to biasing by the reporter (positive and negative), can lack specificity, and often do not correlate well with more direct measures of behavior. Self-reports are also reactive.

In using self-report, the individual is both the observer and exhibitor of behaviors to be observed. As a result, the act of observation, especially when it yields a publicly available record, affects the behavior being observed. All observation is potentially reactive even when its object involves matter at the sub atomic level (cf., Heisenberg, 1999) and self-observation is no exception. A variety of variables have been shown to influence self reporting including timing (in relation to the emission of the behavior), belief or expectancy about the amount and/or direction of change, motivation to change the behavior, value judgments about the behavior, and planned and unplanned consequences of the behavior (Hayes, Barlow, & Nelson-Gray, 1999; Nelson, 1977). Although the reactivity of self-reporting is a substantive barrier to the objectivity and, thus, scientific utility of the data obtained, it can benefit behavioral treatment.

Generally the reactivity of self-recording is therapeutic; that is the direction of change is governed by the desire of the recorder (e.g., prosocial recordings increase). For example, self-recording was a critical component in several of the early behavioral treatment studies on trichotillomania (Friman, Finney, & Christophersen, 1984). A major reason for using a self-report involves accessibility. As indicated several times above, important aspects of behavior are either not observable by another person (e.g., thinking, feeling) or are observable in principle but rarely in practice (e.g., theft, drug use, sexual behaviors). Thus self-reports are often used as a supplement to, or substitution for, more direct observations. For example, pain is a private event and, although it is associated with byproducts that are directly observable, pain itself is not. Nonetheless, asking a pain patient to self-report the location, quality, and quantity of pain can assist an investigator who seeks to strategically focus treatment and assess its effects. More generally, self-reporting can supply investigators with potentially helpful subjective information about the private aspects of any clinical concern, including those discussed previously such as anxiety or depression (e.g., Antony, Orsillo, & Roemer, 2001). But the problem of reactivity, along with potential biasing, distortion, inaccuracy, and inconsistency of self reports, limits their objective value in behavior assessment, especially when they are not supplemented by data from more objective sources. For example, several studies on treatment of trichotillomania used self-reported urges to pull as part of a behavioral assessment of pulling. However, the more influential of these studies supplemented data on urges with more objective measures such as observations of pulling, surface measurement of alopecia, and photographs (Friman et al., 1984). As another example, research on pain often includes self-reports of pain sensations, but these are usually supplemented with more objective measures such as direct observation of behavioral byproducts of pain (e.g., wincing, guarding), blood pressure, heart rate, and biochemical indices. The previous edition of this book supplied some evaluative criteria to consider as self-report methods are incorporated into behavior assessment (see Hartmann, 1984) and they will be briefly described below:

1. The instrument should be capable of being administered repeatedly to clients or participants. If the instruments form or content does not allow for repeated administrations, or if the outcomes from it vary systematically with repeated administrations, it is not suitable as a primary dependent measure in a single subject type experiment. However, it may be useful in the selection of participants, settings, target behaviors, or interventions.
2. The instrument should provide the required degree of pertinent information about the target behavior(s).
3. The instrument should be sufficiently sensitive to detect even minor changes in target behaviors that are occurring as a function of an intervention.
4. The instrument needs to be constructed in a way that provides maximal protection against biases that are common to the self-report methodology (e.g., impression management, item difficulty, ambiguous wording, etc.).
5. The instrument should meet minimum standards for reliability and validity and be accompanied by norms for the population(s) of interest in the investigations being conducted.

Physiological measures

An intersection between the fields of psychology and medicine has been growing for decades, and large subfields that utilize behavioral assessment and single-case experiments (e.g., behavioral pediatrics, behavioral medicine) have emerged resulting in the expanded use of physiological measures in behavioral assessment. These measures range in technical complexity and sophistication from simple pressure-activated scales and switches to functional magnetic imaging (MRI) and computer assisted (CAT) and positron emission tomographies (PET). The most commonly used physiological measures include blood pressure, heart rate (HR), electroencephalography (EEG), electromyography (EMG), galvanic skin response (GSR), and electrodermal activity (EDA), including skin resistance (SRL), skin conductance (SCL), respiration rate, pupil size and activity, salivation, and body temperature. In addition to supplementing behavior assessment, the advance of physiological measures has led to the development of entire fields of endeavor, specialized research societies, and major areas of clinical expertise.

Perhaps the best example of such development is biofeedback, an assessment (and treatment) method that uses sensors attached to strategic parts of the body to amplify physiological responses (e.g., heart rate, skin temperature, muscle tension), allowing the subject to perceive them more vividly than would otherwise be possible. Typically, the responses are "fed" back to the subject using a computer enhanced visual or auditory display. A wide variety of feedback modalities are used, the most common of which are EEG, EMG, EDA and HR. Biofeedback, similar to other forms of reactive assessment, can be used strictly for assessment purposes or to enhance treatment (e.g., Schwartz & Andrasik, 2003).

An example of biofeedback based-assessment involves the use of batteries of psychophysiological responses including EMG, skin temperature, skin resistance, and HR to predict behavioral responses to behavioral treatment for chronic headache in adults (Blanchard et al., 1983). Examples of biofeedback-based assessment and treatment include the use of thermal (e.g., skin temperature) based (e.g., Blanchard, Theobold, Williamson, Silver, & Brown, 1978; Gauthier, Bois, Allaire, & Drolet, 1981) and EMG-based biofeedback for various headache conditions in adults, as well as numerous other clinical conditions ranging from urinary incontinence in geriatric women (Johnson, Burgio, Redden, Wright, & Goode, 2005) to rare voice disorders in adults (Watson, Allen, & Allen, 1993).

There are also multiple examples of biofeedback used with children. For example, some children with chronic fecal incontinence suffer from extreme constipation, fecal retention, and distension of their rectum and sometimes the walls of their descending colon. This distension reduces the peristaltic function of the colon and the sensory stimulation that typically results from that process. Biofeedback informed research has shown that encopretic children often do not detect a full bowel until their intracolonic pressure exceeds extraordinary levels, sometimes more than 10 times the pressure needed to establish detection in nonencopretic children (Meunier, Mollard, & Marechal, 1976). As a result, these children often fail to detect peristalsis, have grossly delayed urges to defecate, exhibit infrequent and very large bowel movements, and have chronic fecal accidents. Enhancing the sensations of bowel fullness with biofeedback (e.g., manometry, EMG) allows them to detect bowel fullness at much lower levels of intracolonic pressure and, thus, makes them much more likely to succeed at behavior programs designed to produce full continence with more normative bowel movement size and frequency (Loening-Baucke & Younoszai, 1984).

Biofeedback assessments have also been used to identify a clinical subgroup of encopretic children who exhibit a paradoxical response when attempting to defecate. At the distal end of the colon is the rectum, the exterior end of which is chambered by internal and external sphincter muscles. The internal sphincter muscle is controlled by the autonomic nervous system and the external sphincter is controlled by the central nervous system. When the stretch receptors in the rectum are stimulated by fecal matter, the internal sphincter is reflexively relaxed and the external sphincter is voluntarily contracted, and this coordinated action allows the rectum to fill. Successful defecation requires that both sphincters be relaxed. Some children, however, actually tighten the external sphincter as they "bear down" for a bowel movement, thus attempting and preventing a successful movement with the same action (Loening-Baucke & Cruikshank, 1986). The potential value of supplementing behavioral assessment with biofeedback is clear in such cases. No dimension of conventional behavioral assessment would be sensitive to the abnormal defecation dynamics in these children and, absent knowledge of them, the children would likely be subject to a series of increasingly invasive but ultimately ineffective treatment regimens. The biofeedback findings, however, allow the dynamics to be detected and corrected through a behavioral intervention and establish thereby a skill-based foundation for effective treatment of fecal incontinence (Friman, 2003; Friman & Jones, 1998).

There are many other behaviors whose assessment (and treatment) have been enhanced by biofeedback and, as with the assessment of defecation dynamics, a central target of these assessments usually involves an anatomical/physiological domain that is not presently under volitional control, either because it is subject to the autonomic nervous system or because the sensations generated by stimulation or activation of it occur beneath awareness. This domain is typically either too relaxed (e.g., urinary incontinence in postpartum and geriatric populations) or too tense (e.g., tension headache, back pain). Data from biofeedback supplement data from more conventional behavioral assessments and help clarify the diagnostic picture of a presenting problem (e.g., pain), inform and enhance treatment (e.g., location-based relaxation), and yield data on treatment outcome.

Physiological Measures to Support Readily Observable Behavior. There are many other types of physiological measures (besides biofeedback) that can be used to supplement behavior assessment. Some are used to supplement assessments that focus on behaviors that are readily observable. For example, compliance with a specialized diet is a critical dimension of effective treatment for diabetes. A conventional behavioral assessment would focus upon the number and content of meals eaten over select time periods. However, blood-sugar levels are critical disease marker variables for diabetes and are directly affected by diet. Therefore, regular blood sugar measures are an integral part of the behavior assessment of dietary compliance with diabetes treatment regimens. There are many other types of physiological enhancement of behavior assessment focused on readily observable behaviors (e.g., blood serum markers and medical compliance, carbon dioxide concentrations and smoking, penile tumescence and inappropriate sexual stimulation, etc.).

Physiological Measures to Support Measures of Behavior that is not Readily Observable. Behavior assessments also focus on behaviors that are not readily observable (e.g., sexual responses) or psychological phenomena that are, in principle, not observable by other persons (e.g., pain, cognitive activities, emotional processing) and must rely on self-reports for assessment data. Physiological measures can be critical to the credibility of accounts from such assessments. As indicated in the self-report section, the accuracy of such reports is very difficult to verify and, absent other more objective supplemental measures, scientific and clinical confidence in them is limited. However, when self-reports are supplemented by physiological measures, their presumed objective status, and resulting confidence in them, increases. For example, assessment of anxiety disorders almost always includes self reports of worry, distress, and fear. Because of the limited objectivity of these reports, studies on anxiety frequently also include physiological measures (e.g., HR, GSR, EDA) to supplement the reports (Barlow, 2002). For example, an early study reported simultaneous measures of HR and anxious avoidance in nine cases of anxiety disorders (Leitenberg, Agras, Butz, & Wincze, 1971). However, the objectivity problems that can occur when assessment involves constructive conditions such as anxiety often emerge in attempts to correlate physiological measures with other aspects of conditions. For example, in the Leitenberg et al. study, measures of HR and approach did not correlate well. In some cases they were parallel, in others they diverged in opposite directions, and in still others one changed and the other did not. This variable correspondence between HR and other measures of anxiety, also found in other anxiety studies (e.g., Barlow, Mavissakalian, & Schofield, 1980), underscores the cardinal value of behavioral measures in behavioral assessment and the supplementary value of physiological measures. Avoidance behavior, broadly conceived, is the most critical clinical dimension of anxiety disorders. The experience of fear typified by a racing pulse can certainly be distressing, but if it is not accompanied by avoidance of any kind, the diagnostic criteria for impairment in anxiety disorders are less likely to be met.

Electrodermal Activity Measures.   Another physiological measure that accompanies many laboratory studies of fear and anxiety as well as a variety of psychological and behavioral conditions involves electrodermal activity (EDA), involving either conductance (SCL) or resistance (SRL). EDA measures are obtained from electro-sensitive monitoring equipment that targets output from the eccrine sweat glands, and the measures are viewed as physiological markers of activation or autonomic arousal. The measures have many related potential uses a prominent one of which involves supplementing accounts of fear or anxiety (e.g., correlations with responses to stimuli that arouse fear, outcome measures for interventions designed to reduce fear, etc., Barlow, 2002). They have also been used in studies of orienting, habituation and depression, and deception. As with virtually all physiological measures, however, EDA measures do not necessarily correlate closely with the behavioral measures that they accompany, especially when the target of the assessment does not involve directly observed behavior. EDA readings can be influenced by a wide range of variables that are extraneous to the intent of the assessment, including competing stimuli, measurement methods, and anatomical site. Additionally, as with anxiety and HR, in some persons EDA activity simply does not correlate well with overtly exhibited target behavior with which EDA is assumed to be closely associated.

Neuroanatomical Activity. The newest line of investigation utilizing physiological measures to inform behavior assessment, one whose influence is rapidly mounting (although more in scientific than clinical contexts), combines measures such as EDA with measures of brain activity such as those made available by MRI, PET, or CAT. For example, neuroanatomical activity correlates have been established for a broad array of behaviors and events associated with fear and pain (e.g., Fredrikson, Wik, Fischer, & Andersson, 1995). These studies have limited clinical value at present and are conducted by laboratory investigators with access to highly expensive and sophisticated equipment that would not be available to the typical person conducting a behavioral assessment for clinical or clinical research purposes. Additionally, the findings from such research, although certainly informative at the level of theory, have mostly shown correlations between brain activity and other indices of behavior and, thus, cannot be interpreted as showing a functional relationship. And functional relations are the sin qua non outcome of behavioral research (see section on assessment of function below). Nonetheless, these measures do extend behavioral assessment into a domain of activity that has historically been impenetrable to science. As the technology used to obtain them improves, especially in the areas of sensitivity and specificity, the possibility of filling gaps in behavioral assessments with functionally associated measures of neuroanatomical activity increases.

The examples of physiological measures provided above involve a very small sample of the broad range of methods and targets for their application. Although the use of such methods is expanding, a great deal of behavior assessment is conducted in their absence. Part of the reason for limited use is feasibility. The equipment can be very expensive and using it can require considerable technical expertise. Additionally, although such measures can be critical to a complete assessment of some disorders (e.g., abnormal defecation dynamics) their value in others can be limited (e.g., simple phobia, oppositional defiant disorder). There is also a range of variables that can affect the validity of these measures, only a sample of which will be mentioned here. There is a potential problem with false positives and, as a specific example, the urine alarm used for assessment and treatment of diurnal and nocturnal enuresis can be activated by perspiration as well as urine. Reactivity is also a concern. For example, the heart rate and blood pressure of some persons increase in the presence of medical equipment and personnel and the resulting artificially high measures are a potential problem with them. Many people experience high anxiety as they enter an MRI tube. Repeated exposure to an activating stimulus can also result in habituation, and the related reduced responding could artificially affect outcomes from the assessment of other variables. There are many other possibilities and, collectively, they underscore the importance of standardized use of physiological measures preferably in accordance with established application guidelines (cf., Hartmann, 1984; Cacioppo & Bernston, 2000) These limitations notwithstanding, physiological measures can enhance a behavioral assessment and many relatively nontechnical affordable measures are available (e.g., home-based drug screens, glucose monitors, blood pressure cuffs).

4.3. SETTINGS FOR ASSESSMENT

Contrived versus naturalistic settings and observations

There is a range of variables to consider in the selection of settings for behavioral observations, most notably whether the observations will be of behavior occurring in a naturalistic context or whether the context will be contrived in some way in order to bring behaviors of concern into a more informative and acceptable observational context. Naturalistic observations involve observing the subject without intentionally altering the observational situation in any way (or doing it minimally—the mere act of observation involves some alteration). Contrived observation involves deliberate modifications of the observational settings to differentiate it from the setting in which the behavior of concern naturally occurs. Naturalistic observations may seem ideal because of high ecological and ostensibly high functional validity. For example, if the behavior of concern involves child aggression on the playground, it would probably be more informative to conduct the assessment there rather than in a laboratory setting. Additionally, the aggression most likely would be differentially exhibited across time on the playground. For example, children who miss breakfast may be very hungry by first recess. If hunger is an establishing event for aggression (Friman & Oliver-Hawkins, 2006), first recess would probably be a more informative setting than the recess immediately after lunch. As another example, playground aggression can be powerfully affected by the presence of supervising teachers, thereby making assessment at times with teachers absent a potentially more accurate means of estimating a child's aggressive behaviors than times when teachers are present.

Although naturalistic observation has many advantages, there are times when it is simply not possible, permissible, or feasible. In the behavior assessment of panic, for example, laboratory based observation is a feasible option. Panic attacks may or may not occur during intense situational exposure (although they often do), but laboratory provocation is more reliable. There are multiple methods for provoking panic in the laboratory that include biochemicals (e.g., isoproterenol, caffeine, cholecystokinn, lactate), respiration alteration (e.g., exercise, hyperventilation, carbon dioxide infusion), and movement (e.g., vestibular stimulation via rapid circular movements). One of the earliest exemplar studies of laboratory provoked panic involved the injection of 5 mg of adrenaline into army recruits suffering from "irritable heart syndrome" the term then used for panic disorder and members of a control group (Wearn & Sturgis, 1919).

Both groups reported physiological symptoms, but only but the recruits with "irritable heart" reported multiple symptoms associated with anxiety and panic. A detailed and thorough reference source for information on laboratory provoked panic and anxiety is the recent book on anxiety by David Barlow (2002).

There are many other examples of contrived observational assessment. For example, behavior assessments of skills in risk situations are typically conducted in contrived settings because of the danger of exposing children to actual risky situations. As an example involving fires, an early study evaluated whether children could escape from a fire in their homes. Obviously, setting a fire in those homes would not have been permissible. Instead the investigators created a bedroom-like setting at the participating children's school and assessed a range of fire safety responses under simulated fire conditions there (e.g., feeling bedroom door for heat, avoiding smoke inhalation) (Jones, Kazdin, & Haney, 1981). As an example involving guns, a series of studies on training gun-safety skills to children assessed child responses to an available gun in a setting without adults present. The studies used disabled hand-guns to conduct the assessments. The assessments recorded the occurrence of targeted responses (e.g., tell an adult) before and after training (e.g., Miltenberger et al., 2004). As a similar example involving abduction, a series of studies on training child stranger-protection skills assessed child responses to requests from a stranger to leave a safe setting with the stranger (Johnson et al., 2005). The studies used persons, known to the researchers (but not to the children), as the "stranger." The assessments recorded the occurrence of targeted child responses (e.g., say "no") before and after safety training.

A continuum of contrivance

Observational contrivance can occur within and across locations, and both observations and locations for observations can be contrived or naturalistic. Yet it may be helpful to view differences as a matter of degree rather than as categorical or fundamental distinctions (see Kazdin, 1982, for an alternate view). No matter how naturalistic observations and locations are, the mere presence of an observer involves a contrivance of sorts and, thus, it may be most accurate to view assessment methods as occurring along a continuum of contrivance with minimal contrivance on one end and maximal contrivance on the other. For example, at the lowest end of the contrivance continuum would be assessments conducted in naturalistic locations in which the only alteration would be the presence of observers. The assessment of aggression on the playground discussed above is an example of this.

Minimal Contrivance. Also included at the lower end of the contrivance continuum are assessments occurring in a naturalistic location and in which some observations are contrived and others are naturalistic. For example, in a study on training formerly abusive mothers to teach their infants to avoid danger, parent/infant interactions were assessed in three naturalistic observational conditions (bathing, dressing, and play) and in one contrived observational condition, structured play. In the naturalistic contexts, the mothers were merely observed interacting with their infants. In the structured play context, however, mothers were required to interact with their infants in specific ways because the researchers were assessing the mothers' methods for controlling infant behavior (Mathews, Friman, Barone, Ross, & Christophersen, 1987).

Moderate Contrivance. Further up the contrivance continuum are assessments conducted in naturalistic locations but in which all the observational methods are contrived. For example, in a study on the effects of talking about tics on the emission of tics by children with Tourette's syndrome, the assessment location was a clinic setting, which was naturalistic because the hypothesis of the study was that tic talk in therapy sessions may actually increase tic rate and produce an artificially high estimate of tic severity. The observations were contrived by the specific programming of the presence and absence of tic talk in alternating conditions (Woods, Watson, Wolfe, Twohig, & Friman, 2001). Further still are assessments wherein the observational methods are naturalistic, but the assessment location is contrived. For example, a study on pica and lead poisoning assessed children with a history of eating paint (the majority of lead poisoning in children involves lead-based paint—Finney & Friman, 1988). Because the actual eating of lead-based paint presents a clear and present danger to children, it would not be permissible to observe them in the act and not intervene. Using a creative assessment contrivance, a group of researchers created a laboratory facsimile—one that resembled play areas in settings with lead-based paint. In the laboratory preparation, the facsimile was a room whose walls were "painted" with a mixture of flour, water, and food coloring that had a consistency closely resembling paint. Children with a history of eating lead-based paint chips were placed in the room and allowed to play. The target of the assessment was their rates of chipping and eating the faux paint (Finney, Russo, & Cataldo, 1982).

Major Contrivance. Toward the far end of the contrivance continuum are assessments that are conducted in contrived locations and use contrived observations. An example involves one the most sensational experiments conducted in modern psychology, the Stanford Prison Study (Haney, Banks, & Zimbardo, 1973; Zimbardo 2007). The contrived setting for the study involved a functional simulation of a prison in which 21 male undergraduates acted as prisoners and guards over a one-week period. The focus of the study was the assessment of interpersonal dynamics in a prison environment and the methods included direct observations, continuous video-taping, questionnaires, interviews, and self report scales. The results were sobering and remain controversial to this day. The simulated environment elicited intense, realistic, and often pathologic response. The latter results included abusive treatment by the "guards" and emotional disturbance in the "prisoners."

A less controversial and more applied example of major contrivance involves a study on insect phobia. The participant, a 14-year-old African American boy, exhibited the most fearful responses in classroom settings, and his academic performance was detrimentally affected whenever insects were even thought by him to be present. His fear responses were so disruptive that he often had to be removed from class. Direct classroom observations were not feasible because of the infrequency of the presence of insects and the disruptive effect deliberate placement of them would have had on the classroom at large. More technically, there is a growing literature in cognitive behavior science that employs overt behaviors to make inferences about cognitive processes (e.g., Greenwald et al., 2002)

Direct observations were also not permissible because of the unwanted and potentially stigmatizing attention that might have been drawn from peers. The treatment for the phobia involved an exposure-based program. Assessments were conducted in an analogue classroom setting, with academic materials on a table, and with the intermittent presence and absence of 2–3 insects (crickets) on the floor. The dependent measure involved number of compled of math problems (selected for the study by the boy's teacher). In the early part of the study, the boy could (would) not complete a single problem unless the entire room was checked and shown to be free of insects. At the study's end, he completed numerous problems easily (and accurately) even when insects were obviously present in the room (Jones & Friman, 1999). As another example, there is a very large literature on an assessment method referred to as functional analysis (which will be discussed below). Functional analyses usually involve contrived locations and observational methods (e.g., Hanley, Iwata, & McCord, 2003), both of which are also usually made topographically similar to locations and interactions that are natural for the participants.

Maximal Contrivance. At the extreme end of the contrivance continuum are assessments that occur in contrived settings and use contrived observations that are unique to the assessment. These assessments usually involve laboratory locations and technologically enhanced observational methods. Currently, one of the most frequently published examples of single-case experiments using such contrived assessment focuses on what is called derived relational responding. One of the historical mysteries of human language development is the extraordinary amount of language behavior that appears to occur in the absence of direct language training. This mystery has led some notable scientists to assert that human language is "hard-wired" neurologically and is not learned directly, but rather unfolds at critical developmental stages (Chomsky, 1965). Assessments of derived relational responding have addressed this mystery and countered the assertion about "hard wiring" by showing that untrained language expansion may actually be derived and expand indirectly (and exponentially) from directly trained language performances. At a very elementary level of analysis, if subjects are trained that A is equivalent to B and B to C, they come to "know" a number of relations that were not trained (e.g., B is equivalent to A, C to B, A to C and C to A). Some investigators assert that derived relational responding is actually at the heart of language development (Hayes, Barnes-Holmes, & Roche, 2001) as well as various forms of psychopathology (e.g., Friman et al., 1998). In order to show derived relational responding, the relevant behavioral assessments have to control for the potential influence of language that exists in the repertoire of research participants. To do so, nonsense symbols are substituted for letters or numbers (e.g., γ is equivalent to ξ), relations are directly trained using computer-based, forced choice, match-to-sample experimental preparations and untrained but "learned" derived relations are assessed.

In sum, increases and decreases in contrivance present advantages and disadvantages for the single case experimenter and they are essentially mirror images of each other. The major advantage of minimally contrived methods is a maximally natural sample of behavior, that is, the more the data obtained is likely to reflect the behavior as it is exhibited in the normal lives of persons being assessed. The major disadvantage involves the reduction in control the researcher has over the observational methods and locations. With reduced control comes a reduction in the researcher's capacity to obtain data safely, in a sufficient quantity for an informative analysis, within an efficient time frame, and in an economically feasible, socially acceptable and ethically sanctionable way. As contrivance increases, these advantages and disadvantages reverse themselves. The researcher gains control over observational methods and locations, but the behaviors observed may bear a decreasing resemblance to what normally happens in participants' lives. Choices made by a researcher are governed by a sort of calculus of advantage versus disadvantage in relation to the research question. For example, if the question involves a clinically significant behavior that appears to be situationally determined (e.g., fear of public speaking), the assessment should occur in conditions that are as similar to those settings as possible. But if the question involves a more fundamental and generically exhibited form of behavior (e.g., derived relational responding), the assessment can be conducted in highly contrived conditions and still be very informative.

Defining the behaviors to be observed

Although some discussion of defining target behaviors was supplied earlier, especially in the section on selection of behavior to assess, it will be covered more fully now because optimal definitions actually incorporate important aspects of the topics covered thus far. Behavior definitions are "operationalized," that is, they involve very clear, very precise, detailed descriptions of what is to be observed and recorded. These include various inclusion and exclusion criteria, subsets of which include topographical, temporal, dimensional, and functional features. For example, in research on response effort, behaviors to be recorded could include criterion levels of force exerted for criterion levels of time (Friman & Poling, 1995). Some of the effort research has employed functional definitions and thus any response that meets or exceeds specified thresholds is counted. For example, any response that depressed a lever sufficiently far to meet a definitional force criterion would be included in the functional category. Other effort research has incorporated topographical features. For example, only responses that involved hands depressing the lever would be counted.

Researchers strive to have their definitions be sensitive and specific, yet increases in one can result in decreases in the other. For example, in a study on hair-pulling in a 19-year-old woman, pulling was defined as any contact between the woman's right hand and her hair (Rapp, Miltenberg, Ellingson, Galensky, & Long, 1999). This definition was sensitive enough to capture any instance of hair pulling, but not specific enough to exclude more adaptive responses such as grooming or scratching. Conversely, an early study on digit-sucking defined it as two lips enclosed around a thumb. This definition was sensitive enough to capture all instances of thumb-sucking, but specific enough to exclude the sucking of toes and other fingers (Friman, 1988).

Functional definitions ultimately provide more valuable clinical information than topographical ones, but great care must be taken to avoid bringing non-observable components into the definitional category. For example, aggression is a construct with an almost unavoidable subjective (i.e., not observable) aspect. A representative definition is "an act whose goal response is injury to another organism" (Dollard, Doob, Miller, Mowrer, & Sears, 1939, p. 11). A tacit component of this definition is the intention of the aggressor and intentions cannot be observed, only inferred. A more operationalized definition would be "an act directed toward another person resulting in contact that produced injury." Obviously, this is not a perfect definition because it is not sensitive enough to capture aggressive acts that are unsuccessful. The problem is that aggression is a category with abstract aspects, and these are difficult to operationalize. Some researchers use much smaller categories that are more concrete (e.g., hitting) while others disregard the subjectivity problem and proceed with the larger definition (e.g., Dollard et al., 1939). The primary risk with the former is that important features of behavior may be missed. The primary risk of the latter is unreliable measurement (to be discussed further below). The primary message to be drawn from both is that establishing workable operational definitions is a critical, and sometimes difficult, part of behavior assessment.

Selecting observers

Another important domain of behavioral assessment involves who (or what) shall collect the assessment data. In most single case experiments, the primary assessment data are obtained via the direct observations of human observers. There are a variety of criteria to consider when selecting observers. Some are self-evident. Observers should be able to focus attention for extended periods, objectively note, discriminate, code and record various behaviors at one time. These and other criteria have been described in a variety of published papers (e.g., Foster & Cone, 1986; Hartmann, 1984; Hayes et al., 1999; Kazdin, 1982). One criterion emphasized especially by Hayes et al. (1999) involves the extent to which observers participate in the normal life of the person being observed. As with the contrivance of observational settings, there is a continuum of observer participation and corresponding advantages and disadvantages to high and low participation. The continuum extends from close family members at the high end to ad hoc observers, selected by the investigator, who not only do not meet the person to be observed but may not even be detectable by them as observations are conducted. Between these endpoints are persons known to subjects such as therapists, employers, fellow employees, school teachers, school psychologists, and ad hoc observers who have been introduced to participants or who are detectable in the observational settings.

Among the major advantages of close observer participation is proximity to the participant and reduced reactivity. For example, as described above, a series of thumb-sucking studies used time-sampling over the two-hour period when children were most likely to suck their thumbs at home (Friman, 1990; Friman et al., 1986; Friman & Leibowitz, 1990). These periods could occur at virtually any point during the day or night and it was most convenient to utilize parents because they would be more uniformly available across the day than nonparticipant observers. More generally, participant observers are preferred when behavior is situationally specific (e.g., occurs only at home) or has a very low rate. In these instances, it is often simply impractical to use nonparticipant observers. Another advantage of participant observers involves reduced reactivity. In the thumb-sucking studies parents were a part of their children's normal environment, were therefore less obtrusive than observers brought into the homes would have been, and thus less reactive. Another advantage for using participant versus ad hoc observers involves cost. The act of observation involves labor, and persons who have no participatory role in the life of the persons being observed are likely to require compensation for their services.

The disadvantages of using participant observation mostly involve potentially limited technical experience, training, availability, objectivity, and motivation. When necessary, these limitations are addressed by recruiting, training, and using nonparticipant observers. For example, if a behavior is continuous or at a very high rate, it may be impractical to use participant observers, because obtaining representative samples of behavior may require observer availability that challenges the daily schedule of persons who are close to the person being observed. The assessment situation most benefited by well trained, nonparticipant observers involves simultaneous observations of multiple responses that are distinguished from the observed person's generic flow of behavior by complex operational definitions.

A well known example involves facial action coding systems developed by Paul Ekman for assessing emotion (Ekman, 2003). Through specialized training with the systems, observers learned to discriminate subtle aspects of facial expressions (i.e., micro expressions) thus allowing them to more accurately assess a range of emotional states in others and even the extent to which verbal behavior of others was truthful. Another well-known example involves methods for observing and coding interactions between married couples. This research has been most notably conducted by John Gottman (e.g., Gottman, 1979) and the observational coding system used therein has evolved into a virtual scientific method in its own right known as sequential analysis (e.g., Bakeman & Gottman, 1997). The assessment research on marital interaction has produced outcomes that can be used to determine the quality of a marriage and even the probability of divorce (e.g., Gottman & Levenson, 1999). An intriguing subfinding in this research involves the ratio between positive (e.g., favors, affection) and negative (criticism, insults) exchanges between couples. A robust body of data shows that when a positive exchange ratio of 5:1 is exceeded, regardless of interactional style and marriage type, marriages tend to be stable (Gottman, 1979; 1994). A final example involves observation and coding of parent-child interaction, an assessment method that is central to a large body of literature on assessment and treatment of children with instructional control problems (e.g., McMahon & Forehand, 2003). The observations typically focus on multiple responses from the parent (e.g., commands, questions, praise statements, descriptions, criticisms) and their children (e.g., compliance, noncompliance). Accurately distinguishing between responses can be difficult and require intensive training and regular practice. For example, a parent statement can have the grammatical form of a description (e.g., "you are making a tower") but an interrogative tone (e.g., "you are making a tower?") and, thus, actually be a question. Children can refuse to follow an adult command verbally while fully complying with it motorically. There are many other examples (e.g., praise offered with a sarcastic or accusatory tone).

Technically enhanced observation

A major challenge for observers is the transitory nature of behavior. As a response is emitted, an observer has only one opportunity to observe, and no option to review, it. To address this problem, behavioral researchers employ technically-enhanced observational methods. For example, advances in computer technology have led to a number of semi-automated systems for collecting observational data in real time. There are far too many of these to discuss here, but a review covering 15 different systems was provided by Kahng and Iwata (1998). Most of these systems use widely available computer software (e.g., IBM compatible systems with DOS or Windows) and prices range from no cost to over $1500. These systems all have the flexibility to record the most important dimensions of behavior, including frequency, duration, interresponse time, and latency, and they can accommodate interval and time-sample recording.

Although computer-enhanced technology is increasingly available, many researchers use less sophisticated methods often involving only audio or video recordings. For example, with real-time video-recording, behavior is recorded in contrived or natural settings, and the tape is scored for the occurrence of target behaviors at a later time. One representative group of researchers uses VHS and sets the timer on the VCR to zero at the start of the observation session, recording the exact time (in seconds) of the onset and offset of the target behavior by noting the corresponding time on the VCR timer (e.g., Miltenberger, Rapp, & Long, 1999). These investigators establish the exact time of the occurrences of the behavior by using a data sheet that lists the 600 consecutive seconds in a 10-minute observation period. With behavior onset and offset, observers mark the corresponding seconds on the data sheet. Because the behaviors of interest are captured on videotape, and the VCR timer is set at zero at the start of sessions, observers can pause or rewind the tape and observe any segment multiple times, thus facilitating data collection and observer training. As video-recording equipment mounts in sophistication, so too does the ease of real-time recordings. For example, some video cameras display the running time of the tape on the tape itself so that the timer on the VCR does not have to be reset each time the tape is viewed.

If a researcher's budget is too limited for either computer or video-enhanced assessment, and if behaviors of interest have a crucial auditory dimension, simple audio recordings can be used to supplement other observations. For example, a recent series of studies evaluated a treatment for child resistance to bedtime. Among the primary dependent measures were children's crying and calling out from their bedrooms. In two of the studies, parent recordings of crying and calling out were used (Freeman, 2006; Friman et al., 1999). In a third, however, audio recorders were placed in unobtrusive locations in the children's bedrooms and data on crying and calling out were obtained from nightly tapes (Moore, Fruzetti, & Friman, 2007). Although the use of audio recordings in these studies involved relatively low technology methods, there is a broad range of technical sophistication in devices that can be used for recording, as a survey of any area of audio-based research (e.g., infant crying) will show (Lester & Boukydis, 1985).

Training observers

Once observers have been selected, the next critical order of business is adequately training them. From a metaphorical perspective, observers are instruments employed by researchers to record an element of nature. Similar to recording equipment, they too have to be calibrated (e.g., turned on, aimed, focused, turned off, etc.). Critical aspects of observer calibration involve the definitions of the behaviors to be observed, the dimensions to be obtained, and the time frame employed. Once these aspects have been established, observers are then trained to record behavior in strict accordance with them. A variety of training methods are available and one of the more authoritative systems was covered in the previous edition of this book (Hartmann, 1984). Although it focuses primarily on training of non-participant observers, it could certainly be adapted for use with participant observers as well. There are six general steps to the training system that include general orientation (e.g., nature of study, time frames, expectations, level of covertness, etc.), learning the observation system (e.g., memorizing operational definitions, scoring procedures, etc.), practicing observations outside the actual assessment context (i.e., analogue practice), practicing observations inside the assessment context (i.e., in situ practice), repetition with feedback, retraining and recalibration, and review with debriefing. Although it may sound grossly impersonal, the closer an observer comes to operating like a mechanical recording device, the better the observational outcomes. Thus, training should focus on minimizing observer-generated variance from problems that beset human observers such as attentional drift, fatigue, boredom, initiative, or hypotheses about the project. Training should actually involve over-training so that methods are over learned and require little conscious reflection for effective use. Additionally, questions from observers stemming from confusion, doubt, procedural problems or disagreements should be encouraged and regularly addressed. The point of training is to make observers as machine-like as possible and then to recalibrate the machine as needed.

Reliability and validity

Key issues pertaining to data from behavioral assessment involve the extent to which they are reliable and valid. Reliability involves the stability of the methods used to obtain the data. High reliability occurs when changes in the data are due to changes in the behavior being assessed and not to the method used to obtain the data. Validity involves the extent to which the data represent the phenomenon being assessed. High validity occurs when the data obtained closely compare with other measures of the phenomenon, especially when the other measures have well established validity themselves. Said differently, estimating the reliability of data involves obtaining similar measures of the same thing. Estimating the validity of data involves obtaining dissimilar measures of the same thing. For example, in assessments on behaviors associated with cardiovascular health, heart rates are widely used as a measure. Training observers to obtain rates from participants using a touch method applied to an artery near the participants' wrists would be an economical means of obtaining data. One method of establishing the reliability of the rates obtained would be to have a second observer periodically obtain rates simultaneously on the participants' other wrist and compare them. One method for estimating the validity of the touch-based rates would be to simultaneously obtain rates on a sample of participants' heart rates using other, well established methods such as a stethoscopes, finger pulse monitors, or EKGs and compare them.

In assessments that involve measures of behavior as defined here, reliability is likely to be a more important issue than validity. That is, when behavior observations are analyzed merely as a sample of a larger class of functionally or topographically similar behavior, validity, or the extent to which the observations accurately represent the object of the assessment is not a large concern. The object of such assessments is the behavior that is being observed. For example, in thumb-sucking research, direct observation of sucking during select time periods is analyzed merely as a sample of overall sucking, and the question of the validity of the sample is not likely to be raised. However, when behavior observations are analyzed as a sign of something else, then validity is a critical concern. For example, when self reports of racing, fearful, or panicky thoughts are taken as a sign of an anxiety disorder, other measures such as direct observations of escape responses or physiological measures of bodily responses to fear are often employed to gauge the validity of the reports (Barlow, 2002). Validity is an extraordinarily important topic in traditional psychological assessments because such assessments almost always involve measures that are viewed as a sign of something else. Vocabulary is seen as a sign of intelligence, impulsiveness of attention deficit disorder, racing thoughts of panic, self-induced vomiting of bulimia, and the list goes on to involve almost all of psychological assessment. Validity is crucial because the measures of interest and the conditions for which they are a sign often involve qualitatively different phenomenon. In fact, the majority of such assessments involve hypothetical constructs that actually do not have a verifiable material existence. For these reasons, validity will not be addressed further here, but those interested in more information need not look far. There is a very large literature on the validity of measurement and virtually all textbooks on psychological assessment contain large sections devoted to the topic (e.g., Cohen & Swerdlik, 2002; Millon & Davis, 1996; Sattler, 2002).

Reliability, however, is a crucial issue in all assessment, especially behavior assessment. Although there are a variety of methods for estimating reliability, the most widely used in behavior assessment involves inter-observer agreement (IOA). To establish IOA, observations are obtained simultaneously and independently from two or more observers, compared to ascertain agreement, and quantified for a mathematical estimate of consistency across observers or, reliability. In the prototypical assessment setting there is a primary observer who observes all sessions and from whom all of the data are used for the analysis and secondary reliability observers who merely observe a percentage of sessions. Although there is no set standard, 15 to 25% of sessions are conventional for IOA assessments. The data from the reliability observers are not integrated into the primary analysis but, rather, are compared with data from the primary observer, and the results from the corresponding calculations are reported separately as an estimate of reliability. There is also no established standard for an acceptable level of agreement, but 80% or higher is conventional, and 90% is preferred. High IOA is critical because it reflects stability in the observational method and increases the extent to which changes in the obtained data can cogently be attributed to changes in the behavior being observed while decreasing the extent to which changes are attributed to variance in the method.

The methods for calculating IOA change in accord with the dimension of behavior used in the assessment, and the results are always expressed as percentages. Note that there are always at least two sources of data in the calculation of

IOA: one from the primary observer and one from the secondary or reliability observer. On occasion, more than one reliability observer is used but the description here will involve instances where there is only one. For frequency measures, IOA is calculated by dividing the smaller frequency by the larger and multiplying the result by 100%. For example, if the frequency from the primary observer is 10 and from the reliability observer is 9, the reliability estimate is 90%. Similarly, for duration measures, IOA is calculated by dividing the smaller duration by the larger duration and multiplying the result by 100%. For example, if the primary observer records 10 minutes of exercise, and the reliability observer records 9 minutes, the reliability estimate is again 90%. For interval recording (from time sampling), agreement between observers is determined on an interval by interval basis. The number of intervals with agreement between observers is divided by the total number of intervals (i.e., those with agreements and disagreements) and the result is multiplied by 100%. Agreement is defined as intervals in which both observers record the same result (i.e., occurrence or nonoccurrence). Some investigators report agreement on occurrences and nonoccurrences, especially with low rate behaviors because high agreement on nonoccurrence could obscure low agreement on occurrence and vice versa. For example, if in a time sample of 10 one-minute intervals, the primary observer recorded occurrences in all but the last two intervals, and the reliability observer recorded occurrences in all but the last interval, occurrence agreement would be 89% (8/9 × 100% = 89%) but nonoccurrence agreement would only be 50% (1/2 × 100% = 50%). There are other examples and they correspond with the dimension of behavior used. There are also more precise statistics that can be used, such as the *kappa* coefficient that incorporates agreement on occurrence and nonoccurrence with chance agreements stemming from low base rates. There is also *phi*, a statistic that employs correlations between observations. For more information, there are multiple authoritative sources on the selection of appropriate reliability indexes and their calculations (e.g., Suen, 1988; Suen, Ary, & Covalt, 1990) and on the use of IOA (e.g., Foster & Cone, 1986), including the chapter on behavior assessment in the previous edition of this book (Hartmann, 1984).

4.4. THE ASSESSMENT OF FUNCTION

One of the largest and fastest growing domains of behavior assessment involves the assessment of behavioral function. Functional assessment was recommended early in the history of behavior assessment (e.g., Kanfer & Phillips, 1970) and its literature has grown very large. It now includes numerous edited books (e.g., Repp & Horner, 1999), training manuals (e.g., Nelson, Roberts, & Smith, 1998), research papers (Iwata, Dorsey, Slifer, Bauman, & Richman, 1982), theoretical reviews (e.g., Carr, 1977), and research reviews (Hanley, Iwata, & McCord, 2003). A decade ago, an entire issue of the *Journal of Applied Behavior Analysis*, the flagship applied journal in the field of behavioral psychology, was devoted entirely to the topic (Neef, 1994) and that journal has published numerous related studies since then (e.g., Rehfeldt & Chambers, 2003). The use of functional assessment is predicated on the foundational assumption of behavioral psychology, specifically, that behavior occurs as a function of environmental circumstances, and the most determinative circumstances involve contingent consequences (e.g., Skinner, 1938; 1953). When variations in the exhibition of a behavior can be linked to variations in the consequences generated by that behavior, the behavior and the consequences are said to be functionally related. Said differently, the consequences are then seen as a "cause" of the behavior. Functional assessment is a search for such functional (causal) relations. When discovered, those relations are used to inform treatment. Although functional assessment was suggested as an important part of behavioral assessment early on, it yielded little research until it was used to assess the self-injurious behaviors exhibited by persons with developmental disabilities (e.g., Carr, 1977; Iwata et al., 1982). Since then, its use has extended well into mainstream clinical contexts, and it has been used to assess problem behavior associated with most of the major diagnostic categories in the DSM-IV-TR. Examples range from problematic mealtime behavior (Piazza et al., 2003) to trichotillomania (Rapp et al., 1999) and it is rapidly becoming one of most frequently used methods for conducting behavioral assessment of school-based behavior problems in general (Hoff, Ervin, & Friman, 2005) and ADHD in particular (e.g., Ervin, Dupaul, Kern, & Friman, 1998).

The clinical utility of functional assessment was made dramatically apparent when it was used to show that social attention directed towards individuals exhibiting dangerously high levels of self-injurious behavior often led to increases in frequency, duration, and intensity. Intuitively, such individuals often appeared to be seeking attention maladaptively, through their injurious behavior. Results from functional assessments, however, showed that the self-injurious behavior often had the opposite function; it was reinforced by escape from or avoidance of social attention or, more colloquially, its purpose was to keep people away (e.g., Carr, 1977; Iwata et al., 1982). Thus well-intentioned staff attempting to prevent self-injury, or to comfort and console persons engaging in it, often actually worsened the problem.

The most rigorous version of functional assessment, one that is most pertinent to single case experimental design, involves experimental functional analysis. Reviews of numerous data sets on function yielded four general functional categories of consequences: (1) automatic (e.g., self-stimulation); (2) social (e.g., approval); (3) escape or avoidance (e.g., avoiding or escaping from a demand situation); and (4) tangible (e.g., candy, toys, money) (e.g., Iwata et al., 1982). Although there are variations on these categories (e.g., constant versus partial attention, social ignoring, different types of tangibles, control), most reports use some or all of the four mentioned here. Functional analyses are usually conducted in moderately to highly contrived conditions wherein the behavior of participants is repeatedly exposed to consequences drawn from relevant categories. If the analyses yield functional relations between key behaviors and any of the consequences, the findings are used to design programmed consequences for treatment programs. The prototypical analytical tool involves an alternating treatment design (also referred to as a multi-element research design; see chapter 8).

Prior to conducting a functional analysis, researchers typically develop some plausible hypotheses about possible functions. These are the result of interviews with participant observers (e.g., teachers, parents), less formal observations, historical documents (e.g., case files), or other types of assessment (e.g., preference assessments). Subsequently, researchers select the categories of consequences that they hypothesize may be functionally related to the behavior of participants. In some instances, all the major categories and variations within them may be used. For example, a study conducting functional analyses of bizarre speech in dually diagnosed adults used seven categories: alone, constant attention, demand, control, ignore, social attention, and tangibles. The analyses revealed a social attention function, and subsequent treatment involving non-contingent access to attention substantially reduced the problematic speech (Blake et al., 2004). In other instances, only a limited number of consequence categories are used. For example, in a study conducting a functional analysis of a vocal tic, only the attention and tangible categories were tested. The results from the analysis indicated an attentional function and, thus, cessation of attention (i.e., extinction) was subsequently used in a treatment to successfully eliminate the tic (Watson & Sterling, 1998).

There are other versions of functional assessment and analysis but all methods are united by the underlying assumption described above (i.e., behavior occurs as a function of environmental circumstances). Some methods test for the preferences of participants. For example, reinforcers can be difficult to identify for individuals with profound developmental disabilities. Significant advances were made with the development of a reinforcer assessment procedure in which a variety of stimuli were presented to clients, and approach behaviors to them were assessed and then used to differentiate preferred from nonpreferred stimuli (Pace, Ivancic, Edwards, Iwata, & Page 1985). Since that early study, this method has been used widely to inform behavior assessment, especially with regard to function (Fisher et al., 1992). Other methods involve observational systems focused upon the ABCs of behavior (i.e., antecedents, behaviors, consequences). When using these, observers record instances of target behavior along with events that occur before and after them. The rigor of the ABC methods range from simple descriptive systems to complex checklist and interval recording systems (e.g., Miltenberger, 2001). Other methods integrate a broad range of variables including behavior (e.g., response rate), physiological measures (e.g., blood pressure), and hypothetical psychological conditions (e.g., depression) (e.g., Haynes & O'Brien, 2000). Absent an experimental functional analysis, however, data from these methods can only lead to hypotheses about function; they cannot be used to establish it.

4.5 SUMMARY AND CONCLUSIONS

Behavioral assessment is integral to single case experimental designs for the social sciences. One way of understanding their relationship to each other is once again to think of a continuum. At one end of the continuum would be instances where the single-case experiment actually is the assessment. This is the case in many studies involving experimental functional analysis as well as treatment outcome studies. At the other end of the continuum would be instances where assessment measures merely supplement the single-case experiment. This is the case in many studies that use pre- and post-behavior rating scales, baseline and outcome physiological measures, and self reports. A critical point to bear in mind is that the ultimate concern of behavioral assessment is actual behavior. The definition emphasized here restricts behavior to what people do that can be observed by others, at least in principle. However, this definition excludes important aspects of human behavior that are private (e.g., thinking, emotionally processing) or that are understood mostly via abstract categories or constructs such as anxiety or depression. Granted, as behavioral assessment moves toward a conclusive outcome, it often addresses these aspects of human behavior along the way. But the ultimate emphasis is on what actually happens in the lives of persons being assessed, that is, what they actually do in their lives. And the most important portions of what is done involve behavior that fits the definition used here. Anything that moves the assessment toward its ultimate outcome should be of interest to the behavior assessor. Therefore, the discussion in this chapter included assessments of psychological conditions and self-reports of private events, because these can contribute to the assessment and, ultimately, to the single-case experimental analysis of selected behaviors. A cautionary note, however, is that such measures cannot or should not solely comprise the assessment or the research. The ultimate outcome is behavior that is on display in the world in which we live.

This chapter covered a broad range of topics including how to select behaviors to assess, measure the behavior selected, expand the view of the behavior by incorporating proximal, supplementary, or indirect measures, select and train observers to provide primary measures, address validity and, especially, reliability, and to assess function. A primary goal of sciences that use single-case experiments is to increase understanding of, and solutions for, social problems. Ultimately, social problems occur as a function of what people do (or do not do) and behavior assessment is a method for obtaining a credible account of determining what is being done, where, and why. The single-case experiment, either as the assessment itself or as an event informed by the assessment, is one of the best methods for confirming or disconfirming the account.

CHAPTER 5

BASIC A-B-A WITHDRAWAL DESIGNS

5.1. INTRODUCTION

This chapter examines the prototype of single-case experimental designs—the A-B-A design—and its many variants. The objective of this chapter is to familiarize the reader with the advantages and limitations of each design strategy, while providing illustrative examples from the many different applications of these designs reported in the literature. The development of the A-B-A design will be traced, beginning with its roots in the clinical case study and in the application of "quasi-experimental designs" (Campbell & Stanley, 1966). Procedural issues discussed at length in chapter 3 will also be revisited here as they apply to each of the specific design options reviewed. Both ideal and problematic examples will be used for illustrative purposes.

Since the publication of the earlier editions of this book (Hersen & Barlow, 1976; Barlow & Hersen, 1984) the literature has been replete with examples of A-B-A designs. However, there actually has been little change with respect to basic procedural issues. Therefore, we have retained most of the original design considerations and illustrations discussed in these earlier editions, but have added some more recent examples to illustrate how these designs continue to be a valuable tool for clinical researchers.

Limitations of the case study approach

Descriptions of uncontrolled case studies have appeared in the psychoanalytic, psychotherapeutic, and psychiatric literatures for many decades (see chapter 1). Despite the development of applied behavioral methodology (presumably based on sound theoretical underpinnings) in the late 1950s and early to mid-1960s, the case study approach was still the primary method for reporting the efficacy of innovative treatment techniques (cf. Ashem, 1963; Barlow, 1980; Barlow et al., 1983; Lazarus, 1963; Ullmann & Krasner, 1965; Wolpe, 1958, 1976).

There is no doubt that the case history method has long held a valuable place in the clinical research armamentarium (e.g., Freud, 1933; Watson &

Raynor, 1920). Among the advantages of the case study method are that it can be used to: (1) foster clinical innovation, (2) cast doubt on prior theoretical assumptions, (3) permit study of rare phenomena (e.g., selective mutism, dissociative identity disorder), (4) develop new technical skills, (5) buttress theoretical views, (6) result in the refinement of clinical techniques, and (7) provide clinical data to be used as a point of departure for subsequent controlled investigations. These many strengths are among the reasons the case study method has been effectively used since the earliest days of clinical science and continues to serve an important purpose. Indeed, journals such as the newly developed *Clinical Case Studies* (founded in 2002) are dedicated exclusively to this method and provide volumes of articles describing useful applications of the case study approach.

These many strengths notwithstanding, there are significant limitations associated with the use of a case study approach. Perhaps most importantly, the multitude of uncontrolled factors present in each study does not permit one to draw causal conclusions. Even when the case study method is applied at its best, the lack of precise measures of target behaviors and the absence of experimental control remain serious mitigating factors. Indeed, the case study approach typically relies on a retrospective, subjective description of the treatment administered and the resulting behavioral changes as recalled by the clinician. Several techniques usually are administered simultaneously, precluding an analysis of the relative merits of each procedure. Moreover, evidence for improvement usually is based on the clinician's global impression rather than on the use of specific, observable, and replicable measurement of an identified target behavior. Thus, there is a strong possibility of bias in such evaluations, as well as an inability to control for threats to internal and construct validity, such as history, maturation, client expectancies for change, and attention from the clinician.

As Kazdin (1981; 2003) has argued, one can draw some valid inferences from the case study approach, especially in situations where methodological rigor can be incorporated into standard clinical procedures. At the most basic level, one could collect pre-assessment and post-assessment data from a single subject. This is the single-case equivalent of the uncontrolled pre- and post-assessment strategy often used in group-based research and associated threats to validity apply. A slightly more rigorous strategy would be to conduct repeated assessment over the course of treatment and to demonstrate marked changes (e.g., Nock et al., 2004; Vonk & Thyer, 1995). An even more rigorous approach is to examine multiple cases with continuous assessment and stability information. Each of these would provide an improvement over the standard case study approach; however, despite such improvement, threats to internal validity are still present to some degree.

5.2. A-B DESIGN

The A-B design, although the simplest of the single-case experimental strategies, corrects for some of the deficiencies of the case study approach. In this design the target behavior is clearly specified, and repeated measurement is taken throughout the baseline (A) and treatment (B) phases of experimentation. As in all single-case experimental research, the A phase involves a series of baseline observations of the natural frequency of the target behavior(s) under study. In the B phase the treatment variable is introduced, and changes in the dependent measure are noted. Thus, *with some major reservations*, changes in the dependent variable are attributed to the effects of treatment (Barlow & Hersen, 1973; Campbell, 1969; Campbell & Stanley, 1966; Cook & Campbell, 1979; Hersen, 1982; Kazdin, 1982; Kratochwill, 1978).

Let us now examine some of the important reservations. In their evaluation of the A-B strategy, Wolf and Risley (1971) argued that "The analysis provided no information about what the natural course of the behavior would have been had we not intervened with our treatment condition" (pp. 314–315). That is to say, it is very possible that changes in the B phase might have occurred regardless of the introduction of treatment or that changes in B might have resulted as a function of correlation with some fortuitous (but uncontrolled) event. For instance, at the same point in time when the design changed from A to B, the person under study may have experienced some significant change in their living situation, begun another treatment, started a new relationship, etc. When considered in this light, the A-B strategy does not permit a full experimental analysis of the controlling effects of the treatment inasmuch as its correlative properties are quite apparent. Indeed, Campbell and Stanley (1966) referred to this strategy as a "quasi-experimental design."

Risley and Wolf (1972) presented an interesting discussion of the limitations of the A-B design with respect to predicting, or "forecasting," the B phase on the basis of data obtained in A. Two hypothetical examples of the A-B design were depicted, with both showing a mean increase in the amount of behavior in B over A. However, in the first example, a steady and stable trend in baseline is followed by an abrupt increase in B, which is then maintained. In the second case, the upward trend in A is continued in B. Therefore, despite the equivalence of means and variances in the two cases, the importance of the trend in evaluating the data is underscored. Some tentative conclusions can be reached on the basis of the first example, but in the second example the continued linear trend in A permits no conclusions as to the controlling effects of the B treatment variable.

In further analyzing the difficulties inherent in the A-B strategy, Risley and Wolf (1972) contended that:

> The weakness in this design is that the data in the experimental condition is compared with a forecast from the prior baseline data. The accuracy of an assessment of the role of the experimental procedure in producing the change rests upon the accuracy of that forecast. A strong statement of causality therefore requires that the forecast be supported. This support is accomplished by elaborating the A-B design. (p. 5)

Such elaboration is found in the A-B-A design discussed and illustrated in section 5.3 of this chapter.

Despite these aforementioned limitations, it is shown how in some settings, such as where control-group analysis or repeated introduction and withdrawals of treatment variables are not feasible, the A-B design can be of some utility (Campbell & Stanley, 1966; Cook & Campbell, 1979). For example, the use of the A-B strategy in the private-practice setting has previously been recommended in section 3.2 of chapter 3 (see also Barlow, Hayes, & Nelson, 1984; Hayes, Barlow, & Nelson-Gray, 1999).

The use of the A-B strategy in field experiments where more traditional forms of experimentation are not at all possible (e.g., the effects of modifying traffic laws on the documented frequency of accidents) has been a valuable tool for many years, as discussed in detail by Campbell (1969). Indeed, the A-B design can be used to study groups of individuals and the use of repeated assessment of the dependent variable offers a valuable advantage over standard pre- and post-intervention assessment because the experimenter can show that behavior was stable over the course of baseline, and changed precisely when the intervention was initiated in the B phase (e.g., Cox, Cox, & Cox, 2000; Porritt, Burt, & Poling, 2006). However one uses the quasi-experimental design, Campbell cautioned the investigator as to the numerous threats to internal validity (history, maturation, instability, testing, instrumentation, regression artifacts, selection, experimental mortality, and selection-maturation interaction) and external validity (interaction effects of testing, interaction of selection and experimental treatment, reactive effects of experimental arrangements, multiple-treatment interference, irrelevant responsiveness of measures, and irrelevant replicability of treatments) that may be encountered. The interested reader is encouraged to read Campbell's (1969) classic article for a full discussion of the issues involved in large-scale retrospective or prospective field studies.

In summary, it should be apparent that the use of a quasi-experimental design such as the A-B strategy while more rigorous than the case study, ultimately yields rather weak conclusions. This design is subject to the influence of a host of confounding variables and is best applied as a last-resort measure when circumstances do not allow for more extensive experimentation. Examples of such cases will now be illustrated.

A-B with follow-up

An improvement on the A-B design is the inclusion of follow-up assessment. One early example of an A-B design with follow-up was provided by Epstein and Hersen (1974), who assessed the effects of reinforcement on the frequency of gagging in a 26-year-old psychiatric inpatient. The patient's symptoms had persisted for approximately 2 years despite repeated attempts at medical intervention. During the baseline (A) phase, the patient was instructed to record the time and frequency of each gagging episode on an index card, collected by the experimenter the following morning at ward rounds. Treatment (B) involved presenting the patient with $2.00 in canteen books (exchangeable at the hospital store for goods) for any decrease in gagging from the previous daily frequency. In addition, zero rates of gagging were similarly reinforced. In order to facilitate maintenance of gains after treatment, no instructions were given as to how the patient might control his gagging. Thus, emphasis was placed on self-management of the behavior. At the conclusion of his hospital stay, the patient was requested to continue recording data at home for a period of 12 weeks. In this case, treatment conditions were not withdrawn during the patient's hospitalization because of clinical considerations.

The results of this study are plotted in Figure 5.1. Baseline frequency of gagging fluctuated between 8 and 17 episodes per day but stabilized to some extent in the last 4 days. Initiation of the reinforcement procedures resulted in a decline to zero episodes of gagging within 6 days. However, on Day 15, frequency of gagging rose again to seven daily episodes. At this point, the criterion for obtaining reinforcement was reset to that originally planned for Day 13. Renewed improvement was then noted between Days 15–18, and treatment was continued through Day 24. Thus, the B phase was twice as long as the A phase but it was extended for obvious clinical reasons.

The 12-week follow-up period revealed a zero level of gagging, with the exception of Week 9, when three gagging episodes were recorded. Follow-up data were corroborated by the patient's wife, thus precluding the possibility that

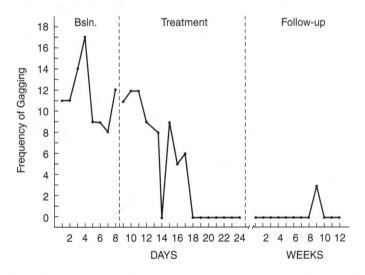

FIGURE 5.1   Frequency of gagging during baseline, treatment, and follow-up. (Figure 1, p. 103, from: Epstein, L. H., & Hersen, M. (1974). Behavioral control of hysterical gagging. *Journal of Clinical Psychology*, **30**, 102–104. Copyright 1974 by American Psychological Association. Reproduced by permission.)

treatment only affected the patient's verbal report rather than diminution of actual problem behavior.

Although treatment appeared to be the effective ingredient of change in this study, particularly in light of the longevity of the patient's condition, it is conceivable that some unidentified variable coincided with the application of reinforcement procedures and actually accounted for observed changes. The A-B design does not permit a definitive answer to this question. It is notable that this design (baseline, treatment, and follow-up) could be easily carried out in an outpatient setting with minimal difficulty and with no deleterious effects to the patient.

A-B with multiple target measures and follow-up

The clinical researcher often is interested in using multiple measures of a single target behavior, or in changing multiple target behaviors. The A-B design is well-suited for this purpose. An example of an A-B design with multiple target measures and follow-up assessment is provided by de Kinkelder and Boelens (1998), who studied the effects of habit reversal on stuttering behavior in two boys. Habit reversal training consists of teaching a person to become aware of the undesirable behavior to be modified and training in the performance of a behavior that is incompatible with the undesired behavior. In this study, the boys were recorded having conversations at school, at home, and at a speech clinic and the primary dependent variables included the percentage of syllables stuttered from among the first 300 syllables recorded at each assessment point, as well as the overall rate of speech and naturalness of speech as rated by independent coders. Each case began with a two- or three-week baseline phase (A) during which the boys' speech was recorded multiple times in each setting. After baseline behavior was observed to be stable, the intervention phase (B) was initiated, which consisted of four procedures: awareness training, training in regulated breathing, training in positive attitudes, and social support from parents. The treatment phase lasted for 21 sessions for the first boy and 31 sessions for the second.

Examination of the data in Figure 5.2 indicates that there were substantial decreases in stuttering for both boys during the treatment phase. Moreover, data collected for both boys also showed that improvements occurred across all three settings, that there were also substantial improvements in speech rates and naturalness across settings, and that these improvements appeared to be maintained at post-treatment and follow-up assessments. This, then, from a design standpoint, fits in nicely with Kazdin's notion of repeated assessment with marked changes and stability information improving the quality of case study. But, in spite of this, the A-B design *does not* allow for a clear demonstration of the controlling effects of the treatment. For that we require an A-B-A or A-B-A-B strategy.

Another example of the use of an A-B design with multiple target measures and follow-up assessment is provided by O'Donohue, Plaud, and Hecker (1992). These experimenters tested the effects of a contingency management program

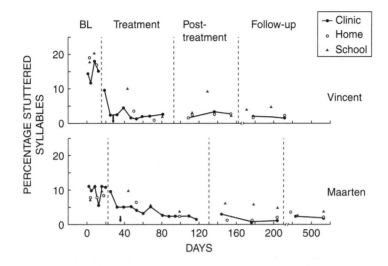

FIGURE 5.2 Stuttering frequencies during baseline, treatment, posttreatment, and follow-up for each child in each setting (clinic, home and school). The frequencies are shown as a function of time since the beginning of the study. The arrows indicate the end of awareness training. BL = Baseline. Figure 1, p. 264, from: de Kinkelder, M., & Boelens, H. (1998). Habit-reversal treatment for children's stuttering: Assessment in three settings, *Journal of Behavior Therapy and Experimental Psychiatry*, **29** (3), 261–269.

on engagement in out-of-home behaviors in a 42-year-old woman with agoraphobia. The subject in this case had not left her home for the previous 7.5 years. During a 30-day baseline phase (A), the experimenters collected data on total time spent out of the home. The experimenters also collected data on the subject's level of depression as measured by the Beck Depression Inventory (BDI) (Beck, Ward, Mendelson, Mock, & Erbaugh, 1961) as well as level of fear and avoidance on the agoraphobia subscale of the Fear Questionnaire (Marks & Mathews, 1979), both administered at several points over the course of the study. Data also were collected during the baseline phase on the subject's engagement in pleasurable activities while in the home, and this information was used to develop the intervention.

After the 30-day baseline phase, an 18-day intervention phase (B) was initiated during which the subject agreed to only engage in several identified pleasurable/rewarding activities while *outside* of her home (e.g., watching television, but only at a friend's house). The experimenters collected data over a 60-day follow up period, which was itself followed by 18-months of more traditional cognitive behavior therapy at the request of the subject. Thus, this design might be considered an A-B-A (given the extensive follow-up phase) or an A-B-A-C (given the addition of a second intervention phase). Given measurement occurred much less frequently over the second intervention phase, we focus more specifically on the A-B phases and follow-up period described in more detail in this report.

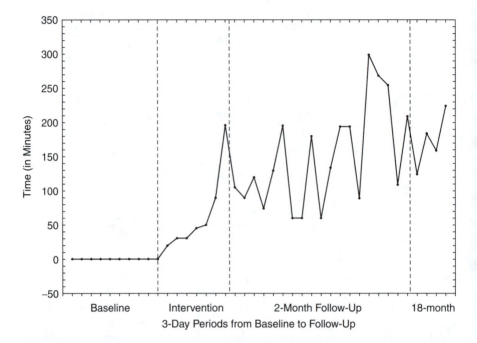

FIGURE 5.3 Total time spent outside of the home (in minutes). (Figure 1, p.308, from: O'Donohue, W., Plaud, J. J., & Hecker, J. E. (1992). The possible function of positive reinforcement in home-bound agoraphobia: A case study. *Journal of Behavior Therapy and Experimental Psychiatry*, **23** (4), 303–312.

The results of the initial intervention are presented in Figure 5.3. As shown, time spent outside the home remained at a zero level across the baseline phase (A), but increased substantially during the intervention phase. This increase was maintained across the two-month follow-up period. Results also revealed that BDI scores had a decreasing-increase trend over the baseline phase, but that this trend was reversed during the intervention phase, and continued on a decreasing trend over the course of follow-up. Interestingly, fear and avoidance decreased during baseline, and increased over the course of the intervention. However, they decreased once again during follow-up and continued to do so during the last phase. The increases observed on the Fear Questionnaire during the treatment phase may have been due to the nature of the intervention, which required the subject to engage in feared activities.

A-B with follow-up and booster treatment

In our next illustration of an A-B design, clinical considerations necessitated a short baseline period and also contraindicated the withdrawal of treatment procedures (Harbert, Barlow, Hersen, & Austin, 1974). However, during the course of extended follow-up assessment, the patient's condition deteriorated and required the reinstatement of treatment in booster sessions. Renewed improvement immediately followed, thus lending additional support for the treatment's efficacy. When examined from a design standpoint, the conditions of the more complete A-B-A-B strategy are approximated in this experimental case study.

Harbert et al. (1974) examined the effects of covert sensitization therapy on self-report (card sort technique) and physiological (mean penile circumference changes) indices in a 52-year-old male inpatient who complained of a long history of incestuous episodes with his adolescent daughter. The card sort technique consisted of 10 scenes (typed on cards) depicting the patient and his daughter. Five of these scenes were concerned with normal father-daughter relations; the remaining five involved descriptions of incestuous activity between father and daughter. The patient was asked to rate the 10 scenes, presented in random sequence, on a 0-4 basis, with 0 representing no desire and 4 representing much desire. Thus, measures of both deviant and non-deviant aspects of the relationship were obtained throughout all phases of study. In addition, penile circumference changes scored as a percentage of full erection were obtained in response to audio-taped descriptions of incestuous activity and in reaction to slides of the daughter. The inclusion of objective data that do not rely on self-report is an important aspect of the single-case experimental design. Three days of self-report data and 4 days of physiological measurements were taken during baseline (A phase). It is notable that while most single-case studies have historically used observations of motor behavior, the use of physiological or other behavioral measures (e.g., Gray, Brown, MacCulloch, Smith, & Snowden, 2005; Nock & Banaji, 2007) can be valuable additions to such designs (see chapter 4).

Covert sensitization treatment (B phase) consisted of approximately 3 weeks of daily sessions in which descriptions of incestuous activity were paired with the nauseous scene as used by Barlow, Leitenberg, and Agras (1969). However, as nausea proved to be a weak aversive stimulus for this patient, a "guilt" scene—in which the patient is discovered engaging in sexual activity with the daughter by his current wife and a respected priest—was substituted during the second week of treatment. The flexibility of the single-case approach is exemplified here inasmuch as a "therapeutic shift of gears" follows from a close monitoring of the data. Follow-up assessment sessions were conducted after termination of the patient's hospitalization at 2-week, and 1-, 2-, 3-, and 6-month intervals. After each follow-up session, brief booster covert sensitization was administered.

The results of this study are presented in Figures 5.4 and 5.5. Inspection of Figure 5.5 indicates that mean penile circumference changes to audiotapes in baseline ranged from 18% to 35% (mean = 22.8%). Penile circumference changes to slides ranged from 18% to 75% (mean = 43.5%). Examination of Figure 5.5 shows that non-deviant scores remained at a maximum of 20 for all three baseline probes; deviant scores achieved a level of 17 throughout.

The introduction of standard covert sensitization, followed by the use of guilt imagery resulted in decreased penile responding to audio-tapes and slides

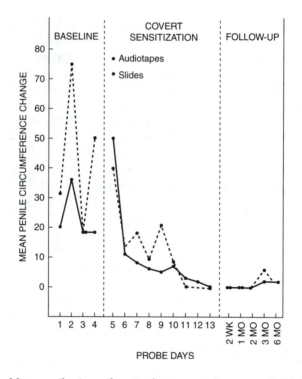

FIGURE 5.4 Mean penile circumference change to audiotapes and slides during baseline, covert sensitization, and follow-up. (Figure 1, p. 83, from: Harbert, T. L., Barlow, D. H., Hersen, M., & Austin, J. B. (1974). Measurement and modification of incestuous behavior: A case study, *Psychological Reports*, **34**, 79–86. Copyright 1974 by Psychological Reports. Reproduced by permission.)

(see Figure 5.4) and a substantial decrease in the patient's self-report of deviant interests in his daughter (see Figure 5.5). Non-deviant interests, however, remained at a high level.

Follow-up data in Figure 5.4 reveal that penile circumference changes remained at zero during the first three probes but increased slightly at the 3-month assessment. Similarly, Figure 5.5 data show a considerable increase in deviant interests at the 3-month follow-up. This coincides with the patient's reports of marital disharmony. In addition, non-deviant interests diminished during follow-up (at that point the patient was angry at his daughter for rejecting his positive efforts at being a father).

As there appeared to be some deterioration at the 3-month follow-up, an additional course of outpatient covert sensitization therapy was carried out in three weekly sessions. The final assessment period at 6 months appeared to reflect the effects of additional treatment in that (1) penile responding was negligible, and (2) deviant interests had returned to a zero level.

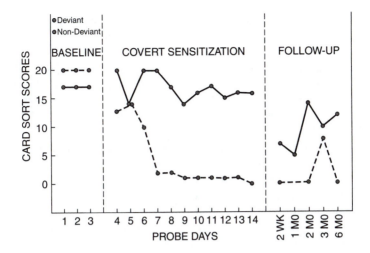

FIGURE 5.5   Card sort scores on probe days during baseline, covert sensitization, and follow-up. (Figure 2, p. 84, from: Harbert, T. L., Barlow, D. H., Hersen, M., & Austin, J. B. (1974). Measurement and modification of incestuous behavior: A case study. *Psychological Reports*, **34**, 79–86. Copyright 1974 by Psychological Reports. Reproduced by permission.)

5.3. A-B-A DESIGN

The A-B-A design is the simplest of the experimental analysis strategies in which the treatment variable is introduced and then withdrawn. For this reason, this strategy as well as those that follow, are most often referred to as *withdrawal designs*. Whereas the A-B design permits only tentative conclusions as to a treatment's influence, the A-B-A design allows for an analysis of the controlling effects of its introduction and subsequent removal. If after baseline measurement (A) the application of a treatment (B) leads to improvement and there is deterioration after it is withdrawn (A), one can conclude with a high degree of certainty that the treatment variable is the agent responsible for observed changes in the target behavior. Unless the natural history of the behavior under study were to follow identical fluctuations in trends (see chapter 3, section 3.6 on cyclic variation), it is *most improbable* that observed changes would be due to any influence (e.g., some correlated or uncontrolled variable) other than the treatment variable that is systematically changed. Also, replication of the A-B-A design in different subjects strengthens conclusions as to power and controlling forces of the treatment (see chapter 10).

Although the A-B-A strategy is acceptable from an experimental standpoint, it has one major undesirable feature when considered from the clinical context. Unfortunately for the patient or subject, this paradigm ends on the A or baseline phase of study, therefore denying him or her the full benefits of experimental treatment. Along these lines, Barlow and Hersen (1973) have argued that:

> On an ethical and moral basis it certainly behooves the experimenter-clinician to continue some form of treatment to its ultimate conclusion subsequent to completion of the research aspects of the case. A further design, known as the A-B-A-B design, meets this criticism as study ends on the B or treatment phase. (p. 321).

However, despite this limitation, the A-B-A design is a useful research tool when temporal factors (e.g., premature discharge of a patient) or clinical aspects of a case (e.g., necessity of changing the level of medication in addition to reintroducing a treatment variable after the second A phase) interfere with the correct application of the more comprehensive A-B-A-B strategy.

A second problem with the A-B-A strategy concerns the issues of multiple-treatment interference, particularly sequential confounding (Bandura, 1969; Cook & Campbell, 1979). The problem of sequential confounding in an A-B-A design, and its variants, also somewhat limits generalization to the clinic. As Bandura (1969) and Kazdin (1973, 2003) have noted, the effectiveness of a therapeutic variable in the final phase of an A-B-A design can only be interpreted in the context of the previous phases. Change occurring in this last phase may not be comparable to changes that would have occurred if the treatment had been introduced initially. For instance, in an A-B-BC-B design, when A is baseline and B and C are two therapeutic variables, the effects of the BC phase may be more or less powerful than if they had been introduced initially. This point has been demonstrated in studies by O'Leary and colleagues (O'Leary & Becker, 1967; O'Leary, Becker, Evans, & Saudargas, 1969), who noted that the simultaneous introduction of two variables produced greater change than the sequential introduction of the same two variables.

The clinical researcher should keep in mind that the purpose of subsequent phases in an A-B-A design is to confirm the effects of the independent variable (internal validity) rather than to generalize to the clinical situation. The results that are most generalizable, of course, are data from the first introduction of the treatment. When two or more variables are introduced in sequence, the purpose again is to test the separate effects of each variable. Subsequently, order effects and effects of combining the variable can be tested in systematic replication series, as was the case with the O'Leary, Becker, Evans, and Saudergas (1969) study.

A-B-A from the adult literature

It must be borne in mind that in many stances the re-introduction of a baseline phase will not lead to a change in behavior and the absence of such behavior change during the second A phase significantly weakens any inferences that can be drawn about the controlling effects of the intervention. In one recent

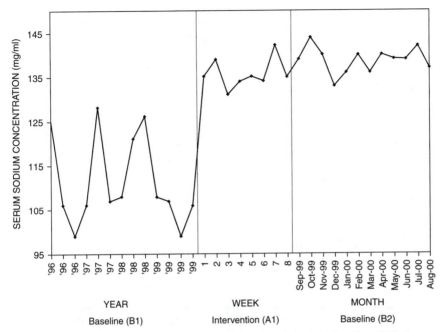

Figure 5.6 Serum sodium concentration documented through baseline (B1), intervention (A1) and post treatment (B2) phases. The time interval from the last baseline (B1) assessment to the first intervention (A1) point was one week and the time interval from the last intervention (A1) point to the first post-treatment (B2) point was 2 weeks. (Figure 1, p. 245, from: Thomas, J. L., Howe, J., Gaudet, A., & Brantley, P. J. (2001). Behavioral treatment of chronic psychogenic polydipsia with hyponatremia; A unique case of polydipsia in a primary care patient with infractable hiccups. *Journal of Behavior Therapy and Experimental Psychiatry*, **32**, 241–250.)

example, Thomas and colleagues (Thomas, Howe, Gaudet, & Brantley, 2001) used in A-B-A design in examining the treatment of polydipsia (compulsive fluid consumption) and chronic hiccups (for 20 years) using an intervention composed of education about hiccups, reinforcement for decreased fluid consumption, and relaxation training. Results, presented in Figure 5.6, revealed a significant improvement during the intervention (B) phase, but no return to baseline functioning during the reintroduction of the A phase. This is good for clinical reasons as it suggests maintenance of treatment effects; however, such findings preclude the experimenters from drawing firm conclusions about the controlling effects of the intervention.

A-B-A from child literature

A classic example of an A-B-A design is provided by Walker and Buckley (1968) in their functional analysis of the effects of an individualized educational

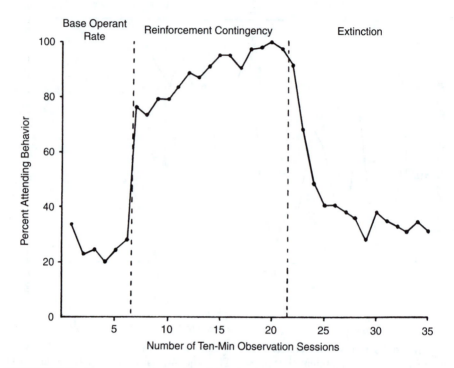

FIGURE 5.7   Percentage of attending behavior in successive time samples during the individual conditioning program. (Figure 2, p. 247, from: Walker, H. M., & Buckley, N. K. (1968). The use of positive reinforcement in conditioning attending behavior. *Journal of Applied Behavior Analysis,* **1**, 245–250. Copyright 1968 by Society for the Experimental Analysis of Behavior, Inc. Reproduced by permission.)

program for a $9\frac{1}{2}$-year-old boy whose extreme distractibility in the classroom interfered with task-oriented performance (see Figure 5.7). During baseline assessment (A), percentage of attending behavior was recorded in 10-minute observation sessions while the boy was working on programmed learning materials. Following baseline measurement, a reinforcement contingency (B) was instituted whereby the boy earned points (exchangeable for a model of his choice) for maintaining his attention (operationally defined for him) to the learning task. A progressively increasing time criterion for attending behavior over sessions was required (30 to 600 seconds of attending per point). The extinction phase (A) involved a return to original baseline conditions.

Examination of baseline data shows a slightly decreasing trend followed by a slightly increasing trend, but within stable limits (mean = 33%). Institution of the reinforcement procedures led to an immediate improvement, which increased to its asymptote in accordance with the progressively more difficult criterion. Removal of the reinforcement contingency during extinction resulted in a decreased percentage of attending behaviors to approximately baseline levels.

After completion of experimental study, the subject was returned to his classroom where a variable interval reinforcement program was used to increase and maintain attending behaviors in that setting.

A few design issues warrant brief comment. Walker and Buckley (1968) used a short initial A phase (6 data points) followed by longer B (15 data points) and A phases (14 data points). In view of the fact that a large and immediate increase in attention was obtained during reinforcement, the possible confound of time when using disparate lengths of phases (see section 3.6, chapter 3) *does not* apply here. Moreover, the shape of the curve during extinction (A) and the relatively equal lengths of the B and A phases further dispel doubts as to the confound of time. Regarding the decreasing-increasing baseline obtained in the first A phase, although it might be preferable to extend measurement until full stability is achieved (see section 3.3, chapter 3), the range of variability is very constricted here, thus delimiting the importance of the trends.

5.4. A-B-A-B DESIGN

Perhaps the most widely known single-case experimental design is the A-B-A-B design. This design strategy is more rigorous than the A-B-A design and controls for the deficiencies present in that design. More specifically, the A-B-A-B design ends on a treatment phase (B), which then can be extended beyond the experimental requirements of study for the purposes of providing good clinical care. The A-B-A-B design also provides for two occasions for demonstrating the positive effects of the treatment variable (B to A and then A to B). This strengthens the conclusions that can be drawn regarding the controlling effects of the intervention (Barlow & Hersen, 1973).

In the following subsections we provide five examples of the use of the A-B-A-B strategy. In the first, we present examples from the child literature that illustrate ideal procedures. In the second, we examine a situation in which the return to baseline is not completely under experimental control and so experimental manipulation is only approximated. In the third, we examine problems that can develop when improvement fortuitously occurs during the second baseline period. In the fourth, we illustrate the use of the A-B-A-B design when concurrent behaviors are monitored in addition to targeted behaviors of interest. Finally, in the fifth, we examine the advantages and disadvantages of using the A-B-A-B strategy without the experimenter's knowledge of results throughout the different phases of study.

A-B-A-B from child literature

The A-B-A-B design strategy has been used countless times in the examination of interventions for child behavior problems. One excellent example is provided by R. V. Hall et al. (1971). In this study, the effects of contingent teacher attention were examined when applied to a 10-year-old boy with mental retardation whose "talking-out" behaviors during special education classes was disruptive, especially because other children were copying his talking out behaviors. Baseline observations of *talk-outs* were recorded by the teacher (reliability checks indicated 84% to 100% agreement) during five daily 15-minute sessions. During these first five sessions (A), the teacher responded naturally to talk-outs by attending to them. However, in the next five sessions (B) the teacher was instructed to ignore talk-outs but to provide increased attention to the child's productive behaviors. The third series of five sessions involved a return to baseline conditions (A), and the last series of five sessions consisted of reinstatement of contingent attention (B).

The results of this study are plotted in Figure 5.8. The use of equal phases facilitates the analysis of results. Baseline data are stable and range from three to five talk-outs, with three of the five points at a level of four talk-outs per session. Institution of contingent attention resulted in a marked decrease that achieved a zero level by Sessions 9 and 10. Removal of contingent attention led to a linear increase of talk-outs to a high of five. However, reinstatement of contingent attention once again brought talk-outs under experimental control. Thus application and withdrawal of contingent attention clearly demonstrates its controlling effects on talk-out behaviors. This is twice-documented, as seen in the decreasing and increasing data trends in the second set of A and B phases.

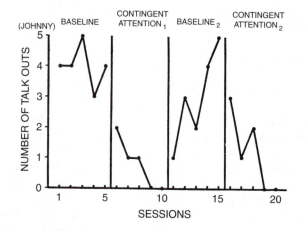

FIGURE 5.8   A record of talking out behavior of an educable mentally retarded student. Baseline₁—before experimental conditions. Contingent Teacher Attention₁—systematic ignoring of talking out and increased teacher attention to appropriate behavior. Baseline₂—reinstatment of teacher attention to talking out behavior. (Figure 2, p. 143, from: Hall, R. V., Fox, R., Willard, D., Goldsmith, L., Emerson, M., Owen, M., Davis, T., & Porcia, E. (1971). The teacher as observer and experimenter in the modification of disputing and talking-out behaviors. *Journal of Applied Behavior Analysis*, **4**, 141–149. Copyright 1971 by Society for the Experimental Analysis of Behavior, Inc. Reproduced by permission.)

A more recent example from the child literature is a study by Facon, Beghin and Riviere (2007) in which two visually impaired boys with a history of making inappropriate verbalizations were treated using planned ignoring of inappropriate verbalizations and differential reinforcement of appropriate verbalizations. The intervention was tested in each boy using an A-B-A-B design.

During all phases, the child was observed interacting with a therapist for 12 to 30 minute sessions. Each session was divided into 10 second intervals and the percentage of intervals during which appropriate and inappropriate verbalizations were made by the child were calculated (inter-observer agreement was 91%). During the baseline (A) phases, therapists responded to all verbalizations with a neutral response. During both treatment (B) phases, therapists ignored inappropriate verbalizations (i.e., did not speak until 10 seconds after the end of the verbalization) and responded to appropriate verbalizations with statements expressing strong interest in the child's statements.

The results of this study are presented in Figure 5.9. As shown for both children, inappropriate verbal responses occurred more frequently than appropriate responses during the initial baseline. During the intervention phase, this pattern changed significantly and appropriate verbalizations occurred much more frequently than inappropriate ones. The return to baseline showed an immediate reversal back to baseline levels, and the second intervention phase showed an immediate return of the intervention effects.

With respect to design considerations, we have here a very clear demonstration of the efficacy of the intervention on two occasions. As was the case in our prior example (R. V. Hall et al., 1971) baselines (especially the second) were shorter than treatment phases. However, in light of the immediate and dramatic improvements as a result of the intervention, the possible confound of time and length of adjacent phases does not apply in this analysis.

A-B-A-B when phase change is not under complete experimental control

As mentioned above, although the use of the A-B-A-B design allows the experimenter to draw strong inferences about treatment effects, it is not always clinically desirable or feasible to withdraw an effective intervention during the second baseline phase, particularly in the case of dangerous or harmful behaviors such as aggressive or self-injurious behaviors. Thus, it is possible that an experimenter begins an A-B-A-B design and is unable to withdraw treatment and must abandon this design in favor of an A-B design or an A-B-A-B with an abbreviated second baseline.

Another possibility, though, is that the subject him- or herself stops participating in the intervention during the first B phase, thus creating a quasi-experimental return to baseline. In such cases, the experimenter can flexibly continue with the investigation, but is now limited in the inferences that can be drawn given there is no longer complete experimental control over study procedures. As an example, Wallenstein and Nock (2007) tested the effects of aerobic

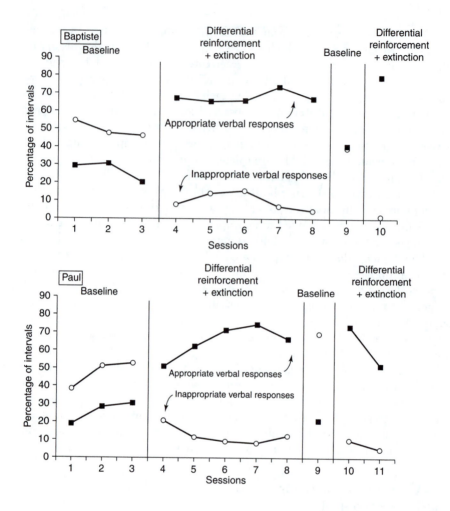

FIGURE 5.9 Percentage of intervals with appropriate and inappropriate verbal responses across experimental conditions for Baptiste and Paul. (Figure 1, p. 26, from: Facon, B., Beghin, M., & Riviere, V. (2007). The reinforcing effect of contingent attention on verbal preserverations of two children with severe visual impairment. *Journal of Behavior Therapy and Experimental Psychiatry*, **38** (1), 23–28.)

exercise on engagement in non-suicidal self-injury (NSSI; e.g., skin cutting) in a 26-year-old woman with a 13-year history of such behavior. In this study, the subject kept a daily log of self-injurious urges and behaviors across all phases. The study was planned as an A-B-A-B design, with treatment consisting of the subject engaging in a 60-minute aerobic exercise regimen (guided by an exercise video) three times per week and in response to any urges to engage in NSSI.

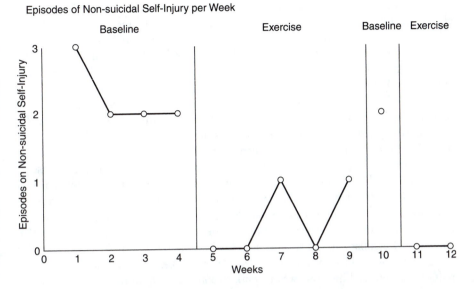

FIGURE 5.10   Treatment of nonsuicidal self-injurer with exercise intervention over a 12 week period. (Data are from: Wallenstein, M. B., & Nock, M. K. [2007]. Physical exercise for the treatment of non-suicidal self-injury: Evidence from a single-case study. *American Journal of Psychiatry*, **164**, 350–351.)

As presented in Figure 5.10, the subject reported a significant decrease in NSSI during the first, 5-week treatment (B) phase. Before the experimenters instructed the subject to discontinue use of the exercise regimen, the subject voluntarily decided to do so. During this quasi-experimental return to baseline (A), the subject reported a return of self-injurious urges and behaviors to initial baseline levels. This was followed by an instruction to re-introduce the exercise regimen (B), which was associated with a return of treatment effects. The quasi-experimental nature of this design precludes the experimenters from drawing causal inferences about the effects of the intervention, as unmeasured historical factor (e.g., break-up with significant other, problems in treatment) may have caused the subject to both stop exercising (i.e., begin the second A phase) and start engaging in NSSI once again. Nevertheless, these data provide some evidence for the effectiveness of this treatment approach and offer a basis for future experimental replications.

A-B-A-B with unexpected improvement in baseline

Difficulties can arise when interpreting the results of an A-B-A-B design if improvement occurs unexpectedly during baseline assessment. As an example, Epstein, Hersen, and Hemphill (1974) used an A-B-A-B design to study the effects of feedback on frontalis muscle activity in a patient who had suffered from chronic headaches for 16-years. EMG recordings were obtained while the patient relaxed in a reclining chair in the experimental laboratory for 10 minutes following 10 minutes of adaptation during each of six baseline (A) sessions. During the six feedback (B) sessions, the patient's favorite music (prerecorded on tape) was automatically turned on whenever EMG activity decreased below a preset criterion level. In contrast, responses above that level turned off the music. The patient was instructed to "keep the music on" during the treatment phase. The intervention phase was followed by a six session return to baseline (A), which was itself followed by a six session return to feedback (B). The patient also was instructed to keep a record of the intensity of headache activity across all phases.

The results of this study are presented in Figure 5.11. As shown, EMG activity during baseline ranged from 28 to 50 seconds (mean = 39.18) per minute that contained integrated responses above the criterion microvolt level. Institution of feedback procedures resulted in decreased activity (mean = 23.18). Removal of feedback in the second baseline initially resulted in increased activity in Sessions 13–15. However, an *unexplained but decreased trend* was noted in the last half of that phase. This downward trend, to some extent, detracts from the interpretation that music feedback was the responsible agent of change during the first B phase. The importance of maintaining equal lengths of phases is highlighted here. If baseline measurement had been concluded on Day 15, an unequivocal interpretation (though probably erroneous) would have been made. However, despite the downward trend in baseline, mean data for this phase (30.25) were higher than for the previous feedback phase (23.18).

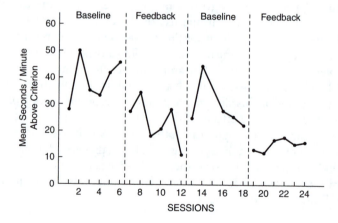

FIGURE 5.11   Mean seconds per minute that contained integrated responses above criterion microvolt level during baseline and feedback phases. (Figure 1, p. 61, from: Epstein, L. H., Hersen, M., & Hemphill, D. P. (1974). Music feedback as a treatment for tension headache: An experimental case study. *Journal of Behavior Therapy and Experimental Psychiatry, 5*, 59–63. Copyright 1974 by Pergamon. Reproduced by permission.)

In the final phase, feedback resulted in a further decline that was generally maintained at low levels (mean = 14.98). Unfortunately, it is not clear whether this further decrease might have occurred naturally without the benefits of renewed introduction of feedback. Therefore, despite the presence of statistically significant differences between baseline and feedback phases and confirmation of EMG differences by self-reports of decreased headache intensity during feedback, the downward trend in the second baseline prevents a definitive interpretation of the controlling effects of the feedback procedure.

When the aforementioned data pattern results, it is recommended that variables that might have caused improvement during baseline be examined through additional experimental analyses. However, time limitations and pressing clinical needs of the patient or subject under study usually preclude such additional study. Therefore, the next best strategy involves a replication of the procedure with the same subject—or with additional subjects bearing the same kind of diagnosis (see chapter 10).

A-B-A-B with monitoring of concurrent behaviors

Most studies reporting on the use of the A-B-A-B design test the effects of an intervention on only one target behavior. However, a number of reports have highlighted the importance of monitoring concurrent (non-targeted) behaviors as well. This is of particular importance when side effects of treatment are possibly negative (see Sajwaj, Twardosz, & Burke, 1972). Kazdin (1973) has noted some of the potential advantages in monitoring the multiple effects of treatment on operant paradigms:

> One initial advantage is that such assessment would permit the possibility of determining response generalization. If certain response frequencies are increased or decreased, it would be expected that other related operants would be influenced. It would be a desirable addition to determine generalization of beneficial response changes by looking at behavior related to the target response. In addition, changes in the frequency of responses might also correlate with topographical alterations. (p. 527)

The examination of potential collateral effects of an intervention of course should not be restricted to operant paradigms, but can be examined more generally whenever using experimental single-case designs.

As an example, Twardosz and Sajwaj (1972) used an A-B-A-B design to evaluate the efficacy of an intervention designed to increase sitting behavior in a 4-year-old, hyperactive, mentally retarded boy who was enrolled in an experimental preschool class. Beyond the assessment of the primary target behavior (sitting), the experimenters examined the effects of treatment on a variety of concurrent behaviors (posturing, walking, use of toys, and proximity of children). Observations were made during a free-play period (one-half hour) in which class members could choose their playmates and toys. During baseline (A), the teacher gave the child instructions (as she did to all others in class) but did not prompt him to sit or praise him when he did. Institution of the sitting program (B) involved prompting the child (placing him in a chair with toys before him on the table), praising him for remaining seated and for evidencing other positive behaviors, and awarding him tokens (exchangeable for candy) for in-seat behavior. The sitting program was withdrawn in the third phase (A) and reinstated in the fourth phase (B).

The results of this study appear in Figure 5.12. Examination of the top part of the graph shows that the sitting program, with the exception of the last day in the first treatment phase, led to improvement over baseline conditions on both occasions. Continued examination of the figure reveals that posturing decreased during the sitting program, but walking remained at a consistent rate throughout all phases of study. Similarly, use of toys and proximity to children increased during administrations of the sitting program. In discussing their results, Twardosz and Sajwaj (1972) stated that:

> This study . . . points out the desirability of measuring several child behaviors, although a modification procedure might focus on only one. In this way the preschool teacher can assess the efficacy of her program based upon changes in other behaviors as well as the behavior of immediate concern. (p. 77)

However, in the event that non-targeted behaviors remain unmodified or that deterioration occurs in others, additional behavioral techniques can then be applied (Sajwaj, Twardosz, & Burke, 1972). Under these circumstances it might be preferable to use a multiple baseline strategy in which attention to each behavior can be programmed in advance (see chapter 7).

A-B-A-B with no feedback to experimenter

As mentioned in Chapter 3, one of the main advantages of single-case experimental designs is that they provide the experimenter with ongoing feedback about the target behavior(s) and also allow the experimenter to flexibly modify the intervention over the course of the study. Thus, changes from one phase to the next are accomplished with the experimenter's full knowledge of prior results. Although these factors benefit the experimental clinician, they can introduce problems from a purely experimental standpoint. Critics of single-case experimental designs have suggested that the experimenter could introduce bias in the evaluation of the target behavior and in the actual application and withdrawal of specified techniques. One method of preventing such "bias" is to determine lengths of baseline and experimental phases on an *a priori* basis, while keeping the experimenter uninformed as to trends in the data during their collection. A problem with this approach, however, is that decisions regarding choice of baselines and those concerned with appropriate timing of institution and removal of therapeutic variables are left to chance rather than adjusted in order to display stability in the data.

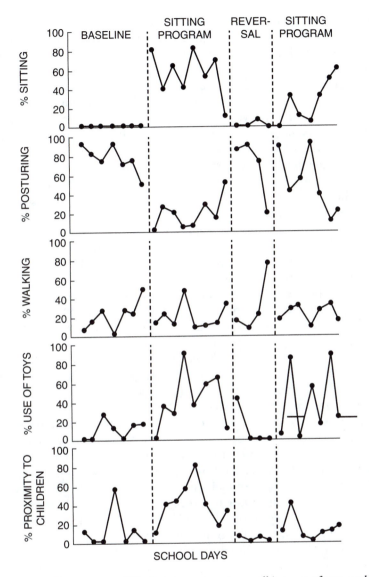

FIGURE 5.12   Percentages of Tim's sitting, posturing, walking, use of toys, and proximity to children during freeplay as a function of the teacher's ignoring him when he did not obey a command to sit down. (Figure 1, p. 75, from: Twardosz, S., & Sajwaj, T. (1972). Multiple effects of a procedure to increase sitting in a hyperactive retarded boy. *Journal of Applied Behavior Analysis*, **5**, 73–78. Copyright 1972 by Society for the Experimental Analysis of Behavior, Inc. Reproduced by permission.)

The use of an A-B-A-B design with a set number of sessions per phase and no feedback to the experimenter (i.e., data were obtained from videotaped recordings for all phases after the experiment ended) appears in a report by Hersen, Miller, and Eisler (1973). The authors examined the effects of varying conversational topics (non-alcohol and alcohol-related) on duration of looking and duration of speech in four heavy drinkers and their wives in *ad libitum* interactions videotaped in a television studio. Following 3 minutes of "warm-up" interaction, each couple was instructed to converse for 6 minutes (A phase) about any subject *unrelated* to the husband's drinking problem. Instructions were repeated at 2-minute intervals over a two-way intercom from an adjoining room to ensure maintenance of the topic of conversation. In the next 6 minutes (B phase) the couple was instructed to converse *only* about the husband's drinking problem (instructions were repeated at 2-minute intervals). The last 12 minutes of interaction consisted of identical replications of the A and B phases.

The results of this study are presented in Figure 5.13 as mean data for all four couples. As shown, speech duration data showed no trends across experimental phases for either husbands or wives. Similarly, duration of looking did not vary across phases for husbands. However, duration of looking for wives was significantly greater during alcohol- than non-alcohol-related segments of interaction. In the first non-alcohol phase, looking duration ranged from 26 to 43 seconds, with an upward trend in evidence. In the first alcohol phase (B), duration of looking ranged from 57 to 70 seconds, with a continuation of the upward linear trend. Reintroduction of the non-alcohol phase (A) resulted in a decrease of looking (38 to 45 seconds). In the final alcohol segment (B), looking once again increased, ranging from 62 to 70 seconds.

An analysis of these data does not allow for conclusions with respect to the initial A and B phases inasmuch as the upward trend in A continued into B. However, the decreasing trend in the second A phase succeeded by the increasing trend in the second B phase suggests that topic of conversation had a controlling influence on the wives' rates of looking. We might note here that if the experimenters were in position to monitor their results throughout all experimental phases, the initial segment probably would have been extended until the wives' looking duration achieved stability in the form of a plateau. Then the second phase would have been introduced.

5.5. B-A-B DESIGN

An important variant of the A-B-A design is the B-A-B design, in which the first phase (B) typically involves the application of a treatment. In the second phase (A) the treatment is withdrawn and in the final phase (B) it is reinstated. Some investigators have introduced an abbreviated baseline session prior to the major B-A-B phases, resulting in the popular A-B-A-B design. Clinically, the B-A-B design is superior to the A-B-A design because the study begins and ends with the

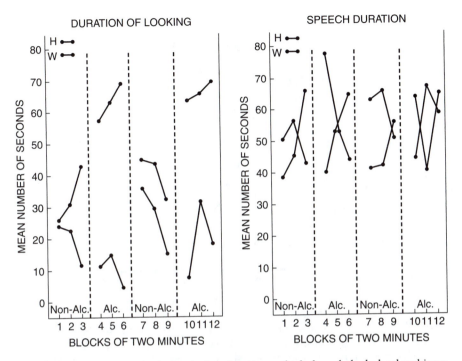

FIGURE 5.13   Looking and speech duration in nonalcohol- and alcohol-related inter-actions of alcoholics and their wives. Plotted in blocks of 2 minutes. Closed circles—husbands; open circles—wives. (Figure 1, p. 518, from: Hersen, M., Miller, P. M., & Eisler, R. M. (1973). Interactions between alcoholics and their wives: A descriptive analysis of verbal and non-verbal behavior. *Quarterly Journal of Studies on Alcohol,* **34,** 516–520. Copyright 1973 by Journal of Studies on Alcohol, Inc. New Brunswick, N.J. 08903. Reproduced by permission.)

administration of treatment. However, absence of an initial baseline phase precludes an analysis of the effects of treatment over the natural frequency of occurrence of the targeted behaviors under study. Therefore, the use of the more complete A-B-A-B design is preferred for assessment of singular therapeutic variables. Below we review two classic examples of the B-A-B design to illustrate this strategy.

B-A-B with group data

Ayllon and Azrin (1965) used the B-A-B strategy on a group basis in their evaluation of the effects of token economy on the work performance of 44 patients with psychosis. During the first 20 days (B phase) of the experiment, subjects were awarded tokens (exchangeable for a large variety of "backup" reinforcers) for engaging in work activities in their hospital inpatient unit. Over the next

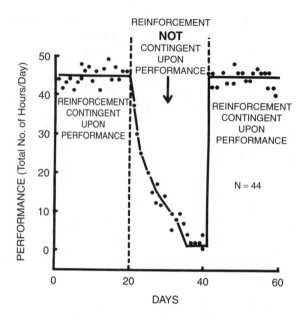

FIGURE 5.14 Total number of hours of on-ward performance by a group of 44 patients, Exp. III (Figure 4, p. 373, redrawn from: Ayllon, T., & Azrin, N. H. (1965). The measurement and reinforcement, of behavior of psychotics. *Journal of the Experimental Analysis of Behavior*, **8**, 357–383. Copyright 1965 by Society for the Experimental Analysis of Behavior, Inc. Reproduced by permission.)

20 days (A phase) subjects were given tokens on a non-contingent basis, regardless of their work performance. Each subject received tokens daily, based on the mean daily rate obtained in the initial B phase. In the last 20 days (second B phase) the contingency system was reinstated. Notably, this design also could be labeled a B-C-B design, as the middle phase is not a true measure of the natural frequency of occurrence of the target measure (see section 5.6).

The results of this study appear in Figure 5.14. During the first B phase, the entire group averaged about 45 hours of work per day. Removal of the contingency in the A phase resulted in a marked decrease to a level of one hour per day on Day 36. Reinstitution of the token reinforcement program in the second B phase led to an immediate increase in hours worked to a level approximating the first B phase. Thus, Ayllon and Azrin (1965) presented the first experimental demonstration of the controlling effects of token economy over work performance in state hospital psychiatric patients.

Importantly, when single-case experimental strategies are used on a group basis, it behooves the experimenter to show that a majority of those subjects exposed to and then withdrawn from treatment provide supporting evidence for its controlling effects. Individual data presented for selected subjects can be quite useful, particularly if data trends differ. Otherwise, difficulties inherent in the traditional group comparison approach (e.g., averaging out of effects, effects due to a small minority while the majority remains unaffected by treatment) will be carried over to the experimental analysis procedure. In the current example, Ayllon and Azrin (1965) showed that 36 of their 44 subjects decreased their performance from contingent to non-contingent reinforcement. Conversely, 36 of 44 subjects increased their performance from non-contingent to contingent reinforcement. Eight subjects were totally unaffected by contingencies and maintained a zero level of performance in all phases.

Extending the previous point, virtually all of the designs discussed in this chapter can be used on a group basis. The overall strategy remains the same, but the specific procedures used and inferences permitted may differ on a case by case basis. For instance, Caruso and Kennedy (2004) used an A-B-A-B design to study the effect of a journal reviewer prompting strategy on the timeliness of reviews. Rather than following the same individual(s) over time, the authors observed the timeliness of journal article reviews during normal baseline phases (A) and during experimental phases (B) that consisted of an e-mail reminder to reviewers 7 days prior to the date the review was due. Results of this study revealed that prompting led to more on-time reviews and less variability in return times. The use of this design on a group basis provides compelling data about the effectiveness of the intervention; however, difficulties inherent in the use of group designs mentioned above remain.

B-A-B from rogerian framework

Although single-case experimental designs often are discussed within the context of the cognitive behavioral paradigm, these strategies can be easily and flexibly employed to study other psychological treatments. For instance, Truax and Carkhuff (1965) provided an earlier example of this in their well-known study on Rogerian therapy. These authors systematically examined the effects of high and low "therapeutic conditions" on the responses of 3 psychiatric patients during the course of initial 1-hour interviews. Each of the interviews consisted of the three 20-minute phases. In the first phase (B) the therapist was instructed to evidence high levels of "accurate empathy" and "unconditional positive warmth" in his interactions with the patient. In the following A phase the therapist experimentally lowered these conditions, and in the final phase (B) they were reinstated at a high level.

Each of the three interviews was audiotaped. From these audiotapes, five 3-minute segments for each phase were obtained and rerecorded on separate tapes. These tapes were then presented to raters (naive as to which phase the tape originated in) in random order. Ratings made on the basis of the Accurate Empathy Scale and the Unconditional Positive Regard Scale confirmed (graphically and statistically) that the therapist followed directions as indicated by the dictates of the experimental design (B-A-B). The effects of high and low therapeutic conditions were then assessed in terms of depth of the patient's intrapersonal exploration.

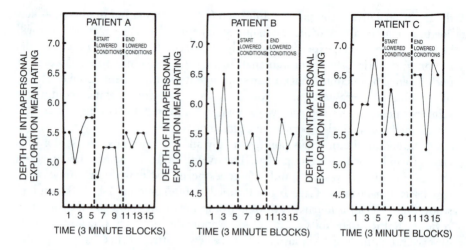

FIGURE 5.15   Depth of intrapersonal exploration. (Figure 4, p. 122, redrawn from: Truax, C.B., & Carkhuff, R. R. (1965). Experimental manipulation of therapeutic conditions, *Journal of Consulting Psychology*, **29**, 119–124. Copyright 1965 by the American Psychological Association. Reproduced by permission.)

Once again, 3-minute segments from the A and B phases were presented to "naive" raters in randomized order. These new ratings were made on the basis of the Truax Depth of Interpersonal Exploration Scale (reliability of raters per segment = .78).

Data on depth of intrapersonal exploration are plotted in Figure 5.15. Visual inspection of these data indicates that depth of intrapersonal exploration, despite considerable overlapping in adjacent phases, was *somewhat* lowered during the middle phase (A) for each of the three patients. Although these data are less than ideal (i.e., overlap between phases), this study illustrates that the controlling effects of therapist relational factors *can be investigated systematically using the experimental analysis of behavior model.*

5.6. A-B-C-B DESIGN

Another important variant of the A-B-A-B design is the A-B-C-B design, in which only the first two phases of experimentation consist of baseline and contingent reinforcement phases. In the third phase (C), instead of returning to baseline observation, reinforcement is administered in proportions equal to the preceding B phase but on a totally *noncontingent* basis. This phase controls for the added attention ("attention-placebo") that a subject receives for being in a treatment condition and is analogous to the A_1 phase (placebo) used in drug evaluations (see chapter 6). In the final phase, contingent reinforcement procedures are reinstated. Thus the last three phases of study are identical to those in the B-A-B study used by Ayllon and Azrin (1965) in the example described in section 5.5. In the A-B-C-B design the A and C phases are not comparable, inasmuch as experimental procedures differ. Therefore, the main experimental analysis is derived from the B-C-B portion of study. However, baseline observations are of some value, as the effects of B over A are suggested (here we have the limitations of the A-B analysis).

A-B-C-B from the child literature

Goldstein, Kaczmarek, Pennington, and Shafer (1992) examined the effects of a peer-mediated intervention on social interaction among 5 children diagnosed with autism. During all phases of the study observers coded audio- and video-taped interactions between five triads of children, each triad containing one autistic child and two non-autistic peers trained in facilitation strategies designed to increase social interaction behaviors performed by the target children.

During baseline (A phase) all children in each triad were instructed to talk and play with their friends. During the intervention phase (B), peers were instructed to use the facilitation strategies to increase social interaction behaviors performed by the target child in the triad. During the next experimental phase (C), peers were instructed to continue using their social interaction skills, but not to direct them only at the target child, and they were praised only for interactions with the other (non-autistic peer). Importantly, peers were allowed to interact with target children, but were only praised for interactions with non-target children. The authors note that they selected such an A-B-C-B design rather than a withdrawal (A-B-A-B) design in order to demonstrate that behavior change was related to the treatment variable itself, and not merely to the presence of any peer interaction. Finally, the last phase (B) in this design consisted of a return to the intervention in which peer facilitation strategies were directed at the target child.

The results from this study were presented individually for each target child. The results from one of those children are presented in Figure 5.16. As shown, the total number of communicative acts performed by the target child increased substantially during the peer intervention. This pattern was reversed during the reversal (C) phase, during which the frequency of social behaviors and total communicative behaviors directed toward the target children decreased to baseline (A) levels. Reintroduction of the peer intervention in the final phase (B) showed a return of the treatment effects, providing evidence of the controlling effects of the intervention. This pattern of results was observed in 4 of the 5 target children studied.

A-B-C-B in a group application and follow-up

An interesting application of the A-B-C-B design to a group of subjects was reported by Porterfield, Blunden, and Blewitt (1980). Subjects in this experimental analysis were "profoundly mentally handicapped" adults attending a center for those with mental retardation. The behavior targeted for modification

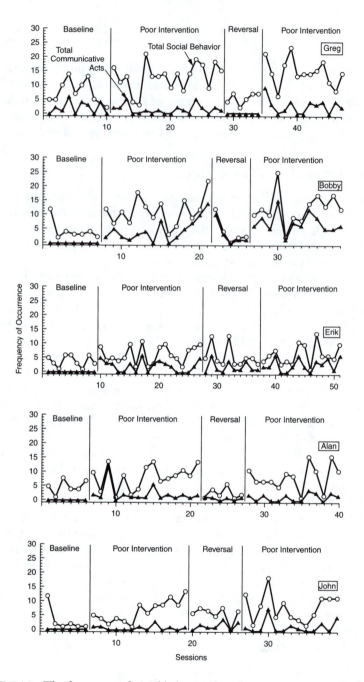

FIGURE 5.16 The frequency of social behavior demonstrated by target children. The circles indicate the total number of social behaviors, and the triangles indicate the total number of communicative acts. (Figure 2, p. 297, from: Goldstein, H., Kaczmarek, L., Pennington, R., & Shafer, K. (1992). Peer-mediated intervention: Attending to, commenting on, and acknowledging the behavior of preschoolers with autism. *Journal of Applied Behavior Analysis*, **25** (2), 289–305.)

was participation in activities during a 1-hour period so designated during the 19 days of the study. Participation was defined by 12 separate activities and involved some of the following: watching television, dancing, responding to a verbal command, talking to another subject, and eating without assistance.

The baseline phase (A) lasted 3 days, with three staff members interacting with subjects in normal fashion. No specific instructions were given at this point. The B phase (room manager) lasted 5 days, with two staff members alternating for half-hour periods. Subjects in this condition were prompted and differentially reinforced for their participation. The C phase (no distraction) lasted 6 days and involved a maximum of two prompts to engage in activity, but subjects were not differentially reinforced. In the fourth phase (B) the room manager condition was reinstated. Then there was a 69-day follow-up period involving the room manager condition in the absence of the experimenter.

Data appear in Figure 5.17 and are presented as the percentage of subjects (i.e., trainees) engaged in activity. It is clear that baseline (A) functioning was poor, ranging from 25.7% to 37.9% participation. Introduction of the room manager (B) condition led to marked increases in participation (72.9% to 90.9%). However, when the no-distraction (C) condition was introduced, participation

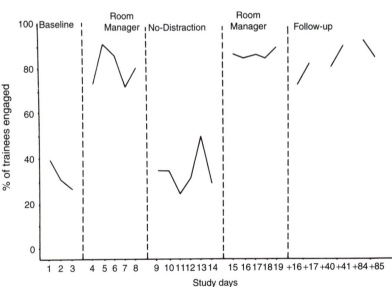

FIGURE 5.17   Percentage of trainees engaged during the activity hour for 19 days and follow-up days. (Figure 1, p. 236 from: Porterfield, J., Blunden, R., & Blewitt, E. (1980). Improving environments for profoundly handicapped adults: Using prompts and social attention to maintain high group engagement. *Behavior Modification, 4,* 225–241. Copyright 1980 by Sage Publications. Reproduced by permission.)

decreased to near baseline levels (21.5% to 48.0%). When the room manager condition was reintroduced, in the second B phase, level of participation once again increased to 84.7% to 88.1%. This second application of the room manager condition clearly documented the controlling effects of the contingency. Furthermore, data in follow-up confirmed that participation could be maintained (71.5% to 91.1%) in the absence of experimental prompting.

There are two noteworthy features in this particular example of the A-B-C-B design. First, even though the A and C phases were technically dissimilar, they were functionally quite similar. That is, the data pattern was the same as would be observed in an A-B-A-B design. However, contrary to the A-B-A-B design, where there are two instances of confirmation of the contingency, only the B-C-B portion of the design truly reflected the controlling aspects of the room manager intervention. Second, by making the dependent measure the "percentage of trainees engaged," the experimenters obviated the necessity of providing individual data. However, from a single-case perspective, data as to percentage of time active *for each trainee* would be most welcome.

EXTENSIONS OF THE A-B-A DESIGN, USES IN DRUG EVALUATION AND INTERACTION DESIGN STRATEGIES

6.1. EXTENSIONS AND VARIATIONS OF THE A-B-A WITHDRAWAL DESIGN

The A-B-A design provides a fundamental structure from which the clinical experimenter can flexibly make modifications to address a multitude of clinical research questions. Although all of the possible variations on this design are too numerous to list exhaustively, one should be aware of five major categories of designs that follow from the A-B-A withdrawal design. The first category consists of designs in which the A-B pattern is replicated several times (e.g., A-B-A-B). There are several advantages to this design, such as the repeated demonstration of control of the treatment variable and the fact that extended study can be conducted until full clinical treatment has been achieved. There are myriad examples of the A-B-A-B-A-B design (and its close variations), ranging from the examination of methods for enhancing eating and nutrition among infants (Wenzl et al., 2003), to the evaluation of methods for increasing the use of seatbelts among motorists (Austin, Alvero, & Olson, 1998), to the effects of strategies for improving foul shooting among basketball players (Savoy & Beitel, 1996). The wide range of studies employing this design strategy highlights the great value and flexibility of this approach.

In the second category, separate treatment variables are compared with performance during baseline, as outlined in the discussion of A-B-A-C-A designs in section 3.4 of chapter 3. In that section it was pointed out that the comparison of the relative effectiveness of B and C variables is difficult when both variables appear to effect change over baseline levels. This can be addressed using a slight variation, the A-B-A-B-A-C-A design, in which the individual controlling effects of B and C variables can be determined. It is important to note the distinction between these designs and those in which the interactive effects of variables are studied (e.g., A-B-A-B-BC-B-BC). The former examines the independent effects of C (administered in this case after B), while the latter tests the effects of adding C to B. In summary, in the A-B-A-C-A design the effects of B and C over A can be evaluated. However, interpreting the *relative* efficacy of B and C is problematic in this strategy.

In the third category, specific variations of the treatment procedure are examined during the course of experimentation. For example, the treatment procedure might be tapered or faded out over subsequent phases or different levels or "doses" of the treatment variable may be tested across different phases or in graduated progression following demonstration of the controlling effects of variables in the A-B-A-B portion of the design. Such *parametric* design strategies have proven useful in group designs (Kazdin, 2003; Nock, Janis, & Wedig, 2008) and are equally valuable, although perhaps more easily and flexibly conducted, using a single-case experimental design.

In the fourth category, the additive or interactive effects of combining two or more treatment variables are examined through variations in the basic A-B-A design. In such designs, the effects of each treatment variable are first examined independently and then in combination. This extends beyond analysis of the separate effects of two therapeutic variables over baseline as represented by the A-B-A-C-A type design described in the second category. It also extends a step beyond merely adding a variation of a therapeutic variable on the end of an A-B-A-B series (e.g., A-B-A-B-BC), since no experimental analysis of the additive effects of BC is performed. Conducted properly, interaction designs are complex and usually require more than a single subject (see section 6.5.).

The fifth category consists of the changing-criterion design and its variant, the range-bound changing criterion design (McDougall, 2005). In the changing-criterion design, baseline is followed by treatment until a preset criterion is met. This then becomes the new baseline, and a new criterion is set. Such repetition, of course, continues until eventually the final criterion is reached (see Nock, et al., 2007; Photos et al., 2008). The following subsections present examples of extensions and variations, with illustrations selected from each of the five major categories.

6.2. A-B-A-B-A-B DESIGN

Austin and colleagues (1998) provide an interesting example of an A-B-A-B-A-B design in which they tested the effectiveness of using verbal prompts to increase the use of safety belts among patrons leaving a restaurant. They conducted this test in a mid-western branch of a national restaurant chain at which the hostess typically said "good-bye" to patrons as they exited the restaurant. The experimenters recruited 10 hostesses to participate in the study. The dependent variable was percentage of patrons observed using an over-the-shoulder safety belt

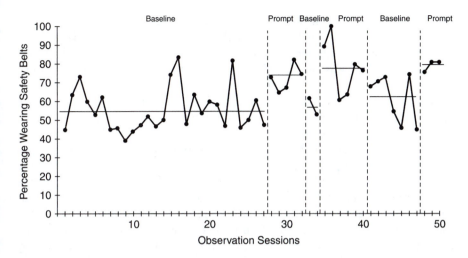

FIGURE 6.1 The percentage of patrons wearing safety belts across baseline and verbal prompt phases. (Figure 1, p. 657, from: Austin, J., Aluero, A. M., & Olsen, R. (1998). Prompting patron safety belt use at a restaurant. *Journal of Applied Behavior Analysis*, **3**, 655–657.)

while exiting the restaurant during two 1-hour sessions on Thursday–Sunday evenings, as observed by an independent rater stationed in a parked car near the exit and with inter-rater reliability at 97%. During baseline phases (A), hostesses gave their standard farewell as patrons exited the restaurant, and the rater observed and recorded the percentage of people wearing a safety belt under these conditions. During the intervention phases (B), hostesses added "Don't forget to buckle up" to their customary farewell, and the same observation procedures were used. Baseline and treatment phases were repeated in an A-B-A-B-A-B design.

The results of this study for are plotted in Figure 6.1. Inspection of data show a higher percentage of safety belt use when the prompt to wear a safety belt was given (B) relative to that during baseline conditions (A). Overall, safety belt use was 57% across all baseline phases and 77% across all intervention phases. Moreover, the controlling influence of the prompt to wear a safety belt on actual safety belt use was demonstrated repeatedly over the course of the study.

6.3. COMPARING SEPARATE TREATMENT VARIABLES/COMPONENTS

A-B-A-C-A-C'-A design

One classic study by Wincze et al. (1972) included a series of 10 single-case experimental designs examining the effects of feedback and token reinforcement on the verbal behavior of delusional psychiatric patients. One of these studies used an A-B-A-C-A-C'-A design, with B and C phases representing feedback and token reinforcement, respectively. During all phases of this particular study, a delusional patient was questioned daily (15 questions selected randomly from a pool of 105) by his clinician to elicit delusional material. The percentage of his responses that contained delusional verbalizations was recorded, as was the patient's percentage of delusional talk on the unit (token economy unit), which was monitored by nursing staff on a randomly distributed basis 20 times per day.

During baseline (A), the patient received "free" tokens as no contingencies were placed with respect to delusional verbalizations. During feedback (B), the patient continued to receive tokens noncontingently, but corrective statements in response to delusional verbalizations were offered by the clinician in individual sessions. The third phase (A) consisted of a return to baseline procedures. In the fourth phase (C), a stringent token economy system embracing all aspects of the patient's life on the inpatient unit was instituted. Tokens could be earned by the patient for "talking correctly" (nondelusionally) both in individual sessions and on the unit. Tokens were exchangeable for meals, luxuries, and privileges. The fifth phase (A), once again involved a return to baseline. In the sixth phase (C'), token bonuses were awarded on a predetermined percentage basis for talking correctly (e.g., speaking delusionally less than 10% of the time during designated periods). This condition was incorporated to counteract the tendency of the patient to earn tokens merely for increasing frequency of nondelusional talk while still maintaining a high frequency of delusional verbalizations. In the last phase of experimentation (A), baseline conditions were again reinstated.

Results of this experimental analysis for one subject appear in Figure 6.2. Percentage of delusional talk in individual sessions and on the unit did not differ substantially during the first three sessions, suggesting the ineffectiveness of the feedback variable. Institution of token economy in the fourth phase, however, resulted in a marked decrease of delusional talk in individual sessions, but failed to effect a change in delusional talk on the unit. Removal of token economy in the fifth phase led to a return to initial levels of delusional talk during individual sessions. Throughout the first five phases, percentage of delusional talk on the unit was consistent, ranging from 0% to 30%. Introduction of the token bonus in the sixth phase again resulted in a drop of delusional verbalizations in individual sessions. Additionally, percentage of delusional talk on the unit decreased to zero. In the last phase (baseline), delusional verbalizations rose both on the unit and in individual sessions.

In this case, feedback (B) proved to be an ineffective therapeutic agent. However, token economy (C) and token bonuses (C'), respectively, controlled percentage of delusional talk in individual sessions and on the unit. Had feedback also effected changes in behavior, the comparative efficacy of feedback and token economy would be difficult to ascertain using this design. Such analysis would require the use of a group comparison design. This is because one variable, token reinforcement, follows the other variable, feedback. Therefore, it is

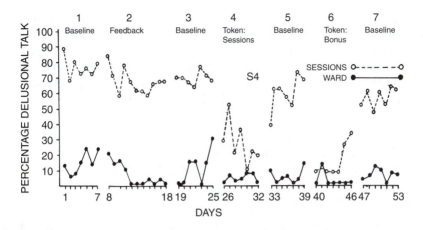

FIGURE 6.2 Percentage of delusional talk of Subject 4 during therapist sessions and on ward for each experimental day. (Figure 4, p. 256, from: Wincze, J. P., Leitenberg, H., & Agras, W. S. [1972]. The effects of token reinforcement and feedback on the delusional verbal behavior of chronic paranoid schizophrenics. *Journal of Applied Behavior Analysis*, **5**, 247–262. Copyright 1972 by Society for the Experimental Analysis of Behavior, Inc. Reproduced by permission.)

conceivable that tokens were effective only if instituted *after* a feedback phase and would not be effective if introduced initially. Thus a possible confound of order effects exists. Of course, the more usual case is that the first treatment would be effective to an extent that it would not leave much room for improvement in the second treatment. In other words, a "ceiling" effect would prevent a proper comparison between treatments, due to the order of their introduction.

To compare two treatments in this fashion, the investigator would have to administer two treatments with baseline interspersed to two different individuals (and their replications), with the order of treatments counterbalanced. For example, 3 subjects could receive A-B-A-C-A, where B and C were two distinct treatments, and 3 could receive A-C-A-B-A. In fact, Wincze et al. (1972) carried out this necessary counterbalancing with half of their subjects in order to analyze the effects of feedback on token reinforcement.

This design, then, approximates the group crossover design or the counterbalanced within-subject group comparison, with the exception of the presence of repeated measures and individual analyses of the data. Each design option suffers from possible multiple-treatment interference or carryover effects (see chapter 8 for a discussion of multiple-treatment interference). In group designs, any carryover effects are averaged into group differences and treated statistically as part of the error. In the A-B-A-C-A single-case design, on the other hand, data are usually presented more descriptively, with visual analysis sometimes combined with statistical descriptions (rather than inferences) to estimate the effect of each treatment. Wincze et al. (1972) did an excellent job of this in their series, which is fully described in chapter 10. Analysis depends on comparing individuals experiencing different orders of treatments. Thus the functional analysis cannot be carried out within one individual with all of the experimental control that it affords. Other alternatives to comparing two treatments include a between-groups comparison design or an alternating-treatments design (see chapter 8). As noted above, this particular direct replication series will be discussed in greater detail in chapter 10.

6.4. PARAMETRIC VARIATIONS OF THE SAME TREATMENT VARIABLE/COMPONENT

A-B-A-B-B_1-B_2-B_3-B_N design

Our example from the third category of extensions of the A-B-A design is drawn from the clinical child literature. Ducharme and Worling (1994) systematically tested the effects of using high-probability requests (HPRs—requests likely to elicit compliance) immediately prior to low-probability requests (LPRs) in order to establish behavioral momentum of child compliance with adult requests. Although the effectiveness of pairing high- and low-probability requests had been demonstrated previously, the authors sought to test the usefulness of incorporating phases focused on fading HPRs in order to enhance the durability of behavior change. The authors tested the effects of pairing of high- and low-probability requests in a 5-year-old boy and 15-year-old girl both treated and assessed within their homes. The primary dependent variable was percentage of compliance to LPRs, framed as both "do" and "don't" requests. This variable was coded from video-taped sessions recorded in the homes and was scored by independent observers, with agreement averaging ⩾88% across all study phases.

During baseline (A), parents made a series of randomly ordered LPRs and provided verbal praise for compliance and no praise for noncompliance. During the initial HPR phase (B), parents followed the same procedure as in baseline, but immediately before making each LPR (i.e., 5 seconds before) they gave three HPRs spaced 10 seconds apart, with no interaction with the child during the 5 and 10 second delays. The parents then instituted a return to baseline (A) and a re-introduction of the treatment variable (B) in order to test the controlling influence of the treatment variable on child compliance with adult requests. Thus, in the initial stage of this study a standard A-B-A-B design was followed. Next, however, the clinical researchers tested the effect of fading the treatment variable over time. They did this by sequentially fading or reducing the magnitude of the HPR treatment variable as well as its temporal proximity to the LPR. This was done in six separate phases. In the first two fading phases the number of HPRs was reduced from three to two (B_1), then from two to one (B_2). In the third fading phase the parent increased the delay between compliance to the

HPR and introduction of the LPR from 5 seconds to 10 seconds (B_3). This delay was subsequently increased to 15 seconds (B_4) and 20 seconds (B_5). In the final fading phase, parents maintained the 20 second delay, but now were allowed to interact with the child during the delay in order to approximate a more natural situation (B_6). Thus, the design was an A-B-A-B-B_1-B_2-B_3-B_4-B_5-B_6. In addition, follow-up data were collected at 1-, 3-, 6-, 8-, and 16-week intervals.

Data for the 5-year-old boy (Ralph) are plotted in Figure 6.3, with separate plots for "do" and "don't" requests. Examination of the figure shows that administration of the HPR intervention increased child compliance over baseline levels. This was confirmed on two occasions in the A-B-A-B portion of study. Data from the sequence fading phases demonstrate that a high level of compliance was maintained even as the HPR intervention was faded over time. Moreover, data from the follow-up period provides further evidence of the maintenance of the behavior change resulting from this intervention. As demonstrated in this study, this variation on the A-B-A-B is well suited to examine the maintenance of changes resulting from psychological or drug treatments.

A-B- B_1-B_2-A-B_1 design

Another excellent example of a potential variation on the same treatment variable/component appears in a study by Conrin et al. (1982), in which the clinical researchers used differential reinforcement of other behaviors (DRO) to treat chronic rumination in a mentally retarded individual. The subject was a 19-year-old male who was profoundly retarded and had a 17-year history of rumination (i.e., emesis of previously chewed food, rechewing food, and reswallowing food).

The study used was an A-B-B_1-B_2-A-B_1 design. The primary dependent variable was duration of rumination (i.e., cheek swelling, chewing, and swallowing) occurring during assessment periods, which began one hour after the subject finished his meals. Interrater reliability for behavioral observations ranged from 94% to 100%. After an initial baseline phase (A), a DRO procedure (B) was implemented. This consisted of giving the subject small portions of cookies or bits of peanut butter contingent on *no rumination*. Initial, reinforcement was provided if no rumination occurred for 15 seconds or more (IRT > 15"). In the next phase (B_1) reinforcement was provided if no rumination occurred for 30 seconds (IRT > 30"), followed by an IRT > 60" in phase B_2. This was followed by a return to baseline (A) and a subsequent reintroduction of IRT > 30 (B_1).

The results of this study are presented in Figure 6.4. Observation of these data reveals a high duration of rumination (5 to 22 minutes; mean = 7 minutes) during baseline (A). Introduction of DRO (IRT > 15") resulted in a zero duration after 18 sessions, which was maintained during the thinning of the reinforcement schedule in B_1 (IRT > 30") and B_2 (IRT > 60"). A return to baseline conditions (A) resulted in marked increases in rumination (mean = 10 minutes per session), but was once again reduced to zero when DRO procedures (IRT > 30") were

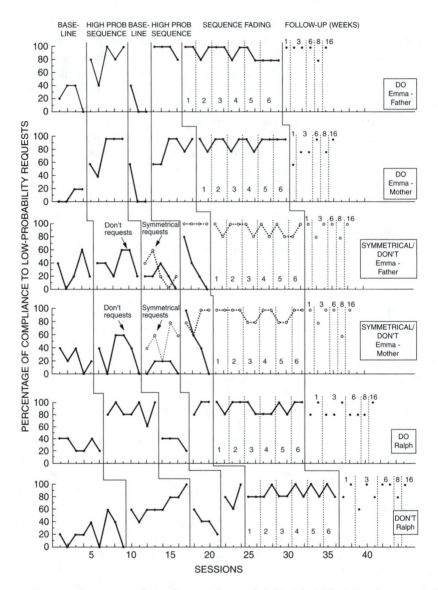

FIGURE 6.3 Percentage of compliance to low-probability "do," "don't," and symmetrical "do" requests, by subject and parent. (Figure 1, p. 643, from: Ducharme, J. M., & Worling, D. E. (1994). Behavioral momentum and stimulus fading in the acquisition and maintenance of child compliance in the home. *Journal of Applied Behavior Analysis,* **27** (4), 639–647.)

reintroduced in the B₁ phase. In summary, this experimental analysis clearly documents the controlling effects of DRO over rumination. It also shows how it was possible to thin the reinforcement schedule from IRT > 15" to IRT > 60" and still maintain rumination at near zero levels.

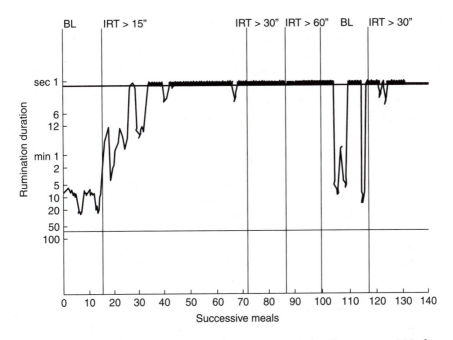

FIGURE 6.4 Duration of ruminations after meals by Bob. (Figure 2, p. 328, from: Conrin, J., Pennypacker, H. S., Johnston, J. M., & Rast, J. [1982]. Differential reinforcement of other behaviors to treat chronic rumination of mental retardates. *Journal of Behavior Therapy and Experimental Psychiatry*, **13**, 325–329. Copyright 1982 by Pergamon. Reproduced by permission.)

6.5. DRUG EVALUATIONS

The examination of the effects of drugs on behavior has become an increasingly large and important endeavor over the past several decades, and the group comparison approach has predominated in this area of clinical research. Indeed, there are numerous examples in the literature of large, multi-site randomized controlled trials testing the effects of various drugs on human behavior (e.g., Barlow, Gorman, Shear, & Woods, 2000; Gerin et al., 2007). Clinical researchers have long encouraged the use the within-subject withdrawal design in assessing drug-environment interactions (e.g., Liberman et al., 1973). For instance, some 30 years ago Liberman and colleagues contended that:

Useful interactions among the drug-patient-environment system can be obtained using this type of methodology. The approach is reliable and rigorous, efficient and inexpensive to mount, and permits sound conclusions and generalizations to other patients with similar behavioral repertoires when systematic replications are performed. . . . (p. 433)

Although single-case experimental designs are very well suited to evaluate the effects of drugs on behavior, they have not been as widely used for this purpose as they have in the study of psychological treatments. In the following sections we review issues that arise in the use of single-case experimental designs that are specific to drug evaluations as well as the many design options available. We provide examples from the literature throughout these sections to highlight the potential usefulness of single-case designs in this area.

Issues specific to drug evaluations

All of the basic procedural issues discussed in chapter 3 apply just the same when the treatment variable is a pharmacological rather than psychosocial agent. However, there are several considerations specific to this area of research including: (1) nomenclature, (2) carryover effects, and (3) single- and double-blind assessments.

Regarding nomenclature, A typically is designated as the baseline phase, A_1 as the placebo phase, B as the phase evaluating the first active drug, and C as the phase evaluating the second active drug (if included). The A_1 phase is an intermediary phase between the baseline and active drug phase in this design and controls for factors such as the subject's expectancy of improvement as a result of ingesting a pill or meeting with the clinician providing the drug.

Of course, some of these considerations were examined in section 3.4 of chapter 3 in relation to changing one variable at a time across experimental phases. With regard to this one-variable rule, it becomes apparent, then, that A-B, A-B-A, B-A-B, and A-B-A-B designs in drug research involve the manipulation of two variables (expectancy and condition) at one time across phases. However, under certain circumstances where time limitations and clinical considerations prevail, this type of experimental strategy is justified. Of course, when conditions permit, it is preferable to use strategies in which the systematic progression of variables across phases is carefully followed (see Table 6.1, Designs 4, 6, 7, 9–13). For example, this would be the case in the A_1-B-A_1 design strategy, where only one variable at a time is manipulated from phase to phase. Further discussion of these issues will appear in the following section, in which the different design options available to drug researchers will be outlined.

Regarding carry-over effects, considerations associated with the carryover of treatment effects from one phase to the next also has already been discussed (see section 3.6 of chapter 3). In that section we made some specific recommendations regarding short-term assessments of drug effects and the concurrent monitoring of biochemical changes during different phases of study. In this connection, Barlow and Hersen (1973) have noted that "Since continued measurements are in effect, length of phases can be varied from experiment to experiment to determine precisely the latency of drug effects after beginning the dosage and the residual effects after discontinuing the dosage" (p. 324). This may, at times, necessitate the inequality of phase lengths and the suspension of

TABLE 6.1   Single-Case Experimental Drug Strategies

NO.	DESIGN	TYPE OF BLIND	POSSIBLE
1.	A-A_1	Quasi-experimental	None
2.	A-B	Quasi-experimental	None
3.	A_1-B	Quasi-experimental	Single or double
4.	A-A_1-A	Experimental	None
5.	A-B-A	Experimental	None
6.	A_1-B-A_1	Experimental	Single or double
7.	A_1-A-A_1	Experimental	Single or double
8.	B-A-B	Experimental	None
9.	B-A_1-B	Experimental	Single or double
10.	A-A_1-A-A_1	Experimental	Single or double
11.	A-B-A-B	Experimental	None
12.	A_1-B-A_1-B	Experimental	Single or double
13.	A-A_1-B-A_1-B	Experimental	Single or double
14.	A-A_1-A-A_1-B-A_1-B	Experimental	Single or double
15.	A_1-B-A_1-C-A_1-C	Experimental	Single or double

Note: A = no drug; A_1 = placebo; B = drug 1; C = drug 2.

active drug treatment until biochemical measurements (based on blood and urine studies) reach an acceptable level. For example, the experimenter may want to include a baseline (A) "wash-out" period within the design during which no active drug or placebo are administered in order to decrease the potential impact of carry-over effects.

A third issue specific to drug evaluation involves the use of single- and double-blind assessments. The double-blind placebo-controlled trial is considered the current gold standard in the evaluation of drug effects because it controls for possible experimenter bias and patient expectations of improvement under drug conditions when drug and placebo groups are being contrasted. In such designs, subjects are randomly assigned to receive either the active drug or a placebo, which are identical in size, shape, markings, and color. Neither the experimenters nor the subjects know to which condition each person has been assigned, and the blind is not "broken" (i.e., condition revealed) by the experimenter until the subject has completed all study assessments.

While the double-blind procedure is readily adaptable to group comparison research, it is difficult to engineer for some of the single-case strategies and impossible for others. Moreover, in some cases (see Table 6.1, Designs 1, 2, 4, 5, 8) even the single-blind strategy (where only the subject remains unaware of whether s/he is in the drug or placebo condition) is not applicable. In these designs the changes from baseline observation to either placebo or drug conditions obviously cannot be disguised in any manner.

One of the greatest difficulties in conducting a double-blind trial using a single-case experimental design is related to the experimenter's monitoring of data. Namely, in being blind to the study condition the experimenter losses the ability to make decisions regarding when baseline observation should be ended and other study phases introduced and withdrawn. Of course, it is possible to program phase lengths on an *a priori* basis, but this too eliminates the experimenter's ability to flexibly adjust the study procedures, which is one of the major advantages of the single-case strategy. However, one important consideration is that even if the experimenter controlling the study is aware of treatment condition, the spirit of the double-blind trial can be maintained by keeping the observer (often a research assistant or nursing staff member) unaware of drug and placebo changes. We should note here additionally that despite the use of the double-blind procedure, the side effects of drugs in some cases, and the marked changes in behavior resulting from removal of active drug therapy in other cases often betray to nursing personnel whether a placebo or drug condition is currently in operation. This problem is equally troublesome for researchers using group comparison designs.

Design options

In order to facilitate the use of single-case experimental designs in the evaluation of drug effects on behavior, in this section we outline the basic quasi-experimental and experimental analysis design strategies for evaluating singular application of drugs. Specific advantages and disadvantages of each design option will be considered. Where possible, we will illustrate with actual examples selected from the research literature. However, to date, most of these strategies have not yet been implemented.

A number of possible single-case strategies suitable for drug evaluation are presented in Table 6.1. The first three strategies fall into the A-B category and are quasi-experimental designs in that the controlling effects of the treatment variable (placebo or active drug) cannot be conclusively determined. Indeed, it was noted in section 5.2 of chapter 5 that changes observed in B might result from the action of some uncontrolled variable (e.g., time, maturational changes, expectancy of improvement). These quasi-experimental designs are perhaps best suited for instances in which the clinical researcher is working in an applied clinical setting (e.g., consulting room practice) where limited time and facilities preclude more formal experimentation. In the first design (Table 6.1, number 1) the effects of placebo over baseline conditions are *suggested* (i.e., but not determined conclusively due to the exclusion of a return to baseline); in the second the effects of active drug over baseline conditions are *suggested*; in the third the effects of an active drug over placebo are *suggested*.

Design strategies 4–6 are essentially A-B-A designs in which the controlling effects of the treatment variable can be ascertained. In Design 4 the controlling effects of a placebo manipulation over no treatment can be assessed experimentally. This design has great potential in the study of behaviors where attentional factors are presumed to play a major role. Also, the use of this type of design in evaluating the therapeutic contribution of placebos in a variety of psychosomatic disorders could be of considerable importance to clinicians. In Design 5, the controlling effects of an active drug are determined over baseline conditions. However, as previously noted, two variables are being manipulated here at one time across phases (i.e., attention/expectancies and administration of the drug). Design 6 corrects for this deficiency, as the active drug condition (B) is preceded and followed by placebo (A_1) conditions. In this case the one-variable rule across phases is correctly observed.

Returning to Table 6.1, strategies 7–9 can be classified as B-A-B designs, and the same advantages and limitations previously outlined in section 5.5 of chapter 5 apply. One recent example of a B-A_1-B-A_1-B-A_1-B-A_1-B design is a study by Kelley and colleagues (2006) in which the authors tested the effects of stimulant medication (i.e., Adderall®) versus placebo pill on performance of compliant and destructive behaviors (holding constant the antecedents and consequences for these behaviors). The subject in this study was an 11-year-old boy diagnosed with moderate mental retardation and attention deficit hyperactivity disorder (ADHD) and a history of destructive behavior. In this study, the subject's destructive (e.g., throwing objects, face slapping, spitting) and compliant (e.g., initiation of requested task within 5 seconds) behaviors were carefully defined and observed during daily systematic assessment periods with strong inter-observer agreement for both destructive (97%) and compliant (98%) behaviors. The treatment variable in this study was administration of either stimulant medication (B) or placebo pill (A_1), which were administered on a daily, alternating basis in a double-blind fashion, with only the school nurse aware of which pill was administered each day. The results of this study are presented in Figure 6.5. As shown, relative to administration of placebo, administration of stimulant medication was associated with a lower frequency and percentage of destructive behavior and a higher frequency and percentage of compliant behavior. This pattern was repeated multiple times over the course of the study, and the double-blind nature of the design rule out the potential influence of subject or experimenter expectancies on the results.

Strategies 10–12 fall into the general category of A-B-A-B designs and are superior to the A-B-A and B-A-B designs because (1) the initial observation period involves baseline or baseline-placebo measurement; (2) there are two occasions in which the controlling effects of the placebo or the treatment variables can be demonstrated; and (3) the concluding phase ends on a treatment variable. A classic example of the use of an A-B-A-B design to assess the effects of drug treatment on behavior is provided by Agras (1976), who tested the effects of thorazine on disruptive behavior. The subject in this study was a 16-year-old male inpatient with brain damage who had a history of clinically significant disruptive behaviors including temper tantrums, stealing food, eating with his fingers, exposing himself, hallucinations, and begging for money, cigarettes, or food. A token economy program was developed in which performance of positive

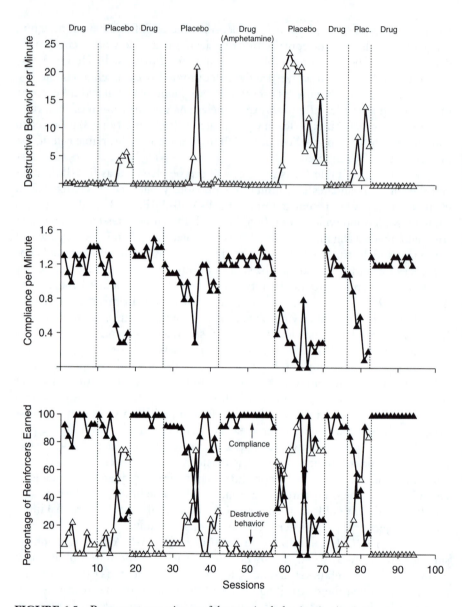

FIGURE 6.5 Responses per minute of destructive behavior (top), responses per minute of compliance (middle), and percentages of reinforcers earned via destructive behavior and compliance (bottom) during drug (amphetamine) and placebo conditions. (Figure 1, p. 246, from: Kelley M. E., Fisher, W. W., Lomas, J. E., & Sanders R. Q. (2006). Some effects of stimulant medication on response allocation: A double-blind analysis. *Journal of Applied Behavior Analysis*, **39** (2), 243–247.)

behaviors resulted in the provision of tokens, and inappropriate behaviors resulted in penalties. The number of tokens earned and number of tokens fined were the two dependent measures in this study.

The results of this investigation are presented in Figure 6.6. In the first baseline phase (A), although improvement in appropriate behaviors was noted, the patient's disruptive behaviors continued to increase markedly, resulting in his being fined many times. This occurred in spite of the addition of a timeout contingency. On Hospital Day 9, thorazine (300 mg per day) was introduced (B phase) in an attempt to decrease the subject's disruptive behavior. This dosage was subsequently decreased to 200 mg per day, as the subject became noticeably drowsy. Examination of Figure 6.6 reveals that fines decreased to a zero level whereas tokens earned for appropriate behaviors remained at a stable level. In the return to baseline (A) thorazine was temporarily discontinued, resulting in an increase in fines for disruptive behavior. This phase lasted only 2 days, as the patient's renewal of disruptive activities caused nursing personnel to demand reinstatement of his medication. When thorazine was reintroduced in the final phase (B), number of tokens fined once again decreased to a zero level. Thus the controlling effects of thorazine over disruptive behavior were demonstrated.

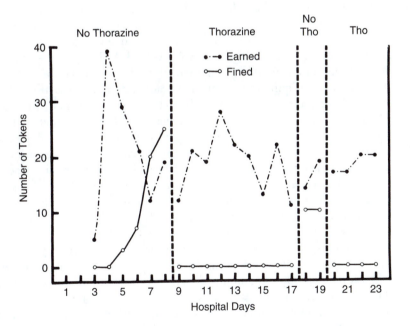

FIGURE 6.6 Behavior of an adolescent as indicated by tokens earned or fined in response to chlorpromazine, which was added to token economy. (Figure 15.3, p. 556, from: Agras, W. S. [1976]. Behavior modification in the general hospital psychiatric unit. In H. Leitenberg [Ed.], *Handbook of behavior modification.* Englewood Cliffs, NJ: Prentice-Hall. Copyright 1976 by H. Leitenberg. Reproduced by permission.)

Agras (1976) raised the question as to the possible contribution of the token economy program in controlling this patient's behavior. Unfortunately, time considerations did not permit him to systematically tease out the effects of that variable. The current use of A-B-A-B designs to study the effects of drugs on human behavior typically focus on the evaluation of novel drug applications prior to examination in larger randomized controlled trials (Kaplan, Crawford, Gardner, & Farrelly, 2002; Woodard, Groden, Goodwin, & Bodfish, 2007), and in rarer cases such designs have been used to experimentally test different facets of drug administration, such as whether effects differ based on self- versus experimenter-administration (e.g., Donny, Bigelow, & Walsh, 2006).

It also is notable that in A-B-A-B drug designs in which single- or double-blind trials are not feasible, staff and patient expectations of success during the drug condition are a possible confound with the drug's pharmacological actions. Designs listed in Table 6.1 that show control for these factors are 12 (A_1-B-A_1-B) and 13 (A-A_1-B-A_1-B). Design 13 is particularly useful in this instance. In the event that administration of the placebo fails to lead to behavioral change (A_1 phase of experimentation) over baseline measurement (A), the investigator is in a position to proceed with assessment of the active drug agent in an experimental analysis whereby the drug is twice introduced and once withdrawn (the B-A_1-B portion of study). If, on the other hand, the placebo exerts an effect over behavior, the investigator may wish to show its controlling effects as in Design 10 (A-A_1-A-A_1), which then can be followed with a sequential assessment of an active pharmacologic agent (Design 14: A-A_1-A-A_1-B-A_1-B). This design, however, does not permit an analysis of the interactive effects of a placebo (A_1) and a drug (B). This would require the use of an interactive design (see section 6.6).

An excellent example of the A-A_1-B-A_1-B strategy appears in the classic series of drug evaluations conducted by Liberman et al. (1973). In that study, the effects of a placebo pill and an active pharmacological agent, trifluperazine (stelazine), were examined on social interaction and content of conversation in a 21-year-old, withdrawn, male inpatient whose behavior had progressively deteriorated over a 3-year period. Two dependent measures were selected for study: (1) willingness to engage in 18 daily, randomly time-sampled, one-half minute chats with a member of the nursing staff, and (2) percentage of the chats that contained irrational or delusion content.

Before the experiment began, the patient was already receiving 20 mg of stelazine per day. The patient's medication was discontinued during the baseline phase (A). Next, a placebo was administered (A_1). In the third phase (B) stelazine was administered (60 mg per day), which was followed by a repetition of the A_1 and B phases. A double-blind trial was used in which neither the patient nor the nursing staff was aware of placebo and drug alternations.

Results of this study with regard to the patient's willingness to partake in brief conversations appear in Figure 6.7. In the baseline phase (A) a marked increase in number of asocial responses was observed. Institution of the placebo (A_1) first led to a decrease, followed by a renewed increase in asocial responses,

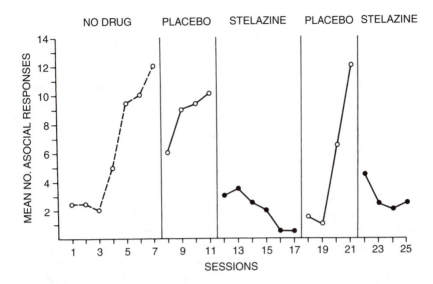

FIGURE 6.7   Average number of refusals to engage in a brief conversation. (Figure 2, p. 435, from: Liberman, R. P., Davis, J., Moon, W., & Moore, J. [1973]. Research design for analyzing drug-environment-behavior interactions. *Journal of Nervous and Mental Disease*, **156**, 432–439. Copyright 1973 Williams & Wilkins. Reproduced by permission.)

suggesting the overall ineffectiveness of the placebo condition. In the third phase (B) administration of stelazine resulted in a substantial decrease in asocial responses. However, a return to placebo conditions (A_1) again led to an increase in refusals to chat. In the final phase (B), reintroduction of stelazine affected a decrease in refusals. To summarize, the effects of an active pharmacological agent were documented twice, as indicated by the decreasing data trends in the stelazine phases. Data regarding the content of conversation were not presented graphically, but the authors indicated that under stelazine conditions, rational speech increased. However, administration of stelazine did not appear to modify frequency of delusional and hypochondriacal statements in that they remained at a constant level across all phases of study.

Finally in Table 6.1, in Design 15 (A_1-B-A_1-C-A_1-C) the controlling effects of two drugs (B and C) over placebo conditions (A_1) can be assessed. However, as in the A-B-A-C-A design, cited in section 6.1, the comparative efficacy of variables B and C are not subject to direct analysis, as a group comparison design would be required.

It is important to note that many extensions of these 15 basic drug designs are possible, including those in which differing levels of the drug are examined. This can be done within the structure of these 15 designs during active drug treatment or in separate experimental analyses where dosages are systematically varied (e.g., low-high-low-high) or where pharmacological agents are evaluated after possible failure of behavioral strategies (or vice versa). However, as in the A-B-A-C-A design cited in section 6.1, the comparative efficacy of variables B and C is subject to a number of restrictions and is, in general, a rather weak method for comparing two treatments.

The following A-B-C-A-D-A-D experimental analysis illustrates how, after two behavioral strategies (flooding, response prevention) failed to yield improvements in ritualistic behavior, a tricyclic (imipramine) led to some behavioral change, but only when administered at a high dosage (Turner, Hersen, Bellack, Andrasik, & Capparell, 1980).

The subject was a 25-year-old woman with a 7-year history of hand-washing and tooth-brushing rituals. She had been hospitalized several times, with no treatment proving successful (including ECT). Throughout the seven phases of the study (with the exception of response prevention), mean duration of hand-washing and tooth-brushing was recorded. Following a 7-day baseline period (A), flooding (B) was initiated for 8 days, and then response prevention (C) for 7 days. Then there was a 5-day return to baseline (A). Imipramine (C) was subsequently administered in increasing doses (75 mg to 250 mg) over 23 days, followed by withdrawal (A) and then reinstitution (C). In addition, 4 weeks of follow-up data were obtained.

Resulting data in Figure 6.8 are fairly clear-cut. Neither of the two behavioral strategies effected any change in the two behaviors targeted for modification. Similarly, imipramine, until it reached a level of 200 mg per day was ineffective. However, from 200–250 mg per day the drug appeared to reduce the duration of hand-washing and tooth-brushing. When imipramine was withdrawn, hand-washing and tooth-brushing increased in duration but decreased again when

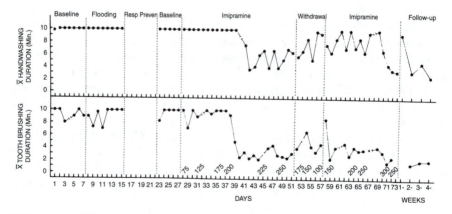

FIGURE 6.8 Mean duration of hand-washing and toothbrushing per day. (Figure 3, p. 654, from: Turner, S. M., Hersen, M., Bellack, A. S., Andrasik, F., & Capparell, H. V. [1980]. Behavioral and pharmacological treatment of obsessive-compulsive disorders. *Journal of Nervous and Mental Disease*, **168**, 651–657. Copyright 1980 The Williams and Wilkins Co., Baltimore. Reproduced by permission.)

it was reinstated. Improvement was greatest at the higher dosage levels and was maintained during the 4-week follow-up.

From a design perspective, phases 4–7 (A-C-A-C) essentially are the same as Design 11 (A-B-A-B) in Table 6.1. Of course, the problem with the A-B-A-B design is that the intervening A' or placebo phase is bypassed, resulting in two variables being manipulated at once (i.e., ingestion and action of the drug). Therefore, one cannot discount the possible placebo effect in the Turner et al. (1980) analysis, although the long history of the disorder makes this interpretation unlikely.

6.6. STRATEGIES FOR STUDYING INTERACTION EFFECTS

Most psychological treatments, and many drug treatments, contain a number of potentially therapeutic components. For instance, cognitive behavior therapy typically contains a psycho-educational component, a behavioral activation or behavioral practice component, a cognitive restructuring component, and an exposure-based component. One important task of the clinical researcher is to experimentally analyze these components to determine which are effective and which can be discarded, resulting in a more efficient treatment (Foa et al., 2005; Jacobson et al., 1996). Breaking a treatment down to its basic components and analyzing the separate effects of each component is one way to identify which components are most important. However, these components may have different effects when interacting with other treatment components. In advanced stages of the construction of complex treatments it becomes necessary to determine the nature of these interactions. Within the group comparison approach, statistical techniques, such as analysis of variance, are quite valuable in determining the presence of interactions. However, these techniques are not capable of determining the nature of the interaction or the relative contribution of a given variable to the total effect in an individual.

To evaluate the interaction of two (or more) variables, one must analyze the effects of both variables separately and in combination in one case, followed by replications. However, one must be careful to adhere to the basic rule of not changing more than one variable at a time (see chapter 3, section 3.4).

Before discussing examples of strategies for studying interaction effects, it will be helpful to examine some examples of designs containing two or more variables that are *not* capable of isolating interactive or additive effects. The first example is one where variations of a treatment are added to the end of a successful A-B-A-B, such as in an A-B-A-B-BC design in which C is a different therapeutic component. If the combined variable (BC) produces an effect over and above the previous phase (B), this provides a clue that an interaction exists, but the controlling effects of the BC phase will not have been demonstrated. To do this, one would have to return to the B phase and reintroduce the BC phase once again.

Another design option in which an analysis of interaction effects is not possible is one in which the clinical researcher performs an experimental analysis of the effect of adding one variable against a background of one or more variables already present. For example, Cote, Thompson, and McKerchar (2005) tested the effects of two different strategies for increasing toddlers' compliance during transitions (e.g., termination of play period and initiation of clean-up of toys): warning prior to transition (e.g., "two-minutes until clean-up") and access to preferred objects during the transition (e.g., ability to continue to have a toy while cleaning up). Although these techniques are both used quite commonly, they have not been well-evaluated, and Cote and colleagues aimed to determine the relative effectiveness of these treatment components. The authors tested the effects of these two strategies among three toddlers attending a day-care program. Results revealed that following a baseline phase (A), neither administration of a warning prior to transition (B) nor access to a toy (C) increased compliance or decreased problem behavior during transitions. However, addition of extinction procedures (D) to both of these strategies (i.e., BD and CD phases) resulted in significant improvement across all three children. Results were reversed during a return to baseline (A), and re-appeared during a re-initiation of the combined intervention (i.e., CD). Although this experiment demonstrated that warning plus extinction and toy plus extinction works in this setting, the role of the first two variables is not completely clear. It is possible that either of those variables or both are necessary for the effectiveness of the extinction program, or at least to enhance its effect. On the other hand, the initial two variables may not contribute to the therapeutic effect.

A third example where the analysis of interaction effects is not possible occurs in the test of a composite treatment package. An example of this strategy was presented in section 3.4 of chapter 3. More specifically, the effects of covert sensitization on pedophilic interest were examined (Barlow, Leitenberg, & Agras, 1969). Covert sensitization, where a patient is instructed to imagine both unwanted arousing scenes in conjunction with aversive scenes, contains a number of variables such as therapeutic instruction, muscle relaxation, and instructions to imagine each of the two scenes. In this experiment, the whole package was introduced after baseline, followed by withdrawal and reinstatement of one component—the aversive scene. The design can be represented as A-BC-B-BC, where BC is the treatment package and C is the aversive scene. In this particular case more than one variable was changed during the transition from A-BC; however, this was in accordance with an exception to the guidelines outlined in chapter 3, section 3.4.

Figure 3.13 shows that pedophilic interest decreased during administration of the treatment package, increased when the aversive scene was removed, and decreased again after reinstatement of the aversive scene. Once again, these data indicate that the noxious scene is important against the background of the other variables present in covert sensitization. However, the contribution of each of the other variables, and the nature of these interactions with the aversive scene, has not been demonstrated, nor was this the purpose of the study. In this case, it would *seem* that an interaction is present because it is hard to conceive of the aversive scene alone producing these decreases in pedophilic interest. However, an understanding of the nature of the interaction awaits further experimental inquiry.

While the designs reviewed so far can hint at interaction and set the stage for further experimentation, a thorough evaluation of interaction effects requires an experimental analysis of two or more variables both separately and in combination. To illustrate this process, we present two classic series of experiments that both analyze the effects of feedback and reinforcement in two separate populations: those with a specific phobia and those with anorexia nervosa.

In one series of experiments, Leitenberg and colleagues (1968) treated a subject with a severe knife phobia. The target behavior was the amount of time (in seconds) that the subject was able to remain in the presence of a knife. The design involved a baseline phase (A) and treatment components involving: feedback (B), which consisted of simply informing the subject after each trial of the amount of time spent looking at the knife, and praise (C), which consisted of providing the subject with verbal reinforcement whenever he exceeded a progressively increasing time criterion. The experimental arrangement of phases was B-BC-B-A-B-BC-B, with each session consisting of 10 trials.

The results of the study are presented in Figure 6.9 (and were briefly presented in Figure 3.9). As is clear from this figure, there was a marked upward trend in time spent looking at the knife during the feedback phase (B). The addition of praise (BC) did not appear to add to the therapeutic effect. Similarly, the removal of praise in the next phase (B) did not subtract from the effect. At this point, it appeared that feedback was responsible for the therapeutic gains. Withdrawal and reinstatement of feedback in the next two phases (A-B) confirmed the controlling effects of feedback. Finally, the addition and removal of praise in the remaining two phases (BC-B) replicated the beginning of the experiment.

Although this experiment provides rich information about the effect of the treatment components, it does not entirely elucidate the nature of the interaction. Two tentative conclusions are possible: either praise has no effect on phobic behavior, or praise has an effect but it was masked by the powerful effect of feedback. Consistent with the general guidelines of analyzing both treatment variables separately and in combination, the next experiment in this series reversed the order of the introduction of variables in a second subject with a knife phobia (Leitenberg, 1973). Once again, the target behavior was the amount of time the subject was able to remain in the presence of the knife. The design replicated the first experiment, with the exception of the elimination of the last phase. Thus the design can be represented as B-BC-B-A-B-BC. This time, however, B refers to praise and C to feedback.

The results of this study are presented in Figure 6.10. As is clear from this figure, there was little progress during the first praise phase (B). However, when feedback was added to praise (BC) performance increased steadily. This suggests, in combination with the results from the prior study, that feedback is the active

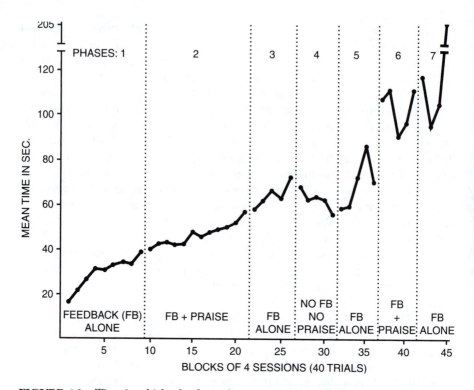

FIGURE 6.9   Time in which a knife was kept exposed by a phobic patient as a function of feedback, feedback plus praise, and no feedback or praise conditions. (Figure 2, p. 136, from: Leitenberg, H., Agras, W. S., Thomson, L. E., & Wright, D. E. [1968]. Feedback in behavior modification: An experimental analysis in two phobic cases. *Journal of Applied Behavior Analysis*, **1**, 131–137. Copyright 1968 by Society for the Experimental Analysis of Behavior, Inc. Reproduced by permission.)

treatment component. Interestingly, this rate of improvement was maintained when feedback was removed (B). After a sharp gain, performance stabilized when both feedback and praise were removed (A). Once again, the introduction of praise alone did not produce any further improvement (B), and the addition of feedback to praise (BC) again resulted in marked improvement.

Direct replication of this experiment with four additional subjects, each with a different phobia, produced similar results. The overall results of these interaction analyses indicate that feedback is the most active component because marked improvement occurred during both feedback alone and feedback plus praise phases, while praise alone had little or no effect, although it was capable of maintaining progress begun in a prior feedback phase in some cases. So a more efficient treatment package for people with a specific phobia would emphasize the feedback or knowledge-of-results aspect and deemphasize the social reinforcement component. Since these studies, feedback of behavioral progress has

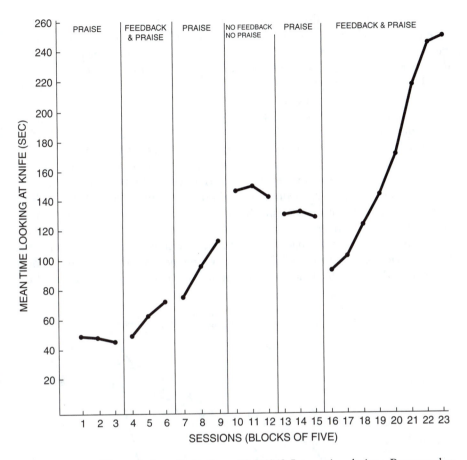

FIGURE 6.10   (Figure 1, from: Leitenberg, H. [1973]. Interaction designs. Paper read at the American Psychological Association, Montreal, August. Reproduced by permission.)

become an important component of exposure-based treatment programs for phobia (Barlow, 2002).

Of course, feedback and reinforcement are important components of psychological treatments more generally, and their effects have long been demonstrated beyond the area of specific phobias. For instance, another classic series of studies tested the interaction of reinforcement and feedback among those with anorexia nervosa (Agras et al., 1974). From the perspective of interaction designs, this particular experiment is interesting because the contribution of a third therapeutic variable, *size of meals*, also was tested. Here we review several experiments from this series in order to illustrate the usefulness of an interaction design strategy. All of the patients included in this series were hospitalized and presented with 6,000 calories per day, divided into four meals of 1,500 calories each. Two measures of eating behavior were recorded as dependent variables: weight and caloric intake. Patients also were asked to record number of mouthfuls eaten at each meal. Reinforcement consisted of granting privileges based on increases in weight. For instance, if weight gain exceeded a certain criterion the patient could leave her room, watch television, play table games with the nurses, and so on. Feedback consisted of providing precise information on weight, caloric intake, and number of mouthfuls eaten.

In one experiment the effect of reinforcement (C) was examined against a background of feedback (B). The design can be represented as B-BC-BC¹-BC, where C¹ represents noncontingent reinforcement. During the first feedback phase (B), labeled *baseline* in Figure 6.11, slight gains in caloric intake and weight were observed. These gains increased substantially when reinforcement was added to feedback (BC). Noncontingent reinforcement produced a drop in caloric intake and a slowing of weight gain (BC¹), while reintroduction of reinforcement (BC) once again produced sharp gains in both measures. These data show hints of an interaction effect in that caloric intake and weight rose slightly during the first feedback phase but the addition of reinforcement produced increases over and above those for feedback alone. The drop and subsequent rise of caloric

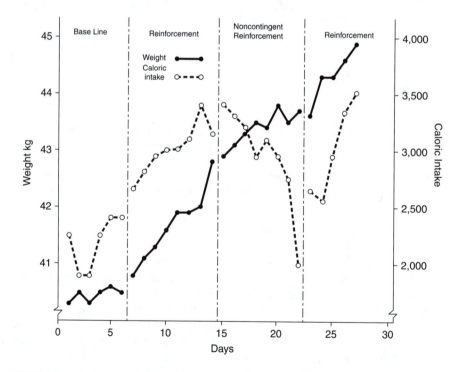

FIGURE 6.11   Data from an experiment examining the effect of positive reinforcement in the absence of negative reinforcement (Patient 3). (Figure 2, p. 281, from: Agras, W. S., Barlow, D. H., Chapin, H. N., Abel, G. G., & Leitenberg, H. [1974]. Behavior modification of anorexia nervosa. *Archives of General Psychiatry, 30,* 279–286. Copyright 1974 American Medical Association. Reproduced by permission.)

intake and rate of weight gain during the next two phases demonstrated that reinforcement is a controlling variable *when combined with feedback*—hence the interaction effect.

These data only hint at the presence of an interaction effect given that some improvement did occur during the initial feedback phase. Moreover, this experiment did not provide an analysis of the independent effects of reinforcement. However, two subsequent experiments were conducted where feedback was introduced against a background of reinforcement to address this issue. We review only one experiment here, although data from both experiments are quite similar in nature, and the interested reader is encouraged to read the original report for more details. This experiment included baseline (A), reinforcement (B), and feedback (C) phases, presented in an A-B-BC-B-BC design. In this experiment, the subject also was presented with 6,000 calories per day.

The results of this experiment are presented in Figure 6.12. As shown, caloric intake actually declined during baseline (A). The introduction of reinforcement (B) did not result in any increases and the decline actually continued. However, adding feedback to reinforcement (BC) produced increases in both weight and caloric intake, which stopped during withdrawal of feedback (B), and re-emerged when feedback was reintroduced (BC).

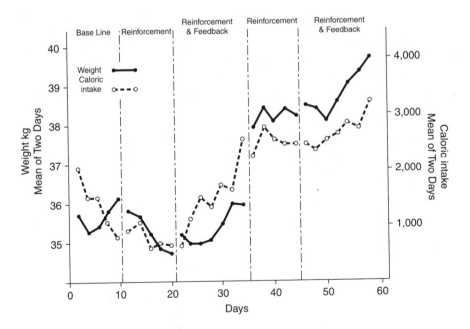

FIGURE 6.12 Data from an experiment examining the effect of feedback on the eating behavior of a patient with anorexia nervosa (Patient 5). (Figure 4, p. 283, from: Agras, W. S., Barlow, D. H., Chapin, H. N., Abel, G. G., & Leitenberg, H. [1974]. Behavior modification of anorexia nervosa. *Archives of General Psychiatry*, **30**, 279–286. Copyright 1974 American Medical Association. Reproduced by permission.)

This experiment (and its replications) provides the data needed to begin to draw some conclusions about the nature of this complex interaction. More specifically, when both variables were presented alone, as in the initial phases in the respective experiments, reinforcement produced no increases, but feedback produced some increase. When presented in combination, reinforcement added to the feedback effect and, against a background of feedback, became the controlling variable in that caloric intake decreased when contingent reinforcement was removed. Feedback, however, also exerted a controlling effect when it was removed and reintroduced against a background of reinforcement. Thus, it seems that feedback can maximize the effectiveness of reinforcement to the point where it is a controlling variable. However, feedback alone is capable of producing therapeutic results, which is not the case with reinforcement. Feedback, thus, is the more important of the two variables, although both contribute to treatment outcome. It is notable that this rich and valuable information about the interacting influences of these two treatment components is available from careful experiments conducted with only a few subjects, and that this level of detail and clarity would be significantly more difficult to obtain using a group comparison approach.

It was noted earlier that the contribution of a third variable—size of meals—was also examined within the context of this interaction. In keeping with the guidelines of analyzing each variable separately and in combination with other variables, phases were examined when the large amount of 6,000 calories was presented without the presence of either feedback or reinforcement. The baseline phase of Figure 6.12 represents one such instance. In this phase caloric intake declined steadily. Examination of other baseline phases in the replications of this experiment revealed similar results. To complete the interaction analysis, size of meal was varied against a background of both feedback and reinforcement. The design can be represented as ABC-ABC^1-ABC, where A is feedback, B is reinforcement, C is 6,000 calories per day, and C^1 is 3,000 calories per day.

Under this condition, size of meal did have an effect, in that more was eaten when 6,000 calories were served than when 3,000 calories were presented (see Figure 6.13). In terms of treatment, however, even large meals were incapable of producing weight gain in those phases where it was the only therapeutic variable. Thus this variable is not as strong as feedback. The authors concluded this series by summarizing the effects of the three variables alone and in combination across five patients:

> Thus large meals and reinforcement were combined in four experimental phases and weight was lost in each phase. On the other hand, large meals and feedback were combined in eight phases and weight was gained in all but one. Finally, all three variables (large meals, feedback, and reinforcement) were combined in 12 phases and weight was gained in each phase. These findings suggest that informational feedback is more important in the treatment of anorexia nervosa than positive reinforcement, while serving large meals is least important. However, the combination of all three variables seems most effective. (Agras et al., 1974, p. 285)

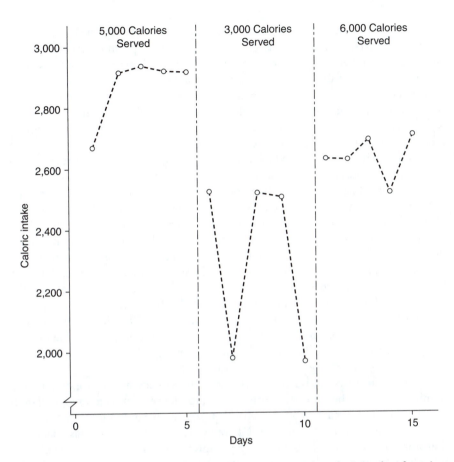

FIGURE 6.13   The effect of varying the size of meals upon the caloric intake of a patient with anorexia nervosa (Patient 5). (Figure 5, p. 285, from: Agras, W. S., Barlow, D. H., Chapin, H. N., Abel, G. G., & Leitenberg, H. [1974]. Behavior modification of anorexia nervosa. *Archives of General Psychiatry*, **30**, 279–286. Copyright 1974 American Medical Association. Reproduced by permission.)

As in the previous series focused on specific phobias, the juxtaposition of variables within the general framework of analyzing each variable separately and in combination provided information on the interaction of these variables.

Let us now consider two more recent applications of the interaction design strategy to illustrate other variations on this approach. One recent example is a study by Saunders, McEntee, and Saunders (2005) that tested the interaction of the use of varied reinforcement schedules and the provision of a materials organizer on work-related behavior among three adult men diagnosed with mental retardation. Each of these men was referred to the study because they engaged in very low levels of work and displayed high levels of off-task behaviors, such as stereotyped behaviors, self-injury, and leaving their work station. In this study, the men came to a simulated workshop each day in the experimenters' behavioral laboratory, and were asked to engage in 20 minutes of "work," which involved shredding pieces of paper. The primary dependent variables in this study were percentage of each session spent engaging in on-task behavior (e.g., shredding paper), off-task behavior (e.g., walking around the room), and aberrant behavior (e.g., stereotypy, self-injury, etc.), each coded with strong inter-observer agreement ($\geq 90\%$ across all behaviors for each subject).

The design used differed slightly for each subject, so we will review data from the first subject for illustrative purposes. During a baseline phase (A), the subject engaged in paper shredding and received a consumable reinforcer (e.g., M&Ms, ice cream) for engaging in on-task behavior on a variable interval schedule. In the next phase (B), the schedule was changed to a fixed ratio schedule in which reinforcers were provided after each on-task behavior (FR1). In the subsequent phase, the experimenters added the use of a materials organizer that contained the paper to be shredded (C). This phase could be labeled BC. This was followed by a removal of the organizer (B), and then a reinstatement of the organizer (BC). At this point, we have an A-B-BC-B-BC design. The results of this study, shown in Figure 6.14, reveal that the use of a FR schedule is not associated with an increase in on-task behavior; however, the addition of the organizer is associated with an increase, and the controlling influence of the organizer is demonstrated via the use of a withdrawal design.

In the next several phases, the experimenters systematically increased the number of on-task behaviors required to earn reinforcement from one in phase B and BC, to 2 (B_1C), then 3 (B_2C), then 4 (B_3C). As shown in Figure 6.14, this thinning of the reinforcement schedule did not lead to a decrease in on-task behavior. The final thinning to a FR5 schedule (B_4C) appeared to decrease on-task behavior initially; however, it subsequently returned to earlier levels. Interestingly, the experimenters then again removed the organizer (B_4) and subsequently reinstated it (B_4C), providing a second demonstration of the controlling influence of this treatment component.

Although the findings for this subject suggest a controlling effect of the organizer component (C), it is important to remember that study of the interaction effects is not yet possible because C was not analyzed in isolation, but only against a background of B. Thus, it is possible that introducing C first would have a somewhat different effect, as might adding B *after* the introduction of C rather than the other way around. As pointed out in chapter 5 and discussed more fully in chapter 8, the latter phases of experiments such as this are subject to multiple-treatment interference. In other words, the effect of a treatment or interaction in the latter phases may depend to some extent on experience in the earlier phases. But if the interaction effect is consistent across subjects, both early and late in the experiment, and across different "orders" of introduction of the interaction then one has greatly increased confidence in both the fact and the generality of the effect. As with A-B-A withdrawal designs, however, the most

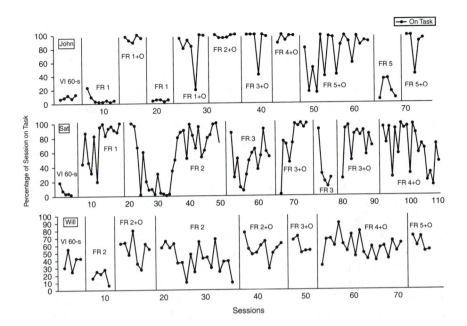

FIGURE 6.14   Percentage of each experimental session on task for each participant. (Figure 1, p. 168, from: Saunders, R. R., McEntree, J. E., & Saunders, M. D. (2005). Interaction of reinforcement schedules, a behavioral prosthesis, and work-related behavior in adults with mental retardation. *Journal of Applied Behavior Analysis*, **38** (2), 163–176.)

easily generalizable data from the experiment to applied situations are the early phases before multiple treatments build up. This is because the early phase most closely resembles the applied situation, where the treatment would also be introduced and continued without a prior background of several treatments.

Our final example of an interaction design is a creative one in which Huybers, Van Houten, and Malenfant (2004) examined the effects of street sign prompts and pavement markings on reducing conflicts between motorists and pedestrians across multiple intersections. In this instance, the experimenters conducted two studies, one using an A-B-B$_1$-BC design and the other an A-C-CB design, to test two strategies alone and in combination aimed at decreasing pedestrian injuries and fatalities. Given the relative infrequency of pedestrian injuries and fatalities, the dependent variable in this study was "evasion conflicts," which involve instances of a motorist engaging in abrupt braking or swerving to avoid a pedestrian or of a pedestrian running or jumping out of the street to avoid being struck by a vehicle. The experimenters arranged for trained observers to collect data on the occurrence of evasion conflicts at four different crosswalks in study 1 and two different crosswalks in study 2, with perfect inter-observer agreement on number of conflicts in both studies (100%).

In the first experiment, observers first collected data during a baseline phase (A) on the first 20 pedestrians to cross the crosswalk, recording the percentage of pedestrians for whom an evasion conflict occurred (data were also collected on the distance at which motorists stopped from the crosswalk, see Huybers et al., 2004). In the next phase (B), the experimenters posted white street signs before the crosswalks that read "Yield here to pedestrians." In the next phase (B₁), an identical sign was used with the exception being that instead of white the signs were fluorescent yellow-green, with the hypothesis that this novel color would enhance the effectiveness of the sign. In the final phase (BC), the white sign was replaced and pavement markings made of reflective material were added in the street in advance of the crosswalk. The purpose of this condition was to examine the additive effect of the pavement markings.

The results of the first experiment are presented in the top half of Figure 6.15A. As shown, baseline assessment across all four crosswalks revealed relatively equal percentages of evasion conflicts at approximately 10-20%. The addition of the signs in the next two phases did not appear to consistently decrease the occurrence of evasion conflicts across the four crosswalks, although some decrease is noticeable in the third and fourth sites. The addition of the markings in the final phase, however, is associated with a clearer reduction in evasion conflicts across all sites, suggesting that the pavement markings are a more effective component. However, this design does not allow for strong inferences about the controlling effect of pavement markings given there is no withdrawal condition. Moreover, concerns about the failure to independently examine the latter treatment component mentioned above applied here.

In a second experiment, Huybers et al. (2004) used similar assessment and treatment procedures to that in the first experiment (although now across only two sites); however, after a baseline phase (A), they next implemented the pavement markings alone (C), followed by a combination of the markings and white signs (BC). As shown in Figure 6.15, results again supported the conclusion that the pavement markings are associated with a decrease in evasion conflicts, with the presentation of white signs showing no additional benefit. Taken together, these two experiments suggest that pavement markings are associated with a decrease in conflicts between motorists and pedestrians, while the posting of street signs is minimally effective and does not have an additive benefit over and above pavement markings. Some notable strengths of these experiments are the replication of these results across multiple sites in each experiment, as well as the independent and combined examination of each component, and evaluation of different ordering of treatment components. However, it also is notable that the evidence in support of the study conclusions would be considerably stronger with the inclusion of a treatment withdrawal phase in order to increase confidence in the controlling influence of the treatment components. Although a withdrawal would be possible in a traffic study such as this, it is not always possible or desirable. In such instances, alternative designs such as changing criterion and multiple-baseline designs can be especially valuable.

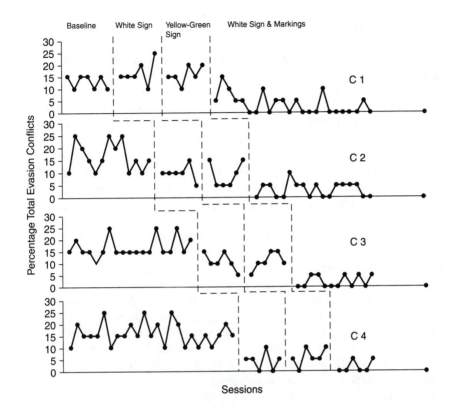

FIGURE 6.15A   Percentage of total evasion conflicts during each session of Experiment 1. (Figure 3, p. 450 & 453, from: Huybers, S., Van Houten, R., & Malenfant, J. E. (2004). Reducing conflicts between motor vehicles and pedestrians: The separate and combined effects of pavement markings and a sign prompt. *Journal of Applied Behavior Analysis*, **37** (4), 445–456.)

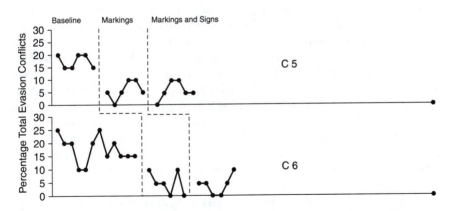

FIGURE 6.15B   Percentage of total evasion conflicts (top panel) and drivers who yielded more than 3 m (middle panel) and 6 m (botom panel) in advance of the crosswalk during each session of Experiment 2.

6.7. CHANGING CRITERION DESIGNS

The changing criterion design is one in which after a brief baseline (A) phase an intervention is administered and the criterion for reinforcement of that behavior is changed over the course of the evaluation such that increasing levels of behavior are required in order for reinforcement to occur. In such designs, there is no withdrawal of treatment; however, a causal relation between treatment and behavior change may be supported by showing that behavior changes when and only when the criterion for reinforcement is changed. The result of this experimental arrangement should be a step-like pattern of behavior change that matches the changing criterion. As in other variations on the A-B design strategies discussed earlier, decisions regarding when to change phases (i.e., when to change the criterion) are made by the experimenter, but typically occur once there is stability in the target behavior. The criterion typically is changed in the same direction over the course of the study; however, the experimenter may incorporate mini-reversals to increase the strength of evidence supporting the controlling effect of the treatment variable. Alternatively, on a more extended basis one can reverse the procedure and experimentally demonstrate successive increases in a targeted behavior following initial demonstration of successive decreases. This is referred to as *bidirectionality*. As with other designs, the study continues until the behavior is changed and maintained at an acceptable level.

Kazdin (1982) pointed out that some experimenters have dealt with the problem of excessive behavioral variability by showing that the mean performance over adjacent subphases reflects the stepwise progression desired in changing criterion designs. This is an acceptable solution, but of course not one that is ideal. It behooves researchers using this design to demonstrate close correspondence between the changing criterion and actually observed behavior.

Hartmann and Hall (1976) presented a classic illustration of the changing-criterion design in which a smoking-deceleration program was evaluated. Baseline level of smoking is depicted in panel A of Figure 6.16. In the treatment phase (B), the criterion rate was set at 95% of the baseline rate (i.e., 46 cigarettes per day). An increasing response cost of $1 was established for smoking each additional cigarette (i.e., $1 for cigarette 47, $2 for cigarette 48, etc.). In contrast, an escalating bonus of $0.10 per cigarette was established if the subject smoked less than the criterion number set. Subsequently, in phases C–G, the criterion for each succeeding phase was established at 94% of the previous one. Examination of Figure 6.16 clearly shows that treatment reduced cigarette smoking by $\geq 2\%$ in each phase. From the experimental analysis perspective, there were six replications of the contingencies applied. Experimental control was documented in each instance, with the treatment phase serving as baseline with respect to the decreasing criterion for the next phase.

One recent variation on the classic changing criterion design is the range-bound changing criterion design (McDougall, 2005). This variation addresses concerns about behavioral variability while also providing the experimenter with

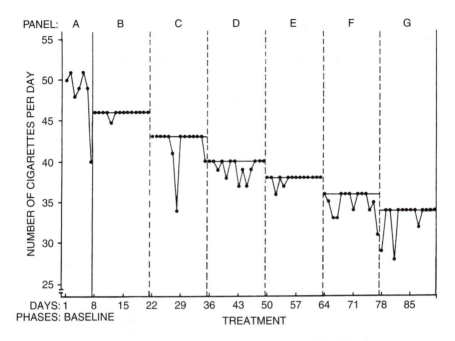

FIGURE 6.16   Data from a smoking-reduction program used to illustrate the stepwise criterion change design. The solid horizontal lines indicate the criterion for each treatment phase. (Figure 2, p. 529, from: Hartmann, D. P., & Hall, R. V. [1976]. The changing criterion design. *Journal of Applied Behavior Analysis, 9,* 527–532. Copyright 1976 by Soc. for the Experimental Analysis of Behavior. Reproduced by permission.)

a method of increasing the inferences one can draw about the relation between the treatment variable and the target behavior. While the classic changing criterion design requires that the target behavior surpass a pre-defined criterion in order to be reinforced, the range-bound changing criterion design requires that the target behavior occur within an established upper and lower criterion during each intervention phase. These criteria create a bounded range of performance— and the demonstration that behavioral performance remains within (i.e., rather than beyond) this range across each experimental phase increases the strength of the inference that can be drawn between the treatment variable and target behavior (see McDougall, 2005).

Although not as widely used as the A-B and A-B-A variations described earlier, there are numerous examples of the changing criterion design in various literatures, including the increasing food consumption (Kahng, Boscoe, & Byrne, 2003), decreasing involuntary muscle activity (e.g., paradoxical vocal fold motion) (Warnes & Allen, 2005), and reducing excessive blood glucose monitoring in a patient with diabetes (Allen & Evans, 2001). In addition to the flexibility of changing criterion designs, a major strength and perhaps the factor that makes such designs among the most attractive clinically is that there is no reversal or withdrawal, and the goal is continued gradual improvement over the course of the intervention. This feature makes such designs well suited in the treatment of dangerous behaviors (e.g., self-injury, violent behaviors), and in treating maladaptive behaviors more generally.

■ ■ ■ ■ ■

CHAPTER 7

MULTIPLE BASELINE DESIGNS

7.1. INTRODUCTION

Withdrawal or reversal designs may be undesirable or even inappropriate when treatment variables cannot be withdrawn or reversed due to ethical considerations, practical limitations, or problems in subject or staff cooperation. The researcher's goal of identifying which treatment components are most effective and of demonstrating the controlling influence of these components by returning undesirable behavior in their absence is often at odds with the desires of the subject and clinical staff, who most often want the undesirable behaviors to go away quickly, and not to return.

Ethical considerations are of paramount importance when the treatment variable is effective in reducing self-injurious or aggressive behaviors. Here the withdrawal of treatment is obviously unwarranted, even for brief periods of time. Variations of the withdrawal design may be used in such instances, such as quasi-experimental withdrawal designs (e.g., Wallenstein & Nock, 2007), but these present limitations on the causal inferences that can be drawn. In still other instances, withdrawal of treatment, despite absence of harm to the subject or others in his or her environment, may be undesirable because of the severity of the disorder. Here the importance of preserving therapeutic gains is given priority, especially when a disorder has a lengthy history and previous efforts at remediation have failed.

A related concern is environmental cooperation. Even if the behavior in question does not have immediate destructive effects on the environment, if it is considered to be aversive (i.e., by family, parents, teachers, or clinical staff) the experimenter will not obtain sufficient cooperation to carry out withdrawal or reversal of treatment procedures. Under these circumstances, it is clear that the researcher must seek alternative experimental strategies.

Another potential limitation that can arise is one in which carryover effects appear across adjacent phases of study, such as in the case of therapeutic instructions or drugs with long-lasting effects. Also, when multiple behaviors within an individual are targeted for change, withdrawal designs may not provide the most elegant strategy for evaluation. In summary, in many situations withdrawal or reversal designs may not be the best methodological option.

There are three main design options the clinical researcher should consider as strong alternatives to withdrawal or reversal designs when presented with the problems mentioned in the preceding paragraphs. One option is the use of a changing criterion design, which was discussed earlier (see chapter 6). A second option is the use of a multiple-baseline design, which is the focus of the current chapter. The third option, use of an alternating treatment design, will be discussed in the next chapter (see chapter 8).

In this chapter we present the rationale and procedures for multiple baseline designs. Examples of the three principal varieties of multiple baseline strategies will be presented for illustrative purposes. In addition, we will consider the more recent varieties and permutations, including the nonconcurrent multiple baseline design across subjects and the multiple-probe technique. Finally, specific issues that may arise in the use of multiple baseline designs in drug evaluations will be discussed.

7.2. MULTIPLE BASELINE DESIGNS

Historically, the first uses of multiple-baseline designs appeared in the clinical science literature approximately forty years ago. The rationale for the multiple baseline design first appeared in the applied behavioral literature in 1968 (Baer et al.), in which they explained:

> In the multiple-baseline technique, a number of responses are identified and measured over time to provide baselines, against which changes can be evaluated. With these baselines established, the experimenter then applies an experimental variable to one of the behaviors, produces a change in it, and perhaps notes little or no change in the other baselines. (p. 94)

Since that time, the multiple baseline design has become the most well-known and widely used of the three alternatives to withdrawal or reversal designs noted above. Indeed, a brief search on PubMed (an electronic text-based article search and retrieval system available on the internet at www.pubmed.gov) reveals that as of June 6, 2007: 30 articles are listed using the term "changing criterion," 123 articles using the term "alternating treatments," and 1,036 articles using the term "multiple baseline."

Multiple-baseline designs are those in which the treatment variable is introduced in temporal sequence to different behaviors, subjects, or settings. The power of such designs comes from demonstrating that *change occurs when, and only when,* the intervention is directed at the behavior, setting, or subject in question. As with reversal designs, multiple-baseline designs begin with a baseline phase that continues until behavioral stability is demonstrated, at which time the treatment variable is introduced. As mentioned above, a change in behavior that occurs only when the intervention is introduced suggests that the intervention caused the change; however, the influence of other factors (e.g., history, maturation, etc.) must be ruled out in order to increase the validity of this claim. Rather than using a withdrawal or reversal, multiple baseline designs replicate the effect of the treatment variable across different behaviors, settings, or individuals. The temporal sequencing element is vital in order to rule out the likelihood that history, maturation, or other extraneous factors could account for the observed behavior change.

Each baseline and introduction of the treatment variable can be conceptualized as separate A-B designs, with the A phase further extended for each of the succeeding baselines (i.e., behaviors, subjects, or settings) until the treatment variable is applied. The experimenter is assured that the treatment variable is effective when a change in rate appears after its application while the rate of concurrent (untreated) behaviors remains relatively constant. A basic assumption is that the targeted behaviors are independent from one another. If they happen to covary (i.e., change is observed across all baselines when the intervention is administered to the first behavior), then the controlling effects of the treatment variable are subject to question, and limitations of the A-B analysis fully apply (see chapter 5).

In some cases, when independence of behaviors is not found, application of the alternating treatment design may be recommended (see chapter 8). In other cases, application of the multiple baseline design across different subjects might yield useful information. Kazdin and Kopel (1975) offered three additional recommendations for dealing with instances in which the effects of the treatment variable may be general rather than specific. The first is to include baselines that topographically are as distinct as possible from one another, although this may be difficult to ascertain on an *a priori* basis. The second is to use four or more baselines rather than two or three. However, there is the statistical probability that interdependence will be enhanced with a larger number. The third (on an *ex post facto* basis) is to withdraw and then reintroduce treatment for the correlated baseline (as in the B-A-B design), thus demonstrating the controlling effects over that targeted response. Even though the multiple baseline strategy was implemented in the first place to avoid treatment withdrawal, the rationale for such temporary (or partial) withdrawal in the multiple baseline design across behaviors seems reasonable when independence of baselines cannot be documented.

The issue regarding how many baselines are needed to establish confidence in the controlling effects of treatment is one that has been debated a bit in the literature. Baer et al. (1968) initially considered this issue to be an "audience variable" and were reluctant to specify the minimum number of baselines required. Theoretically, only two baselines are needed to derive useful information. However, consistent with earlier views on this topic (e.g., Barlow and Hersen, 1973; Kazdin and Kopel, 1975; Wolf and Risley, 1971), we recommend using at least three baselines, with the use of four or more baselines increasing the strength of the design, if practical and experimental considerations permit.

Although demonstration of the controlling effects of a treatment variable is weaker in the multiple baseline design than in withdrawal designs, a major advantage of the former is that it facilitates the simultaneous measurement of multiple target behaviors. This is significant for two reasons. First, the monitoring of concurrent behaviors allows for a closer approximation to naturalistic conditions, where a variety of responses are occurring at the same time. Second, examination of concurrent behaviors fosters an analysis of covariation among the targeted behaviors. The co-occurrence of maladaptive behaviors has long been of interest to epidemiologists (e.g., Angold, Costello, & Erkanli, 1999; Kessler, Chiu, Demler, Merikangas, & Walters, 2005), basic behavioral researchers (Goodwin & Gotlib, 2004; Lewinsohn, Rohde, Seeley, Klein, & Gotlib, 2003), and those studying the treatment of maladaptive behaviors (Doss & Weisz, 2006; Kazdin & Whitley, 2006). In fact, in their introduction to a special journal section focused on the treatment implications of comorbid psychopathology, Kendall and Clarkin (1992) called comorbidity "the premier challenge facing mental health professionals" (p. 833). The single-case experimental design in general, and the multiple baseline strategy in particular, is especially well suited to advance understanding of how treatment variables may influence not only the key target behavior, but other behaviors as well. Kazdin (1973) cogently underscored the importance of measuring concurrent (untreated) behaviors when assessing the efficacy of reinforcement paradigms in applied settings in stating that:

> While changes in target behaviors are the *raison d'être* for undertaking treatment or training programs, concomitant changes may take place as well. If so, they should be assessed. It is one thing to assess and evaluate changes in a target behavior, but quite another to insist on excluding nontarget measures. It may be that investigators are short-changing themselves in evaluating the programs. (p. 527)

Types of multiple baseline designs

There are three basic types of multiple baseline designs. In the first, the *multiple baseline design across behaviors*, the same treatment variable is applied sequentially to separate (independent) target behaviors within a single subject. A possible variation of this strategy, of course, involves the sequential application of a treatment variable to targeted behaviors for an entire group of subjects (e.g., Malott, Glasgow, O'Neill, & Klesges, 1984). Of course, in such cases it would be best if the experimenter presents data for individual subjects, demonstrating that sequential treatment applications to independent behaviors affected most subjects in the same direction.

In the second design, the *multiple baseline design across subjects*, a particular treatment is applied in sequence across matched subjects presumably exposed to "identical" environmental conditions. Thus, as the same treatment variable is applied to succeeding subjects, the baseline for each subject increases in length. In contrast to the multiple baseline design across behaviors (which is a within-subject multiple baseline design), in the multiple baseline design across subjects a single targeted behavior serves as the primary focus of inquiry. Of course, there is no experimental contraindication to monitoring concurrent (untreated) behaviors as well. On the contrary, it is likely that the monitoring of concurrent behaviors will lead to additional findings of merit.

As with the multiple baseline design across behaviors, a possible variation of the multiple baseline design across subjects involves the sequential application of the treatment variable across entire groups of subjects (e.g., Porritt et al., 2006). Here too, however, it is best if the experimenter demonstrates that a large majority of individual subjects from each group evidenced the same effects of treatment. Notably, the multiple baseline design across subjects has also been labeled a *time-lagged control* design (e.g., Allen & Shriver, 1997; Gottman, 1973). In fact, this strategy was followed by Hilgard (1933) some 75 years ago in a study in which she examined the effects of early and delayed practice on memory and motoric functions in a set of twins (method of co-twin control).

In the third design, the *multiple baseline design across settings*, a particular treatment is applied sequentially to a single subject or a group of subjects across independent situations. For example, in a classroom situation, one might apply time-out contingencies for unruly behavior in sequence across different class-room periods. The baseline period for each succeeding classroom period, then, increases in length before application of the treatment. As in the across-subjects design, assessment of treatment is usually based on rate changes observed in a selected target behavior. However, once again the monitoring of concurrent behaviors might prove to be of value and should be encouraged where possible. Here too, this multiple baseline strategy may be used to study groups of subjects rather than individual subjects (e.g., Lohrmann & Talerico, 2004). In the follow-ing three subsections we provide illustrations of the use of these basic multiple baseline strategies, as well as variations on these designs, selected from various clinical literatures.

Multiple baseline design across behaviors

An early example of a multiple baseline design across behaviors appeared in a study by Bornstein, Bellack, and Hersen (1977). These authors used this design to assess the effects of social skills training in the social performance of an unassertive 8-year-old third grader (Tom) whose passivity led to derision by his peers. Generally, if Tom experienced conflict with a peer, he cried or reported the incident to his teacher. Three target behaviors were selected for modification as a result of role-played performance in baseline: ratio of eye contact to speech duration, number of words spoken, and number of requests made. In addition, independent evaluations of overall assertiveness, based on role-played perfor-mance, were obtained. As can be seen in Figure 7.1, baseline responding for tar-geted behaviors was low and stable. Following baseline evaluation, Tom received three weeks of social skills training consisting of three 15–30 minute sessions per

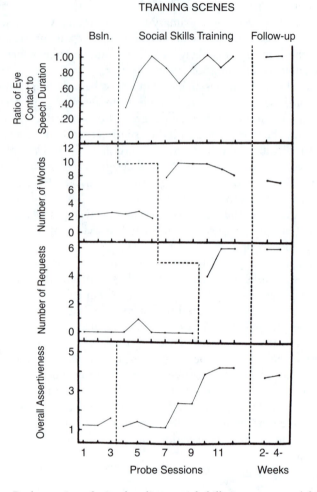

FIGURE 7.1 Probe sessions during baseline, social skills treatment, and follow-up for training scenes for Tom. A multiple baseline analysis of ratio of eye contact while speaking to speech duration, number of words, number of requests, and overall assertiveness. (Figure 3, p. 190, from: Bornstein, M. R., Bellack, A. S., Hersen, M. (1977). Social-skills training for unassertive children: A multiple-baseline analysis. *Journal of Applied Behavior Analysis,* **10,** 183–195. Copyright 1977 by Society for Experimental Analysis of Behavior. Reproduced by permission.)

week. These were applied sequentially and cumulatively over the three-week period. Throughout training, six role-played scenes were used to evaluate the effects of treatment. In addition, three scenes (on which the subject received no training) were used to assess generalization from trained to untrained scenes.

The results for training scenes appear in Figure 7.1. Examination of the graph indicates that institution of social skills training for ratio of eye contact to speech duration resulted in marked changes in that behavior, but rates for number of words and number of requests remained constant. When social skills training was applied to number of words itself this behavior increased, while the rate for number of requests remained the same. Finally, when social skills training was directly applied to number of requests, marked changes were noted. Thus, the finding that each behavior changed markedly *when and only when* the treatment variable targeted each behavior provides evidence for the effectiveness of social skills training. Independence of the three behaviors and the absence of generalization effects from one behavior to the next facilitate interpretation of these data. On the other hand, had non-treated behaviors covaried following application of social skills training, unequivocal conclusions as to the controlling effects of the training could not have been reached without resorting to Kazdin and Kopel's (1975) solution to withdraw and reinstate the treatment.

It is notable that while overall assertiveness was not treated directly, independent ratings evinced gradual improvement over the three-week period, with treatment gains for all behaviors maintained in follow-up (see bottom of Figure 7.1). Examination of data for the *untreated* generalization scenes indicates that similar results were obtained, confirming that transfer of training occurred from treated to untreated items. Indeed, the patterns of data for Figures 7.1 and 7.2 are remarkably consistent.

A more recent example of a multiple baseline design across behaviors is provided in a study by Nock (2002) that examines the effects of a treatment package including modeling, graduated exposure and contingency management on increasing food consumption in a four-year-old boy with food phobia. The boy in this case consumed only water and protein drinks since the age of seven months, when he choked on baby food with chunks of solid food in it. His parents had tried repeatedly to introduce various foods and drinks without success, and several previous psychodynamic and occupational therapy interventions also had failed.

In this study, the parents learned and applied the modeling, graduated exposure and contingency management strategies in weekly therapy sessions and applied them at home. The dependent variable was number of servings of four different types of food consumed by the boy each week: fluids other than water (e.g., juice), soft foods (e.g., pudding), hard foods (e.g., cookies), and chewy foods (e.g., chicken). The treatment strategies were directed at each of these four types of foods one at a time using a multiple baseline design.

The results of this study, presented in Figure 7.3, show that the boy's consumption of fluids increased immediately after the treatment targeted this behavior (panel A), while the other three behaviors remained unchanged. Figure 7.3 shows a similar pattern for each of the other three behaviors (panels B-D), each increasing when and only when the treatment targeted that behavior, with increases in each behavior maintained at two- and six-month follow-up. Two additional aspects of this study are notable. First, there is a slight increase in consumption of chewy foods before the treatment targeted this behavior. This may have occurred because the parents began targeting this behavior before being

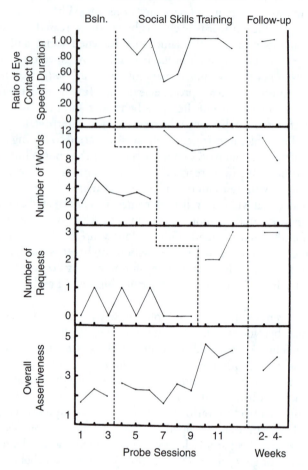

FIGURE 7.2 Probe sessions during baseline, social skills treatment, and follow-up for generalization scenes for Tom. A multiple baseline analysis of ratio of eye contact while speaking to speech duration, number of words, number of requests and overall assertiveness. (Figure 4, p. 191, from: Bornstein, M. R., Bellack, A. S., & Hersen, M. [1977]. Social-skills training for unassertive children: A multiple-baseline analysis. *Journal of Applied Behavior Analysis*, **10**, 183–195. Copyright 1977 by Society for the Experimental Analysis of Behavior. Reproduced by permission.)

instructed to do so by the experimenter. Although certainly understandable clinically, this pattern slightly decreases the strength of the findings. Second, an additional problem behavior, vomiting, was designated for study during the second baseline and a line mapping the frequency of this behavior appears in panel B. More specifically, the boy began vomiting on occasion after consuming soft foods (e.g., pudding, bread). The parents and clinician suspected that this

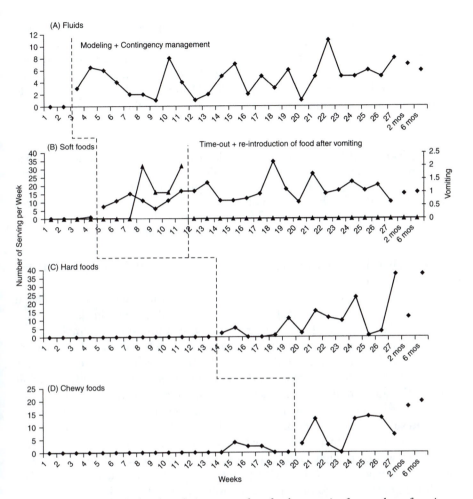

FIGURE 7.3 Multiple-baseline design across four food categories for number of servings per week and vomiting. *Note:* In all four graphs, the lines marked with diamonds represent the number of servings of each food type consumed each week. The line marked with triangles in Graph B represents the number of vomiting episodes each week. (Figure 1, p. 221, from: Nock, M. K. (2002). A multiple-baseline evaluation of the treatment of food phobia in a young boy. *Journal of Behavior Therapy and Experimental Psychiatry*, **33** (3–4), 217–225.)

behavior was somewhat under the boy's behavioral control, and so instituted a treatment variable of time-out plus re-introduction of soft food (i.e., extinction) whenever vomiting occurred. The initiation of this intervention is represented by the second vertical line in panel B, and as shown, led to an immediate cessation of vomiting. This last feature provides one example of how multiple baseline designs can be flexibly modified during the course of the study to address newly emerging problem behaviors.

In another example of a multiple baseline design across behaviors, a psychological measure (erectile strength as assessed with a penile gauge) was used to determine efficacy of covert sensitization in the treatment of a 21-year-old married male, admitted for inpatient treatment of exhibitionism and obscene phone calling (Alford, Webster, & Sanders, 1980). History of exhibitionism began at age 16, and obscene phone calling had taken place over the previous year. During baseline assessment:

> Audiotapes of both deviant and non-deviant sexual scenes were used to elicit arousal during physiological monitoring sessions. Deviant stimulus material included three tapes depicting various obscene phone calls . . . and three tapes of exhibitionism. . . . Two non-deviant tapes . . . that depicted normal heterosexual behavior were also used. . . . They consisted of verbal descriptions designed to closely parallel the patient's own sexual behavior and fantasy. (p. 17)

These included one taped description of intercourse with his wife and another with different sexual partners.

Covert sensitization sessions were conducted twice daily in the hospital at various locations. This treatment consisted of imaginally pairing the deviant sexual approach (i.e., obscene phone calls, exhibitionism) with aversive stimuli such as suffocation, nausea, and arrest. Each session involved 20 pairings of the deviant scenarios with aversive imagery. Following baseline assessment, covert sensitization was first applied to obscene phone calling and then to exhibitionism. In addition to therapist-conducted treatment sessions, the patient was instructed to use covert imagery on his own initiative whenever he experienced deviant sexual urges.

Results from this study are presented in Figure 7.4. During baseline evaluation, penile tumescence in response to tapes of obscene phone calling and exhibitionism was quite high. Similarly, tumescence was above 75% in response to nondeviant tapes of sexual activity with females other than his wife, but only slightly higher than 25% in response to lovemaking with his wife.

Institution of covert sensitization for obscene phone calling resulted in marked diminution in penile responsivity to taped descriptions of that behavior, eventually resulting in only a negligible response. However, such treatment also appeared to affect changes in penile response to one of the exhibitionism tapes (Ex. 1), even though that behavior had not yet been specifically targeted. (We have here an instance where the baselines are not independent from one another.) However, when treatment subsequently was directed to exhibitionism itself, there was marked diminution in penile response to tapes Ex. 2 and Ex. 3 in addition to continued decreases to tape Ex. 1. During the course of treatment, penile responsivity to nondeviant heterosexual interactions remained high, increasing considerably with respect to lovemaking with the wife.

It is notable that "the patient was preloaded with 36 oz of beer 90 to 60 minutes prior to Assessments 10 and 11" (Alford et al., 1980, p. 19). This was incorporated because the subject claimed that alcohol had disinhibited deviant

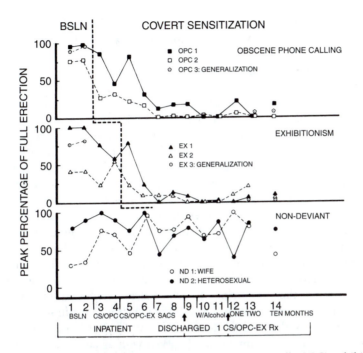

FIGURE 7.4 Percentage of full erection to obscene phone call (OPC) exhibitionistic (EX), and heterosexual stimuli (ND) during baseline, treatment, and follow-up phases. (Figure 1, p. 20, from: Alford, G. S., Webster, J. S., & Sanders, S. H. [1980]. Covert aversion of two interrelated deviant sexual practices: Obscene phone calling and exhibitionism. A single case analysis. *Behavior Therapy,* **11,** 13–25. Copyright 1980 by Association for the Advancement of Behavior Therapy. Reproduced by permission.)

sexuality. However, experimental data did not seem to confirm this. One-, two-, and 10-month follow-up assessments indicated that all gains were maintained, with the exception of decreased penile responsivity to taped descriptions of intercourse with the wife. In addition, 10-month collateral information from the subject's wife, parents, and attorney, as well as police, court, and telephone company records revealed no incidents of sexual deviance.

Our illustration reveals a clinically successful intervention evaluated through the multiple baseline design. However, because of some correlation between the first two baselines (obscene phone calling and exhibitionism) the experimental control of the treatment over targeted behaviors remains unclear. Retrospectively, a more elegant experimental demonstration might have ensued if the experimenters had temporarily withdrawn treatment from the second baseline and then reinstated it (in B-A-B fashion), in order to show the specific controlling power of the aversive strategy. However, from the clinical standpoint, given the length of the disorder, it is most likely that the aversive intervention was responsible for ultimate change.

A variation on the multiple baseline design across behaviors in which a changing criterion design was used in applying treatment to each behavior was illustrated by Rassau and Arco (2003). The experimenters tested the effect of a internet-based administration of cognitive behavior therapy (CBT) on three school-related behaviors in an undergraduate student experiencing academic difficulties. The target behaviors in this study were hours of study per day, number of pages read per day, and quality of note-taking per day (scored using standard scoring criteria with greater points awarded for factors such as the use of subheadings, etc.). The treatment variable was administered 6 times per week in 45-minute sessions over a 57-day period. The treatment first targeted hours of study per day, then number of pages read, then points for note-taking, with the target criterion for each behavior increasing over the course of the intervention.

The results of this study are presented in Figure 7.5. As shown, in the top panel, hours of study increased in variability following the initiation of the treatment variable and performance far exceeded the criterion level on most days with a sharp increase several days into the treatment phase, which then immediately decreased. Similarly, there is a sharp increase in the second behavior, number of pages read, during the baseline period, which also then decreased. Both of these patterns suggest the treatment variable did not exert a controlling influence over these behaviors in the early course of the study, but rather the behaviors increased due to the assignment due (marked with asterisks) at that time. It is notable, however, that after the first assignment performance on both of the first two behaviors closely matched the established criterion, and increased commensurate with increases in the criterion level, suggesting a controlling influence of the treatment variable. Similarly, the third behavior, points for note taking, increased substantially when the treatment variable was directed at this behavior, providing further support for the intervention.

A notable limitation of this study is the reliance on self-report of behavior over the course of the study, which introduces questions about the accuracy and validity of the data collected. Although the early stages of this study did not provide strong support for the effectiveness of this intervention, the measurement of an extraneous factor that likely influenced these behaviors (i.e., assignment due dates)—which was a nice feature of this study—and the subsequent increases in performance and confirmation to the established criterion levels increases the strength of the findings.

An excellent, early example of a multiple baseline design across behaviors in which treatment was applied to entire group of subjects was provided by Barton, Guess, Garcia, and Baer (1970). Sixteen severely and profoundly retarded males served as subjects in an experiment designed to improve their mealtime behaviors through the use of time-out procedures. Several undesirable behaviors were selected as targets for study during preliminary observations. They included *stealing* (taking food from another resident's tray), *fingers* (eating food with the fingers that should have been eaten with utensils), *messy utensils* (e.g., using a utensil to push food off the dish, spilling food), and what was termed

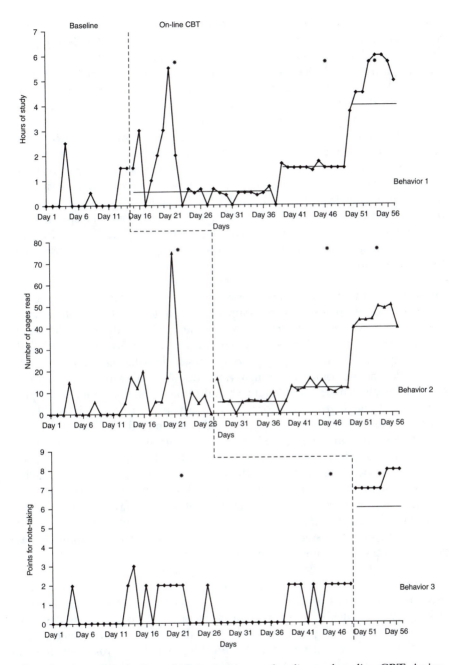

FIGURE 7.5 Participant's study behaviors across baseline and on-line CBT. Assignment due dates are indicated by asterisks. (Figure 1, p. 380, from: Rassau, A., & Arco, L. (2003). Effects of chat-based on-line cognitive behavior therapy on study related behavior and anxiety. *Behavioural and Cognitive Psychotherapy,* **31,** 377–381.)

pigging (eating spilled food from the floor, a tray, etc.; placing mouth directly over food without the use of a utensil). Observations of these behaviors were made 5 days per week during the noon and evening meals by using a time-sampling procedure. Independent observations were also obtained as reliability checks. The treatment—time-out—involved removing the subject from the dining area for the remainder of a meal or for a designated time period contingent upon his evidencing undesirable mealtime behavior.

After 6 days of baseline assessment, the treatment was applied to *stealing*. Time-out contingencies for *fingers, messy utensils,* and *pigging* were then applied in sequence, each time maintaining the contingency in force for the previously treated behavior. During the application of time-out for *fingers* the contingency involved time-out from the entire meal for 11 subjects, but only 15 seconds time-out for five of the subjects. This differentiation was made in response to the nursing staff's concerns that a complete time-out contingency for the five subjects might jeopardize their health. Time-out procedures for *messy utensils* and *pigging* were limited to 15 seconds per infraction for all 16 subjects.

The results of this study are presented in Figure 7.6. Examination of the graph indicates that when time-out was applied to *stealing* and *fingers*, rates for these behaviors decreased. However, application of time-out to *fingers* also resulted in a concurrent increase in the rate for *messy utensils*. But subsequent application of time-out for *messy utensils* affected a decrease in rate for that behavior. Finally, application of time-out for *pigging* proved successful in reducing its rate.

Independence of the target behaviors was observed, with the exception of *messy utensils*, which increased in rate when the time-out contingency was applied to *fingers*. Although group data for the 16 subjects were presented, it would have been desirable if the authors had presented data for individual subjects. Unfortunately, the time-sampling procedure used by Barton et al. (1970) precluded obtaining such information. However, this factor should not overshadow the clinical and social significance of this study, in that (1) mealtime behaviors improved significantly; (2) a result of improved mealtime behaviors was a concomitant improvement in staff morale, facilitating more favorable interactions with the subjects; and (3) staff beyond those involved with the study subjects were sufficiently impressed with the results of this study to begin to implement similar mealtime programs for their own residents.

It is notable that studies demonstrating behavior change for an entire group of subjects can be very useful; however, in co-opting behavior analytic procedures, one must be careful to present as much individual data as possible. Whenever group data are presented, all of the problems of averaging described in previous chapters apply to the obtained data. That is, some subjects could show the very steady changes apparent in the group data across measurement sessions, whereas others might demonstrate opposite or cyclic patterns. Presenting data in this way does not allow one the option of examining sources of variability (e.g., treatment moderators) where it might be important. Moreover, when it is not clear how many individuals changed in clinically significant ways, estimates of the replicability of the procedures used across individuals and iden-

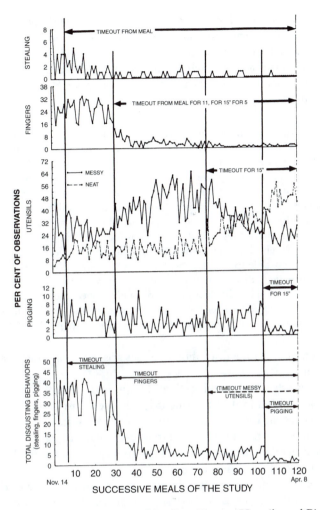

FIGURE 7.6   Concurrent group rates of Stealing, Fingers, Utensils, and Pigging behaviors, and the sum of Stealing, Fingers, and Pigging (Total Disgusting Behaviors) through the baseline and experimental phases of the study. (Figure 1, p. 80, from: Barton, E. S., Guess, D., Garcia, E., & Baer, D. M. [1970]. Improvement of retardates' mealtime behaviors by time-out procedures using multiple baseline techniques. *Journal of Applied Behavior Analysis*, **3**, 77–84. Copyright 1970 by Society for Experimental Analysis of Behavior, Inc. Reproduced by permission.)

tification of individual predictors of success and failure are not possible (see chapter 10). In summary, when using group designs the presentation of as much individual data as possible is strongly recommended.

In an interesting solution to the problem of averaging when a number of subjects are treated simultaneously, Kelly (1980) argued for the use of a design referred to as the *simultaneous replication design*, which can be used within a multiple baseline format. The specific example cited involves application of social skills training *in group format* to 6 subjects for three components of social skill on a time-lagged basis. However, although applied on a group basis, behavioral assessment of each subject follows each group session. Thus individual data for each treated subject are available and can be plotted *individually* (see Figure 10.6). As noted by Kelly (1980):

> The use of this group multiple baseline-simultaneous replication design is particularly useful in applied clinical settings for several reasons. First, it eliminates the need for elaborate and/or untreated control groups to establish group treatment effects and rule out many alternative hypotheses which cannot be adequately controlled by other one group designs. Second, by analyzing the social skills behavior change effects of a *group* treatment procedure, it is possible to demonstrate more compellingly cost- or time-effectiveness than if each subject had been laboriously handled as an *individually treated* case study using single subject procedures. Because subjects all received the same group training but are individually evaluated after each group, it is possible to examine "within subject" response to group treatment with greater specificity than in "between groups" designs. Since data for each subject in the training group is individually measured and graphed, each subject also serves as a simultaneous replication for the training procedure and provides important information on the generality (or specificity) of the treatment. (pp. 206–207)

(See also section 10.2 for a discussion of issues arising from this strategy relevant to replication.)

Although the multiple baseline design is frequently used in clinical research when withdrawal of treatment is considered to be detrimental to the patient, on occasion withdrawal procedures have been instituted following the sequential administration of treatment to target behaviors (e.g., Russo & Koegel, 1977). If treatment is reintroduced after a withdrawal, a powerful demonstration of its controlling effects can be documented.

A recent example of a multiple baseline design across behaviors with an embedded withdrawal (A-B-A-B) design is provided in a study by Clayton, Helms, and Simpson (2006). In this study, the experimenters tested the effectiveness of active prompting (i.e., posting street signs) on decreasing cell phone use and increasing seat belt use among motorists passing through a four-way intersection. The primary dependent variables in this study were cell phone use and cell phone hang-ups while driving through the intersection, as well as seat belt use and buckling up while driving through the intersection. Using a multiple baseline design across behaviors, the experimenters tested the effectiveness of first posting a sign asking motorists to hang up their cell phones (i.e., "Please Hang Up, I Care"), and subsequently to buckle their seat belts (i.e., "Please Buckle Up, I Care"). Each of these behaviors was recorded by independent observers and scored with strong inter-observer agreement (>95% for all behaviors).

The results of this study are presented in Figure 7.7. As shown, cell phone use occurred at a fairly stable rate of 6% during the baseline phase, with 0% of

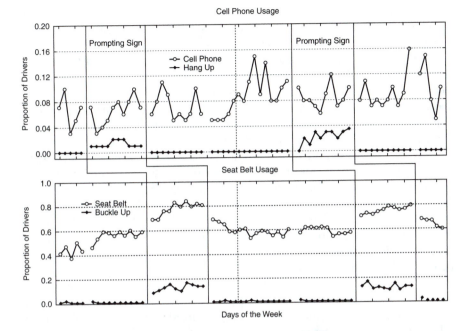

FIGURE 7.7   Proportion of drivers using cell phones and hanging up, and drivers wearing seat belts and buckling up during the study. The broken phase line at the midpoint indicates when the second season began, about 1 year later. Open circles: proportion of drivers using a cell phone upon approaching the observers (top) and proportion of drivers wearing a seat belt (bottom). Closed circles: proportion of drivers hanging up upon approaching the observers (top) and proportion who fastened their seat belts (bottom). Open circles represent a change in behavior over time, and closed circles represent an immediate response to the displayed prompt. (Figure 2, p. 345, from: Clayton, M., Helms, B., & Simpson, C. (2006). Active prompting to decrease cell phone use and increase seat belt use while driving. *Journal of Applied Behavior Analysis*, **39** (3), 341–349.)

motorists actually hanging up their cell phone when they passed through the intersection. The percentage of motorists hanging up their cell phone increased following posting of the cell phone hang up sign, although the overall rate of cell phone use remained unchanged. The experimenters then instituted a withdrawal of the hang up sign, during which the rate of hang ups returned to 0%, followed by a subsequent reinstatement of the hang up sign, which again increased the rate of hang ups. The hang up sign was removed in the final phase, again returning the rate of hang ups to 0%. Thus, the experimenters used an A-B-A-B-A design for the cell phone behaviors to demonstrate the controlling effect of the intervention on cell phone hang ups, with minimal impact on overall cell phone use.

Notably, the use of seat belts and rate of buckling up were not affected during the phases involving posting of the hang up sign. Instead, both buckling up and overall seat belt use increased when and only when the buckle up sign was posted (bottom panel of Figure 7.7). The experimenters again used an A-B-A-B-A design for seat belt use and buckling up to demonstrate the controlling influence of active prompting (i.e., posting street signs) on these behaviors.

In summary, this study by Clayton, Helms, and Simpson (2006) illustrates the use of the multiple baseline design across behaviors, demonstrating clear independence of target behaviors. Sequential application of active prompting showed the controlling effects of the intervention. Additional experimental manipulations (withdrawal and reintroduction of the intervention) further confirmed the controlling effects of the treatment.

In our final example of a multiple baseline design across behaviors, the effect of booster sessions on subject behavior (i.e., rather than a full withdrawal or reversal design) subsequent to deterioration during follow-up was tested (Van Hasselt, Hersen, Kazdin, Simon, & Mastantuono, 1983). The subject in this case was a blind female child attending a special school for the blind. Baseline assessment of social skills through role playing revealed deficiencies in posture and gaze, a hostile tone of voice, inability to make requests for new behavior, and a general lack of social skills (see Figure 7.8).

The sequential and cumulative application of social skills training resulted in marked improvements in role-played performance, thus documenting the controlling effects of the treatment. However, data for the four-week post-treatment follow-up revealed a decrement for two of the four specific behaviors targeted: gaze and requests for new behavior. Examination of Figure 7.8 shows that treatment provided in booster sessions for those behaviors resulted in a renewed improvement, extending through the eight- and 10-week follow-up assessments. Thus, our multiple baseline analysis permitted a clear assessment of which behaviors were maintained after treatment in addition to those that required booster treatment. This study again highlights the specificity and flexibility afforded by the use of single-case experimental designs.

Multiple baseline design across subjects

Our first example of the multiple baseline strategy across subjects is a fairly basic application of this design taken from the child literature. Miltenberger and colleagues (Miltenberger et al., 2005) tested the effectiveness of teaching firearm safety skills on the prevention of playing with guns found in the home or school setting. Participants in this study were 10 children recruited from a local pre-school program. The dependent variable in this study was demonstration of firearm safety skills scored on a four-point scale (e.g., 0 = touches gun, 1 = doesn't touch gun, 2 = leaves area, 3 = tells adult about gun) in response to finding a gun at home or at school. The guns were unloaded and placed in designated locations by the experimenters where the children were expected to find them, and the children's behavior was observed and rated by hidden video-camera and/or an experimenter out of sight from the child. Inter-observer agreement on the dependent variable was 100%. The treatment variable was firearm

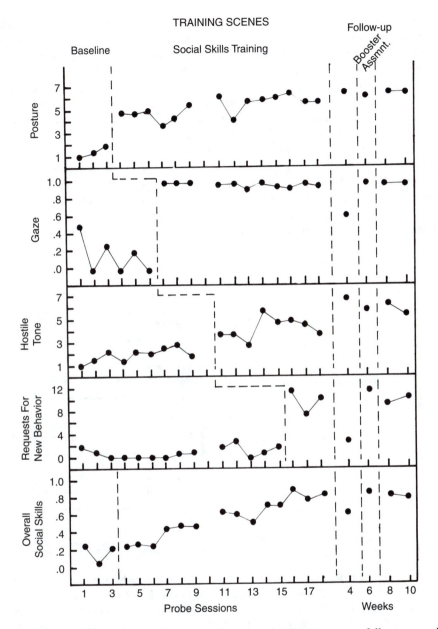

FIGURE 7.8 Probe sessions during baseline, social skills treatment, follow-up, and booster assessments for training scenes for S1. A multiple baseline analysis of posture, gaze, hostile tone, requests for new behavior, and overall social skill. (Figure 1, p. 201, from: Van Hasselt, V. B., Hersen, M., Kazdin, A. E., Simon, J., & Mastantuono, A. K. [1983]. Social skills training for blind adolescents. *Journal of Visual Impairment and Blindness*, **75**, 199–203. Copyright 1983. Reproduced by permission.)

safety training that used instructions, modeling, rehearsal, and feedback to teach the children not to touch firearms and to inform an adult if a firearm is ever found. Over the course of the study, the experimenters placed firearms in designated places at the children's school and home and observed the effects of the treatment, which was administered in a multiple baseline fashion across children.

The results of this study are presented in Figure 7.9. The first three children were observed over two baseline sessions and all touched the gun in each instance (i.e., scored a 0 on the safety skills scale). After introduction of the treatment, all three children showed substantial improvement on firearm safety, with results immediately and consistently going to 3 for Alan and Jessie, but with a one-session latency for Steph (who notably left the pre-school program after five sessions). The next three children were observed over three baseline sessions before receiving the treatment. Notably, they showed no improvement when the first three children received the intervention, but did show an improvement when the treatment was

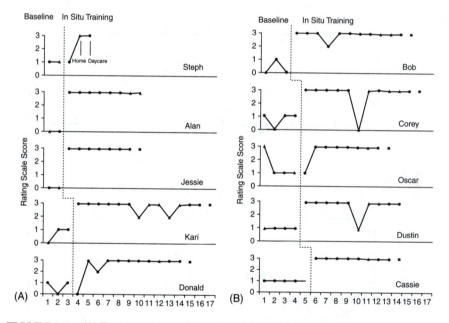

FIGURE 7.9 **(A)** Rating scale scores for 5 participants during baseline and in situ training phases. Circles are day-care assessments, triangles are home assessments, and squares are dyad assessments. The last home or day-care data point for all participants except Steph is a 3-month follow-up assessment. **(B)** Rating scale scores for 5 participants during baseline and in situ training phases. Circles are day-care assessments, triangles are home assessments, and squares are dyad assessments. The last home or day-care data point for all participants is a 3-month follow-up assessment. (Figure 1, p. 397, from: Miltenberger, R. G., Gatheridge, B. J., Scatterlond, M., Egemo-Helm, K. R., Johnson, B. M., Jastad, C., et al. (2005). Teaching safety skills to children to prevent gun play: An evaluation of in situ training. *Journal of Applied Behavior Analysis*, **38** (3), 395–398.)

directed at them, with Kari and Bob showing an immediate and sustained improvement to 3, but with a one-session latency for Donald. The next three children received the treatment after a four-session baseline and the last child after a five-session baseline. The results of this study by Miltenberger and colleagues (2005) clearly demonstrate that the children's behavior improved markedly when and only when they received the treatment, providing evidence for the effectiveness of this intervention. A three-month follow-up assessment was conducted for five of the 10 children and in each case maintenance of safety skills was demonstrated.

Miller and Kelley (1994) used an interesting variation of a multiple baseline strategy across subjects in their assessment of goal setting and contingency contracting on improving homework performance among four children (9–11 years old) who were at risk for academic problems due to poor homework performance. Among the dependent variables measured was accuracy of completed work (percentage of correct solutions on homework problems) and percentage of time spent on-task and off-task while engaged in homework after school each day. Accuracy was calculated by the child's parent each day, and on-task and off-task behaviors were carefully defined and observed by trained graduate and undergraduate raters with strong inter-observer agreement (97% for on-task and 87% for off-task behaviors). Treatment consisted of the experimenter teaching the child's parent goal setting and contingency contracting for homework assignments, and the parent managing the homework intervention with the child (see Miller & Kelley, 1994).

Data on homework accuracy are presented in Figure 7.10. As shown, improved performance only occurred when the treatment was directly applied to each child, thus documenting the controlling effects of treatment. Data clearly indicate that the four baselines were independent of one another. Moreover, additional confirmation of the controlling effects of treatment was noted when introduction of the treatment resulted in improved performance, followed by deterioration when withdrawn and renewed improvement when reinstated. Thus, for each child we have an A-B-A-B demonstration, but carried out sequentially and cumulatively across the four. In short, the study by Miller and Kelley (1994) is an excellent example of the combined use of the A-B-A-B design in multiple baseline fashion across subjects.

Recent technological advances have introduced exciting methodological innovations that can be incorporated into single-case experimental designs, and several recent examples have done so within the context of multiple baseline designs across subjects. As one recent example, Dallery and Glenn (2005) tested the effects of a new internet-based voucher reinforcement program on abstinence from cigarette smoking. Voucher reinforcement programs have been shown to be effective at decreasing smoking; however, such programs often rely on breath carbon monoxide (CO) output as a measure of smoking abstinence (with CO output < 4 parts per million [ppm] indicating abstinence). This is problematic because it requires in-person measurement in order to verify the authenticity of the CO sample.

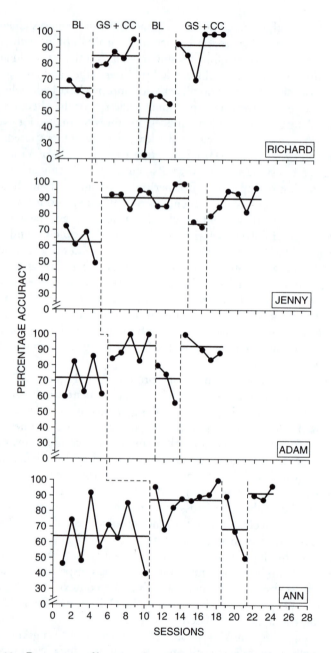

FIGURE 7.10   Percentage of homework completed accurately during baseline and treatment conditions across subjects. Sessions correspond to sequential school days (i.e., Mondays through Thursdays) on which subjects were assigned homework. Data were not collected on days on which homework was not assigned. (Figure 2, p. 80, from: Miller, D. L., & Kelley, M. L. (1994). The use of goal setting and contingency contracting for improving children's homework performance. *Journal of Applied Behavior Analysis, 27* (1), 73–84.)

To address this problem and thus increase the potential application of such protocols, Dallery and Glenn (2005) developed an internet-based protocol in which subjects submitted CO results via the internet (i.e., using a home-based monitor, web-cam, and e-mailing results to the experimenters) and were awarded vouchers via the internet as well (i.e., decreased CO levels were rewarded with monetary vouchers to an on-line shopping mall: www.amazon.com). Subjects in this study were four healthy adults with an 8–30 year history of smoking, who were currently smoking 20–40 cigarettes per day.

As displayed in Figure 7.11, each of the four subjects evidenced levels of CO consistent with cigarette smoking during the baseline phase. Next, a shaping program was administered sequentially across subjects in which each subject earned vouchers for increasingly lower levels of CO. As shown, in each case CO levels decreased during this phase. In the next phase, subjects received vouchers for smoking abstinence (i.e., CO < 4 ppm) and results indicate that three of the four subjects regularly met this criterion. During the next phase the reinforcement schedule was thinned, and finally there was a return to baseline.

Several aspects of these results are notable. First, there was a decrease in CO levels for the second subject during the baseline phase. This weakens the inferences that can be drawn about the controlling influence of the intervention in this case; however, the replication of decreased CO associated with presentation of the intervention across the three other participants provide much stronger evidence for the intervention than would be possible in a single A-B design. Second, the first subject showed a significant increase in smoking during the third (abstinence) phase. This pattern also weakens inferences that can be drawn about the effectiveness of the treatment; however, here the measurement of an extraneous factor that may have contributed to this increase—namely, the experience of significant family-related stress—provides some increased understanding about this increase. Third, although it would be nice clinically to see long-term maintenance of treatment effects during the final phase of the study, the increase in CO levels for the first and third subject as well as increased variability for the fourth, while not supporting the durability of behavior change, do provide some evidence for the controlling influence of the treatment variable. Overall, these results generally support the effectiveness of this internet-based treatment program—which has been further examined and compared with alternative treatment strategies by these authors (Glenn & Dallery, 2007), provide an illustration of the benefits of examining results at the level of each individual, highlight the potential usefulness of single-case designs for demonstrating the feasibility of a newly developed intervention (see also Choate, Pincus, Eyberg, & Barlow, 2005; Moras, Telfer, & Barlow, 1993), and also demonstrate the innovations possible in single-case experiments using recent technological advances.

Another example of a multiple baseline design across subjects that incorporates recent technological advances is provided by Ingvarsson and Hanley (2006). In this study, the experimenters tested the effectiveness of a fully computerized assessment and training tool designed to teach preschool teachers the names and faces of parents so that the teachers could greet the parents by name

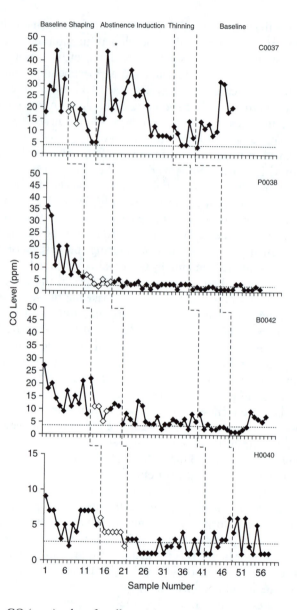

FIGURE 7.11 CO (ppm) values for all participants across baseline, shaping, abstinence induction, thinning, and return to baseline. The dashed horizontal line marks a reading of 4 ppm (4 ppm or below is considered abstinent). The open circles in the shaping condition indicate when the shaping criteria were met. The asterisk indicates the day when C0037 started to experience significant family-related stress. Note that Participant H0040 has a different y axis. (Figure 1, p. 354, from: Dallery, J., & Glen, I. M. (2005). Effects of an Internet-based voucher reinforcement program for smoking abstinence: A feasibility study. *Journal of Applied Behavior Analysis*, **38** (3), 349–357.)

when they dropped their children off at preschool each morning, thus improving parent-teacher communication. Subjects in this study were four student teachers (1 male, 3 female) working at a local preschool. The primary dependent variable was percentage of opportunities during which parents were greeted by name by each teacher (inter-observer agreement = 93%). The computerized training program was administered sequentially to each teacher using a multiple baseline design across subjects.

The results from this study are presented in Figure 7.12. As shown, although each of the four teachers had been instructed to greet parents by name each morning, they rarely did so during the baseline phase. For three of four teachers (1, 2, and 4) the percentage of greetings using parents' names increased markedly when and only when the treatment variable was applied to that teacher. The results from these first two phases suggest the treatment was effective for three of four teachers. In the case of teacher 3, due to lack of a response to the treatment variable, a feedback phase was quickly introduced during which the teacher's supervisor reviewed the previous data for that teacher, encouraged her to use parents' names, and praised that teacher for any instances of parental name use. These procedures were repeated daily for the duration of the feedback phase. The results reveal that addition of this feedback phase led to an increase in name use by teacher 3. The feedback phase was subsequently used to enhance treatment effects for teacher 1 and 4 also, whereas teacher 2 performed at a high level throughout the study and so no feedback phase was added. This study by Ingvarsson and Hanley (2006) provides another example of the flexibility possible using single-case designs and offers an additional illustration of how recent technological advances can enhance such designs, as well as improve behavioral interventions.

A classic example of a multiple baseline design across *groups* of subjects was provided by Epstein et al. (1981). The effects of a behavioral treatment program to increase the percentage of negative urine tests among 19 children with insulin dependent diabetes. Treatment aimed to decrease intake of simple sugars and saturated fats, decrease stress, increase exercise, and adjust insulin intake. Parents were taught to use praise and token economic techniques to reinforce improvements in the children's self-regulating behavior. When treatment began, 10 of the children (ages 8 to 12) were self-administering their insulin; the remaining 9 were receiving shots from their parents.

The primary dependent measure involved a biochemical determination of *any* glucose in the urine. As noted by Epstein et al. (1981), this ". . . suggests that greater than normal glucose concentrations are present in the blood, and the renal threshold has been exceeded" (p. 367). Such testing was carried out on a daily basis during baseline, treatment, and follow-up. The 19 families were assigned on a random basis to one of three groups, with treatment begun under time-lagged conditions two, four, or six weeks after initiation of the 12-week program.

Examination of Figure 7.13 indicates that percentage of negative urines was relatively low for each of the three groups during baseline. Institution of treatment resulted in marked improvements in percentage of negative urines, indicating the

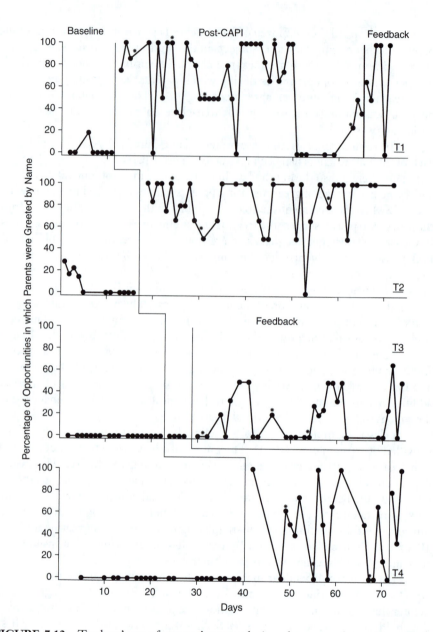

FIGURE 7.12 Teachers' use of parents' names during classroom observations. Each panel represents data from an individual teacher. Each data point represents the percentage of opportunities in which a teacher greeted a parent by name. A data point is not presented for days on which a teacher had no opportunities to greet parents. An asterisk denotes that a refresher training session was implemented. (Figure 2, p. 209, from: Ingvarsson, E. T., & Hanley, G. P. (2006). An evaluation of computer-based programmed instruction for promoting teachers' greeting of parents by name. *Journal of Applied Behavior Analysis,* **39** (2), 203–214.)

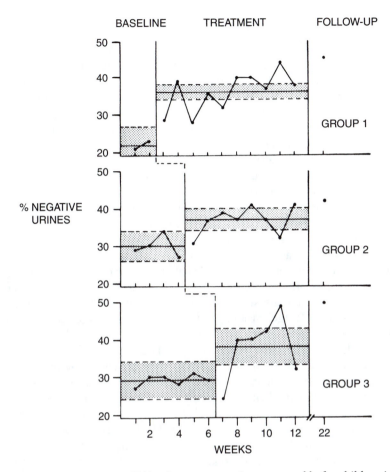

FIGURE 7.13   Percentage of 0% urine concentration tests weekly for children in each group. The mean and standard error of the mean for all the observations in each phase by group are represented by a solid and dotted line, respectively. (Figure 1, p. 371, from: Epstein, L. H., Beck, S., Figueroa, J., Farkas, G., Kazdin, A. E., Daneman, D., & Becker, D. [1981]. The effects of targeting improvements in urine glucose on metabolic control in children with insulin dependent diabetes. *Journal of Applied Behavior Analysis*, **14**, 365–375. Copyright 1981 by Society for Experimental Analysis of Behavior. Reproduced by permission.)

controlling effects of the strategy. Moreover, it appears that these gains were maintained post-treatment, as indicated by the follow-up assessment at 22 weeks.

In summary, Epstein et al. (1981) presented a powerful demonstration of the effects of a behavioral treatment over a biochemical dependent measure (that has serious health implications). From a design standpoint, this study is an excellent illustration of the multiple baseline strategy across small groups of subjects, suggesting how the particular experimental strategy can be used to evaluate treatments in the area of behavioral medicine. However, from a design standpoint, the aforementioned cautions associated with averaging data certainly apply.

Multiple baseline across settings

Our first example of a multiple baseline strategy across settings involves a recent study by Kay, Harchik and Luiselli (2006) that tests the effectiveness of a multi-component treatment package designed to reduce drooling in a 17-year-old high school student, George, diagnosed with autism and mental retardation. The boy had a long history of drooling since childhood that was causing problems at school (e.g., presence of saliva on school materials) and with peers (e.g., other students avoided the subject and complained about his drooling).

During baseline, George's drooling was monitored by his assigned academic aide, who counted the pools of saliva (i.e., saliva present on the surfaces of his immediate area measuring ≥ 1 inch in diameter) present in three different school locations each day: his classroom (three hours per day), community vocation site (two hours per day), and cooking class (one hour per day). Inter-observer agreement was 91–96% across all three sites. The aide wiped each saliva pool dry immediately after it was recorded. As shown in Figure 7.14, during baseline George produced an average of 6–14 pools of saliva per hour in the classroom and community settings, and between 8–16 pools of saliva per hour in cooking class.

Following baseline measurement and formulation of hypotheses about the factors maintaining George's drooling (i.e., skills deficit), George was administered an intervention including instructions, skill acquisition (i.e., swallowing and wiping his mouth), and differential reinforcement of other behavior (DRO; i.e., small edible treats were provided for dry mouth on periodic checks by the aide). This treatment was applied sequentially across settings, focusing initially on George's drooling in the classroom, then in the community setting, then in cooking class.

As shown in Figure 7.14, George's drooling in the classroom decreased substantially when the intervention was applied to that setting, but there was no change in drooling in the other two settings. However, drooling in the community and cooking class settings decreased when and only when the intervention targeted these settings. Behavior change was maintained when the period checks and associated reinforcement strategies were discontinued, demonstrating the maintenance of behavior change

A multiple baseline design across settings with an embedded withdrawal strategy (A-B-A-B) is demonstrated in a study by Singh, Dawson, and Gregory (1980) that tested treatment of hyperventilation in a 17-year-old girl diagnosed with profound mental retardation. The subject in this case suffered from epilepsy (controlled pharmacologically) and had a 6-year history of hyperventilation. Prior attempts to treat her symptoms, which included deep, heavy breathing, accompanied by a grunting noise and up-and-down head movements), were unsuccessful. These symptoms were observed in four separate settings of the residential unit of the state facility in which she lived: classroom, dining room, bathroom, and dayroom. Data were recorded in 10-second intervals throughout 30-minute sessions.

Baseline data were obtained for five sessions in the classroom, 10 in the dining room, 15 in the bathroom, and 20 in the dayroom. Then, under time-lagged conditions, treatment was introduced, removed, and reintroduced in each

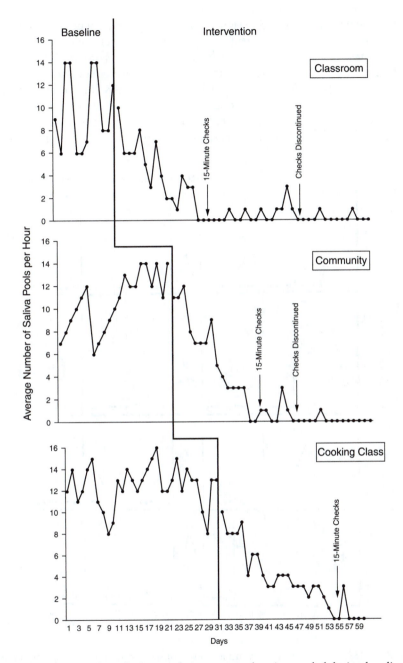

FIGURE 7.14 Number of saliva pools (average per hour) recorded during baseline and intervention phases. (Figure 1, p. 26, from: Kay, S., Harchik, A. E., & Luiselli, J. K. (2006). Elimination of drooling by an adolescent student with autism attending public high school. *Journal of Positive Behavior Interventions*, **8** (1), 24–28.)

setting—yielding an A-B-A-B design in each setting. Treatment consisted of the application of response-contingent aromatic ammonia held under her nose for three seconds whenever an instance of hyperventilation was observed. Finally, during the eight weeks of the generalization phase, nurses were requested to carry out the punishment procedure on an eight-hour-per-day basis. This is in contrast to original treatment that was carried out for only four 30-minute sessions per day.

Results of this study are presented in Figure 7.15. These data clearly indicate the controlling effects of the treatment, both in terms of its initial application on a

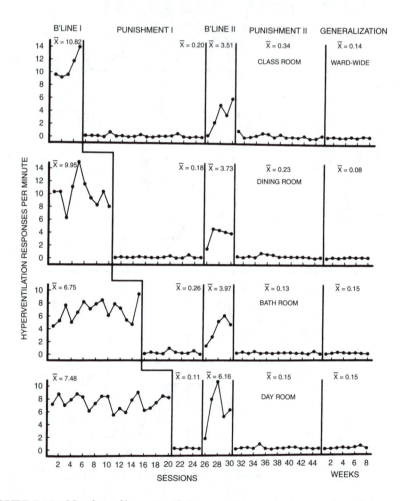

FIGURE 7.15 Number of hyperventilation responses per minute and condition means across experimental phases and settings. (Figure 1, p. 565, from: Singh, N. N., Dawson, J. H., & Gregory, P. R. [1980]. Suppression of chronic hyperventilation using response-contingent dramatic ammonia. *Behavior Therapy, 11,* 561–566. Copyright 1980 by Association for Advancement of Behavior Therapy. Reproduced by permission.)

time-lagged basis (baselines were independent) and when it was removed and reintroduced simultaneously in all four settings. Rate of hyperventilation episodes increased dramatically when the punishment contingency was removed in the second baseline and decreased to near zero levels when it was reintroduced. Moreover, the positive effects of treatment were prolonged and enhanced as a result of the more extensive punishment approach followed in the generalization phase.

Soenksen and Alper (2006) present an interesting application of a multiple baseline design across settings in which they target two behaviors within each setting. They tested a social skills training intervention presented in a story format to a five year-old boy, named TJ, with hyperlexia—a condition characterized by an ability to read far beyond one's comprehension, often accompanied with social deficits including poor eye contact and poor social communication skills. The treatment consisted of reading TJ and several of his classmates a story about a person who communicates with his friends by looking at them and saying their names. This story was read to TJ and his classmates each day, first immediately before recess, then before choice time (during which students could choose from various activities in the classroom), then before math time. The dependent variables in this study were TJ's daily frequency of (1) saying a peer's name and (2) looking at a peer's face when attempting to speak to that person (interobserver agreement = 94.3%).

The results of this study are presented in Figure 7.16. As shown, TJ very rarely engaged in either of the target behaviors during baseline. When the treatment variable was applied to recess, TJ's frequency of both saying peers' names and making eye-contact with them increased to match that of his peers' performance (represented by the solid horizontal line), and remained at that level during the maintenance phase. The frequency of these two behaviors also increased for TJ when the treatment variable was applied to choice time, and subsequently to math time, and in both instances TJ's behavior increased to match that of his peers.

Overall, the results of this study by Soenksen and Alper (2006) suggest this treatment was effective at increasing these two social skill behaviors across these three different settings. Several aspects of these findings warrant comment. First, although the data generally support independence of behavior across these three settings, the brief increases during the baseline phase of choice time and math time slightly weaken the case for independence and for the controlling influence of the intervention. However, given the brevity of the increases one could conclude that the intervention is supported overall. Second, a positive aspect of this study is the maintenance of behavior change, which extends out to follow-up for choice time and math time and highlights the durability of the improvements in social skills associated with this treatment.

A particularly socially relevant example of a multiple baseline design across settings that also measured two related behaviors but in addition included an embedded withdrawal (A-B-A) design was provided by Ludwig, Gray, and Rowell (1998). The experimenters tested the effects of moving recycling receptacles (and associated recycling signs) from hallways to classrooms (where beverages

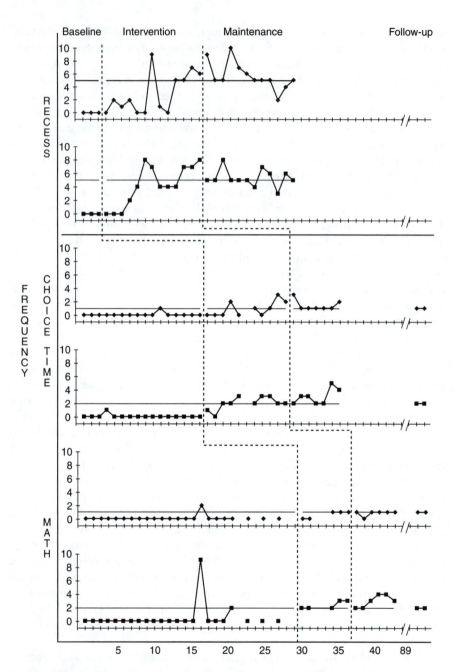

FIGURE 7.16 Frequency of saying a peer's name and looking at a peer's face across three different settings. (Figure 1, p. 41, from: Soenksen, P., & Alper, S. (2006). Teaching a young child to appropriately gain attention of peers using a social story intervention. *Focus on Autism and Other Developmental Disabilities*, **21** (1), 36–44.)

were typically consumed) in academic classrooms in two different buildings on: (1) percentage of recyclable aluminum cans placed in recycling receptacles and (2) percentage of cans thrown in trash containers—and thus not recycled). The results of this study are presented in Figure 7.17. As shown, during baseline cans were more often thrown away in trash containers than in recycling receptacles, and this was true across both buildings studied. After 10 days of baseline measurement, the treatment variable was administered in Building A, at which time the percentages of cans in each type of container switched, with the majority of cans now being thrown away in the recycling receptacles. There was no such change in Building B during this time; however, a similar change was observed

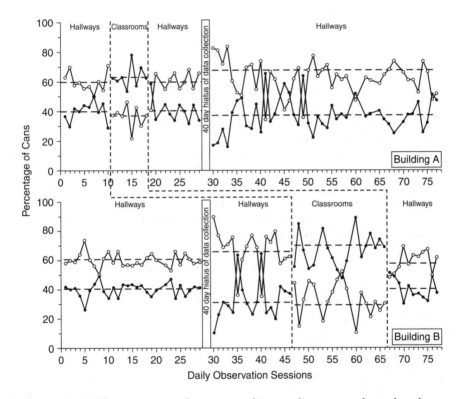

FIGURE 7.17 The percentage of cans counted in recycling receptacles and trash containers per day in Buildings A and B. Daily observation sessions were conducted Monday through Friday. Filled circles represent cans counted in recycling receptacles, and open circles represent cans counted in trash containers. Vertical dashed lines represent the phase changes. Thick dashed horizontal lines represent the mean number of cans counted in recycling receptacles for a given phase. Thin dashed and dotted horizontal lines represent the mean number of cans counted in trash containers for a given phase. (Figure 1, p. 685, from: Ludwig, T. D., Gray, T. W., & Rowell, A. (1998). Increasing recycling in academic buildings: A systematic replication. *Journal of Applied Behavior Analysis*, **31** (4), 683–686.)

in Building B when the treatment variable was administered in that setting (after a 40 day hiatus in both settings due to winter break), although with greater variability observed during both baseline and treatment phases in that setting.

Notably, there was a withdrawal of the treatment variable after 18 days in Building A and after 66 days in Building B and in both settings this resulted in a return to baseline levels of behavior, providing strong support for the controlling influence of the treatment variable. The A-B-A confirmation of the controlling power of the intervention adds substantially to documentation of the time-lagged contingency. Thus we have a very powerful demonstration of this treatment in a multiple baseline design across settings that incorporates A-B-A withdrawal features.

7.3. VARIATIONS OF MULTIPLE BASELINE DESIGNS

Nonconcurrent multiple baseline design

As noted in section 7.2, in the multiple baseline design across subjects, each individual targeted for treatment is exposed to the same environment. Treatment is delayed for each successive subject in time-lagged fashion because of the increased length of baselines required for each. The functional relationship between treatment and target behavior can be determined only when such treatment is applied to each subject in succession. Thus, since subjects are simultaneously available for assessment and treatment, this design is able to control for *history*, a possible experimental contaminant.

However, there are times when one is unable to obtain concurrent observations for several subjects, in that they may be available only in succession (e.g., as for less frequently observed conditions such as food phobia or hyperlexia). Following strictures of the multiple baseline design across subjects, this design ordinarily would not be considered appropriate under these circumstances. However, Watson and Workman (1981) have proposed an alternative—the *nonconcurrent multiple baseline design across individuals*:

> In this . . . design, the researcher initially determines the length of each of several baseline designs (e.g., 5, 10, 15 days). When a given subject becomes available (e.g., a client referred who has the target behavior of interest, and is amenable to the use of a specific treatment of interest), s(he) is randomly assigned to one of the predetermined baseline lengths. Baseline observations are then carried out; and assuming the responding has reached acceptable stability criteria, treatment is implemented at the pre-determined point in time. Observations are continued through the treatment phase, as in a simple A-B design. Subjects who fail to display stable responding would be dropped from the formal investigation; however, their eventual reaction to treatment might serve as useful replication data.

The logic of this variation is graphically portrayed in Figure 7.18. Of course, the major problem with this strategy is that the control for history

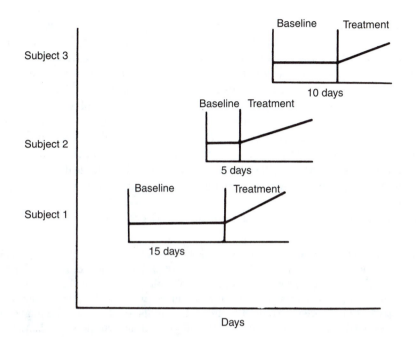

FIGURE 7.18   Hypothetical data obtained through use of a nonconcurrent multiple baseline design. (Figure 1, p. 258, from: Watson, P. J., & Workman, E. A. [1981]. The nonconcurrent multiple baseline across-individuals design: An extension of the traditional multiple baseline design. *Journal of Behavior Therapy and Experimental Psychiatry*, **12**, 257–259. Copyright 1981 by Pergamon. Reproduced by permission.)

(i.e., the ability to assess subjects concurrently) is greatly diminished. Therefore, we view this approach as less desirable than the standard multiple baseline design across subjects and suggest that it should be employed only when the standard approach is not feasible. Moreover, under such circumstances, an increased number of replications (i.e., number of subjects so treated) would enhance the confidence one has in the results. Of course, in the case of rarer disorders this may not be possible. For instance, Frank, Spirito, Stark and Owens-Stively (1997) report on the use of a nonconcurrent multiple baseline design across subjects to demonstrate the effectiveness of scheduled awakenings to eliminate childhood sleepwalking in three young children. The noncurrent multiple baseline design also has been proposed as an especially useful strategy in educational and other settings when more rigorous designs may not be feasible (Harvey, May, & Kennedy, 2004).

Multiple-probe technique

In all of the multiple baseline designs described above, baseline measurement has been continuous. However, there are situations in which repeated measurements will result in reactivity to assessment, in which change occurs simply as a result of repetition of the assessment (Kazdin, 2003). When treatment is subsequently introduced under these circumstances, changes may not be detected or may be masked due to alterations in the baseline as a function of reactivity. In addition, there are instances when continuous measurement is not feasible and when on the basis of prior experimentation an "*a priori* assumption of stability can be made" (Horner & Baer, 1978, p. 193). This being the case, instead of having 6, 9, and 12 assessments in three successive baselines, for example, these can be more interspersed, resulting in perhaps two, three, and four measurement points. An example of this approach is presented in Figure 7.19. Hypothetical probes in our example are represented by closed triangles, whereas actual reported data appear as open circles.

In commenting on this graph, Horner and Baer (1978) argued that:

> The multiple-probe technique, with probes every five days, would have provided one, two, three, and five probe sessions to establish baselines across the four subjects. The multiple-probe technique probably could have provided a stable baseline with five or fewer probe sessions for the subject who had 15 days of continuous baseline in the original study. The use of the multiple-probe procedure might have precluded the increase in irrelevant and competing behaviors by this subject because such behavior began to increase after the tenth baseline session. (p. 195)

It should be noted that several different researchers have applied this variant of baseline assessment in the multiple baseline design over the years (Baer & Guess, 1971; Schumaker & Sherman, 1970; Striefel, Bryan, & Aikins, 1974; Striefel & Wetherby, 1973). In each of these studies the design used was the multiple baseline design across behaviors. But, as in Figure 7.19, it could be across subjects, and it could also be used across settings.

If concerns about reactivity are the primary reason for using this variant, the probe technique should be continued when treatment is instituted. However, if feasibility is questionable in baseline or if an *a priori* assumption of baseline stability can be made, more frequent measurements during treatment may be desirable.

An example of a multiple baseline design across settings that used the multiple probe technique is provided by De La Paz (1999), in which the experimenter tested the effects of specific instructional procedures on 22 students' ability to write longer, more complete, and higher quality essays. Because the dependent variables in this study were derived from student essays, and it was not feasible for students to provide essays on a continuous basis, a multiple probe approach was employed in which students provided essays several times per week over the course of the study. Subjects recruited from three different classroom settings completed a minimum of six essays during the baseline phase, three of which were required to be completed within the week prior to administration of the treatment variable (i.e., the instructional training). All subjects then completed three

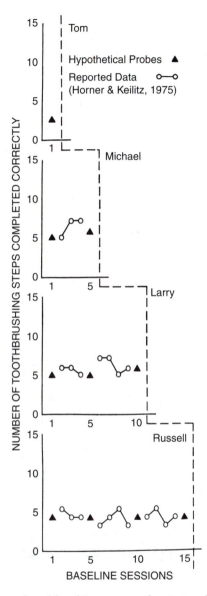

FIGURE 7.19 Number of toothbrushing steps conforming to the definition of a correct response across 4 subjects. (Figure 2, p. 194, from: Horner, R. D., & Baer, D. M. [1978]. Multiple-probe technique: A variation of the multiple baseline. *Journal of Applied Behavior Analysis*, **11**, 189–196. Copyright 1978 by Society for Experimental Analysis of Behavior. Reproduced by permission.)

essays within one week after receiving the treatment variable, and students from the first two classrooms completed a follow-up essay four weeks after the treatment variable. No follow-up was conducted for the third classroom because school ended within one week after the post-instruction essays were completed.

The results from this study regarding essay quality (coded by teachers blind to the study design and hypotheses) are presented in Figure 7.20. Data

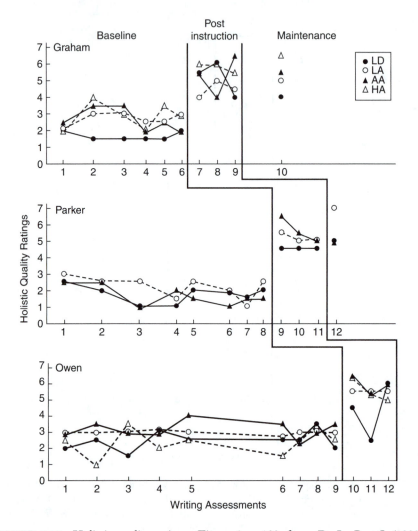

FIGURE 7.20   Holistic quality ratings. (Figure 4, p. 103, from: De La Paz, S. (1999). Self-regulated strategy instruction in regular education settings: Improving outcomes for students with and without learning disabilities. *Learning Disabilities Research & Practice,* **14** (2), 92–106.)

from each classroom are averaged across subjects; however, subjects in each classroom were classified into subgroups based on cognitive ability in order to examine whether effects of the treatment variable differ among those with a learning disability relative to those classified as low-achieving, average-achieving, and high-achieving. As shown, writing quality was fairly stable for all subgroups in all three classroom settings across the baseline phase. The treatment variable was administered in the first classroom after six probes, at which time writing quality increased markedly for all subgroups in this classroom, with no changes in the other classrooms. Similar improvements in writing quality were observed when and only when the treatment variable was administered to subjects in the second and third classrooms, supporting the effectiveness of the instructional training session. The improvements observed were maintained at follow-up.

The probe technique can be quite useful in a number of instances. However, as in the case of the nonconcurrent multiple baseline design, it should not be employed as a substitute for continuous measurement when that is feasible, as data accrued from use of probe measures are *suggestive* rather than confirmatory of the controlling effects of a given treatment.

7.4. ISSUES IN DRUG EVALUATIONS

With the exception of the multiple baseline design across subjects, the multiple baseline strategies are often not well suited for the evaluation of pharmacological agents on behavior. For example, at this point in time it is quite unlikely that any drugs will have the specificity of action to, within the same person, sequentially change different behaviors or even to sequentially change the same behavior across different settings. In this regard, psychological interventions are currently far superior to pharmacological interventions.

However; it would be possible to apply *different drugs* under time-lagged conditions to *separate behaviors* following baseline placebo administrations for each. However, such a design would involve a radical departure from the basic assumptions underlying the multiple baseline strategy across behaviors and would only permit very tentative conclusions based on separate A_1-B designs for each targeted behavior. In addition, the possible interactive effects of drugs might obfuscate specific results. Indeed, the interaction design (see chapter 6) is better suited for evaluation of combined effects of therapeutic strategies.

Overall, of the three multiple baseline design strategies currently in use, the multiple baseline design across subjects is most readily adaptable to drug evaluations. The application of such designs could be most useful when withdrawal procedures (return to A_1—baseline placebo) are unwarranted for either ethical or clinical considerations, such as in the case of suicidal or self-injurious behaviors. Using this type of strategy across matched subjects, baseline administration of a placebo (A_1) could be followed by the sequential administration (under time-lagged conditions) of an active drug (B). Thus a series of A_1-B (quasi-experimental) designs would result, with inferences made in accordance with changes observed when the B (drug) condition was applied.

Many other design options are possible in the application of the multiple baseline design across subjects when evaluating pharmacological effects. For example, Breuning and colleagues (1980) used a multiple baseline design across subjects (small groups) to evaluate the effects of drug, placebo, and response cost conditions. This yields a B (drug), A_1 (placebo), C (response cost) design. Subjects were hospitalized individuals diagnosed with mental retardation who displayed inappropriate behaviors. After three weeks on active neuroleptic drugs, Subjects 12, 15, and 16 were switched to placebo for 10 weeks. After six weeks on active neuroleptic drugs, Subjects 13 and 19 were switched to placebo for seven weeks. Finally, after nine weeks on active neuroleptic drugs, Subjects 14 and 17 were switched to placebo for seven weeks.

The results of this study are presented in Figure 7.21. Examination of drug and placebo data reveals no apparent improvements in inappropriate behavior. However, as might be expected, the switch to placebo for Subject 18 led to an increase in inappropriate behavior, suggesting at least some controlling effects of the drug. When response-cost procedures were instituted in Week 14 for Subjects 12, 13, 15, 16, and 18, and in Week 17 for Subjects 14 and 17, marked improvements in appropriate behavior were observed, beginning almost immediately. Thus, this rather complicated experimental analysis confirmed the efficacy of response cost procedures under time-lagged conditions, but only when the contingency was directly applied. Both neuroleptic drugs and placebo generally seemed to be ineffective.

In this type of drug evaluation it is important to underscore that the prolonged placebo phases are important in that they provide a needed "wash-out" period for possible carryover effects of drugs. This, of course, would have been much more critical had neuroleptic drugs substantially decreased the behavior targeted for change (i.e., inappropriate behavior).

An alternative use of the multiple baseline design in drug evaluations is one in which the investigator tests the effectiveness of combined treatment relative to using either drug treatment or psychological treatment alone. As an example of such a design, Bach, Barlow, and Winze (2004) used a multiple baseline design to test the effectiveness of adding cognitive-behavioral treatment to administration of Sildenafil on erectile dysfunction in a series of six heterosexual couples. This study revealed large and consistent treatment gains associated with administration of cognitive-behavioral treatment above and beyond the effects of Sildenafil (see chapter 10 for further description of this study). Taken together, these studies of drug evaluations provide only a few illustrations of the many variations on the multiple baseline design that can be used to study the effects of psychological and pharmacological treatments on behavior.

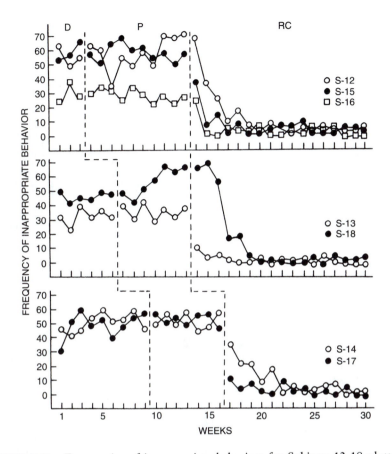

FIGURE 7.21   Frequencies of inappropriate behaviors for Subjects 12-18 plotted as total occurrences per week (summed daily interval totals). During the D condition, the subjects received their drug; during the P condition, the subjects received a placebo, were no longer receiving their drug, and the response cost procedure was not in effect. Drugs were discontinued during the first 3 weeks of the P condition. During the RC condition, the response cost procedure was in effect, and the subjects were not receiving their drug. The dotted vertical lines separate the conditions. (Figure 2, p. 261, from: Breuning, S. E., O'Neill, M. J., & Ferguson, D. G. [1980]. Comparison of psychotropic drug, response cost, and psychotropic drug plus response cost procedures for controlling institutionalized mentally retarded persons. *Applied Research in Mental Retardation*, **1**, 253–268. Copyright 1980. Reproduced by permission.)

CHAPTER 8

ALTERNATING TREATMENTS DESIGN

8.1. INTRODUCTION

As efficacious and effective treatment options are identified (Kazdin & Weisz, 2003; Nathan & Gorman, 2002), the primary questions of the clinical researcher shift from "what works?" to "what works for this particular person?" The most common methodological approach used to address this question has been the traditional group-based research strategy in which either: (a) a single group is administered a treatment and the researcher tests what factors moderate clinical change, or (b) subjects are randomly assigned to two or more treatment conditions and in addition to the relative outcome of the treatments being compared the researcher also tests what factors moderate clinical change. A major limitation to both approaches is that the use of group averages introduces problems in attempting to generalize results from the group average to the individual subjects, as discussed in chapter 2.

To avoid problems with averaging and with inter-subject variability, a better solution would be to administer each treatment to each person. In fact, this strategy would provide one of the most elegant controls for most threats to internal validity—or the extent to which clinical change can be attributed to the treatment variable rather than extraneous factors such as history, maturation, or regression to the mean (Campbell & Stanley, 1966; Cook & Campbell, 1979; Kazdin, 2003; Shadish et al., 2001). Statements about external validity—the generality of findings observed in one subject to other similar subjects—must be made through the more usual process of replication and "logical generalization" (see chapters 2 and 10).

The *alternating treatments design* (ATD; Barlow & Hayes, 1979) is an experimental design that accomplishes this goal. As the name implies, the basic strategy involved in this design is the rapid alternation of two or more treatments or conditions within a single subject. *Rapid* does not necessarily mean quickly within a fixed period of time; as, for example, every hour or every day. In applied research, rapid might mean that each time the client is seen he or she would receive an alternative treatment. For example, if an experimenter were comparing treatments A and B in a client seen weekly, he or she might apply Treatment

A one week and Treatment B the next. If the client were seen monthly, alternations would be monthly. This is in clear contrast to the usual A-B-A withdrawal design where after a baseline the experimenter would need at least three, and usually more, consecutive data points measuring the effect of Treatment A in order to examine any trends toward improvement. For a client seen weekly, at least three weeks would be needed to establish the trend.

Given that the experimenter is interested in comparing two or more treatments rather than in simply showing a trend toward improvement over time, the experimenter does not merely plot the data by connecting data points for Weeks 1, 2, 3, and so on. Instead, the experimenter examines the data by connecting all the data points measuring the effects of Treatment A and then connects all the data points measuring the effects of Treatment B. If, over time, these two series of data points separate (e.g., Treatment B produces greater improvement than Treatment A), then one could say with some certainty that one treatment is more effective. Naturally, these results would then require replication on additional clients with the same problem. Such hypothetical data are plotted in Figure 8.1 for a client who was treated and assessed weekly.

The experimenter should not proceed in a simple A-B-A-B-A-B-A-B fashion, but rather should randomize the order of introduction of the treatments to control for sequential confounding, or the possibility that introducing Treatment A first might bias the results in favor of Treatment A. Notice in the hypothetical data presented in Figure 8.1 that Treatments A and B are introduced in a

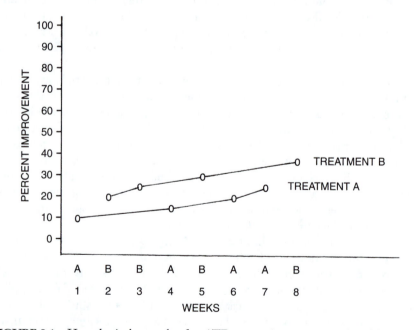

FIGURE 8.1 Hypothetical example of an ATD comparing treatments A and B.

relatively random fashion. Thus, a clinician treating a client using this approach might administer the treatments in an A-B-B-A-B-A-A-B fashion, as in the hypothetical data. For a client in an office setting, these treatment occasions might be twice a week, with the experiment taking a total of 4 weeks. For a child in a school setting, one might alternate treatments 4 times a day, and the experiment would be completed in a total of 2 days. Introducing and alternating treatments in a random fashion, as well as other procedural considerations, will be discussed more fully in section 8.2. In summary, this design requires the comparison of two separate series of data points. For this reason, this experimental design has also been described as falling within a general strategy referred to as *between-series*, where one is comparing results between two separate series of data points. On the other hand, A-B-A withdrawal designs, described in chapters 5 and 6, look at data *within* the same series of data points, and therefore the strategy has been described as *within-series* (see Hayes, Barlow, & Nelson-Gray, 1999).

History and terminology

The ATD strategy has been used for many years; however, a confusing array of terminology has delayed widespread understanding and use of this design. In the first edition of this book, we termed this strategy a *multiple schedule design*. Others have termed the same design a *multi-element baseline design*, *a randomization design*, and *a simultaneous treatment design*. Below we provide a brief historical review of the different terms used to describe the ATD strategy so that the reader can be clear on how and why these different terms have been used.

Sidman (1960) initially used the term *multi-element manipulation* to describe this design. Following this early work, some researchers have continued to use the term *multi-element design* when referring to this strategy (e.g., Neef, McCord, & Ferreri, 2006). Others have used the term *multiple schedule* to refer to this design (e.g., Agras et al., 1969; Leitenberg, 1973). These procedures and terminology were derived directly from basic behavioral research laboratories in which researchers were attempted to apply operant conditioning procedures to the treatment of human behavioral problems. Thus, the term *multiple schedule*, implies not only a distinct reinforcement schedule as one of the treatments, but also a distinct stimulus that allows subjects to discriminate as to when each of the two or more conditions will be in effect. However, in recent years it has become clear that signs or signals functioning as discriminative stimuli (S^D) are either an inherent part of the treatment, and therefore require no further consideration, or are not needed. For example, alternating a pharmacological agent with a placebo, using at ATD design, would be perfectly legitimate, but each drug would not require a discriminative stimulus. In fact, this would be undesirable; hence, the usual double-blind experimental strategies in drug research (see chapter 6). For this reason, the more appropriate analogy within the basic behavioral laboratories would be a mixed schedule rather than a multiple schedule, since a mixed schedule does not have discriminative stimuli. The term *schedule* implies a distinct reinforcement schedule associated with each treatment. Although some studies, particularly those testing operant conditioning procedures do indeed use multiple schedules of reinforcement (e.g., Hagopian, Bruzek, Bowman, & Jennett, 2007; Tiger, Hanley, & Heal, 2006), many and perhaps most specific treatments under investigation do not contain different schedules of reinforcement, and so the terms *multiple schedule* and *mixed schedule* are not really appropriate more generally.

The term *randomization design* originated from a somewhat different perspective. Edgington (1966, 1972) used this term to describe his variation of a time series approach amenable to statistical analysis. He was most interested in exploring statistical procedures applicable to randomly alternated treatments. In this respect he continued a tradition begun by R. A. Fisher (1925), who explored the abilities of a lady to discriminate tea prepared in two different ways. Edgington emphasized the randomness of the alternation as well as the number of alternations in developing his statistical arguments. While these and other statistical approaches discussed below are useful and valuable, they are not essential to the logic of the design in our view.

A final term sometimes used to describe the ATD strategy is the *simultaneous treatment design*. However, this term is a bit confusing because there is actually an infrequently used design in which two or more treatments are actually available simultaneously. Because the treatments are presented simultaneously, what happens is that the subject "chooses" a preferred treatment or condition. Furthermore, this design has also been called the *simultaneous treatment design* (Browning, 1967). In fact, the design has little application in applied research and has not been used since 1967. Therefore, it will be described only briefly at the end of this chapter (see section 8.6). Kazdin (1982) (2003) has used the term *multiple-treatment designs*, very accurately in our view, to refer to both alternating and simultaneous treatment designs. However, since simultaneous treatment designs are so rare and would seem to have such little applicability in applied research, we will concentrate on the description and illustration of the true ATD strategy.

In summary, the basic feature of this design is the "rapid" alternation of two or more different treatments or conditions. For this reason, we suggested the term *alternating treatments design* (Barlow & Hayes, 1979), which most likely because of its descriptive properties has been widely adopted. Although we use the term *alternating treatments*, we note that "treatments" refers to the particular condition in force, not necessarily psychotherapy. Baseline conditions can be alternated with specific therapies as easily as two or more distinct therapies can be alternated. Whether or not this is needed, of course, depends on the specific research question. The use of the term *treatment* in this way continues a long tradition in experimental design of referring to various conditions as *treatments*.

8.2. PROCEDURAL CONSIDERATIONS

Most of the procedures utilized in an ATD are similar to those described earlier in this book for other designs. However, because of the unique purpose of this design—comparing two treatments or conditions in a single subject—and because of the strategy of rapid alternation, some distinct procedural issues arise that the experimenter will want to consider.

Multiple-treatment interference

Multiple-treatment interference raises the issue: Will the results of administering Treatment B in alternation with Treatment A be the same as when Treatment B is administered alone? In other words, is Treatment A somehow interfering with Treatment B, so that we are not getting a true picture of the effects of treatment? Indeed, at first glance there are few clinical situations where treatments are ever alternated. Thus, it may not be immediately apparent to practitioners how the results from an ATD could generalize to their own situations. On closer analysis, however, we suggest that this is a relatively small problem, and in some cases not a problem at all, for clinical researchers (although it is a major issue in basic research). After a discussion of the nature of multiple-treatment interference, the remainder of this section will describe procedures that clinical researchers can use to minimize it.

In a sense, all clinical research is fraught with potential multiple-treatment interference. Unlike the scientifically splendid isolation of experimental animal laboratories where rats are returned to their cages for 23 hours to await the next session, the children and adults who are the subjects of clinical research experience a variety of events before and after each treatment session. A college student on the way to an experiment may have just failed an examination. A subject in a fear-reduction experiment may have been mugged on the way to the session. Another experimental patient may have lost a family member in recent weeks or just had sexual intercourse before the session. It is possible that these subjects respond differently to the treatment than otherwise would have been the case, and it is these historical factors that account for some of the enormous inter-subject variability apparent in between-group designs comparing two treatments. ATDs, on the other hand, control for this kind of confounding experience perfectly by "dividing the subject in two" and administering two or more treatments (to the same subjects) within the same time period. Thus, if a family member died during the previous week, that experience would presumably affect each rapidly alternated treatment equally. However, the one remaining concern is the possibility that one experimental treatment is interfering with the other within the experiment itself. Essentially, there are three related concerns: *sequential confounding, carryover effects,* and *alternation effects* (Barlow & Hayes, 1979; Kazdin, 2003; Ulman & Sulzer-Azaroff, 1975).

Sequential confounding, also called *order effects,* was discussed earlier as referring to the fact that Treatment B might be different if it always followed Treatment A. In such case, much of the benefit of Treatment B might be due simply to the order in which it is administered in relation to other treatments. Sequential confounding with A-B-A withdrawal designs was discussed in section 5.3. The solution, of course, is to arrange for a random (or semi-random) sequencing of treatments. One can view this random order of sequencing treatments in a typical ATD in the hypothetical data presented in Figure 8.1. Such counterbalancing also allows for statistical analyses of ATDs for those who so desire (see chapter 9).

Carryover effects, refer to the influence of one treatment on an adjacent treatment, irrespective of overall sequencing. Terms such as *induction* and, *contrast* have long been used to describe these phenomena (e.g., Rachlin, 1973; G. S. Reynolds, 1968). Several of these terms carry specific theoretical connotations. For our purposes, it will be enough to speak of positive carryover effects and negative carryover effects. Returning to the hypothetical data in Figure 8.1, positive carryover effects would occur if Treatment B were *more* effective, *because it was alternated with Treatment A* than it would be if it were the only treatment administered. Negative carryover effects would occur if Treatment B were *less* effective because it was alternated with Treatment A than if it were administered alone. In other words, Treatment A is somehow interfering with the effects one would see from Treatment B if it were administered in isolation.

Findings from basic research have illuminated the nature and parameters of carryover effects. In basic research laboratories, where the understanding of carryover effects is very important to various theories of behavior, investigators have discovered that such effects are almost always transient and due mostly to the inability of the subject to discriminate among two treatments (e.g., Blough, 1983; Hinson & Malone, 1980; Malone, 1976; McLean & White, 1981). Fortunately for the clinical researcher, the types of experimental situations where carryover effects are observed in basic research rarely occur in applied research. In basic research, treatments (schedules of reinforcement in this particular context) are often alternated by the minute and the treatments themselves are almost impossible to discriminate as they are occurring. For this reason, signs or signals (discriminative stimuli), referred to as S^Ds, are associated with each treatment. As these signals themselves become harder to discriminate (for example, increasingly closer wavelengths of light), carryover effects occur. But even with these difficult-to-discriminate treatments and signals, carryover effects eventually disappear as discriminations are learned. Blough (1983) proposed that in situations where carryover effects are more permanent within this context, individual differences in ability to learn discrimination may be the reason. That is, those subjects (i.e., pigeons or rats) that are slower in learning the discriminations are associated with longer periods of carryover effects, whereas subjects learning the discriminations quickly evidence very short and transient carryover effects. When carryover effects have been noticed in humans (e.g., Haw, Dickinson, & Meissner, 2007; Taylor & Lupker, 2007), experimental operations similar to those employed in the laboratories of basic research were in operation. Presumably the same lack of discriminability was occurring.

In clinical research, this would imply that carryover effects of the type discussed here are a possibility only when learning is occurring. This would exclude most biological treatments, such as pharmacotherapy, where no real learning occurs (although biological multiple-treatment interference will occur if drugs are alternated too quickly, depending on the half-life of the particular drug, see chapter 6). On the other hand, almost all psychological treatments do involve some learning; however, treatments are usually so distinct that they are very easily discriminated even without any sign or signal. In fact, in the examples described below, subjects are usually told which treatment is in effect from session to session, and therefore discriminations are perfect. Even when not told, such as with children switching from the use of time-out to praise in the classroom, subjects are likely to be quite capable of discriminating different treatments very quickly.

The following procedures can be used to limit the influence of carryover effects when implementing an ATD. First, counterbalancing the order of treatments should minimize carryover effects and control for order effects. The remaining steps involve ensuring that treatments are discriminable. Second, separating treatment sessions with a time interval should reduce carryover effects, such as by presenting only one treatment per session (e.g., one treatment session per week, with six days in between). Fortunately, in applied research it is typical that only one treatment is administered per session. Similar procedures have been suggested to minimize carryover effects in the traditional within-subjects group comparison approaches (e.g., Greenwald, 1976). Third, the speed of alternations seems to increase carryover effects, at least until discriminations are formed. This is particularly true in basic research, where treatments may be alternated by the minute. Slower and more discriminable alternations should minimize carryover effects (e.g., Powell & Hake, 1971; Waite & Osborne, 1972). In summary, based on what is known about carryover effects, counterbalancing and insuring discriminability of treatments will minimize this problem. In applied research, where possible, simply telling the subjects which treatment they are getting should be sufficient.

Of course, in the event that some carryover effects may be occurring even with the procedural cautions mentioned above in place, it is important to note that there is no reason to think that these carryover effects would reverse the relative positions of the two treatments. Returning to the hypothetical data in Figure 8.1, Treatment B is seen as better than Treatment A. In this particular ATD, B may not be as effective as it would be if it were the only treatment administered, and A may be more effective, but it is extremely unlikely that carryover effects would make A better than B. Thus, even if carryover effects were observed in the major comparison of treatments, the experimenter would have clear evidence concerning the effectiveness of Treatment B, but would have to emphasize caution in determining exactly how effective Treatment B would be if it were not alternated with Treatment A.

Assessing Multiple-Treatment Interference.   It is possible and sometimes desirable to assess directly the extent to which carryover effects are present. Sidman (1960) suggested two methods. One is termed *independent verification* and entails conducting a controlled experiment in which one or another of the component treatments in the ATD is administered independently. For example, returning to Figure 8.1, Treatments A and B would be compared using an ATD in the manner presented in Figure 8.1, and this experiment would be replicated across two subjects. The investigator could then recruit three more closely matched subjects to receive a baseline condition, followed by Treatment A in an A-B fashion. Treatment B could be administered to a third trio of subjects in the same manner. Any differences that occur between the treatment administered in an ATD or independently could be due to carryover effects. Alternatively, these subjects could receive treatment A alone, followed by the ATD that alternated Treatments A and B, returning to Treatment A alone. An additional three subjects could receive Treatment B in the same manner. Trends and levels of behavior during either treatment alone could be compared with the same treatment in the ATD. Obviously, this type of strategy would also be valuable for purposes of replication and for estimating the generality or external validity of either treatment.

A second, more elegant, method is *functional manipulation* (Sidman, 1960). In this procedure the strength of one of the components is manipulated and the experimenter observes the effect, if any, on the alternate treatment in the subsequent phase. For example, if comparing imaginal flooding (Treatment A) versus reinforced practice (Treatment B) in the treatment of fear, the amount of time in flooding could be doubled at one point. Changes in fear behavior occurring during the second unchanged treatment (reinforced practice) could be attributed to carryover effects.

In an excellent example using these types of strategies, Shapiro, Kazdin, and McGonigle (1982) examined the possible multiple-treatment interference in an experiment with five children diagnosed with mental retardation receiving treatment in a psychiatric inpatient unit. The target behavior was on-task behavior during a specified time period while in a classroom located in the unit. Using a clever and elegant variation on the method of independent verification, the effects of two treatments and a baseline condition were examined within the context of an ATD for increasing on-task behavior. One treatment was token reinforcement for on-task behavior, and the second treatment was a response cost intervention in which tokens were removed following any off-task behavior. These interventions were administered during two 25-minute sessions day: one in the morning and one in the afternoon. Two treatments were administered each day counterbalanced over days. After a four-day phase in which baseline conditions were in effect during both time periods, baseline and token reinforcement were alternated over a six-day phase. This was followed by the alternation of token reinforcement and response cost over a 10-day phase. The experimenters then returned to the baseline versus token reinforcement phase for 6 more days, followed by a return to the token reinforcement versus response cost phase for yet another 6-day period. Finally, this was followed by a phase where token reinforcement was administered during both time periods.

The results of this study are represented in Figure 8.2. This figure depicts the average responses of the five subjects. Individual data also were presented;

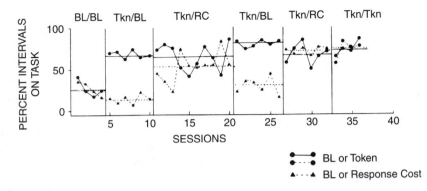

FIGURE 8.2 Group mean percentages of on-task behavior. Paired interventions in each phase consisted of Baseline/Baseline; Token Reinforcement/Baseline; Token Reinforcement/Response Cost; Token Reinforcement/Baseline; Token Reinforcement/Response Cost; Token Reinforcement/Token Reinforcement. (Figure 1, p. 110, from: Shapiro, E. S., Kazdin, A. E., & McGonigle, J. J. (1982). Multiple-treatment interference in the simultaneous- or alternating-treatments design. *Behavioral Assessment*, **4**, 105–115. Copyright 1982 by Association for Advancement of Behavior Therapy. Reproduced by permission.)

however, the data provided in this Figure will suffice for illustrative purposes. As shown in the Figure, this experiment essentially consisted of a baseline phase followed by four separate ATDs in which token reinforcement was alternated with either baseline or response costs, with each of these ATDs repeated twice. The elegance of this design for examining multiple-treatment interference is found in the fact that one can examine the effects of token reinforcement when alternated with either another treatment or baseline. If multiple-treatment interference is evident when token reinforcement is alternated with the other treatment (i.e., response cost) then the effects of token reinforcement should be different during that part of the experiment from when token reinforcement is alternated with baseline.

It is notable that that token reinforcement was clearly effective relative to baseline, and also that both treatments produced strong and comparable effects in increasing on-task behavior. The experimenters concluded that token reinforcement was the preferable treatment because more disruptive behavior occurred during the response-cost procedure than during the token reinforcement procedure.

The investigators reported three different sets of findings from their examination of potential multiple-treatment interference. First, no evidence was found that the overall level of on-task behavior during token reinforcement was different when it was alternated with either baseline or response cost. This is an important finding in terms of estimating what the effects of token reinforcement in this context would be when applied in isolation. In other words, the investigator or clinician can feel somewhat safe in determining that the effects of token reinforcement, when alternated with response costs, are about what they would be if response cost were not present. Of course, this still is not a "pure" test because it is possible that alternating token reinforcement with other conditions yields a different effect from what would be observed if token reinforcement was administered in isolation. Strict adherence to Sidman's method of independent verification would be necessary to estimate if any carryover effects were present when a treatment was alternated with a baseline condition.

Importantly, the investigators note that on-task behavior showed greater variability during token reinforcement when alternated with response cost than when alternated with baseline. Visual inspection of the data indicates that this was particularly true in three of the five subjects. While this finding in no way affects the interpretation of the results, it is an interesting observation that could be followed up in a number of ways. For instance, it is possible that "disruptiveness" noted during response cost temporarily carried over into the next token phase, thereby causing some of the variability. A greater spacing of sessions and subsequent sharpening of stimulus control might have decreased this variability.

Interestingly, the investigators also observed a sequence effect, in that token reinforcement was more effective when applied in the morning session than in the afternoon session. Once again, this demonstrates the importance of counterbalancing. Finally, the investigators observed another possible example of multiple-treatment interference not directly connected with the comparison of the two treatments. More specifically, the first time token reinforcement and baseline were alternated (phase 2) on-task behavior averaged 14%. However, during the alternation of these two conditions (phase 4) on-task behavior averaged approximately 30%. Inspection of individual data revealed that this trend occurred in four out of five children. This may represent a positive carryover or a generalization of treatment effects to the baseline condition. Either way, the first phase probably presents a truer picture of baseline responding. Studies of this type are critical in mapping out the exact nature of multiple-treatment interference and improving our ability to draw causal inferences from ATDs.

Counterbalancing relevant experimental factors

As with any experimental study, all factors extraneous to the treatment/manipulation should be counterbalanced in order to decrease their influence on the dependent variable. For example, if two clinicians were administering Treatments A and B in Figure 8.1, it would be important that one clinician is not always administering Treatment A and the other clinician Treatment B, otherwise, one would be unable to tease apart whether the treatments themselves or some aspect related to the clinicians differentially influenced the dependent variable.

It is up to the clinical researcher to determine which factors to counterbalance in any given study. Naturally, if different clinicians, teachers, or other practitioners are involved in administering the treatments, then they certainly should be counterbalanced. Investigators also should consider counterbalancing setting (e.g., treatment rooms) and time of day during which the procedures are administered if these might have an influence on the dependent variable. Ultimately, it is up to the researcher to make this determination, with the implication being that counterbalancing for an increasing number of factors will lead to a decrease in the likelihood that these experimental factors might account for any observed effects.

Number and sequencing of alternations

The major question to be considered in determining the number of alternations included in an ATD regards the potential for determining differences among two or more treatments. In determining behavior trends within a baseline phase or one of the phases of an A-B-A withdrawal design, we suggested that three data points were the minimum necessary to determine a trend. In the ATD the experimenter is comparing the effects of two treatments rather than examining an overall trend in the data, and therefore we recommend a minimum of two data points for each treatment, although greater numbers of data points are more desirable. The observation of two data points per treatment permits an examination of the relative effects of each treatment and for some tentative conclusions regarding treatment efficacy. However, returning to Figure 8.1, few investigators would be convinced of the superiority of Treatment B if the experiment were stopped after Week 4. Nevertheless, if other practical considerations prevent continuation, the findings might be potentially important, pending replication.

Of course, the frequency of alternations often is limited by practical considerations. For instance, it is possible that treatment and assessment could occur only once per week, or once per month. Such a situation is especially likely in the case of alternating between two drugs with long half-lives, where a meaningful measurement of behavioral or mood changes could occur only after several weeks—such as would be the case with drugs like selective serotonin reuptake inhibitors.

A final but very important point is that in arranging for random alternation of treatments to avoid order effects, one must be careful not to bunch too many administrations of the same treatment together in a row. For instance, if determining the random order of two treatments by coin toss or a random-numbers table, it is conceivable that one might arrive by chance at an order that dictates four (or more) consecutive administrations of the same treatment condition. If the experimenter only has time for eight alternations in total, then this would clearly not be a desirable occurrence, as this would result in an A-B design. To avoid such events, the investigator might consider using a "semi-random" order with an upper limit on the number of consecutive occurrences permitted, with this determination based on the total number of alternations available. For example, if eight alternations were available, as in the hypothetical data in Figure 8.1, then the investigator might want to set an upper limit of three consecutive administrations of one treatment.

8.3. EXAMPLES OF ALTERNATING TREATMENTS DESIGNS

ATDs have been increasingly used by basic and applied researchers. Indeed, a search for scientific articles on ATDs using the various names used to refer to this design strategy on the www.pubmed.gov database yields over 700 research reports (123 using "alternating treatments," 33 using "multielement design," 20 using "randomization design," and 525 using "multiple schedule"). Although variations abound, among clinical researchers ATDs have been used in two primary ways: to compare the effect of treatment and no treatment (baseline) and to compare two distinct treatments. Some examples of ATDs illustrating these strategies are reviewed in the following sections.

Comparing treatment and no treatment conditions

Many studies have compared treatment and no treatment using an ATD. Among early examples, O'Brien, Azrin, and Henson (1969) compared the effect of following and not following suggestions made by chronic mental patients in a group setting on the number of suggestions made by these patients. Doke and Risley (1972) alternated daily the presence of three teachers versus the usual one teacher and noted the effect on planned activities in the classroom. More recent examples include a study by Jordan, Singh, and Repp (1989) in which two treatment approaches, gentle teaching and visual screening, were compared with a control condition among three subjects with severe behavior problems. Another recent example is a study by Northup and colleagues (1999), which included a comparison of methylphenidate versus placebo in the treatment of disruptive and off-task behaviors among four children diagnosed with attention deficit hyperactivity disorder.

A particularly noteworthy example of the use of an ATD to compare treatment and no treatment conditions is provided in a study by Ollendick, Shapiro, and Barrett (1981). These investigators tested the relative effects of two treatments—physical restraint and positive-practice overcorrection—compared to no treatment in the reduction of stereotypic behavior in three children diagnosed with mental retardation. The investigators targeted stereotypic behaviors involving bizarre hand movements, such as repetitive hair twirling and hand posturing. Importantly, the investigators decided against the use of an A-B-A withdrawal design in this case because they considered even temporary increases in stereotypic behavior during withdrawal phases to be unacceptable. Furthermore, previous experience suggested the two treatments might be equally effective, thus, a no treatment condition was considered necessary to determine if these treatments were effective at all. This design decision is not specific to single-case research but also arises in between-group research because if two treatments were equally effective (on the average) a control group would be necessary to determine if any clinical effects occurred over and above no treatment (Nock, Janis, & Wedig, 2008).

Study procedures consisted of the administration of three 15-minute sessions (separated by at least one hour) each day by the same experimenter. Following baseline conditions for all three time periods, the two treatments and the no treatment conditions were administered in a counterbalanced order across sessions. During sessions, each child was escorted to a small table in a classroom and instructed to work on one of several visual motor tasks. One treatment was physical restraint, consisting of a verbal warning and manual restraint of the child's hand on the tabletop for 30 seconds contingent on each occurrence of stereotypic behavior. The second treatment, positive-practice overcorrection, involved the same verbal warning but was followed by manual guidance in appropriate manipulation of the task materials for 30 seconds. Assessment included recording of the number of stereotypic behaviors during each session and performance on the task. When one of the treatments produced a zero or near-zero rate of stereotypic behavior during the alternating treatments phase, that treatment was then selected and implemented across all three time periods during the remainder of the study.

The results for two of the three subjects are presented in Figures 8.3 (for Tim) and 8.4 (for John). As shown in Figure 8.3, data from the alternating treatments phase clearly demonstrate that positive practice is the superior treatment for Tim. In contrast, data presented in Figure 8.4 demonstrate that physical restraint was the superior treatment for John.

Several features of this noteworthy experiment deserve further comment. First, the alternating treatments phase of this experiment was conducted in only three or four days (with three sessions per day), and proper determinations regarding the most effective treatment for each individual were made in each case. This is a relatively brief amount of time for an experiment in applied research, and yet it is typical of ATDs, particularly in this context. This is in stark contrast to prior efforts using group-based research designs, which have been quite disappointing in their ability to effectively match subjects to treatment conditions (e.g., "Matching Alcoholism Treatments to Client Heterogeneity: Project MATCH posttreatment drinking outcomes," 1997).

Second, the inclusion of a baseline phase prior to introduction of the alternating treatments phase allowed for identification of the naturally occurring frequencies of the target problem and the absolute amount of reduction in the target problem when treatments were initiated. Of course, this is not necessary in order to determine which of three conditions was more effective, but it provides important additional information to the investigator.

Third, the alternating treatments phase served as a clinical assessment procedure for each client, since the most effective treatment was immediately applied to eliminate the problem behavior. The rapidity with which the ATD can be implemented makes this design very useful as a clinical assessment tool as well as an experimental strategy (see Barlow, Hayes, & Nelson, 1983).

Fourth, John did better with physical restraint, whereas Tim did better with positive practice intervention. The third subject also did better with positive practice intervention. This is a good example of the handling of inter-subject

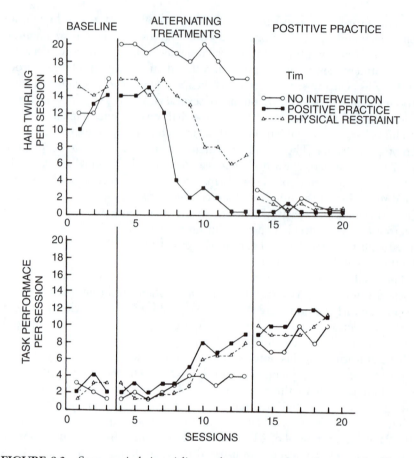

FIGURE 8.3 Stereotypic hair twirling and accurate task performance for Tim across experimental conditions. The data are plotted across the three alternating time periods according to the schedule that the treatments were in effect. The three treatments were presented only during the alternating-treatments phase. During the last phase, physical restraint was used during all three time periods. (Figure 1, p. 573, from Ollendick, T. H., Shapiro, E. S., & Barrett, R. P. (1981). Reducing stereotypic behaviors: An analysis of treatment procedures utilizing an alternating treatments design. *Behavior Therapy*, **12**, 570–577. Copyright 1981 by Association for Advancement of Behavior Therapy. Reproduced by permission.)

variability in an ATD design. As discussed in chapter 2, a between-group strategy would average out rather than highlight these individual differences in response to treatment. By demonstrating this inter-subject variability the investigators were able to speculate on the reasons for these differences and to examine more carefully client-treatment interactions that would predict which treatment would be successful in an individual case. Again, highlighting inter-subject variability in

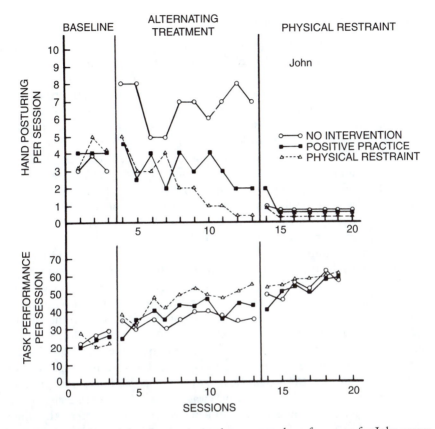

FIGURE 8.4   Stereotypic hand posturing and accurate task performance for John across experimental conditions. The data are plotted across the three alternating time periods according to the schedule that the treatments were in effect. The three treatments were presented only during the alternating-treatments phase. During the last phase, positive practice overcorrection was used during all three time periods. (Figure 2, p. 574, from Ollendick, T. H., Shapiro, E. S., & Barrett, R. P. (1981). Reducing stereotypic behaviors: An analysis of treatment procedures utilizing an alternating treatments design. *Behavior Therapy*, *12*, 570–577. Copyright 1981 by Association for Advancement of Behavior therapy. Reproduced by permission.)

this way can increase the precision with which one can generalize the effects of these specific treatments to other individual clients (see chapter 2).

Fifth and finally, the discerning reader will notice that the target behaviors for both subjects presented were higher during the no treatment condition in the alternating treatments phase then they were during the baseline phase. This may represent a negative carryover effect, because responding during no treatment was worse when it was alternated with treatment than it was observed alone during baseline.

Comparing multiple treatments

In contrast to ATDs that compare treatment(s) with no treatment, the majority of ATDs actually compare the relative effects of two presumably active treatments. For instance, Kearney and Silverman (1990) compared exposure and response prevention and cognitive therapy in the treatment of an adolescent with obsessive-compulsive disorder. Similarly, Carr and Bailey (1996) compared self-monitoring, competing response practice, and dissimilar response practice in the treatment of a nine-year-old boy diagnosed with Tourette's Syndrome. In other applications, rather than decreasing pathological behavior, ATDs have been used to compare treatment approaches for improving positive target behaviors, such as subjective happiness (Davis, Young, Cherry, Dahman, & Rehfeldt, 2004) and academic performance among college students (Neef et al., 2006). While many examples of this application of the ATD exist, several studies provide exemplary illustrations of this approach.

A classic example of such a design is provided by Agras and colleagues (1969) in which the investigators examined the effects of two different exposure-based, fear-reduction strategies. The subject in this case was a 50-year-old woman with severe claustrophobia, whose fears had intensified following the death of her husband seven years earlier. Upon her admission to the treatment program the subject was not able to remain in a closed room for longer than one minute without experiencing significant anxiety, which caused significant impairment. During the study the subject was asked to remain inside a small room (i.e., a closet) until she felt she had to come out, and time in the room was the dependent measure. This procedure was repeated four times each day.

Two clinicians administered treatment. During one treatment, the clinician administered social praise contingent on the subject's remaining in the room for an increasing period of time (reinforcing therapist). In the second treatment, the subject was simply exposed to the closet, with the clinician just outside the door (nonreinforcing therapist). Importantly, the two clinicians alternated sessions. In the original experimental phase the clinicians switched roles, but returned to their original reinforcing and non-reinforcing roles in the third phase.

The results of this study are reported in Figure 8.5. The data clearly indicate that reinforced sessions were consistently superior to non-reinforced sessions, regardless of which clinician administered the treatment. There is significant variability in the first experimental phase, which requires a bit of explanation. During the first four assessments representing treatment, the subject kept her hand on the doorknob. Before the fifth treatment data point (sixth block of sessions), she took her hand off the doorknob, resulting in a considerable drop in time spent in the room.

A few procedural considerations deserve brief comment. First, the counterbalancing was relatively weak given that clinicians switched roles only twice during the whole experiment. Ideally, a more systematic counterbalancing strategy would be incorporated. Second, the treatments were not administered randomly.

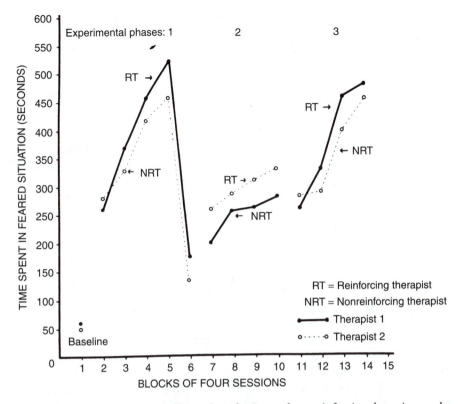

FIGURE 8.5   Comparison of effects of reinforcing and nonreinforcing therapists on the modification of claustrophobic behavior. (Figure 3, p. 1438, from: Agras, W. S., Leitenberg, H., Barlow, D. H., & Thomson, L. E. (1969). Instructions and reinforcement in the modification of neurotic behavior. *American Journal of Psychiatry*, **125**, 1435–1439. Copyright 1969 by the American Psychiatric Association. Reproduced by permission.)

Sessions involving exposure without contingent praise always preceded exposure with contingent praise. Despite this fact, a clear superiority of one treatment over the other emerged. Nevertheless, the experiment would be stronger with counterbalancing of treatments also. Finally, one data point representing a block of four sessions served as a baseline comparison. While formal baseline phases are not necessary for ATD comparisons, and one baseline point is certainly better than none, the examination of trends is always more informative than having simply a one-point pretest (or posttest).

Another excellent example of an ATD is from a study by McKnight, Nelson, Hayes, and Jarrett (1984) that compared the effectiveness of two treatments for depression among nine women diagnosed with severe major depression. While depression is clearly a multifaceted disorder, two common elements are irrational cognitions and deficient social skills. Indeed, current evidence-based treatments for depression focus largely on modifying irrational cognitions (Beck, 2005; Beck, Rush, Shaw, & Emery, 1979) and on increasing behavioral activation and engagement in social interactions (Dimidjian et al., 2006; Jacobson et al., 1996; Martell, Addis, & Jacobson, 2001). This study targeted these two elements using two distinct treatment approaches.

In this study, assessment revealed that three of these depressed subjects were primarily deficient in social skills, with few problems in the area of irrational cognitions. In contrast, another three presented with clear difficulties with irrational cognitions, but problems with social skills. Yet a third group of three subjects displayed problems in both areas. An ATD was used to compare social skills training and cognitive therapy in each of these subjects. The two therapies were repeatedly randomly assigned over an eight week period with the constraint that each subject received four sessions of cognitive therapy and four sessions of social skills therapy.

The results for the first two sets of three subjects mentioned above are presented in Figures 8.6 and 8.7. Upon examining these figures, another experimental design feature that adds to the elegance of this experiment becomes apparent. Specifically, in addition to treatments being compared in individual subjects with an ATD, a multiple baseline across subjects design was implemented in order to observe the effects of treatment, compared to the initial baseline, and to insure that the effects of any treatment occurred only when that treatment was introduced. This strategy controls for potential confounds that are a function of taking multiple measurements and other conditions present during baseline (see chapter 7). Thus, this experimental design allows for a determination of the effects of treatment over baseline by means of a multiple baseline across subjects design, as well as a comparison of two treatments within the ATD portion of the experiment.

As shown in Figure 8.6, social skills training was clearly the more effective treatment for depression in each of the three subjects presenting with social skills deficits, as indicted here by scores on overall depressive symptoms (i.e., on the Lubin Depression Adjective Checklist) as well as on a measure of social skills (i.e., the Interpersonal Events Schedule)—with each of these findings reaching statistical significance. In contrast, no significant differences emerged on a measure of irrational cognitions (i.e., the Personal Beliefs Inventory).

As shown in Figure 8.7, cognitive therapy was clearly the more effective treatment as indicated by measures of depression and irrational cognitions. These findings were also statistically significant. No statistically significant differences emerged on the measure of social skills, however, for people with primarily cognitive deficits.

This very elegant experiment serves as model in many ways for the use of the ATD in clinical situations. The major conclusions derived from these data concern the importance of carefully and specifically assessing a behavioral problem (in this case depression) and all of its components in order to tailor appropriate treatments to the individual. While these data were not necessary for this

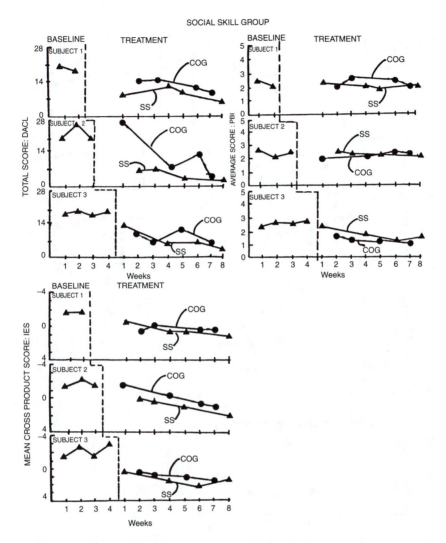

FIGURE 8.6 The effects of each treatment (COG = cognitive treatment; SS = social skill treatment) in a multiple baseline design across the 3 subjects experiencing difficulties in social skills on the weekly dependent measures administered. (Total score on the Lubin Depression Adjective Checklist; Average score on the Personal Beliefs Inventory; Mean cross-product score on the Interpersonal Events Schedule.) (Figure 2, from: McNight, D. L., Nelson, R. O., Hayes, S. C., & Jarrett, R. B. (1984). Importance of treating individually assessed response classes in the amelioration of depression. *Behavior Therapy*. Copyright 1984 by Association for Advancement of Behavioral Therapy. Reproduced by permission.)

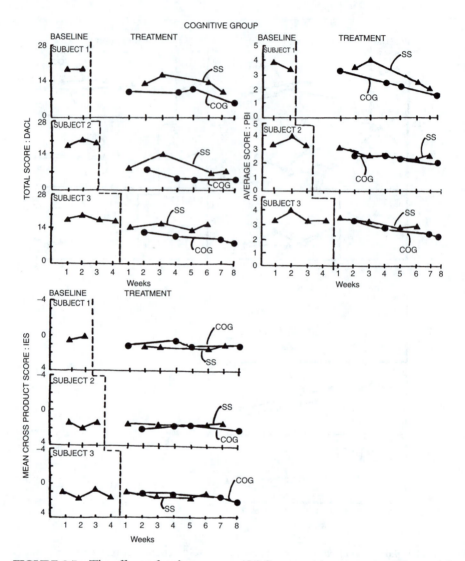

FIGURE 8.7   The effects of each treatment (COG = cognitive treatment; SS = social skill treatment) in a multiple baseline design across the 3 subjects experiencing difficulties in irrational cognitions on the weekly dependent measures administered. (Total score on the Lubin Depression Adjective Checklist; Average score on the Personal Beliefs Inventory; Mean cross-product score on the Interpersonal Events Schedule.) (Figure 4, from: McKnight, D. L., Nelson, R. O., Hayes, S. C., & Jarrett, R. B. (1984). Importance of treating individually assessed response classes in the amelioration of depression. *Behavior Therapy*.)

presentation, the third trio of subjects, displaying both irrational cognitions and social skill deficits, benefited from both treatments. Furthermore, consistent with the advantages of ATDs in investigating other problems, the results were apparent rather quickly after a total of eight treatment sessions. Also, the two treatments require the presentation of somewhat different therapeutic rationales to the patients, but this does not present a problem in our experience, and it did not in this experiment. Usually clients are simply told, correctly, that each treatment is directed at a somewhat different aspect of their, problem and/or that the experimenters are trying to determine which of two treatments might be best for them.

While clinical theory, science, and practice have advanced significantly since these earlier studies, the ATD remains an effective tool to test newly developed theories and to do so across laboratory and clinical settings. As a recent example, Masuda, Hayes, Sackett, and Twohig (2004) used an ATD to test the effectiveness of cognitive defusion techniques at decreasing the discomfort and believability of negative thoughts relative to a control condition and to a thought control condition. Thought defusion techniques are an important element of acceptance and commitment therapy (ACT) as well as more longstanding cognitive behavioral approaches to obsessive compulsive disorder in which the focus has shifted primarily from changing one's behavior or the content of one's thoughts to changing one's awareness of and relation to one's thoughts, behaviors, and emotions (e.g., Hayes, Strosahl, & Wilson, 1999; Linehan, 1993; Segal, Williams, & Teasdale, 2002).

This was a laboratory-based study that included eight female undergraduate students. The dependent variables were self-reported discomfort and believability experienced during six 30-second trials during one laboratory visit. All eight subjects in this study received two alternating treatments randomly assigned over six sessions with the condition that no more than two consecutive trials of the same condition could occur. All subjects received thought defusion training as one of their treatment conditions. In this condition, after learning the rationale for thought defusion—which essentially is that it is possible to change the impact of thoughts or words by changing the context in which they occur—subjects were instructed to repeat a self-relevant negative word for 30-seconds (e.g., "fat" or "dumb"). For the first four subjects, the alternate treatment was a distraction task during which they read a passage about Japan for five minutes (to match the rationale period) and then in 30-second segments (to match the thought defusion trials). For the next four subjects, the alternate treatment was a thought control exercise during which subjects learned the rationale for using thought control techniques—such as positive self-talk, positive imagery, and breathing training—and then were instructed to use one of these techniques during the 30-second trials.

The results of this study are presented in Figure 8.8 and 8.9. As shown in Figure 8.8, thought defusion was clearly and consistently superior to the distraction condition across all four subjects. As shown in Figure 8.9, although the relative effectiveness of thought defusion was not quite as strong when compared to thought control techniques (as would be expected), the thought defusion condition was again clearly and consistently superior at decreasing discomfort and believability of the self-referent negative thoughts across all four subjects.

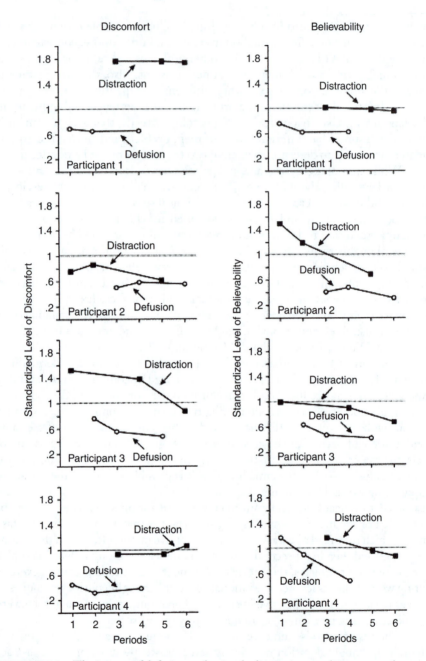

FIGURE 8.8 The impact of defusion and a simple distraction condition across four participants on the discomfort and believability associated with two negative thoughts. (Figure 1, p. 482, from: Masuda, A., Hayes, S. C., Sackett, C. F., & Twohig, M. P. [2004]. Congnitive defusion and self-relevent negative thoughts: examining the impact of a ninety year old technique. *Behaviour Research and Therapy*, **42** (4), 477–485.)

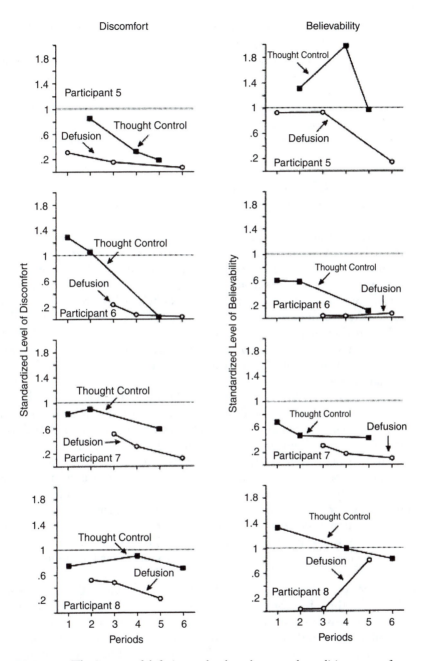

FIGURE 8.9   The impact of defusion and a thought control condition across four participants on the discomfort and believability associated with two negative thoughts. (Figure 2, p. 483, from: Masuda, A., Hayes, S. C., Sackett, C. F., & Twohig, M. P. [2004]. Cognitive defusion and self-relevent negative thoughts: examining the impact of a ninety year old technique. *Behaviour Research and Therapy, 42* (4), 477–485.)

Several methodological issues are notable in this study. The study is limited by its reliance on self-report data on the dependent variables, and also by the fact that it is not exactly clear what subjects did in each case in the thought control condition—as acknowledged by the investigators. This study provides an excellent example of how clinical researchers can test the efficacy of individual treatment components quickly and cogently. This is especially important given the need to identify active components of existing treatments (e.g., Jacobson et al., 1996), the proliferation of new and untested treatment approaches (see Kazdin, 2000).

8.4. ADVANTAGES OF THE ALTERNATING TREATMENTS DESIGN

The first major advantage of the ATD is that it does not require withdrawal of treatment. If two or more therapies are being compared, questions on relative effectiveness can be answered without a withdrawal phase at all. If one is comparing treatment with no treatment, then one still would not require a lengthy phase where no treatment was administered. Rather, no-treatment sessions are alternated with treatment sessions, usually within a relatively brief period of time. This provides an ideal research design for instances in which one does not want to withdraw treatment due to the nature of the problem being treated (e.g., suicidal thoughts, self-injurious behaviors) or to the lack of support from the subject, family, or staff.

The second major advantage of the ATD is that it can supply useful data more quickly than a withdrawal design. This is because the relatively lengthy baseline, treatment, and withdrawal phases necessary to establish trends in A-B-A withdrawal designs are not important in an ATD design. The examples provided in this chapter nicely illustrate this point. In fact, the relative rapidity of an ATD will often make it more suitable in situations where measures can be taken only infrequently. For example, if it is only practical to take measures infrequently, such as monthly, then an ATD will also result in a considerable saving of time. In an example provided in Barlow et al. (1983), it was noted that it often requires several hours and careful testing by two professional staff in a physical rehabilitation center to work up a stroke patient's muscular functioning. Obviously these measures cannot be taken frequently. If one were testing a rehabilitation treatment program using an A-B-A-B design, with at least three data points in each phase, then 12 months would be required to evaluate the treatment, assuming that measures could be taken no more frequently than monthly. On the other hand, if one month of treatment were alternated with one month of maintenance, then useful data within the ATD format would begin to emerge after four months.

A third advantage of the ATD is that it is relatively insensitive to background trends in behavior because one is comparing the results of two treatments or conditions in the context of whatever background trend is occurring. This is in contrast to some other single-case experimental designs in which trends that are extremely variable can introduce problems in the interpretation of results. For example, if a specific behavioral problem is rapidly improving during baseline, it would be problematic to introduce a treatment. However, using an ATD, two treatments could be alternated in the context of this improving behavior, with the potential for useful differences emerging.

A final advantage of the ATD is the overall flexibility afforded with these designs. Single case experimental designs are noted for their flexibility, and this is especially true in the case of the ATD. For instance, the fact that no formal baseline phase is required in an ATD provides the freedom to begin with active treatment, which is very desirable in most clinical settings. Moreover, ATDs are amenable to many of the design variations discussed in our review of other single-case experimental designs throughout this book. For instance, ATD can be quite useful in drug evaluations, and in testing the relative and/or interactive effects of drug treatments and psychological treatments (e.g., Northup et al., 1999; Singh, Landrum, Ellis, & Donatelli, 1993). ATDs also can be used to test the effectiveness of treatments on the behavior of large groups, such as motorists' stopping behavior at traffic intersections (Austin, Hackett, Gravina, & Lebbon, 2006). Overall, the ATD is a strong, flexible, and clinically useful strategy that deserves serious consideration from those preparing a single-case experimental study.

Of course, these advantages relative to other design choices apply only to situations where other design choices are indeed possible. There are, of course, many situations where other experimental designs are more appropriate for addressing the question at hand. Furthermore, ATDs may suffer from the effects of multiple-treatment interference. In any case, when it comes to generalizing the results of single-case experimental investigations to applied situations, there seems little question that the first treatment phase of an A-B-A-B design (or a multiple baseline design) is closer to the applied situation than is a treatment that is rapidly alternated with another treatment or with no treatment. These are only a few of the many factors the investigator must consider when choosing an appropriate experimental design.

8.5. VISUAL ANALYSIS OF THE ALTERNATING TREATMENTS DESIGNS

If enough data points have been collected for each treatment, and if one is so inclined, a variety of statistical procedures are appropriate for analyzing alternating treatment designs (see chapter 9). However, visual analysis should suffice for most ATDs. Throughout this book, the visual analysis of single-case experimental designs is discussed in terms of observation of both levels of behavior and trends in behavior across a phase. Within an ATD, levels and trends in behavior are not necessarily relevant because the major comparison is between two or more series of data points representing two or more treatments or conditions, as noted above. Most investigators using the ATD have been relatively conservative, in that very clear divergence among the treatments is considered necessary to infer that one treatment is superior to the other. In fact, in most cases the series have been non-overlapping. For example, with the exceptions of Points 1 and Points 11, which represented data points immediately following the switch in therapists, the Agras et al. (1969) ATD presented nonoverlapping series (see Figure 8.5). Similarly, Ollendick, Shapiro, and Barrett (1981) demonstrated a clear divergence between treatment and no treatment (see Figures 8.3 and 8.4). When one examines the effects of the two treatments, several data points overlap initially, but the two series increasingly diverge as the ATD proceeds. One must also remember that in this particular experiment there were no clear signs or signals discriminating the treatments, and therefore this overlap may reflect some confusion about which treatment was in effect early in the experiment. Finally, in the study by Masuda and colleagues (2004), 22 of 24 data points for the defusion condition were below (i.e., nonoverlapping with) those from the distraction condition (see Figure 8.8), and 19 of 24 data points for the defusion condition were below those for the thought control condition (see Figure 8.9).

If overlap among the series occurs, then there is little to choose among the treatments or conditions, and most investigators say so. For example, Last, Barlow, and O'Brien (1983) observed overlap between two cognitive therapies and concluded that each was effective. Of course, when some overlap exists, it is possible to utilize statistical procedures to estimate if any differences that do exist are due to chance or not (e.g., McKnight et al., 1984, Figure 8.7; Shapiro et al., 1982, Figure 8.2). However, as discussed in chapter 9, one must then decide if these rather small effects, even if statistically significant, are clinically useful. Our recommendation for these designs, and throughout this book, is to be conservative and to look for large visually clear, clinically significant effects.

8.6. SIMULTANEOUS TREATMENT DESIGN

Earlier in this chapter we noted the existence of a little-used design that actually presents two or more treatments simultaneously to an individual subject. In the first edition of this book, we referred to this design as a *concurrent schedule design*; however, the implication that a distinct schedule of reinforcement is attached to each treatment produces the same unnecessary narrowness as calling an alternating treatments design a multiple schedule design, which we argued against earlier in this chapter. Browning's (1967) term, *simultaneous treatment design* (STD), seems both more descriptive and more suitable. Nevertheless, both terms adequately describe the fundamental characteristic of this design—the concurrent or simultaneous application of two or more treatments in a single-case. This contrasts with the alternation of two or more treatments in the ATD.

The only example of the use of this design in applied research of which we are aware is the original Browning (1967) experiment, also described in Browning and Stover (1971). In this experiment, Browning (1967) obtained a baseline on incidences of grandiose bragging in a 9-year-old child. After 4 weeks, three treatments were used simultaneously: (1) positive interest and praise contingent on bragging, (2) verbal admonishment, and (3) ignoring. Each treatment was administered by a team of two therapists who were staff in a residential college for emotionally disturbed children. To control for possible differential effects with individual staff, each team administered each treatment for one week in a counterbalanced order. For example, the second group of two therapists admonished the first week, ignored the second week, and praised the third week. All six of the staff involved in the study were present simultaneously to administer the treatment. Browning hypothesized that the boy ". . . would seek out and brag to the most reinforcing staff, and shift to different staff on successive weeks as they switched to S's preferred reinforcement contingency" (p. 241). The data from Browning's subject (see Figure 8-10) indicate a preference for verbal admonishment, as indicated

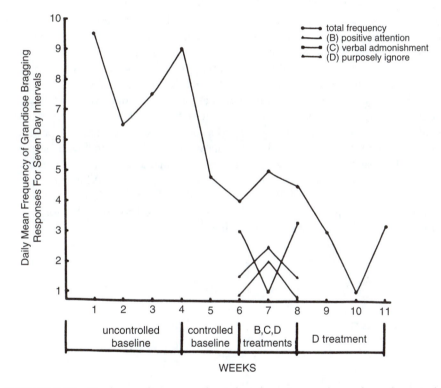

FIGURE 8.10   Total mean frequency of grandiose bragging responses throughout study and for each reinforcement contingency during experimental period. (Figure 3, p. 241, from: Browning, R. M. (1967). A same-subject design for simultaneous comparison of three reinforcement contingencies. *Behaviour Research and Therapy*, **5**, 237–243. Copyright 1967 by Pergamon Press. Reproduced by permission.)

by frequency and duration of bragging, and a lack of preference for ignoring. Thus ignoring became the treatment of choice and was continued by all staff.

In this experiment the effects of three treatments were observed, but it is unlikely that a subject would be equally exposed to each treatment. In fact, the very structure of the design ensures that the subject won't be equally exposed to all treatments because a choice is forced (except in the unlikely event that all treatments are equally preferred). Thus this design is unsuitable for studying differential effects of treatments or conditions.

The STD might be useful anytime a question of individual preferences is important. Of course, in some cases preferences for a treatment may be an important component of its overall effectiveness. For example, if one is treating a phobia, and either one of two cognitive procedures combined with exposure-based therapy is equally effective, the client's preference becomes very important. Presumably a client would be less likely to continue using, after treatment is terminated, a fear-reduction strategy that is less preferred or even mildly aversive. But the more preferred or least aversive treatment procedure would be likely to be used, resulting most likely in a more favorable response during follow-up. Similarly, one could use an STD to determine the reinforcing value of a variety of potential consequences before introducing a program based on selective positive reinforcement. But it is also possible that a particular subject might prefer reinforcing consequences or treatments that are less effective in the long run. The investigator must remember that preference does not always equal effectiveness. The STD, then, awaits implementation by creative investigators studying areas of behavior change or psychopathology where strong experimental determinations of behavioral preference are desired. Presumably, these situations will be such that the self-report resulting from asking a subject about his or her preference will not be sufficient, for a variety of reasons. When these questions arise, the STD can be a very powerful tool for studying preference in the individual subject. But the STD is not well suited to an evaluation of the effectiveness of behavior change procedures.

CHAPTER 9

STATISTICAL ANALYSES FOR SINGLE-CASE EXPERIMENTAL DESIGNS

TIMOTHY T. HOULE, PH.D.*

9.1. INTRODUCTION AND OVERVIEW

Single-case experimental designs bring the experimental rigor that has become the hallmark of group designs to the study of the individual. In this undertaking, a very unique set of analytical challenges is presented to the researcher that is not often encountered in traditional group designs. The nature of these analytical challenges, and hopefully some practical solutions, will be the focus of this chapter.

The first challenge in analyzing the effect of the experiment on the individual is the criterion of evaluation. Specifically, what will be the standard of proof that the independent variable actually influences behavior? The question seems simple enough, although there has been a substantial amount of discussion about what should practically serve as this criterion. Kazdin (1984) delineates between two possible criteria: experimental and therapeutic. The use of an experimental criterion signifies a reliable or veridical difference in behavior under experimental conditions. When using statistical procedures to evaluate an intervention, this criterion is intuitively labeled statistical significance. A therapeutic criterion signifies the clinical significance of any observed differences induced by the independent variable (Kazdin, 1999). This criterion is tantamount to asking, is the effect meaningful to the patient? Applying these two criteria then, an intervention may reliably diminish a problematic behavior (experimental criterion),

*Timothy T. Houle, Department of Anesthesiology, Wake Forest University School of Medicine, Wake Forest University Health Sciences, Medical Center Blvd. Winston-Salem, NC 27157. thoule@wfubmc.edu

yet only to the degree that has very little benefit to the individual's life (lack of therapeutic criterion). Ideally, the analyst will consider both the experimental (statistical) and therapeutic (clinical) significance of any selected criterion that is used to draw conclusions about a conducted intervention.

A second challenge to the single-case researcher is the choice of which methods to use in evaluating the effects of the intervention. Traditionally, this has meant the controversial choice of using either visual inspection or statistical analysis to evaluate the experiment. There have been (and still are) strong proponents of using graphical analysis as the primary method of evaluating differences induced by experimental conditions (Michael, 1974; Parsonson & Baer, 1992; Onghena & Edgington, 2005). The degree of this controversy is best underscored by the fact that the two prior editions of this book contained sections that defended the merits of using statistical analysis as *any* aspect of the analytical process (Hersen & Barlow, 1976; Barlow & Hersen, 1984). Even today the role of visual inspection versus statistical analysis remains controversial leaving some analysts to wonder which to choose.

The easy answer is both. There is simply no replacement for the information provided by graphing the outcome variable as it varies over time (see Wilkonson et al., 1999, for discussion). The time-tested method of visual inspection has no substitute for assessing the volatility of observations, and for communicating the results of the experiment to other researchers or to the patients themselves. However, decades of research have demonstrated that the insular use of graphical analysis to evaluate the single-subject experiment is limited by a number of factors. For instance, researchers may disagree in their interpretation of the data (DeProspero & Cohen, 1979). The method is also affected by the nature of the graphical presentation (i.e., choice of axis scale). Further, the reliance on visual inspection may lead to more Type I errors, especially when there is a great deal of serial dependency (see next section) in the data (Jones, Weinrott, & Vaught, 1978; Knapp, 1983; Matays & Greenwood, 1990a; Matays & Greenwood, 1990b).

The present chapter is predicated on the assumption that the statistical analysis of single-case experimental designs adds an element to the evaluation of studies not present with the insular use of graphical techniques. Indeed, the rest of the chapter will address the unique contributions of several selected statistical tests while considering their unique assumptions and limitations. The choice of which techniques to present is difficult because the choice of which inferential statistic to apply to a study naturally flows from the question that drives it and it is quite impossible to anticipate all possible experimental questions. This limitation leads to descriptions that will be necessarily general in nature as a broad array of applications will be covered. What follows is a description of the nature of single-case time-series data, and subsequently, several statistical approaches that can contribute to the evaluation of single-subject experiments (and quasi-experiments).

9.2. SINGLE-SUBJECT EXPERIMENTS AND TIME-SERIES DATA

Single-subject experimental designs require that one subject be observed on some variable of interest, the dependent variable (DV), while another variable that is thought to affect the DV, the independent variable (IV), is systematically manipulated by the researcher (Kirk, 1995). In this way, a researcher can ascertain what unique effect the IV has on the DV. If the DV is measured without error (a truly objective measure), and if the DV does not exhibit any natural variability, then the experiment can consist of very few measurements; any change in the DV can reasonably be assured to be due to the influence of the manipulated IV. This hypothetical situation describes a *deterministic* system in which a DV can be completely predicted when one knows the level of the IV (e.g., think of a light switch as an IV and amount of light as a DV). In the behavioral sciences, deterministic systems are exceedingly rare. In fact, most behavioral phenomena cannot be thought to be measured without error, and have myriad sources of influence such that any selected DV will vary randomly across measurements, even when the IV is held constant. These types of DVs are called *stochastic* (i.e., probabilistic) and require that the researcher measure them repeatedly across time to better ensure that the observed level of the variable is in fact due to the IV and not simply a random fluctuation in the DV. Collecting repeated observations of the same variable over time is thus almost always necessary in single-case experimental designs and doing so creates a phenomenon called a time-series.

The nature of time-series data

A time-series can be defined as "A sequence of observations taken sequentially in time" (Box, Jenkins, & Reinsel, 1994, p. 1). This sequence of observations can be either continuous or discrete. Continuous time-series involve uninterrupted collection of observations (e.g., hand temperature recorded continuously). A discrete series is one in which the observations are made at equal intervals in time (e.g., daily caloric intake), with the intervals between observations remaining constant throughout the observation period (Box, Jenkins, & Reinsel, 1994; Crabtree, Ray, Schmidt, O'Connor, & Schmidt, 1990; Nelson, 1998). Certainly, data that are continuous in nature could be sampled to create discrete observations. For the sections that follow, the described mathematics applies to time-series data that are discrete.

The nature of single-subject research lends itself to the collection of discrete time-series data. In behavioral research, this collection of discrete time-series occurs quite routinely. Self-report diaries, frequency counts obtained by the researcher, sophisticated physiological monitoring equipment, or other more naturalistic methods could be used to assess the DV as it varies over time in response to an IV. The observations could be made daily or the information could be recorded several times each day (i.e., 8-hour intervals), to increase the amount of data available for analysis (see Stone et al., 2003). These data, observed over time, result in information that is both individual-specific and dynamic in nature, and allow for a host of single-subject statistical analyses.

As previously mentioned, the vast majority of series collected in behavioral research can be considered stochastic. These series are not entirely mathematically determined by any known group of factors. Instead, researchers and clinicians must use statistical models to describe their behavior over time. In the stochastic process of most behavioral data, an observation can be considered to have been influenced by any number of processes that combine to form a realization of those processes. This realization, which is the observed score, can be viewed like a traditional random variable (Shumway & Stoffer, 2000). Thus, a time-series can be re-conceptualized as a sequence of random variables collected in a particular time order. Perhaps these abstract statements can be made more understandable when presented graphically using a DV over time.

Mathematical and graphical description of a time series

A stochastic dependent variable (DV) at a given time (t) can be described using its mean level (μ), plus a unique influence or "shock" (a) driving it up or down from its mean level at that time. This equation is (Yule, 1927):

Equation 9.1: $$DV_t = \mu + a_t$$

The value of a_t can be either positive or negative, depending on the direction of the shock and will necessarily be bounded in magnitude by the scale being used to quantify the DV (e.g., 0 – 10 in a subjective units of distress scale [SUDS]). Figure 9.1 graphically displays the value of a_t for 10 fictitious observations collected on a patient with a spider phobia while approaching a spider in 10 trials (time) while rating SUDS at the end of each trial.

This equation is certainly not a novel mathematical conceptualization of a time-series. Yule (1927), while examining his own single-case study (the fluctuation of sun spots), is credited with coining the term "shocks" (a_t) that influence every observation. Since Yule, the use of a linear filter model, driven by unique shocks or innovations, has been used extensively in many fields, but especially in econometrics (the linear filter is covered later under ARIMA models). The independent shocks are thought to be random drawings from a fixed distribution, which can be argued to be normally distributed with a mean of 0 and variance of σ_a^2 (Box, Jenkins, & Reinsel, 1994). Further, the expected covariance between the shocks is 0, indicating that they represent a "white noise" process (i.e., the value of one shock is a poor predictor of earlier or later shocks). For behavioral data, with a myriad of unique potential influences, the assumptions that shocks are normally distributed and independent would seem especially tenable.

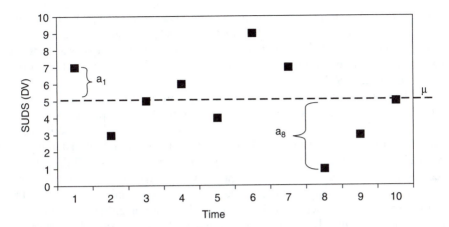

FIGURE 9.1 SUDS (DV) as a function of mean (μ) and a "unique shock" (a_t). Each successive observation can be described using a mean level of the DV ($\mu = 5$) and a shock pushing the observed score above or below the mean. For time $= 1$, the shock ($a_1 = 2$) pushes the observed level of up 2 points to a 7. At time $= 8$, the shock ($a_8 = -4$) pushes the observed level down 4 points to a 1.

Yule's equation applies to many other similarly observed DVs (e.g., acting out behavior, stress level, coping, etc.) that are collected in a discrete time-series format. These variables can also be conceptualized as the realization of a multifactorial (perhaps biopsychosocial; see Houle et al., 2005) process and can be treated as a random variable. Thus, the variance of these variables (or any variables of interest) can be described using a mean level and a unique shock pushing the observed scores above or below the mean. However, the mathematical conceptualization of these variables in this manner does not necessarily imply that they vary meaningfully, and careful attention must be paid to their measurement and interpretation (Onghena & Edgington, 2005). Even under the best of circumstances there are several common mathematical issues with time-series data that are created when a DV is observed over time and that can greatly affect data analysis.

The problem of autocorrelation

When observations of a phenomenon are collected repeatedly over time, subsequent observations tend to be more related than observations more temporally distant (Shumway & Stoffer, 2000). This process has been called autocorrelation, and is the correlation of the series with itself. For example, consider a single-case example of the average daily temperature in Chicago. The average daily temperature is expected to be more similar for two consecutive days in July, than for a particular July and November day. In this example, as in many instances where observations are made in a temporal order, the data are not independent, as one observation can be informative about other observations. As a result of the non-independence, the use of many inferential statistics (e.g., analysis of variance and multiple regression analysis) is inappropriate as most inferential statistics are based on the assumption that observations are independent (West & Hepworth, 1991; Pedhauzer, 1997).

When observations are not independent, as in the case of the average daily temperature, observations close together in time become predictive of one another. This nonindependence creates data structures that when described linearly (as is the case in both ANOVA and Multiple Regression Analysis), produces residuals, or error terms, that are correlated. To illustrate, Figure 9.2 displays the regression of the average daily temperature in Chicago on time over a 7-year period. It is worth noting that the relationship is visually nonlinear but is used to illustrate the problem. Beginning in January and continuing until spring, the linear prediction systematically *over*-represents the data. However, after the occurrence of spring, the predicted values systematically *under*-represent the data. Examination of the residuals in Figure 9.2 illustrates the fact that the magnitude and direction of any current residual is a strong predictor of temporally similar residuals. This data structure leads to residuals that are correlated with near-present (future and past) values, and it is this dependency in the residuals that violates the assumption of many inferential statistics (West & Hepworth, 1991; Jaccard & Wan, 1993).

Autocorrelation in a series is measured by the use of an autocorrelation function (ACF) and partial autocorrelation function (PACF). The ACF consists

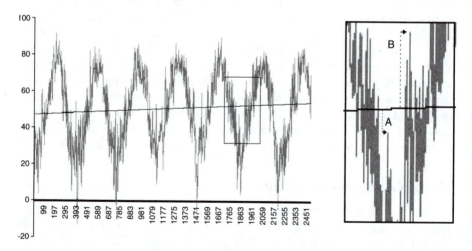

FIGURE 9.2 Regression analysis illustrating autocorrelation in the average daily temperature in Chicago over a 7-year period. Enlargement: Residual A is the degree to which the regression line over predicts temperature. Residual B is the degree to which the regression line under-predicts temperature. Note how residuals close together in time share a similar location in regards to the regression line (either above or below).

of correlations between observations in the series separated by various lags, or temporal distance between them. For instance, the lag 1 autocorrelation represents the degree to which the current observation can be predicted from the observation prior. It would be calculated by correlating the second observation with the first observation, the third with the second, and so on throughout the series (one observation is lost in the calculation as the first observation cannot be correlated with a prior observation). In this way, a researcher can calculate the relatedness (autocorrelation) of previous observations with the present observation using lags of values 1 to k of the series (k = number of observations −1). The PACF is similar as it calculates the correlation of the series with itself at different lags but after partialling out (controlling for) the effects of intervening lags. When displayed graphically, the ACF and PACF are often referred to as a correlogram (Kazdin, 1984). Figure 9.3 displays the ACF for 16 lags of a series collected by a patient who recorded her daily levels of hopelessness for 195 days (graph produced using SPSS).

In single-case research, there are several distinct processes that could potentially introduce autocorrelation into the data. In a following section on time-series analysis, these processes will be described along with several approaches to dealing with them. Before addressing specific analytical approaches, many of which have been designed specifically for dealing with autocorrelation, several important

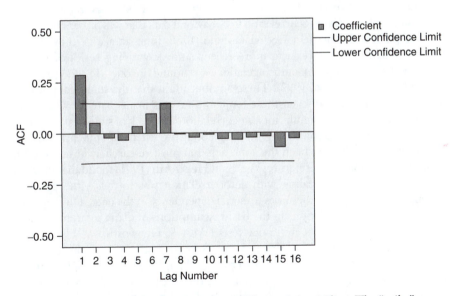

FIGURE 9.3   An autocorrelation function (ACF) examining 16 lags. The "spike" occurring at lag 1 surpasses the upper value of the 95% confidence interval, indicating significant positive autocorrelation of r = .29. Note how little autocorrelation exists between lags 2 and 6, but that significant autocorrelation exists at lag 7 indicating a cyclical (weekly) relationship (i.e., Mondays are similar in terms of reported hopelessness).

questions loom: What is the prevalence of autocorrelation in single-subject experiments that examine human behavior? Or relatedly, do analysts need to worry themselves over autocorrelation in behavioral data?

Autocorrelation and human behavior

Thus far it has been discussed that when it comes to single-subject analyses, there has been a substantial amount of controversy concerning most aspects of the process. So, it should not be shocking to learn that when it comes to the prevalence of autocorrelation in behavioral data, that here too there has been great disagreement among researchers concerning the extent, if even any, that autocorrelation resides in these type of data.

Even a cursory review of the studies that have examined this issue reveal that methodological differences are often confounded with the stated conclusions found by various authors (Sideridis & Greenwood, 1997). For instance, in a review of all studies published in the *Journal of Applied Behavior Analysis* from 1968 to 1977, Huitema (1985) concluded that no autocorrelation existed in these series. However, later studies criticized this conclusion for several reasons, perhaps the most important being that the review may have been biased by the inclusion of studies that contained very few observations (number of observations, n < 10), which may greatly underestimate the true extent of autocorrelation (Matyas & Greenwood, 1991; Sideridis & Greenwood, 1997). This conclusion is in contrast to several studies that have found substantial autocorrelation in behavioral data that was present in 23% to 83% of examined series (Busk & Marascuilo, 1988; Jones et al., 1978; Matyas & Greenwood, 1991). However, a more recent study examining series of n > 30 concluded that significant autocorrelation was found in only 11.65% of series (Sideridis & Greenwood, 1997). These authors admit that the statistical power to detect autocorrelation in even these longer series was inadequate (power <.72), confounding the lack of significant autocorrelation with lack of statistical power.

Considering the conflicting findings about the extent of autocorrelation in behavioral data, what has been the approach that most researchers have taken? In reviewing psychological literature, West and Hepworth (1991) found that the most common approach to dealing with autocorrelation was to *ignore* the problem, effectively assuming that there was no serial dependency in the data. This approach could easily lead to violations in the basic assumptions of many inferential statistics, and produce biased significance tests (West & Hepworth, 1991; Jaccard & Wan, 1993). However, traditional Least Squares estimates of the statistical parameters would remain unbiased (Jaccard & Wan, 1993). For example using the prior regression of average daily temperature on time (Figure 9.2), the parameters defining the line of best fit, remain the best fit. It is the estimated standard errors of these parameters that become biased (Jaccard & Wan, 1993; West & Hepworth, 1991); usually underestimating the actual standard errors of the parameters (Jaccard & Wan, 1993). Underestimation of the standard errors leads to inflation of Type I error, as the values of inferential statistics become recursively inflated.

In the average daily temperature regression, the investigator might overestimate the model's ability to predict temperature as the model's utility is artificially inflated.

General comments

In summary, single-case experiments very often lead to the collection of time-series data. These types of data often contain statistical dependencies (autocorrelation) such that observations close together in time are more similar to each other than with their mean. Autocorrelation may or may not be present in a single-case experiment, but failing to address autocorrelation where it does exist can lead to faulty inference testing in statistical (and perhaps graphical) analysis. Although experts differ in respect to the prevalence of autocorrelation of the *average* series in behavioral research, what is evident from the studies that have been conducted is that at the very least *some* behavioral series will contain this type of serial dependency. Thus, it seems clear that a single-case analyst would be well-advised to examine the data for the existence of autocorrelation, and if present, to select an analytical strategy that addresses autocorrelation. In the sections that follow many such strategies will be discussed.

9.3. SPECIFIC STATISTICAL TESTS

Since Kazdin's (1984) outline of statistical analytic approaches for single-case designs in the previous edition of this book, it is interesting to see how many things have changed, and more interestingly, how many things have not. The types of applicable tests, in particular their assumptions and limitations, mostly have not changed. However, the statistical software used to calculate them, and thus their availability to the average researcher, have greatly improved. In many cases, the performances of tests under a variety of conditions have been better studied and new caveats can be issued.

Depending on the experimental question and resulting types of data, many possible statistical tests could be chosen by an analyst. As in Kazdin's seminal work, the described tests are simply a selection of possible tests that are available. For each test, its assumptions, a description, limitations, and available software will be reviewed.

Conventional t and F tests

Data Assumptions.   Parametric assumptions: normal distribution, homogeneity of variances (and covariances for ANOVA), and independence of observations.

Description.   Because of their ubiquitous use in between-groups analysis and resulting familiarity to most researchers, tests that can assess the reliability of differences between two (t test) or more (ANOVA) groups are a very seductive choice in evaluating a single-case study. In such an application, the "groups" consist of the observations in each phase of the experiment and instead of comparing differences between separate groups of people the tests compare differences between phases. Similarly, within-group variance (error variance) actually becomes within-phase variance. Thus, the tests are calculated by dividing the differences between phases by the pooled variation within-phases (assumed to be equal across phases) in a calculation identical to a standard t or F test.

For instance, in an A-B design, a t test could be used to evaluate the statistical significance of the difference between the mean level of baseline observations (A) compared with the observations collected during an intervention phase (B). If more than one experimental condition is tested (A-B-C) or if the intervention is reversed (A-B-A-B) an analysis of variance (ANOVA) could be used to statistically assess the differences in phases. Permutations of these applications could (and have) been devised combining treatment phases into meaningful groups for statistical comparison (as in combing all A observations and comparing them with all B observations in a t-test).

Limitations.   The use of conventional t and F tests in single-case designs is problematic (Crosbie, 1993; Toothaker et al., 1983) and should be reserved for only rare instances. In fact, it is hard to imagine an application where these tests could be appropriately applied in single-case designs. This is the case for several reasons, all having to do with the probability of single-case designs producing data that violate the assumptions underlying the tests.

First, although these types of tests are quite robust in terms of violations of normality (Kirk, 1995), certain data types push the limits of even this robustness. For example, when examining an intervention's effect on a phenomena that only occurs episodically, such that observations can either be present to some degree or completely absent during an observation period, most observations of a DV are likely to center around a value of zero, with only some non-zero values. This type of data structure greatly violates the assumption of normality and inferences based on these data could be greatly biased (Kirk, 1995). For data of these types, t and F tests should not be used.

Second, the tests assume that observations in each phase are independent, which is tantamount to the series containing no autocorrelation. As previously discussed, single-case behavioral designs may not contain substantial amounts of autocorrelation. However, studies have shown that even small amounts of autocorrelation can bias the conclusions drawn from such tests. For instance, Crosbie (1993) demonstrated that a modest first-order autocorrelation of only $r = .20$ can bias the Type-I error rate from the desired $\alpha = .05$ to $\alpha = .08-.12$, depending on the length of the series. A negative autocorrelation of $r = -.20$ had a similar effect on decreasing the Type-I error rate. These results emphasize how sensitive t and F tests are to even small violations in the assumption of independent observations. Thus, even if a series does not contain statistically significant degrees of autocorrelation (the statistical power of which is based entirely

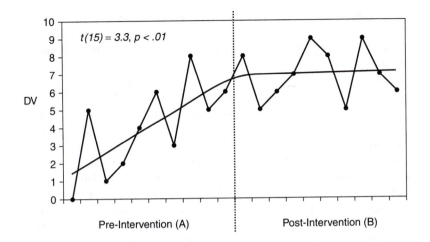

FIGURE 9.4 Example of an inappropriately applied *t* test. Even after adjusting the df for violation of the homogeneity of variances assumption, the *t*-test results in a significant difference between phases. Close inspection of the baseline trend indicates that the DV was improving before the introduction of the intervention. The application of *F* and *t*-tests do not account for trends occurring within a phase.

on the length of the series), it could still contain autocorrelation sufficient to bias the results of *t* or *F* tests.

Finally, because they are computed based on means and variances alone, these tests are insensitive to trends that occur within a phase. It is of note that this is a special case of the violation of independence of observations assumption as trends are a special type of autocorrelation (see ARIMA models). Figure 9.4 displays an improving trend in the baseline phase that is not fully considered in the application of a *t* test. When trends are present in any phase of the experiment, the use of *t* or *F* tests is strongly discouraged.

Available Software. *t* tests and ANOVA (GLM) applications are probably available on all statistical software. SPSS, SAS, Systat, SigmaStat, Statistica, and EXCEL, among many others, all contain routines supporting these analyses.

Randomization tests

Data Assumptions. No assumptions about the distributions of the data (i.e., a distribution-free test) are made. However, it is assumed that experimental conditions are randomly assigned to observation occasions, or groups of occasions.

Description. In recent years, growing attention has been paid to the use of statistical tests that are not reliant on traditional parametric assumptions that base inferences on the populations from which a sample was drawn (see *t* and

F tests). Instead, distribution-free tests that solely utilize information from the sample to evaluate a null hypothesis have been developed. Randomization tests refer to a large family of such tests that all utilize similar logic in evaluating an experiment.

Crucial to the use of these tests is the concept of randomization. In between-groups research subjects are randomly assigned to one of several possible groups that are exactly similar to each other with the exception of the presence and/or degree of the IV that the experimenter is studying. The use of random assignment distinguishes true experimental from quasi-experimental designs in that it neutralizes possible threats to the internal validity of the study by equating the treatment groups on all extraneous variables both known and unknown (Campbell & Stanley, 1966). In single-case experimental designs there is obviously only one entity, so the concept of randomization uniquely translates to the random assignment of treatment condition (IV) to measurement occasion (Onghena & Edgington, 2005). Thus, true experimental single-case designs can be distinguished from quasi-experimental designs by the random assignment of treatment intervention(s) to measurement occasions (Onghena & Edgington, 2005).

Revisiting Figure 9.1 demonstrates the importance of randomization in these designs. Using Yule's equation, it can be seen that every observation occasion (e.g., day) is affected by a unique combination of forces (shocks, a_t) that influence the DV. On some days, like day 1 in Figure 9.1, the combination of shocks is more than typical, which causes the DV to be higher than average. On other days, like day 8, the combination of shocks is less than expected, resulting in lower than average observed levels of the DV. It is interesting to note that these fluctuations in the DV can be the case *even though there is no active intervention*, reflecting only the natural variability of the multitude of forces acting on an entity. The effect of an intervention can be thought of as just another shock that serves to increase or decrease the DV on that measurement occasion. Depending on the nature of an intervention, its effect can intermingle with the naturally occurring extraneous processes obscuring the "true" value of the treatment effect. For this reason it is advantageous to randomly assign the treatment to observation occasions to gain a more reliable estimate of the effect of the intervention under a variety of other naturally occurring shocks.

There are two types of randomization schemes that are entirely based on the nature of the intervention (IV) being studied. The first type assumes that an intervention can be completely alternated on any given measurement occasion. This *alternation* randomization scheme randomly assigns the intervention to given observations using predetermined limitations (e.g., an equal proportion of treatment A and B). This randomization scheme is a natural extension of the alternating treatments design (ATD) and can be adapted to any number of interventions that can be suitably studied using such a design (see chapter 8 for a thorough review of the issues involved). An example of alternation randomization displaying all 20 possible unique combinations of an IV with 2 levels (A & B) with 3 observation occasions per level (6 measurement occasions) is presented by Onghena and Edgington (2005):

AAABBB	BBBAAA
AABABB	BBABAA
AABBAB	BBAABA
AABBBA	BBAAAB
ABAABB	BABBAA
ABABAB	BABABA
ABABBA	BABAAB
ABBAAB	BAABBA
ABBABA	BAABAB
ABBBAA	BAAABB

As can be intuited, the number of possible randomization orders is greatly increased with the addition of more measurement occasions and/or more IVs.

The second randomization scheme, and one that is probably much more common in behavioral research, is employed when it is not feasible to randomly intersperse the intervention among all observation occasions. The implementation of a *phase* randomization scheme is used when the intervention is optimally introduced over the course of several measurement occasions occurring in a predetermined order (Onghena & Edgington, 2005). Phase designs are common for many different types of interventions that are predicted to have cumulative or carry-over effects (see chapter 3). Because the order of the introduction of the intervention effects is usually predetermined (i.e., it is usually advantageous to have the baseline phase precede the intervention phase), it is the *timing* of the phase change that is randomized in these designs. For example, again using an IV with 2 levels and with 6 total measurement occasions (Onghena & Edgington, 2005):

ABBBBB
AABBBB
AAABBB
AAAABB
AAAAAB

The start of the B phase could occur on 1 of 5 possible observation occasions. Because any particular phase is more optimally studied using far more than one observation per phase, limits to the smallest number of observations per phase can be imposed. In practice, experiments of this type are conducted with far more than 6 observations (see below). It is of note that there are far fewer unique combinations of randomly assigned phase change orders than combinations of alternation designs, a fact that will be shown to decrease statistical power.

In sum, when the intervention is randomized to measurement occasion using either an alternation or phase scheme, the use of a randomization test becomes possible. The logic behind these tests is quite simple: If the intervention has no impact on the DV, then the actual observations are not influenced by the IV and the observed scores simply reflect the combination of naturally occurring shocks; the actual order of the IV presentation should not matter. This null hypothesis can be directly tested by rearranging the actual observed scores to all permutations of the possible randomization orders and examining the different outcomes.

For example using a design similar to the alternation scheme presented earlier, suppose a researcher was interested in conducting a 6-day study examining the effect of a novel intervention (B) as compared to baseline (A) on some DV. In the present example, the researcher feels that it is undesirable to have either intervention presented three days in a row, so decides to eliminate the AAABBB, BBBAAA, AABBBA, BBAAAB, ABBBAA, and BAAABB schemes as possibilities, resulting in 14 remaining permutations. Then, the range of acceptable randomization orders is listed, one is randomly selected, and the study is conducted. Table 9.1 lists the acceptable orders and stars the order that was randomly selected. The study is carried out with the intervention presented on days 1, 4, and 5 (BAABBA).

The intervention was potent. The experiment resulted in observed values of the DV of 9, 4, 3, 7, 8, 2. For the present example, the researcher was interested in examining a test statistic of the difference between the mean of observed scores on B days versus the mean of observed scores on A days (test statistic: $\bar{B} - \bar{A}$). The null hypothesis that the intervention had no effect ($\bar{A} = \bar{B}$) is equivalent to testing the order of randomization. The observed scores are treated as if they are fixed but came from each of the different randomization orders. The test statistic is then calculated for each of the possible randomization orders, which in essence assigns the observed scores to a different pattern of presentation of A and B (if A = B, then the order should not matter). For example, although the actual randomization order is known, what if the observed scores had come from AABABB? Table 9.1 calculates the test statistic for all permutations of randomization orders.

As can be seen in the table, the actual randomization order resulted in the greatest positive difference between A and B (indicating that $B > A$). Is this

TABLE 9.1 The 14 Acceptable Randomization Orders and the Test Statistic ($\bar{B} - \bar{A}$) for Each of the Possible Assignments of the Observed Scores (9, 4, 3, 7, 8, 2) to Randomization Order

ASSIGNMENT	$\bar{B} - \bar{A}$	ASSIGNMENT	$\bar{B} - \bar{A}$
AABABB	−2.3	BBABAA	2.3
AABBAB	−3.0	BBAABA	3.0
ABAABB	−1.7	BABBAA	1.7
ABABAB	−2.3	BABABA	2.3
ABABBA	1.7	BABAAB	−1.7
ABBAAB	−5.0	BAABBA*	5.0
ABBABA	−1.0	BAABAB	1.0

*Signifies the observed randomization order and resulting observed test statistic.

difference statistically significant? If the null hypothesis is true, then many of the randomization orders should result in the test statistic being greater than or equal to the observed result simply by chance alone. The p value for a randomization test is thus equal to the proportion of test statistics that are greater than or equal to the observed test statistic. To calculate this using a one-tailed test, the number of scores greater than or equal to the test statistic (including the observed value) is divided by the number of possible randomization schemes. In this case, there are no other test statistics that are greater than or equal to the observed test statistic so the calculation is $p = 1/14 = .071$. That is, assuming the order of randomization does not influence the DV, the chance of observing a test statistic this discrepant is only .071. Applications of randomization tests typically utilize the traditional significant p value (Type-I error rate, α) of .05. Even our potent intervention did not yield a significant result because of low statistical power, highlighting the necessity of more measurement occasions in real studies.

The identical procedure is undertaken to analyze phase designs. The list of possible phase change times are generated (often, a researcher will greatly limit the possible phase change times to allow for a minimally acceptable number of observations in each phase). Then, one randomization order is selected and the study is conducted. To analyze the test statistic, the same procedure is undertaken calculating the proportion of test statistics that are greater than or equal to the observed statistic.

As is hopefully growing evident, the application of randomization tests provides a researcher with a very flexible family of tests that help in the evaluation of experiments. The word "family" is used to describe these tests because any number of test statistics can be evaluated using these techniques. For instance, in the above example, a one-tailed test was used (examining differences in only 1 direction). If a researcher wished to use a two-tailed test (hypothesis: $A \neq B$), the absolute value of the test statistics could have been used (Onghena & Edgington, 2005). In the above example using the alternation design, a two-tailed test would have resulted in a p value $= 2/14 = .14$. Further, any number of test statistics could be evaluated. The listed example comparing two means is simply one type of test statistic; medians, variances, slopes, and many other statistics could be evaluated. Finally, any conceivable permutation of number of treatments, measurement occasions, or other design issues can be evaluated using these tests, as long as there is an element of randomization in the design. Because of the wide-ranging scope of these tests, the preceding discussion was necessarily limited to specific single-case experimental designs (and only a small portion of these). Indeed, several texts have been written on the application of these tests and the reader is referred there for a more comprehensive understanding (e.g., Edgington, 1995).

Limitations. Thus far the use of randomization tests has seemed quite ideal. They do not place unreasonable assumptions on the data and they are applicable in a vast array of different experimental designs. However, despite their efficiency, randomization tests have been called impractical (Bradley, 1968). If these tests lack practicality it is for two very related reasons.

The first reason these tests may be impractical concerns the amount of statistical power that they provide. Although the statistical power provided by alternation designs for a comparison between two means (two treatments) is equivalent to a t test (Onghena & Edgington, 2005), phase designs may be $\leq 10\%$ as efficient in such an application (Ferron & Onghena, 1996). This is the case because the amount of power for these tests is directly proportional to the number of ways that the intervention(s) can be randomized to observations. For an alternation design with two levels of the IV (A & B), the number of different ways that a unique randomization order can be calculated is: $ways = \dfrac{N!}{n_1! n_2!}$, where N = total number of observation occasions and n_1 is the number of observation occasions occurring in A and n_2 in B. Two-phase designs result in far fewer permutations, requiring up to 10 times as many observation occasions as alternation designs with 2 levels. Phase designs do exhibit increasing power with increasing phase changes. For example, ABAB designs with 5 observations per phase reportedly approach the power function of alternation designs (Ferron & Onghena, 1996; Onghena & Edgington, 2005). All of this being the case, how many observations are needed to provide adequate statistical power?

Although it is theoretically possible for 6 total observations to produce a statistically significant result in a two-phase alternation design ($1/20 = .05$), this would be the case under only the largest of interventions. It should be noted that the above calculated example, $p = 1/14$, was incapable of resulting in significance at the .05 level. In terms of effect size, a "Medium" sized intervention (Cohen's $d = .50$) would require 50 observations for each treatment using an alternation design with two levels (see Cohen, 1988, for description of power), and a great many more for a phase design with only 1 phase change (up to 10 times as many as the alternation design; Onghena & Edgington, 2005). Thus, when designing studies that are to be evaluated using randomization tests, like all other statistical tests, statistical power calculations must be considered (Cohen, 1988).

Onghena and Edgington (2005) discuss several other issues that may adversely affect the statistical power of randomization tests in single-case designs. Although previously thought to be unaffected by the effects of autocorrelation (Kazdin, 1984), the power of randomization tests may be diminished with the presence of autocorrelation (Onghena & Edgington, 2005). A delayed response and/or differential carryover effects such that introduction of intervention B takes effect either in subsequent observation periods or lingers in these periods can greatly affect interpretation as well. These limitations can be particularly problematic in alternation designs. The application of the alternating treatments design, including potential limitations of this design, is extensively covered in chapter 8.

The second reason these tests may be impractical concerns their computational burden. Because adequate statistical power requires that a suitable number of observation occasions are collected, and because the number of permutations increases exponentially as observations increase, even small-sized studies require suitable software and processing capability. For instance, using the now-familiar example of a 2 treatment alternation design, only 10 observations per occasion ($N = 20$) produces 184,756 (20!/10!*10!) different permutations that need to be evaluated to calculate the observed p value of the test statistic. A study designed to examine a medium effect size ($N = 100$) would require a back-breaking $1.01*10^{29}$ permutations to be calculated. At the time of this writing, the magnitude of this calculation is non-trivial for even high speed processors.

This computational problem of randomization tests has been addressed using statistical methods based on resampling procedures. In essence, a manageable number of permutations can be randomly selected from the available permutations, the test statistic can be evaluated on only this subset, and the p value can be estimated to a very high degree of accuracy. Although this clever solution effectively addresses the computational limitations, the available software to conduct randomization tests for single-case designs has not been widely available. However, Onghena and Edgington (2005) recently provided a list of viable options.

Available Software. Single-Case Randomization Tests (SCRT; Onghena & Van Damme, 1994), EXCEL routines have been created (Todman & Dugard, 1999), RegRand (Koehler & Levin, 2000), and COMBINE (Edgington & Haller, 1983).

Interrupted time-series analysis (ITSA)

Data Assumptions. The series is equally spaced at meaningful intervals, is weakly stationary (or can be made stationary, see below), consists of at least 50 observations (more adequately 50 observations per phase), has no missing values, and has homoscedastic (i.e., constant) variance (or can be made to have constant variance). The parameters of the ARIMA model (discussed below) do not change as a function of time (i.e., regime stability). For testing the impact of the intervention, it is assumed that the timing of the intervention is known and that the system is closed, in that the intervention is the only external source of systematic influence being modeled (Yaffee & McGee, 2000).

Description. The use of time-series analysis has become increasingly popular over the past 20 years. This increase in use was predicted by Kazdin (1984) who formally recommended it in single-subject analyses. Remarkably, the field of statistical time-series analyses has undergone even more substantial growth during this same period, resulting in a dizzying array of new techniques and applications. Thus, the presentation of these approaches can only serve as an introduction; an analyst would be well-advised to consult with the many cited texts for a complete description. There are now far too many applications of time-series analysis to review each in detail. Instead, only a small subset of these approaches that have particular relevance to the single-subject experimental design will be described.

Interrupted time-series analysis (ITSA) is such an approach that is well-suited for the evaluation of single-case experiments and quasi-experiments. As shall be seen, ITSA addresses a variety of potential types of autocorrelation in the series while also allowing a researcher to model (or describe) a variety of effects that the intervention could potentially have on the DV. Interestingly, this sophisticated technique uses a simple t test to evaluate the differences in levels (means) for different phases of the study, but unlike a traditionally applied t test, can be applied under a variety of conditions including trending baselines, short-acting interventions, delayed response interventions, etc. The technique is certainly not without its limitations and these will be reviewed after a discussion of how ITSA (and other applications based on ARIMA models) addresses autocorrelation, how ITSA models effects, several ITSA modeling strategies, and an example of an applied ITSA model.

Autoregressive Integrated Moving Average (ARIMA) models

Box and Jenkins (1970) provided a comprehensive framework for analyzing time-series data and created a three-stage process for applying the techniques necessary to mathematically model, or if desired, remove autocorrelation. This seminal publication has been revised twice (1976, 1994) to reflect the growing body of research and substantial improvements in computer applications. A brief review of the terminology of the ARIMA subheading, or Autoregressive (AR), Integrated (I), Moving Average (MA) models (i.e., ARIMA) and a description of the 3-stage process suggested by Box and Jenkins (1970) follows.

Each of the different types of ARIMA models begins with Yule's equation (Equation 1.1), which assumes that an observation can be conceived as a mean level (μ), plus a unique shock (a_t) driving its value up or down from that mean at any given time. However, because a series is generated in a time-order, prior influences on the series can often still be present during the current observation. The nature of these processes is what produces autocorrelation in a series. In a clever depiction, Box, Jenkins, and Reinsel (1994) conceive the individual influences (the shocks, which are thought to be independent of each other) as entering a "linear filter," which transforms them into the observed scores that now may contain autocorrelation. Figure 9.5 displays this depiction, which starts with the unique influences at a given time (a_t), and ends with an observed score (Y_t) that contains autocorrelation:

FIGURE 9.5

In essence, ARIMA modeling is an attempt to parsimoniously describe the effect of the linear filter on the unique shocks. Stated differently, ARIMA models describe the nature of the autocorrelation in the series, effectively changing the black box representation of the linear filter into a system that effectively describes the temporal relationship among the observed scores. ARIMA models use three types of parameters to accomplish this task.

Autoregressive parameters (AR), commonly denoted as p, describe the degree to which the current observation is related to prior observations. This parameter, like all ARIMA parameters, can have several "orders." The order, in this case, describes how many past values (i.e., "lags" of the series) can successfully predict the current value. For example, a p(2) model is one where the previous two values can successfully predict the current value. Conceptually, the autoregressive parameter uses lags of the actual series to model autocorrelation produced from temporally similar observations. For example, to model variance due to autocorrelation of an p(1) process, the following regression equation could be used:

Equation 9.2: $$Y_t = \phi Y_{t-1} + a_t$$

In this example, the value of the current observation Y_t is regressed onto itself lagged one observation Y_{t-1}. When the effect of past observations on the current observation is modeled and removed, the remaining variance represents the unique shocks. The value of the parameter weight ϕ can be obtained using ordinary least squares estimates, and if the process that introduces autocorrelation into the series (i.e., the linear filter) is well-represented by a p(1), the residuals from this model (a_t) will be the unique shocks and contain no autocorrelation ("unique" being why they are free of autocorrelation).

Integrated parameters, commonly denoted as d, are often called "differencing" and are used to make the series stationary. Nonstationarity is a complex topic but for the present discussion refers to a series for which the mean, variance, and covariance is changing over time. In terms of Yule's equation, for nonstationary series the constant value (μ) is not actually constant as the observed values are systematically increasing or decreasing over time (or both). If the series is consistently changing over time the process is called a trend, if the series returns to its previous value is it said to drift (McDowall, McCleary, Meidinger, & Hay, 1980).

Like the p parameters, d parameters can have several orders that reflect the degree of nonstationarity of the series. A d(1) reflects a linearly nonstationary series and is computed by subtracting the prior observation from the current observation:

Equation 9.3: $$d(1) = Y_t - Y_{t-1}.$$

A second order difference d(2) is necessary when the series is exponentially changing and can be calculated by differencing the first-order differences. Differenced values conceptually represent the degree of change from observation to observation. When a series has been made stationary using differencing, the differenced values are then used in place of the actual observations. ARIMA models must be made stationary before calculating their parameter weights (AR & MA, or p & q).

Moving average parameters (MA), commonly denoted as q, reflect the effect of past "unique shocks" influencing current observations. Every observation is effected by a unique shock of a presumably random value. However, at times the same effects influencing prior unique shocks can influence the current observation, causing the current observation to be dependent on not only the current value of the unique shock but also past values of unique shocks. When current observations can be predicted from prior unique shocks, a dependency exists that is subtly different than that of the autoregressive type, and can only be removed using either an infinite sum of p parameters or much more simply, a moving average parameter of order q. A first-order MA process can be represented using the following equation:

Equation 9.4: $$Y_t = a_t - \theta a_{t-1}$$

Current observations (Y_t) are regressed onto current (a_t) and past (a_{t-1}) shocks, and θ represents the weight of the first-order MA parameter.

However, there is an inherent mathematical problem in measuring shocks. In regression terminology, unique shocks (a_t) are modeled as the variance in stationary observed scores left over after removing all autocorrelational processes. However, an ARIMA (p, d, q) model cannot be correctly specified until the weights of all parameters are known. Conceptually, this is equivalent to needing the residuals of the model *before* defining the model. This inherent difficulty is usually negotiated using preselected starting values of the parameters in an iterative procedure with maximum likelihood estimates in lieu of least squares criteria (see available software).

An ARIMA model is defined by the order of each of its parameters. Each of the parameters (p, d, q) can be used alone or in combination with each other to model autocorrelation in the series. If a series contains autocorrelation that is able to be modeled using a first-order difference to make it stationary, first-order autoregressive parameter, and a first-order moving average process, its autocorrelation is said to be removed using an ARIMA (1, 1, 1) model. In this case, the residuals of the model would now be absent of autocorrelation. The formula for this ARIMA (1, 1, 1) model could be expressed as:

Equation 9.5: $$Y_t - Y_{t-1} = Z_t = \phi_1 Z_{t-1} + a_t - \theta_1 a_{t-1}$$

Where Z_t represents the differenced observations and where the parameter weights (ϕ θ) are derived using an iterative nonlinear procedure. The most general form of the equation, which reflects the fact that any number of p or q parameters could be used to model a stationary series Y_t (Tsay, 2002):

Equation 9.6: $$Y_t = c + \sum_{i=1}^{p} \phi_i Y_{t-i} - \sum_{j=1}^{q} \theta_j a_{t-j}$$

Where c is the stationary level, and a_t is the unique shock as previously described.

In practice ARIMA parameters above the order of 2 are seldom needed (Box et al., 1994). In many econometric analyses ARIMA (1, 0, 0) are assumed to be the correct model (West & Hepworth, 1991), and it has been suggested that use of this model may successfully eliminate autocorrelation in many time-series applications (Harrop & Velicer, 1985). However, systematic application of this model may not fully address autocorrelational processes of different types and magnitudes, leading to faulty statistical inference (Box et al., 1994). Thus, it is necessary to evaluate the residuals of any conducted model to ensure that any existing autocorrelation is properly addressed (see model building process, below).

Model building process

ARIMA model building is itself a three-stage iterative process. Each step in the process will be conceptually discussed. For a much more detailed description of each step in ARIMA model building see the oft-cited work of Box et al. (1994).

Model Identification. Model Identification is the first step in Model building. The authors have described this step as "inexact," requiring "judgment" and being necessarily "inefficient" (Box et al., 1994, p. 185). This inauspicious description is representative of this step because the series of interest must be examined for a host of potential models that could be selected. In practice, a potential ARIMA model is preliminarily identified using a graphical representation of the autocorrelation function (ACF) and partial autocorrelation function (PACF). Consistent patterns in the ACF and PACF are suggestive of the necessary (p, d, q) parameters and their orders (see Box et al., 1994, for a detailed description). Figures 9.6, 9.7, and 9.8 display three patterns of positive autocorrelation indicative of corresponding ARIMA models.

In practice ACFs and PACFs are seldom as clear as in Figures 9.6 to 9.8, with a typical ACF looking much more similar to that as displayed in Figure 9.3. However, there are some commonly encountered situations that may create divergence from these exemplar figures. The first of these is negative autocorrelation, which will exhibit a negative spike instead of a positive spike in either the ACF (for [0, 0, 1]) or PACF (for [1, 0, 0]), and will exhibit a gradual decay of values alternating in sign as they decay to zero in the other graph. Most of the single-case research conducted on human behavior has shown that the predominant series will contain positive autocorrelation, so the ACFs and PACFs are likely to grossly resemble those in Figures 9.6 to 9.8. Another source of divergence from the very clear patterns in these figures would occur when there are mixed AR & MA processes in the series. Under these circumstances, the ACFs and PACFs contain elements of both types of processes, and a clear model is often not as easily selected. In such cases, an analyst can fit several ARIMA models and assess which model has the best fit (see model estimation and diagnostic checking below).

ARIMA (1,0,0)

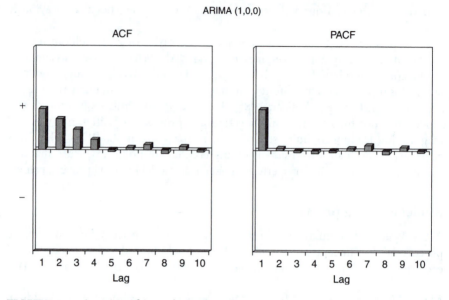

FIGURE 9.6   A positive first-order autoregressive model (1, 0, 0) is suggested if there is a positive or negative spike in the first lag of the PACF, with other lags near zero (it is not unusual that by chance alone many of these lags exhibit small non-zero values). The ACF of such series exhibits a spike at lag one with rapidly decaying spikes in the next several lags, reflecting the decaying influence of past shocks.

ARIMA (0,0,1)

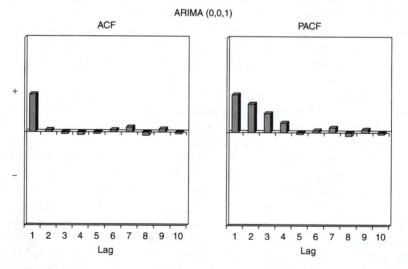

FIGURE 9.7   A positive first-order moving average process (0, 0, 1) is suggested if there is a positive or negative spike in the first lag of the ACF, with other lags near zero. The PACF of such series exhibits a spike at lag one with rapidly decaying spikes in the next several lags, reflecting the decaying influence of past shocks.

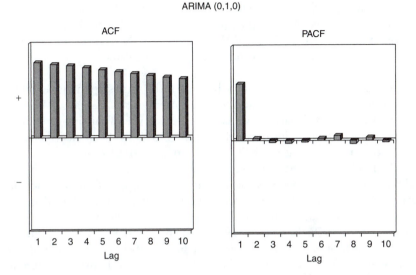

FIGURE 9.8   A series that is non-stationary will have an ACF with spikes at many lags, with a gradual (if any) decay in the magnitude of the correlations. The PACF for such processes exhibits a spike at the first-lag.

A final source of divergence from these figures is a process that can introduce autocorrelation into time series data called seasonality. Seasonality is the regular occurrence of cyclical patterns in the series that often results in autocorrelation in economic and natural science data. Figure 9.2 displays strong seasonality of average daily temperature (the fluctuation of temperature due to the season) in a very visually distinctive manner. Cycles in the data create autocorrelation of a different nature than the previously described AR & MA processes. Seasonal ARIMA models have been created to account for such seasonal autocorrelation. Although it is unlikely that a single-case experiment will produce cyclicality like that seen in Figure 9.2, there are certain types of outcomes that may contain imbedded cycles, such as those found in circadian rhythms. In such cases, iso-lated spikes or spikes with rapid decay will be observed in the ACF or PACF at regularly occurring intervals (i.e., a weekly cycle occurring at 7 days like in Figure 9.3). A complete discussion of seasonality is beyond the scope of the present chapter, but good resources are available to address such issues (Yaffee & McGee, 2000; Box et al., 1994; Shumway & Stoffer, 2000).

Model Estimation.   Model estimation is the second step of model building, which involves estimating the weights of the parameters for the preliminary model that was identified. After a model has been selected, the tentative model's parameters are assigned weights based on a sophisticated mathematical algorithm that is always conducted using statistical software. The ϕ and θ values are calculated at this point based on either maximizing the fit or minimizing the errors.

The parameter statistics very closely resemble that of a standard regression analysis, with the overall fit of the model assessed along with the significance of selected individual AR & MA (ARMA) parameters. Nonsignificant parameters can be dropped from the model and the model recalculated.

Diagnostic Checking. Diagnostic Checking is the third step in model building. Diagnostic checking refers to checking the pattern in the ACF and PACF of the estimated model's residuals to evaluate the occurrence of missing or redundant parameters. The logic holds that if the correct model has been identified and fitted, the remaining variance should be absent of autocorrelation. In terms of ACF and PACF this means that there are no significant spikes at any point in the model and that the residuals now resemble a "white noise" process (random fluctuations near zero). This can be done by visually examining the ACF and PACF for significant spikes at any lag, or by the use of statistics like the portmanteau statistic (Ljung & Box, 1978; Box et al., 1994), which essentially uses the sum of the squared value of autocorrelation over a specified number of lags to index the overall amount of autocorrelation remaining in the residuals. If a significant amount of autocorrelation is found to linger in the residuals, either in a single lag or in the residuals as a whole, the remaining autocorrelation is used to identify a new model that must be identified with the addition or subtraction of parameters. This new model is then re-estimated and checked. Statistical methods can be used to make comparisons between alternative models using model selection criteria such as Akaike's Information Criteria (AIC; Akaike, 1974) or Schwarz's Bayesian Information Criteria (BIC; Schwarz, 1978), both of which include "penalty factors" for the use of higher-order models (encouraging parsimonious representations of the series). This process continues until the simplest possible model is found that best identifies the dependency structure in the series.

Using the iterative three-stage procedure, ARIMA models are tentatively identified, estimated, and checked for parameter significance and modeling of autocorrelation. It is assumed that a fitted ARIMA model describes a time-series equally well throughout the observation period. That is, the parameters of the model should be a good fit both before and after the conducted intervention(s). This concept is called regime stability and signifies that the ARIMA model does not change as a function of time. The residuals of the model, ideally containing only random amounts of autocorrelation, signify that a proper ARIMA model has been found. If all parameters of the model are statistically significant, and if autocorrelation has been sufficiently removed, the model building process ends and the ARIMA model is used in conjunction with the next step of interventional analysis.

Intervention (impact) analysis

Once an ARIMA model (sometimes called a noise model) has been fitted to the data, the effect of the conducted intervention can be properly assessed using impact analysis. Interrupted time-series analysis (ITSA) allows a researcher to model both the change in level of the DV (i.e., mean) and also the change in form (i.e., change in slope) of the DV. For instance, the effect of an intervention can be abrupt or it can gradually cause an effect. Further, its effect can be permanent, altering the mean level of the DV, or temporary, inducing a short-lived effect. Figure 9.9 displays four potential combinations of onset and duration that can be tested (i.e., modeled) using ITSA (McDowall, McCleary, Meidinger, & Hay, 1980).

Any number of interventions can be modeled alone, or in combination, and the analysis can readily be adapted to model treatment withdrawal designs. It is assumed that the starting and ending point of the conducted intervention is known and that the intervention is the only external source of impact on the series. Although each of the examples above displays a stationary baseline, the evaluation of an intervention where the baseline observations are changing over time (i.e., nonstationary) is acceptable as well. Figure 9.10 displays such a nonstationary series that has been affected by an intervention that induced an abrupt, temporary impact.

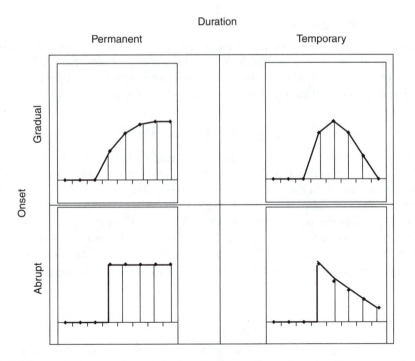

FIGURE 9.9   An intervention can be described according to its onset (abrupt or gradual) and the duration of its effect (permanent or temporary).

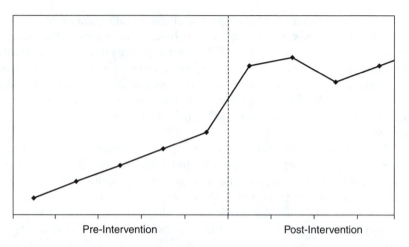

Pre-Intervention   Post-Intervention

FIGURE 9.10   An intervention that caused an abrupt temporary impact on a series with a non-stationary baseline. The resulting impact is short-lived with the series continuing its previous trajectory.

ITSA modeling strategies

There are three major modeling strategies that have been devised to analyze interrupted time-series data (although others exist). The first two utilize variations of ARIMA models and impact analysis, while the third utilizes a slightly different conceptualization. A brief summary of each is provided below.

Box-Jenkins-Tiao strategy (Box & Tiao, 1965)

In this strategy, the analyst creates an ARIMA model based on the pre-intervention series only, applies the ARIMA to the entire series (i.e., re-estimates the selected parameters based on data from the entire series), and then evaluates the impact of the intervention by specifying the expected nature of the impact (as above). It is assumed that the nature of the ARIMA model does not change in response to the intervention, and that only the level or form of the process changes. This strategy has been called preferable to the next (Yaffee & McGee, 2000), but requires that approximately 50 observations be available in the pre-intervention series.

Full series modeling strategy

In this strategy, the analyst identifies an ARIMA model from the entire series (i.e., not just the pre-intervention series) and then evaluates the impact of the intervention. This strategy may be used in situations where there is less than the required number of observations in the pre-intervention series and/or the intervention's effect is transitory, thus not greatly affecting the nature of the ARIMA component (Yaffee & McGee, 2000). An additional variation of this strategy would be to model the intervention component first and then model the ARIMA component (Yaffee & McGee, 2000).

Interrupted time-series experiment (ITSE)

Advanced by Gottman (1981), ITSE is a technique that allows an analyst to examine changes in level and slope induced by an intervention. Similarly to the ARIMA models, the method attempts to account for autocorrelation (using only AR terms, however). The ITSE method calculates an omnibus statistic, an F test, to evaluate if the intervention affects either the slope or level of the DV. If this test is significant, then post-hoc t tests are conducted to examine which aspect was affected, the slope, level, or both. Figure 9.11 displays several examples of differences between starting values and slopes that can be examined using ITSE. From the Figure it can be seen how many different permutations of changing level (a comparison between the ending value of phase I and the starting value of phase 2) and changing slope (a linear rate of change) can be evaluated.

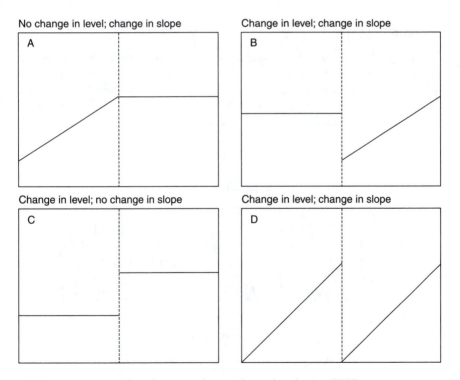

FIGURE 9.11   Examples of patterns that can be analyzed using ITSE.

The method has been expanded with particular emphasis placed on the improved calculation of the AR terms for series with less than 50 observations. A derivation called ITSACORR (Crosbie, 1993) only requires a reported 10–20 observations per phase.

Although these methods have been examined by several researchers (Crosbie, 1995; Gottman, 1981; Greenwood & Matyas, 1990; Harrop & Velicer, 1990) and are often cited, the ITSE and ITSACORR methods have recently been soundly criticized for several substantial shortcomings that may greatly limit their application (Huitema, 2005). For example, it has been shown that flaws in the nature (conceptualization) of the omnibus F test and t tests can be contradictory and/or misleading, depending on the pattern of the data. A good example of this is Figure 9.11D, which Huitema (2005) used as an exemplar situation using simulation data. The F test from data that's linear representation resembled Figure 9.11D was statistically significant (i.e., indicating the slope and/or level of the process differed between phases), yet both of the conducted t tests resulted in non-significant differences (while there is clearly a large difference in level of the post-intervention series). Huitema (2005) presents other situations that highlight the problems with ITSACORR and ITSE as well. At the time of this writing it is not clear how, if at all, these criticisms can be addressed.

Example

The Box-Jenkins-Tiao ITSA modeling strategy is used to model a two-phase intervention using SPSS. The software is included in the Trends module and has both ARIMA modeling and interventional applications. Figure 9.12 displays a series that was created using a random number generator (with induced autocorrelation) and a simulated intervention effect.

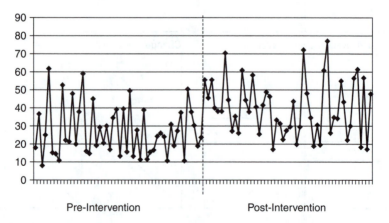

FIGURE 9.12 The pre-intervention series appears to be relatively stable (stationary), and the mean level of the post-intervention series may be somewhat higher.

Identification. The ACF and PACF for the pre-intervention series are:

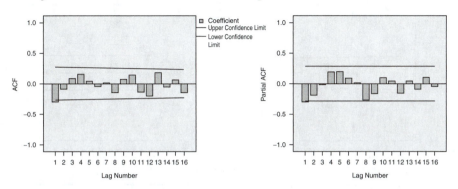

FIGURE 9.13 As suspected, the pre-intervention series does not appear to need differencing, but a solitary negative spike occurring at lag 1 in both the ACF and PACF could be indicative of either an (1, 0, 0) or (0, 0, 1) model.

Because the series might be fit equally well with either a first-order AR or MA parameter, both were conducted for fit comparison. Figure 9.14 (see page 300) displays the ACF and PACF from both models.

Intervention analysis

The effect of the intervention appears to be quite abrupt, and lasts throughout the post-interventional observation period (although it may somewhat diminish). The effect of the intervention was therefore modeled by an "abrupt, permanent" interventional parameter (which is essentially a dummy code of zeros before the intervention and ones afterward). The intervention parameter is evaluated in context with the ARIMA for the pre-interventional series (i.e., the [0, 0, 1] model is now applied to the entire series along with the abrupt permanent interventional parameter). The parameter estimates are displayed in Table 9.2.

TABLE 9.2 The MA Coefficient and Intervention Coefficients are Both Statistically Significant, Indicating that Even after Accounting for Autocorrelation (MA1), the Intervention Induced an Average Change of 12.796 Points in the Post-Intervention Series

	PARAMETER ESTIMATES			
	ESTIMATES	STD ERROR	*t*	APPROX SIG
Non-Seasonal Lags MA1	.205	.100	2.055	.043
Regression Coefficients V2	12.796	2.323	5.507	.000
Constant	27.045	1.648	16.415	.000

Melard's algorithm was used for estimation.

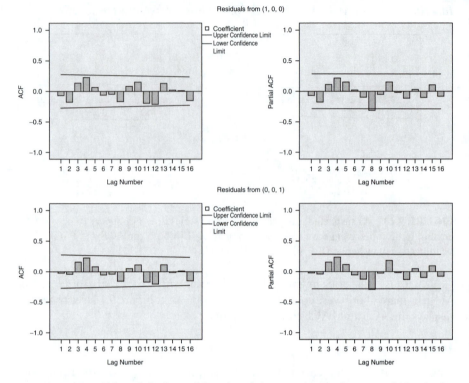

FIGURE 9.14 Although both models reduced the magnitude of autocorrelation in the first-lag, the (0, 0, 1) model more thoroughly reduces autocorrelation in the first 14 lags of the series (portmanteau Q[14] = 16.83 for [1, 0, 0] vs. Q[14] = 13.5 for [0, 0, 1]). Therefore, the (0, 0, 1) model was selected.

Limitations. Although statistical approaches based on interrupted time-series analysis (ITSA) for single-case studies offer a comprehensive approach to modeling autocorrelation and assessing the impact of an intervention, they are limited by a number of factors, mostly having to do with the complexity of the approach.

The success of the strategy hinges on the fitting of a suitable ARIMA model to describe the nature of the autocorrelation in the series, yet the identification process has been shown to be plagued by difficulties that potentially render identified models as insufficient. For instance, Velicer and Harrop (1983) found only modest agreement (36%) between identified models even when the observation period was of sufficient length. A complicated approach, these techniques are not widely known to many researchers and sufficient exposure to ARIMA model building is not routinely encountered in graduate training in psychology. The effect of ARIMA misidentification on impact assessment is not known, but as previously mentioned (see t and F test limitations), unaddressed autocorrelation can substantially bias significance testing.

Another limitation is the required number of observations to conduct the analysis. Because the model identification procedure is so tenuous, the number of observations required for optimal model building is often beyond the scope of many single-case experiments. Fifty observations are recommended for these techniques, but has been seen, 50 observations per phase is often optimal (Box et al., 1994). This is the case because small series ($n < 30$) have been shown to systematically under represent autocorrelation (Bence, 1995). In comparison with other statistical approaches, this number of required observations is not substantially greater; however, for series with less than the recommended number of observations, ITSA has an increased risk of undetected bias in significance testing, which is a flaw that other approaches may not share.

An often assumed limitation is that these approaches are much better suited to the evaluation of phase designs. Although it is possible that a behavioral intervention can be conceived that's effect is limited to the current observation period (i.e., does not systematically carry-over into the next observation or have a delayed response), such that an immediate impact can be modeled using the techniques described above, often this is not the case and ITSA may be a poor choice in evaluating alternation designs. However, this limitation may hold true for ITSA, but general ARIMA models can be employed to evaluate the impact of an intervention on the unique shock induced by such interventions (e.g., correlating the effect of a naturally occurring intervention on the DV in a quasi-experimental design).

Lastly, ITSA techniques share the same distributional assumptions as traditional t and F tests and are poor choices for use with data that fail to meet parametric assumptions. There are now many thoughtful transformations that can be used to make many time-series meet these assumptions, including the family of Box-Cox transformations (Box & Cox, 1964), but there are times when the very nature of the process being studied will produce data that will never meet these assumptions. In such instances, randomization tests appear to be a very attractive alternative (Edgington, 1995).

Available Software. Packages such as SPSS, SAS, Statistica, and several others now contain software that allows both general ARIMA modeling and ITSA. In particular, SPSS and Statistica have very user-friendly interfaces that allow the specification of discrete interventions (e.g., abrupt, temporary impacts). For ITSE, a dedicated package is also available (Williams & Gottman, 1999).

Other statistical tests

Several remaining statistical approaches for single-case designs are now discussed in very brief detail. The approaches in this section may have limited application or simply be too new for adequate comment. These approaches are discussed for the simple purpose of highlighting the array of available tests to the reader.

Revusky's R_n (test of ranks)

When a researcher is interested in examining multiple baselines, the R_n test of Ranks (Revusky, 1967) may be appropriate (Kazdin, 1984). The statistic is applied with logic similar to that of randomization tests, only the ranks of the data are used in lieu of the observed scores. For instance, if a researcher were to compare an intervention's effect on a DV that was being evaluated on several participants (several single-case sub experiments), the intervention could be introduced at different selected times (e.g., on subsequent days) on a participant chosen at random (hence the similarity with randomization tests). The performance of all of the subjects on that day (all but one of which was receiving the same level of the intervention) would be ranked from highest to lowest. The same procedure would be followed on the next day when a different participant would be selected at random to receive the intervention. If the intervention had no effect on the DV, then the sum of the ranks of the intervention-day participants would be expected to be randomly distributed; the conducted significance test examines the degree of departure from randomness of the ranks. Recent examination has confirmed that the test of ranks is susceptible to the effects of autocorrelation (Sierra, Quera, & Solanas, 2000); thus, it shares the limitations of randomization tests.

Split-middle technique

A crafty technique that was developed prior to the wide-spread use of computer applications (White, 1971), this graphical technique essentially describes the linear trend in the data and uses the trend (called the "celeration line") to predict future performance. The technique has been refined to be performed by hand (using graph paper) but can now also be applied using statistical software. For instance, a rate of change (i.e., slope) can be fit to the first phase of an experiment and this linear trend can be used to estimate the subject's performance if the intervention has no effect (using linear regression techniques). Then, the subject's actual performance can be examined in relation to this trend line. If the subject's performance differs from this level of expected performance, the intervention can be concluded to have an effect. In practice, this can be tested by comparing the predicted magnitude of the DV to the actual DV using a binomial test. For example, if chance alone is acting on the post-intervention scores then 50% are likely to be at or below the trend line and 50% are predicted to be at or above it (this is the null hypothesis of the binomial test). Thus, it is deemed statistically significant ($p < .001$) if 10 out of 10 post-intervention observations are greater than the trend line would have predicted. Unfortunately, this technique, too, has been shown to be very susceptible to the effects of autocorrelation (Crosbie, 1987) and has been mostly relegated to a graphical (rather than a statistical) technique.

Double bootstrap method

A promising new method that could be used for interrupted time-series analysis with less than 50 observations is the double bootstrap method (McKnight, McKean, & Huitema, 2000). This iterative technique uses bootstrapping procedures (i.e., statistical resampling methods) to achieve less biased estimates of autocorrelation. The less-biased estimates of the autoregressive terms are then used in conjunction with an existing algorithm (Durbin, 1960) to model the intervention. Simulation results have highlighted the potential of this technique to be applicable to small n single-case experiments. At the time of this writing, the authors were investigating the utility of the technique with a broader range of models.

Evaluation of statistical tests: which test to choose?

The preceding discussion reviewed many selected statistical tests and introduced a host of issues, strengths, and limitations for each test. Perhaps the reader is now left to wonder, which test should I choose?

It is important to remember that even though this chapter focuses on the statistical tests as things-in-themselves, the tests are not designed to be the focus of the experiment. Rather, when proper thought has been given to the type of data and experimental design, the importance of the tests recedes into the background as simply a means for addressing the reason for conducting the experiment in the first place- the experimental question. Thus, the experimental question (hypothesis) and resulting sequelae should drive all aspects of the study including the choice of analytical technique. Very often, the pragmatics of the setting in which the research is conducted will interact with the experimental question to drive the experiment. For instance, the nature of the experimental condition(s) in large part dictates the type of designs that are applicable (e.g., reversal, withdrawal). Further, because of the nature of the intervention, is it best tested in phases or can an alternation design be used? Relatedly, because of the nature of the setting, what is the feasible length of the phases? Each of these questions very much influences the available statistical techniques that can be applied and each of these experimental design decisions are dictated by the experimental question.

Most behavioral single-case experimental research will utilize phase designs (Kazdin, 1984), thus leading to the applicability of the interrupted time-series analyses. Taking the lead from Kazdin (1984), the time-series approaches are recommended whenever feasible. Of the techniques covered, these approaches are deemed preferable because of their comprehensive methods of addressing autocorrelation (ARIMA models), the flexibility of designs that they can be adapted, and their ability to model a variety of intervention effects. The recent advances in these approaches (see the double bootstrap method) may yet serve to eliminate the sample size limitations that have heretofore hamstrung these techniques. As noted however, conducting these analyses is not trivial and a budding time-series analyst will definitely need to consult additional resources to conduct the analyses successfully.

No matter which test is chosen, however, the use of statistical analyses to evaluate the experiment is not sufficient for certain conclusions. First, the use of statistics to calculate the "significance" of the findings does not ensure that the results are in fact meaningful. The clinical relevance of the findings should be used in conjunction with the statistical evaluation to place the intervention effect in context (see chapters 1 and 10). Further, the use of statistical analysis does not "elevate" the experimental design beyond what it is capable. For instance, a significant result obtained using interrupted time-series analysis on data collected from a quasi-experimental design (e.g., the intervention was not manipulated by the researcher), does not indicate that the modeled intervention caused the effect. No selected statistic is able to improve the design of the experiment; statistics simply ensure that the maximum amount of information can be gleaned from it.

9.4. SUMMARY AND CONCLUSION

The present chapter discussed many of the issues involved with the application of statistical approaches to the single-case experimental design. In so doing, the importance of defining the criterion of evaluation was highlighted, with emphasis placed on the difference between the statistical and clinical significance of a finding. The nature of single subject research was briefly reviewed with the notion of stochastic (i.e., probabilistic) processes resulting in the necessity of collecting repeated measures to create time-series data. The nature of time-series data was reviewed and the mathematical properties of these data were discussed, particularly in context with the expected prevalence of autocorrelation in behavioral data. Several statistical approaches that have particular utility in single-case designs were discussed. The approaches were reviewed with respect to their applications, assumptions, limitations, and available software. Finally, interrupted time-series analysis was recommended as the technique of choice, when sample size permits.

The chapter was intended to serve as an introduction to these techniques; care was taken to provide adequate references for the reader to further explore any or all of these approaches. Unfortunately, many techniques could not be included, in particular those techniques that are able to aggregate single-case effects, essentially allowing an analyst to conduct meta-analyses of multiple single-case sub-experiments (see hierarchical linear models: Raudenbush & Bryk, 2002). Further, there are a host of other quasi-experimental applications that have become quite popular in many fields, many of which are based on ARIMA modeling.

Nevertheless, the present chapter provides the researcher with a diverse group of tests for a host of applications. The software to conduct the tests has greatly improved and will very likely continue to do so. Learning one or more of the techniques allows a researcher to greatly increase the types of questions that can be formulated, and knowledge of the tests' assumptions and their corresponding limitations most certainly may improve design and data collection efforts. The use of statistical analysis to evaluate the single-case experiment has seen remarkable growth in the last 20 years, and there is little doubt that the field will continue to improve allowing for more powerful tests and resulting improvements in applications.

CHAPTER 10

BEYOND THE INDIVIDUAL: DIRECT, SYSTEMATIC, AND CLINICAL REPLICATION PROCEDURES

10.1. INTRODUCTION

Replication is at the heart of any science. In all sciences, replication serves at least two purposes: first, to establish the reliability of previous findings; and, second, to determine the generality of these findings under differing conditions. These goals, of course, are intrinsically interrelated. Each time that certain results are replicated under different conditions, this not only establishes generality of findings, but also increases confidence in the reliability of these findings. The emphasis of this chapter is on replication procedures for establishing generality of findings.

In chapter 2 the difficulties of establishing generality of findings in applied research were reviewed and discussed. The problem in generalizing from a heterogeneous group to an individual limits generality of findings from this approach. The problem in generalizing from one individual to other individuals who may differ in many ways limits generality of findings from a single-case experiment. One answer to this problem is the replication of single-case experiments. Through this procedure, the applied researcher can maintain his or her focus on the individual, but establish generality of findings for those who differ from the individual in the original experiment. Sidman (1960) originally outlined two procedures for replicating single-case experiments in basic research: direct replication and systematic replication. In applied research a third type of replication, which we termed *clinical replication* in the first edition of this book, is assuming increasing importance. The term "benchmarking" has been introduced recently to describe a very similar strategy (Wilson, in press). In addition, the beginning of the creation of "practice research networks" provides the infrastructure to facilitate these strategies (Borkovec, Echemendia, Ragusea, & Ruiz, 2001).

The purpose of this chapter is to outline the procedures and goals of replication strategies in applied research. Examples of each type of replication series will be presented and criticized. Guidelines for the proper use of these procedures in future series will be suggested from current examples judged to be successful in establishing generality of findings. Finally, the feasibility of large-scale replication series, in practice research networks or other groups of associated practitioners will be discussed in light of the practical limitations inherent in applied research.

10.2. DIRECT REPLICATION

Direct replication of single-case experiments have often appeared in professional journals. As noted above, these series are capable of determining both reliability of findings and generality of findings across clients. In most cases, however; the very important issue of generality of findings has not been discussed. Indeed, it seems that most investigators employing single-case methodology, as well as editors of journals who judge the adequacy of such endeavors, have been concerned primarily with reliability of findings as a goal in replication series rather than generality of findings. That is, most investigators have been concerned with demonstrating that certain results can or cannot be replicated in subsequent experiments rather than with systematically observing the replications themselves to determine generality of findings. However, since any attempt to establish reliability of a finding by replicating the experiment on additional cases also provides information on generality, many applied researchers have conducted direct replication series yielding valuable information on client generality. Examples of several of these series will be presented below.

Definition of direct replication

For our, purposes, we agree basically with Sidman's (1960) definition of direct replication as ". . . replication of a given experiment by the same investigator" (p. 73). Sidman divided direct replication into two different procedures: repetition of the experiment on the same subject and repetition on different subjects. While repetition on the same subject increases confidence in the reliability of findings and is used occasionally in applied research (see chapter 5), generality of findings across clients can be ascertained only by replication on different subjects. More specifically, direct replication in applied research refers to administration of a given procedure by the same investigator or group of investigators in a specific setting (e.g., hospital, clinic, or classroom) on a series of clients homogeneous for a particular behavioral problem (e.g., agoraphobia, compulsive hand washing). While it is recognized that, in applied research, clients will always be more heterogeneous on background variables such as age, sex, or presence of additional maladaptive behaviors than in basic research, the conservative approach is to match clients in a replication series as closely as possible on these additional variables. Interpretation of mixed results, where some clients benefit from the procedure and some do not, can then be attributed to as few differences as possible, thereby providing a clearer direction for further experimentation. This point will be discussed more fully below.

Direct replication as we define it can begin to answer questions about generality of findings across clients but cannot address questions concerning generality of findings across therapists or settings. Furthermore, to the extent that clients are homogeneous on a given behavioral problem (such as agoraphobia), a direct replication series cannot answer questions on the results of a given procedure on related problems such as claustrophobia, although successful results should certainly lead to further attempts at replication on related problems. A close examination of several direct replication series will serve to illustrate the information available concerning generality of findings across clients.

Example one: two successful replications

The first example concerns one successful experiment and two successful replications of a therapeutic procedure. This early clinical series examined the effects of direct in vivo exposure enhanced by motivational procedures (social reinforcement) on severe agoraphobic behavior in three patients (Agras et al., 1968). This series was also one of the first evaluations of direct-exposure-based treatments for phobia that became the treatment of choice for phobic behavior by the 1970s (Barlow, 2002). The procedure was straightforward.

All patients were hospitalized. Severity of agoraphobic behavior was measured by observing the distance the patients were able to walk on a course from the hospital to a downtown area. Landmarks were identified at 25-yard intervals for over one mile. The patients were asked two or more times a day to walk as far as they could on the course without feeling "undue tension." Their report of distance walked was surreptitiously checked from time to time by an observer to determine reliability, precise feedback of progress in terms of increases in distance was provided, and this progress was socially reinforced with praise and approval during treatment phases and ignored during withdrawal phases. In the first patient, increases in time spent away from the center were praised first, but as this resulted in the patient simply standing outside the front door of the hospital for longer periods, the target behavior was changed to distance. Because baseline procedures were abbreviated, this design is best characterized as a B-A-B design (see chapter 5). The comparison, then, is between direct exposure with and without social reinforcement (praise and approval from a therapist).

For purposes of generality across clients, it is important to note that the patients in this experiment were rather heterogeneous, as is typically the case in applied research. Although each patient was severely agoraphobic, all had numerous associated fears and obsessions. The extent and severity of agoraphobic fears also differed. One subject was a 36-year-old male with a 15-year agoraphobic history. He was incapacitated to the extent that he could manage a 5-minute drive to work in a rural area only with great difficulty. A second patient was a 23-year-old female with only a one-year agoraphobic history. This patient, however, could not leave her home unaccompanied. The third patient, a 36-year-old female, also could not leave her home unaccompanied, but had a 16-year agoraphobic history. In fact, this patient had to be sedated and brought to the hospital in an ambulance. In addition, these three patients presented different background variables such as personality characteristics and cultural variations (one patient was European).

The results from one of the cases (the male) are presented in Figure 10.1. Situational exposure and reinforcement produced a marked increase in distance walked, and withdrawal of the motivational procedure resulted in a small deterioration in performance. Reintroduction of reinforcement in the final phase produced a further increase in distance walked. These results were replicated on the remaining two patients.

At least three conclusions can be drawn from these data. The first conclusion is that motivated situational exposure was effective in modifying agoraphobic

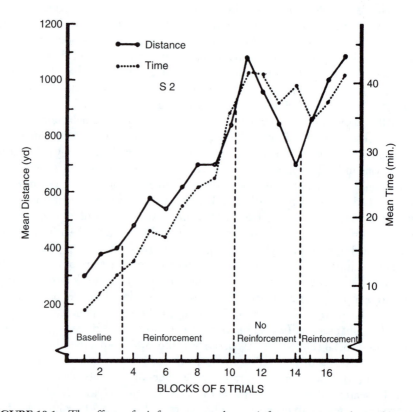

FIGURE 10.1 The effects of reinforcement and nonreinforcement upon the performance of an agoraphobic patient (Subject 2). (Figure 2, p. 425, from: Agras, W. S., Leitenberg, H., and Barlow, D. H., [1968]. Social reinforcement in the modification of agoraphobia. *Archives of General Psychiatry*, **19**, 423–427. Copyright 1968 by American Medical Association. Reproduced by permission.)

behavior. The second conclusion is that within the limits of these data, the results are reliable and not due to idiosyncrasies present in the first experiment, since two replications of the first experiment were successful. The third conclusion, however, is of most interest here. The procedure was clearly effective with three patients of different ages, sex, duration of agoraphobic behavior, and cultural backgrounds. For purposes of generality of findings, this series of experiments would be strengthened by a third replication (a total of 4 subjects). But the consistency of the results across three quite different patients enables one to draw initially favorable conclusions on the general effectiveness of this procedure across the population of patients with agoraphobia through the process of logical generalization (Edgington, 1967, 1996).

On the other hand, if one patient had failed to improve or improved only slightly such that the result was clinically unimportant, an immediate search would have had to be made for procedural or other variables responsible for the lack of generality, across patients. Given the flexibility of this experimental design, alterations in procedure (e.g., adding additional reinforcers, changing the criterion for reinforcement) could be made in an attempt to achieve clinically important results. If mixed results such as these were observed, further replication would be necessary to determine which procedures were most efficacious for given clients (see section 2.2, chapter 2).

In this series, however, these steps were not necessary due to the uniformly successful outcomes, and some preliminary statements about generality across patients were made. The next step in this series, then, was to replicate the results systematically, that is, across different situations and therapists. It is evident that this preliminary series, did not address questions on effectiveness of techniques in different settings or with different therapists. It was entirely possible that characteristics of the therapist or the particular structure of the course that the patient walked facilitated the favorable results. Thus these variables must be systematically varied to determine generality of findings across an important clinical domain. In fact, this goal was accomplished during the 1970s and 1980s to the extent that situational exposure based procedures delivered in the context of a supportive therapist, and, where possible a positive influence from family or significant other, became the treatment of choice for phobic behavior (Barlow, 2002; Craske & Barlow, 2001).

Further experimentation over the ensuing decades demonstrated clearly that reinforcement, feedback, and other similar techniques served primarily to motivate practice with or exposure to feared objects or situations, and that situational exposure was the primary therapeutic ingredient (Barlow, 2002). One strong hint of things to come was the rising baseline in Figure 10.1 where behavior was improving with practice or exposure alone. Ideally, of course, reinforcement should not have been introduced until the baseline stabilized (see section 3, chapter 3). When this was tested properly in subsequent single-case experimentation, the power of pure exposure, even in the absence of external motivating variables such as praise, was demonstrated (Leitenberg, Agras,

Edwards, Thomson, & Wincze, 1970). But the purpose of these illustrations is to examine the process of establishing generality of findings through replication and it is to this topic that we now return.

Example two: four successful replications with design alterations during replications

A second rather early example of a direct replication series will be presented because the behavior is clinically important (compulsive rituals), and the issue of client generality within a direct replication series is highlighted because five patients participated in the study (Mills, Agras, Barlow, & Mills, 1973). In this experiment, what was a new treatment at the time—response prevention—was tested. The basic strategy in this experiment and its replications was an A-B-A design: baseline, response prevention, baseline. During replications, however, the design was expanded somewhat to include controls for instructional and placebo effects. For example, two of the replications were carried out in an A-B-BC-B-A design, where A was baseline, B was a placebo treatment, and C was response prevention.

The addition of new control phases during subsequent replication is not an uncommon strategy in single-case design research because each replication is actually a separate experiment that stands alone. When testing a given treatment, however, new variables interacting within the treatment complex that might be responsible for improvement may be identified and "teased out" in later replications. It was noted in chapter 2 that such flexibility of single-case designs allows one to alter experimental procedures *within* a case. Within the context of replication, if a procedure is effective in the first experiment, one has the flexibility to add further, more stringent controls during replication to ascertain more specifically the mechanism of action of a successful treatment. But, to remain a direct replication series within our definition, the major purpose of the series should be to test the effectiveness of a given treatment on a well-defined problem—in this case compulsive rituals—administered by the same therapeutic team in the same setting. Thus the treatment, if successful, must remain the same, and the comparison is between treatment and no treatment or treatment and placebo control.

The first four subjects in this experiment were patients suffering from OCD with severe compulsive hand washing rituals. The fifth patient presented with a different ritual. All patients were hospitalized on a clinical research unit. All patients with hand washing rituals encountered articles or situations throughout the experiment that produced hand washing. Response prevention consisted of removing the handles from the wash basin wherein all hand washing occurred. The placebo phase consisted of saline injections and oral placebo medication with instructions suggesting improvement in the rituals, but no response prevention. Once again, the design was either A-B-A, with A representing baseline and B representing response prevention, or A-B-BC-B-A, where

A was baseline, B was placebo, and C was response prevention. Both self-report measures (number of urges to wash hands) and an objective measure (occasions when the patient approached the sink, recorded by a washing pen—see chapter 4) were administered.

As in the previous series, the patients were relatively heterogeneous. The first patient was a 31-year-old woman with a 2-year history of compulsive hand washing. Previous to the experiment, she had received over one year of both inpatient and outpatient treatment including chemotherapy, individual psychotherapy, and desensitization. She performed her ritual 10 to 20 times a day, each ritual consisting of eight individual washings and rinsings with alternating hot and cold water. The associated fear was contamination of herself and others through contact with chemicals and dirt. These rituals prevented her from carrying out simple household duties or caring for her child.

The second patient was a 32-year-old woman with a 5-year history of hand washing. Frequency of hand washing ranged from 30 to 60 times per day, with an average of 39 during baseline. Unlike with the previous patient, these rituals had strong religious overtones concerning salvation, although fear of contamination from dirt was also present. Prior treatments included two series of electric shock treatment, which proved ineffective.

A third patient was a 25-year-old woman who had a 3-year history of the hand-washing compulsion. Situations that produced the hand washing in this case were associated with illness and death. If an ambulance passed near her home, she engaged in cleansing rituals. Hand washings averaged 30 per day, and the subject was essentially isolated in her home before treatment.

The fourth patient was a 20-year-old male with a history of hand washing for 1½ years. He had been hospitalized for the previous year and was hand washing at the rate of 20 to 30 times per day. The fifth patient, whose rituals differed considerably from the first four subjects, will be described below.

Representative results from one case are presented below. Hand washing remained high during baseline and placebo phases and dropped markedly after response prevention. Subjective reports of urges to wash declined slightly during response prevention and continued into follow-up. This decline continued beyond the data presented in Figure 10.2 until urges were minimal. These results were essentially replicated in the remaining three hand washers.

Before discussion of issues relative to replication, experimental design considerations in this series deserve comment. The dramatic success of response prevention in this series is obvious, but the continued reduction of hand washing after response prevention was removed presents some problems in interpretation. Since hand washing did not recover, it is difficult to attribute its reduction to response prevention using the basic A-B-A withdrawal design. From the perspective of this design, it is possible that some correlated event occurred concurrent with response prevention that was actually responsible for the gains. Fortunately, the aforementioned flexibility in adding new control phases to replication experiments afforded an experimental analysis from a different perspective.

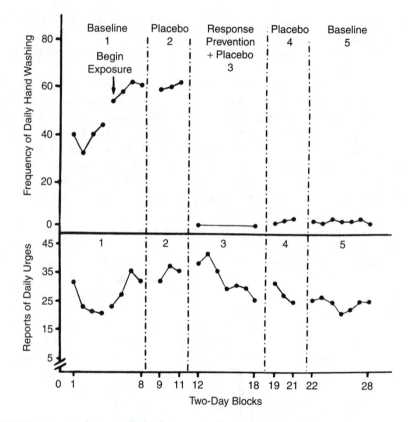

FIGURE 10.2   In the upper half of the graph, the frequency of hand washing across treatment phases is represented. Each point represents the average of 2 days. In the lower portion of the graph, total urges reported by the patient are represented. (Figure 3, p. 527, from: Mills, H. L., Agras, W. S., Barlow, D. H., and Mills, J. R. [1973]. Compulsive rituals treated by response prevention: An experimental analysis. *Archives of General Psychiatry*, **28**, 524–529. Copyright 1973 by American Medical Association. Reproduced by permission.)

In all patients, hand washing was reasonably stable by history and through both baseline and placebo phases. Hand washing showed a marked reduction *only* when response prevention was introduced. In these cases, baseline and placebo phases were administered for differing amounts of time. In fact, then, this becomes a multiple baseline across subjects (see chapter 7), allowing isolation of response prevention as the active treatment.

Again, this series demonstrates that response prevention works, and replications ensure that this finding is reliable. In addition, the clinical significance of the result is easily observable by inspection, since rituals were entirely eliminated in all four patients. More importantly, however, the fact that this clinical result was consistently present across four patients lends considerable confidence to the notion that this procedure would be effective with other patients, again through the process of logical generalization. It is common sense that confidence in generality of findings across clients increases with each replication, but it is our rule of thumb that a point of diminishing returns is reached after one successful experiment and three successful replications for a total of four subjects. At this point, it seems efficient to publish the results so that systematic replication may begin in other settings.

An alternative strategy would be to administer the procedure in the same setting to clients with behavior disorders demonstrating marked differences from those of the first series. Some behavior disorders such as specific phobias lend themselves to this method of replication because a given treatment (e.g., *in vitro* exposure) should theoretically work on many different varieties of specific phobia. Within a disorder such as OCD with compulsive rituals, this is also feasible because several different types of rituals are encountered in the clinic (Rachman & Hodgson, 1980; Steketee & Barlow, 2002). The question that can be answered in the original setting then is: Will the procedure work on other behavior disorders that are topographically different but presumably maintained by similar psychological processes? In other words, would rituals quite different from hand washing respond to the same procedure? The fifth case in this series was the beginning of a replication along these lines.

The fifth subject was a 15-year-old boy who performed a complex set of rituals when retiring at night and another set of rituals when arising in the morning. The night rituals included checking and rechecking the pillow placement and folding and refolding pajamas. The morning rituals were concerned mostly with dressing. This type of ritual is known as *checking* as opposed to previous *washing* rituals. The rituals were extremely time consuming and disruptive to the family's routine. After a baseline phase in which rituals remained relatively stable, the night rituals were prevented, but the morning rituals were allowed to continue. Here again, response prevention dramatically eliminated nighttime rituals. Morning rituals gradually decreased to zero during prevention of night rituals.

The experiment further suggested that response prevention can be effective in the treatment of ritualistic behavior. The implications of this replication, however, are somewhat different from the previous three replications, where the behavior in question was topographically similar. Although the treatment was administered by the same therapists in the same setting, this case does *not* represent a direct replication because the behavior was topographically different. To consider this case as part of a direct replication series, one would have to accept, on an *a priori* basis, the theoretical notion that all compulsive rituals are maintained by similar psychological processes and therefore will respond to the same treatment. Although classification of these under one name (compulsive rituals) implies this, in fact there is some evidence that these rituals are somewhat different and may react differently to response prevention treatments (Rachman & Hodgson, 1980; Barlow, 2002). As such, it was probably inappropriate to include the fifth case in the present series because the clear implication is that response prevention is applicable to all rituals, but only one case was presented where rituals differed.

From the perspective of sound replication procedures, the proper tactic would be to include this case in a second series containing different rituals. This second series would then be the first step in a systematic replication series, in which generality of findings across different behaviors would be established in addition to generality of findings across clients. In fact, response prevention and exposure, combined occasionally with medication, has become the treatment of choice for obsessive-compulsive disorders, based on an extended systematic and clinical replication series that began in the early 1970s (Foa & Franklin, 2001; Rachman & Hodgson, 1980; Steketee & Barlow, 2002). This series, relying on individual experimental analyses and close examination of individual data from group studies, has also begun to identify patient characteristics that predict failure (e.g., Foa, 1979; Foa et al., 1983; Steketee & Barlow, 2002), a critical function of any replication series (see section 10.4).

Example three: mixed results in a multiple baseline design

The goal of this experiment was to examine the effects of supplementing the drug Sildenafil (Viagra) with the use of a cognitive behavioral treatment manual plus minimal therapist contact (Bach, Barlow, & Wincze, 2004) in the treatment of erectile dysfunction. Participants were six heterosexual couples in which the man met criteria for erectile dysfunction and was using Sildenafil. In these participants, erectile dysfunction resulted from psychological factors or a combination of psychological, and organic factors. These individuals were also heterogenous, ranging in age from 31 to 62 with occupations including manual labor, professional, or retired. The couples had been married between a range of two months to 35 years and had suffered from erectile dysfunction from two to twelve years. Each patient had some success using Viagra, which was one of the inclusion criteria for the study. But patients rated their satisfaction with their sexual relationship no higher than 6 on the 0-10 scale. In fact, this pattern of some improvement in physiological functioning but limited improvement in sexual satisfaction characterizes the majority of individuals using this drug.

In this multiple baseline design, participants completed a period of 4, 6, or, 8 weeks during which they used Sildenafil alone while measures were taken, and this procedure was replicated on another three participants for a total of six patients. During the experimental treatments which lasted six weeks, the patients read the manual and had brief weekly phone contacts with a therapist. Measures included assessments of erectile functioning, measures of overall sexual functioning filled out by both the husband and the spouse, general measures of adjustment in the marriage, and Likert scales of satisfaction with the sexual relationship from both the husband and the spouse. It is this latter measure that will be presented below.

The results indicated that for five out of six couples, manualized CBT treatment was associated with increases in sexual satisfaction among men with some accompanying increases among their partners, as well as an increase in the frequency of sexual intercourse. For those who improved, these gains were largely maintained over the course of a 4–10 months follow-up. Specifically, normative functioning for sexually healthy males on this scale is 8 out of 10 or above when rating satisfaction with their sexual relationship. None of the men in the study had reached this level using Sildenafil alone. After manualized treatment, five of the six men evidenced a substantial increase in sexual satisfaction, with four out of six reaching a level of at least 8 out of 10. A representative case is presented in Figure 10.3A.

A sixth participant, however, showed no change with the addition of manualized treatment. His data are also presented in Figure 10.3B.

In fact, on some other measures, this couple actually worsened. Using intensive clinical observation, two possible explanations for these differences were highlighted. First, it became clear during treatment that the partners had very different attitudes regarding sex that had not been resolved. Second, both partners indicated that they were coping with a number of substantial life stressors and that they were both generally dissatisfied with life.

Once again, conclusion in three general areas can be drawn from these data. First, addition of a psychological treatment to those individuals achieving some increased erectile response on Viagra enhances sexual satisfaction of the couple. Second, to the extent that the result was replicated directly on five

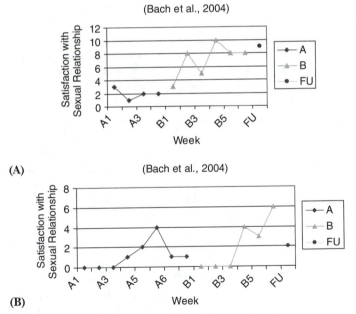

(A)

(B)

FIGURE 10.3 Satisfaction with sexual relationship across baseline, treatment, and follow-up for one of the five men who responded positively to the congnitive behavioral treatment administered in the treatment phase of the study. (From: Bach, A. K., Barlow, D. H., & Wincze, J. P. [2004]. The enhancing effects of manualized treatment for erectile dysfunction among men using sildenafil: A preliminary investigation. *Behavior Therapy*, **35**, 55–73. Copyright 2004 by Association for Advancement of Behavior Therapy. Reproduced by permission).

patients, the data are reliable and are not due to idiosyncrasies in the first case. It does not follow however that generality of findings across patients has been firmly established. Although the results were quite clear and clinically significant for five patients, results from the sixth patient showed no therapeutic effect on the measures presented. Thus, while functional relationships between treatment and response was evident, broad generality across patients was not demonstrated and the task remains to pinpoint differences between this patient and remaining patients to ascertain possible causes for the limitations on client generality. Continuing with measures of sexual functioning and satisfaction while directly addressing differing attitudes toward sexuality in this couple and helping to resolve life stress might have shed some light on these issues.

It should also be noted in this experiment that while the multiple baseline design isolated the manualized treatment as contributing to sexual functioning over and above the drug, it did *not* isolate mechanisms of action in this treatment. While the results are clinically useful, it would be helpful to go further and examine whether this particular manualized approach was clinically effective or if the results could be attributed to "common factors", such as spending more time focusing on sexual issues that was afforded by reading a manual.

Another good example of mixed results was presented in the study by Ollendick et al. (1981) in chapter 8 (Figures 8.3 and 8.4). In this comparison of two treatments in an ATD, one treatment was more effective than another for two children, but just the opposite was true for a third child. Results for two children illustrating the differential effectiveness of these treatments comprise the data for Figures 8.3 and 8.4. Because the investigators were close to the data, they speculated on one seemingly obvious reason for this discrepancy; specifically, physical restraint, one of the interventions, was more aversive for this subject. Thus, pending a subsequent test of their hypothesis, they have already taken the first step on the road to tracking down intersubject variability and establishing guidelines for generality of findings. The investigators themselves are always in the best position to identify, and subsequently test, putative sources of lack of generality of findings.

The issue of interpreting mixed results and looking for causes of failure illustrates an important principle in replication series. We noted above that subjects in a direct replication series should be as homogeneous as possible. If subjects in a series are not homogeneous, the investigator is gambling (Sidman, 1960). If the procedure is effective across heterogeneous subjects, he or she has won the gamble. If the results are mixed, he or she has lost. More specifically, if one individual differs in three or four definable ways from previous individuals, but the data are similar, then the experimenter has won the gamble by demonstrating that a procedure has client generality *despite* these differences. If the results differ in any significant manner, however, as in the example above, the experimenter cannot know which of the three, four, or more variables was responsible for the differences. The task remains, then, to explore systematically the effects of these variables and track down causes of intersubject variability.

In basic research with animals, one seldom sees this type of gamble in a direct replication series, because most variables are controlled and subjects are highly homogeneous. In applied research, however, clients always bring to treatment a variety of historical experiences, personality variables, and other background variables such as age and sex. To the extent that a given treatment works on three, four, or five clients, the applied researcher has already won a gamble even in a direct replication series, because a failure could be attributed to any one of the variables that differentiate one subject from another. In any event, we recommend the conservative approach whenever possible, in that subjects in a direct replication series should be homogeneous for aspects of the target behavior as well as background variables. The issue of gambling arises again when one starts a systematic replication series because the researcher must decide on the number of ways he or she wishes the systematic replication series to differ from the original direct series.

Example four: simultaneous replication in a group

Finally, a method of conducting simultaneous replications has been suggested by J. A. Kelly (Kelly, 1980; Kelly, Laughlin, Clairborne, & Patterson, 1979). This procedure is very useful when one is intervening with a coexisting group. Examples would be group therapy for any of a number of problems such as phobia and social deficiencies, or interventions in a classroom or on a hospital ward. In this procedure, any number of individuals in the group can be treated simultaneously in a particular experimental design, but individual data would be plotted separately. Figure 10.4 illustrates this strategy with hypothetical data originally presented by J. A. Kelly et al. (1979). In this hypothetical strategy, the experimental design was a multiple baseline across behaviors for six individuals. Three different aspects of social skills were repeatedly assessed by role playing. Intervention then proceeded for all six clients on the first social skill, followed by the second social skill, and so on. In this hypothetical example, of course, all clients did very well, with particular aspects of social skills improving only when treated. Naturally, this strategy need not be limited to a multiple-baseline-across-behaviors design. Almost any single-subject design, such as an alternating treatments design or a standard withdrawal design, could be simultaneously replicated.

From the point of view of replication, this is a very economical and conservative way to proceed. It is economical because it is less time consuming to treat six clients in a group than it is to treat six clients individually. But one still has the advantage of observing individual data repeatedly measured from six different subjects. Naturally, this is only possible where opportunities for group therapy exist. Furthermore, the procedure is conservative because fewer variables are different from client to client. The gamble taken by the investigator in a replication series with increasing heterogeneity or diversity of subjects or settings was mentioned above. To repeat, if a replication fails, the more differences there are in subjects, settings, timing of the intervention, and so forth, the harder it is to track

(RATINGS OF EACH SUBJECT'S INDIVIDUAL SOCIAL SKILLS ROLE-PLAYS)

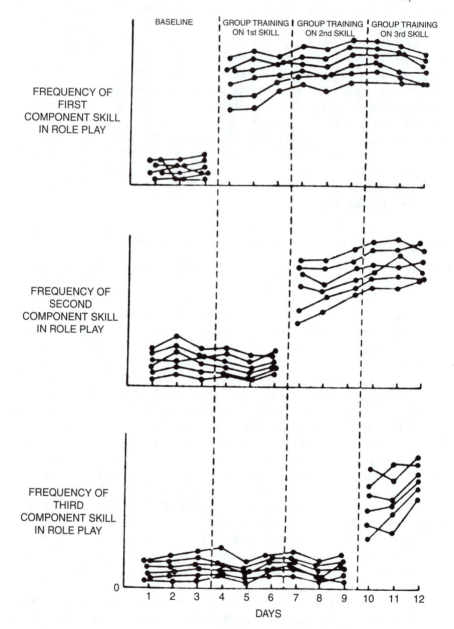

FIGURE 10.4 Graphed hypothetical data of simultaneous replications design. (Figure 2, p. 306 from: Kelly, J. A., Laughlin, C., Claiborne, M., & Patterson, J. [1979]. A group procedure for teaching job interviewing skills to formerly hospitalized psychiatric patients. *Behavior Therapy*, **10**, 299–310. Copyright 1979 by Association for Advancement of Behavior Therapy. Reproduced by permission.)

down the cause of the failure for replication during subsequent experimentation. If all subjects are treated simultaneously in the same group, at the same time, then one can be relatively sure that the intervention procedures, as well as setting and temporal factors, are identical. If there is a failure to replicate, then the investigator should look elsewhere for possible causes, most likely in background variables or personality differences in the subjects themselves.

Of course, treating clients in group therapy creates its own special kind of setting. If one were interested in the generality of these findings to individual treatment settings, the first step in a systematic replication series would be to test the procedure in subjects treated individually. Also, when groups of individuals are treated simultaneously, one cannot stop the series at just any time to begin examining for causes of failures if they occur. However, this is not really a problem as long as the groups remain reasonably small (e.g., three to six), such that the investigator would be unlikely to accumulate a large number of failures before having an opportunity to begin the search for causes.

Guidelines for direct replication

Based on prevailing practice and accumulated knowledge on direct replication, we would suggest the following guidelines in conducting a direct replication series in applied research:

1. Therapists and settings should remain constant across replications.
2. The behavior disorder in question should be topographically similar across clients, such as a specific phobia.
3. Client background variables should be as closely matched as possible, although the ideal goal of identical clients can never be attained in applied research.
4. The procedure employed (treatment) should be uniform across clients, until failures ensue. If failures are encountered during replication, attempts should be made to determine the cause of this intersubject variability through improvised and fast-changing experimental designs (see section 2.3, chapter 2). If the search is successful, the necessary alteration in treatment should be tested on additional clients who share the characteristics or behavior of the first client who required the alteration. If the search for sources of variability is not successful, differences in that particular client from other successful clients should be noted for future research.
5. One successful experiment and three to five successful replications are usually sufficient to generate systematic replication of topographically different behaviors in the same setting or of the same behavior in different settings. This guideline is not as firm as those preceding, because results from a study containing one unusual or significant case may be worth publishing, or an investigator may wish to continue direct replication if experimentally successful but clinically "weak" results are obtained. Generally, though, after one experiment and three to five successful replications, it is time to go on to systematic replication.

On the other hand, if direct replication produces mixed success and failure, then investigators must decide when to stop the series and begin to analyze reasons for failure in what is essentially a new series, because the procedure or treatment presumably will change. If one success is followed by two or three failures, then neither the reliability of the procedure nor the generality of the finding across clients has been established, and it is probably time to find out why. If two or three successes are mixed in with one or two failures, then the reliability of the procedure would be established to some extent, but the investigator must decide when to begin investigating reasons for lack of client generality. In any case, it does not appear to be sound experimental strategy to continue a direct replication series indefinitely, when both successes and failures are occurring.

6. Broad client generality cannot be established from one experiment and three to five replications. Although a practitioner can observe the extent to which an individual client who responded to treatment in a direct replication series is similar to his or her client and can proceed accordingly with the treatment, chances are the practitioner may have a client with a topographically similar behavior disorder who is different in some clinically important way from those in the series. Fortunately, as clinical and systematic replication ensues with other therapists in other settings, many more clients with different background variables are treated, and confidence in generality of findings across clients, which was established in a preliminary manner in the first series, is increased with each new replication.

10.3. SYSTEMATIC REPLICATION

Sidman (1960) noted that where direct replication helps to establish generality of findings among members of a species ". . . systematic replication can accomplish this and at the same time extend its generality over a wide range of situations" (p. 111). In applied research, we have noted that direct replication can begin to establish generality of findings across clients but cannot answer questions concerning applicability of a given procedure or functional relationship in different therapeutic settings or by different therapists. Another limitation of the initial direct replication series is an inability to determine the effectiveness of a procedure proven effective with one type of behavior disorder on a related but topographically different behavior disorder.

Definition of systematic replication

We can define systematic replication in applied research as any attempt to replicate findings from a direct replication series, varying settings, behavior change agents, behavior disorders, or any combination thereof. It would appear that, any successful systematic replication series in which one or more of the above-mentioned factors is varied also provides further information on generality of findings across clients because new clients are usually included in these efforts.

Example: differential attention in children

One of the most extensive and advanced systematic replication series began in the early 1960s. The purpose of this series has been to determine the generality of the effectiveness of a single intervention technique, often termed *differential attention*. Differential attention consists of attending to a client contingent on the emission of a well-defined desired behavior. Usually such attention takes the form of positive interaction with the client consisting of praise, smiling, and so on. Absence of the desired behavior results in withdrawal of attention, hence "differential" attention. This series, consisting of over 100 articles, has provided practitioners with a great deal of specific information on the effectiveness of this procedure in various settings with different behavior disorders and behavior change agents.

What is perhaps more important is that articles in this series have noted certain occasions when the procedure fails, leading to a clearer delineation of the generality of this technique in all relevant domains in the applied area. The effects of this procedure were studied extensively in adults with, for example psychotic behaviors (Wincze et al., 1972), somataform disorders (Brady & Lind, 1961), and marital difficulties (Goldstein, 1971). It was discovered that even Carl Rogers himself differentially reinforced his clients to good effect (Truax, 1966). But the greatest number of experimental inquiries on the effectiveness of differential attention have been conducted with children, and this series represents what is probably the most comprehensive systematic replication series to date. It is also important to note that the bulk of this work occurred in the late 1960s and early 1970s, with a decrease in published research since that time. Unlike the examples above, this is due to the fact that many of the goals of this systematic replication series were completed and differential attention was then incorporated into other more comprehensive approaches used by many clinicians today such as parent training (Kazdin, 2005; Forehand & Kotchick, 2002), various interventions in the schools (Kazdin, 2001; Crone, Homer, & Hawken, 2003), and with developmental disabilities (Lovaas, 2003; Rhodes, 2003), among other problems. Thus, this series provides an excellent context to examine the process of systematic replication. We will discuss this issue further below.

One of the earliest studies on the application of differential attention to behavior problems of a child was reported by C. D. Williams (1959), who instructed parents to withdraw attention from nightly temper tantrums. When an aunt unwittingly attended to tantrum behavior, tantrums increased and were extinguished once again by withdrawal of attention.

Table 10.1 presents summaries of replication efforts in this series since that time. Studies reported in this table used differential attention as the sole or, at least, a very major treatment component. Studies where differential attention

TABLE 10.1 Summary of Studies on Differential Attention with Children

AUTHORS	CLIENTS	N	BEHAVIOR	SETTING	THERAPIST	EXPERIMENTAL ANALYSIS
C. D. Williams (1959)	18-mo.-old female	1	Tantrums	Home	Parents	No
E. H. Zimmerman & Zimmerman (1962)	11-yr.-old males	2	Unproductive classroom behavior	Residential treatment center	Teachers	No
Allen, Hart, Buell, Harris, & Wolf (1964)	4-yr.-old female	1	Isolate behavior	Lab preschool	Teacher	Yes
Harris, Johnston, Kelley, & Wolf (1964)	3-yr.-old female	1	Crawling behavior	University nursery school	Teacher	Yes
Hart, Allen, Buell, Harris, & Wolf (1964)	4-yr.-old males	2	Crying	Preschool	Teachers	Yes
Davison (1965)	10-yr.-old male	2	Autistic behavior	Private daycare center	Under-graduates	No
Wahler, Winkel, Peterson, & Morrison (1965)	4–6-yr.-old males	3	Oppositional behavior	Lab playroom	Mother	Yes
Allen & Harris (1966)	5-yr.-old female	1	Scratching behavior	Lab preschool and home	Mother	No
Hawkins, Peterson, Schwied, & Bijou (1966)	4-yr.-old male	1	Tantrums and oppositional behavior	Home	Mother	Yes
Holmes (1966)	9-yr.-old male	1	Underachievement in school and disruptive behavior	Classroom	Teacher	No
M. K. Johnston, Kelley, Harris, & Wolf (1966)	3-yr.-old male	1	Physical activity	Preschool	Teacher	Yes
Allen, Henke, Harris, Baer, & Reynolds (1967)	4½-yr.-old male	1	Short attention span	Lab preschool	Teachers	Yes

Study	Subjects	N	Behavior	Setting	Change agent	Lab
Etzel & Gerwitz (1967)	6- and 20-wk.-old infant	2	Crying	Lab	Professional	Yes
R. V. Hall & Broden (1967)	5- and 6-yr.-old males and 9-yr.-old female with CNS dysfunction	3	Behavior considered by staff to be interfering with developmental progress	Experimental educational unit	Parents and teachers	Yes
Sloane, Johnston, & Bijou (1967)	4-yr.-old male	1	Extreme aggression, temper tantrums, and excessive fantasy play	Remedial nursery school	Teachers	Yes
Buell, Stoddard, Harris, & Baer (1968)	3-yr.-old female	1	Lack of cooperative play and participation in preschool programs	Preschool program	Teacher	Yes
Carlson, Arnold, Becker, & Madsen (1968)	8-yr.-old female	1	Tantrums	Classroom	Teacher	No
Ellis (1968)	4- and 5-yr.-old males	5	Aggressive behavior	Lab school	Teacher and helper	Yes
B. V. Hall, Lund, & Jackson (1968)	Elementary school pupils	6	Disruptive and dawdling study behavior	Poverty area classroom	Teachers	Yes
R. V. Hall, Panyan, Rabon, & Broden (1968)	3 classrooms, 1st, 6th; 7th grades, 5-yr.-old female	24	Study Behavior	Classroom	Teachers	Yes
Hart, Reynolds, Baer, Brawley, & Harris (1968)	5-yr.-old female	1	Uncooperative play	Preschool	Teacher	Yes
Madsen, Becker, & Thomas (1968)	Elementary school pupils	3	Classroom disruption	Classroom	Teachers	Yes
N.J. Reynolds & Risley (1968)	4-yr.-old female	1	Low frequency of talking	Preschool	Teacher	Yes

(continued)

TABLE 10.1 Continued

AUTHORS	CLIENTS	N	BEHAVIOR	SETTING	THERAPIST	EXPERIMENTAL ANALYSIS
D. R. Thomas, Becker, & Armstrong (1968)	6–11-yr.-old males and females	10	Disruptive behavior	Classroom	Teacher	Yes
D. R. Thomas, Nielson, Kuypers, & Becker (1968)	6-yr.-old male	1	Disruptive behavior	Classroom	Teacher	Yes
Wahler & Pollio (1968)	8-yr.-old male	1	Excessive dependency and lack of aggressive behavior	University clinic	Parents and therapist	Yes
Ward & Baker (1968)	1st-grade children	4	Disruptive behavior	Classroom	Teacher	Yes
Zeilberger, Sampen, & Sloane (1968)	4½-year-old male	1	Disobedience and aggressive behavior	Home	Mother	Yes
Brawley, Harris, Allen, Fleming, & Peterson (1969)	7-yr.-old male	1	Autistic behavior	Hospital daycare unit	Professional	Yes
Cormier (1969)	6th and 8th-grade classes	18	Disruptive behavior and lack of motivation	Classroom	Teacher	Yes
McCallister, Stachowiak, Baer, & Conderman (1969)	High school English class	25	Inappropriate talking and turning around	Classroom	Teacher	Yes
O'Leary, Becker, Evans, & Saudargas (1969)	2nd-grade males	7	Disruptive classroom behavior	Special education class	Teacher	Yes
Wahler (1969a)	Elementary-school-age males	2	Oppositional behavior	Home	Parents	Yes
Wahler (1969b)	5–8-year-old males	2	Oppositional and disruptive behavior	Home and classroom	Parent and teacher	Yes
Broden, Bruce, Mitchell, Carter, & Hall (1970)	2nd grade males	2	Disruptive behavior	Poverty area classroom	Teacher	Yes

Study	N	Behavior	Setting	Mediator	Reversal
Broden, Hall, Dunlap, & Clark (1970)	7th- and 8th-grade males and females	13	Disruptive classroom behavior	Special education class	Teacher	Yes
J. C. Conger (1970)	9-yr.-old male	1	Encopresis	Home	Mother	Yes
Goodlet, Goodlet, & Dredge (1970)	5- and 7-year-old males	2	Disruptive behavior	University lab classroom	Teacher	Yes
Schutte & Hopkins (1970)	4- to 6-yr.-old females	5	Instruction following	Classroom	Teacher	Yes
Smeets (1970)	18-yr.-old male	1	Rumination and regurgitation	Hospital room	Teacher	Yes
Wahler, Sperling, Thomas, Teeter, & Luper (1970)	4- and 9-yr.-old males	2	"Beginning" stuttering and mildly deviant behavior	Hearing and speech center	Parents	Yes
J. Wright, Clayton & Edgar (1970)	Severely retarded children	15	Negative behaviors	State residential institution	Ward technicians	No
Buys (1971)	9 problem and 9 control elementary school pupils	18	Deviant classroom behavior	Classroom	Teacher	Yes
Corte, Wolf, & Locke (1971)	Profoundly retarded adolescents	4	Self-injurious behavior	Classroom	Teacher	Yes
R. V. Hall et al. (1971)	Individual pupils and classroom groups from 1st grade to junior high school	Ex : N 1 : 1 2 : 1 3 : 1 4 : 1 5 : 30 6 : 27	Disruptive and talking-out behavior	White, middle-class, and black poverty classroom	Teacher	Yes

(continued)

TABLE 10.1 Continued

AUTHORS	CLIENTS	N	BEHAVIOR	SETTING	THERAPIST	EXPERIMENTAL ANALYSIS
Laws, Brown, Epstein, & Hocking (1971)	Severely disturbed 8- and 9-yr.-old males	3	Behavior that interferes with speech and language	State hospital	Speech therapist	Yes
Nordquist (1971)	5½-year-old male	1	Enuresis and oppositional behavior	Home	Parents	Yes
Skiba, Pettigrew, & Alden (1971)	8-yr.-old females	3	Thumb sucking	Classroom	Teacher	Yes
J. D. Thomas & Adams (1971)	Well-behaved and remedial primary school pupils	16	Task-related behavior and lowering sound levels	Classroom	Teacher	Yes
Veenstra (1971)	5- to 14-yr.-old siblings	4	Disruptive behavior	Home	Mother	Yes
Vukelich & Hake (1971)	18-yr.-old severely retarded female	1	Choking and grabbing	State hospital	Ward staff	Yes
Yawkey (1971)	7-yr.-old female 7-yr.-old males	2	Poor attending behavior	Classroom	Teacher	Yes
Barnes, Wooton, & Wood (1972)	3- and 4-yr.-old males and females	24	Immature play	Mental health center	Public health nurse	Yes
R. V. Hall et al. (1972)	4- and 8-yr.-old males and 5- and 10-yr.-old females	4	Whining and failure to wear orthodontic device	Home	Parents	Yes
Hasazi & Hasazi (1972)	8-yr.-old male	1	Digital reversal	Classroom	Teacher	Yes

Study	Subjects	N	Target behavior	Setting	Change agent	Professional
Herbert & Baer (1972)	5-yr.-old male and female	2	Inappropriate behavior in home	Home	Mother	Yes
Kirby & Schields (1972)	13-yr.-old male	1	Nonattending and poor arithmetic	Classroom	Teacher	Yes
Sajwaj, Twardosz, & Burke (1972)	7-yr.-old retarded male	1	Excessive conversation with teacher	Remedial preschool	Teacher	Yes
Twardosz & Sajwaj (1972)	4-yr.-old hyperactive retarded male	1	Sitting	Remedial preschool	Teacher	Yes
Cossairt, Hall, & Hopkins (1973)	3½-year-old female	1	Noncompliance with instruction-following behavior	Elementary schools	Teachers	Yes
Herbert et al. (1973)	5- and 6-yr.-old females, 5-, 7- and 8-yr.-old males	6	Deviant	Preschool classroom and observation lab	Mothers	Yes
Pinkston, Reese, LeBlanc, & Baer (1973)	3½-yr.-old male	1	Aggressive behaviors with peers and low peer interaction	Preschool classroom	Teacher	Yes
Budd, Green, & Baer (1976)	3-yr.-old female	1	Noncompliance with instructions and considerable demands for attention	University lab room	Mother	Yes
Munford & Liberman (1978)	13-yr.-old male	1	Operant coughing	1. hospital 2. home	1. hospital staff 2. parents	Yes
Varni, Russo, & Cataldo (1978)	11-yr.-old male	1	Delusional speech	Psychiatric hospital	Graduate student	yes

Note: Professional usually refers to Ph.D., Psychologist, or Psychiatrist.

was a minor part of a treatment package were for the most part omitted. It is certainly possible that a few additional studies were inadvertently excluded. In the table, it is important to note the variety of clients, problem behaviors, therapists, and settings described in the studies, because generality of findings in all relevant domains is entirely dependent on the diversity of settings, clients, and the rest employed in such studies.

Most replication efforts through 1965 presented an experimental analysis of results from a single-case (see Table 10.1). A good example of these early studies was presented by Allen et al. (1964), who reported that differential attention was responsible for increased social interaction with peers in a socially isolated preschool girl. The setting for the demonstration was a classroom, and the behavior change agent, of course, was the teacher. While most of the early studies contained only one case, the experimental demonstration of the effectiveness of differential attention in different settings with different therapists began to provide information on generality of findings across all-important domains. These replications increased confidence in this procedure as a generally effective clinical tool. In addition to isolate behavior, the successful treatment of such problems as regressed crawling (Harris, Johnston, Kelley, & Wolf, 1964), crying (Hart, Allen, Buell, Harris, & Wolf, 1964), and various behavior problems associated with the autistic syndrome (e.g., Davison, 1965) also suggested that this procedure was applicable to a wide variety of behavior problems in children while at the same time providing additional information on generality of findings across therapists and settings.

Although studies of successful application of differential attention to a single-case demonstrated that this procedure is applicable in a wide range of situations, a more important development in the series was the appearance of direct replication efforts containing three or more cases within the systematic replication series. Although reports of single-cases are uniformly successful, or they would not have been published, exceptions to these reports of success can and do appear in series of cases, and these exceptions or failures begin to define the limits of the applicability of differential attention.

For this reason, it is particularly impressive that many series of three or more cases reported consistent success across many different clients, with such behavior disorders as inappropriate social behavior in disturbed hospitalized children (e.g., Laws, Brown, Epstein, & Hocking, 1971), disruptive behavior in the elementary classroom (e.g., Cormier, 1969; R. V. Hall et al., 1971; R. V. Hall, Lund, & Jackson, 1968), or high school classroom (e.g., Schutte & Hopkins, 1970), chronic thumb-sucking (Skiba, Pettigrew, & Alden, 1971), disruptive behavior in the home (Veenstra, 1971; Wahler, Winkel, Peterson, & Morrison, 1965), and disruptive behavior in brain-injured children (R. V. Hall & Broden, 1967). These improvements occurred in many different settings such as elementary and high school classrooms, hospitals, homes, kindergartens, and various preschools. Therapists included professionals, teachers, aides, parents, and nurses (see Table 10.1).

The consistency of their success was impressive, but as these series of cases accumulated, the inevitable but extremely valuable reports of failures began to appear. For instance, early investigations suggested that differential attention was not effective with self-injurious behavior in children. Tate and Baroff (1966) noted that in the length of time necessary for differential attention to work, severe injury would result. Initial alternative attempts in place of differential attention found that a strong aversive stimulus—electric shock—proved effective in suppressing this behavior. Later, Corte, Wolf, and Locke (1971) found that while differential attention was ineffective on mild self-injurious behavior in retarded children but, again, electric shock proved effective. Because there were no reports of success in the literature using differential attention for self-injurious behavior, it is unlikely that these cases would have been published at all if differential attention had not proven effective on other behavior disorders. Thus this is an example of a systematic replication series setting the stage for reports of limitations of a procedure. Of course, aversive stimuli quickly became discredited in the 1980s as intrusive and unnecessary and reports using this approach declined significantly over time. In contrast, the results of single-case experimental designs testing behavioral treatments for self-injurious behaviors have accumulated over the years. As clinical investigators have learned more about the function of self-injurious behaviors effective behavioral treatments have emerged (Iwata et al., 1994; Nock & Prinstein, 2004; 2005). Studies in this area have demonstrated that a range of behavioral interventions are effective in the treatment of self-injurious behavior, including differential reinforcement, extinction, antecedent manipulations, response blocking, and functional communication training (Durand, 1990; Kahng, Iwata, & Lewin, 2002).

More subtle limitations of the procedure are reported in series of cases wherein the technique worked in some cases, but not in others. In an early series, Wahler et al. (1965) trained mothers of young, oppositional children in differential attention procedures. The setting was an experimental preschool. In two out of three cases the mothers were quite successful in modifying oppositional behavior in their children, and an experimental analysis isolated differential attention as the important ingredient. In a third child, however, this procedure was not effective, and an additional punishment (time-out) procedure was necessary. The authors did not offer any explanation for this discrepancy, and there were no obvious differences in the cases that could account for the failure based on descriptions in the article. The authors did not seem concerned with the discrepancy, probably because it was an early effort on the replication series, and the goal was to control the oppositional behavior, which was accomplished when time-out was added. This study was important, however, for it contained the first hint that differential attention might not be effective with some cases of oppositional behavior.

In a later series, after differential attention was well established as an effective procedure, further failures to replicate did elicit concern from the investigator (Wahler, 1968, 1969). Wahler trained parents of children with severe oppositional behavior in differential attention procedures. Results indicated that differential attention was ineffective across five children, but the addition of time-out again produced the desired changes. Replication in two more cases of oppositional behavior confirmed that differential attention was only effective when combined with a time-out procedure.

In the best tradition of science, Wahler (1969) did not gloss over the failure of differential attention, although his treatment "package" was ultimately successful. Contemplating reasons for the failure, Wahler hypothesized that in cases of severe oppositional behavior, parental reinforcement value may be extremely low; that is, attention from parents is not as reinforcing. After treatment using the combination of time-out and differential attention, oppositional behavior was under control, even though time-out was no longer used. Employing a test of parental reinforcement values, Wahler demonstrated that the treatment package increased the reinforcing value of parental attention, allowing the gain to be maintained. This was the first clear suggestion that therapist variables are important in the application of differential attention, and that with oppositional children particularly, differential attention alone may be ineffective due to the low reinforcing value of parental attention.

Although differential attention occasionally was found ineffective in other settings, such as the classroom (O'Leary et al., 1969), other investigators actually observed deleterious effects under certain conditions (e.g., Herbert et al., 1973; Sajwaj & Hedges, 1971). For example, Herbert et al. (1973) trained mothers in the use of differential attention in two separate geographical locations (Kansas and Mississippi). Although preschools were the settings in both locations, the design and function of the preschools were quite dissimilar. Clients were children with a variety of disruptive and deviant behaviors, including hyperactivity, oppositional behavior, and other inappropriate social behaviors. These young children presented different background variables, from familial retardation through childhood autism and Down's syndrome, and they came from differing socioeconomic backgrounds. The one similarity among the six cases (two from Mississippi, four from Kansas) was that differential attention from parents was not only ineffective but detrimental in many cases, in that deviant behavior increased, and dangerous and surprising side effects appeared. Deleterious effects of this procedure were confirmed in extensions of A-B-A designs, where behavior worsened under differential attention and improved when the procedure was withdrawn.

These results were, of course, surprising to the authors, and discovery of similar results in two settings through personal communication prompted the combining of the data into a single publication. In this particular report the investigators were unable to pinpoint reasons for these failures. As the authors note, ". . . the results were not peculiar to a particular setting, certain parent-child activities, observation code or recording system, experimenter or parent training procedure. Subject characteristics also were not predictive of the results obtained" (Herbert et al., 1973, p. 26). But in one case where time-out was added, disruptive behavior declined. In fact, Sajwaj and Dillon (1977) analyzed a large portion of their systematic replication series and found a ratio of 87 individual successes to only 27 individual failures. In many of the cases that failed, the addition of another procedure, such as time-out, quickly converted the failure to a success. Other studies replicated the finding that adding time-out corrects differential attention failures (Roberts, Hatzenbuehler, & Bean, 1981).

As noted above, this series was largely complete by 1980, as is evident in Table 10.1. This was due to widespread confidence in the general applicability of differential attention, and so the field moved on. Differential attention was fully incorporated into a treatment program, often referred to as *parent training* (e.g., Forehand & Kotchik, 2002; Forehand & McMahon, 1981; Kazdin, 2005). This package consists of additional components to differential attention, such as time-out and training in the discrimination of certain instructions or commands. Since this package has been well worked out, the field then became more concerned with results from a clinical replication analysis of the entire treatment package than with continued systematic replication of the differential attention procedure in isolation.

Comment on replication

In our view, data on failures are a sign of the maturity of a systematic replication series. Only when a procedure is proven successful through many replications, do negative results assume this importance. But these failures do not detract from the successful replications. The effectiveness of differential attention has been established repeatedly. These data do however indicate that there are conditions that are not fully understood that limit generality of effectiveness and that practitioners must proceed with caution (Wahler et al., 1979).

In conclusion, this advanced systematic replication series on differential attention generated a great deal of confidence among practitioners. The evidence indicates that it can be effective with children with a variety of behavioral problems in most any setting. The clinically oriented books and monographs widely advocating its use, most often in combination with other procedures as part of a treatment package (Crone et al., 2003; Forehand & Kotchick, 2002; Kazdin, 2001; Kazdin, 2005, Lovaas, 2003; Rhodes, 2003), have made this procedure available to numerous professionals concerned with behavior change, as well as to the consuming public. Similarly differential attention was incorporated into many adult programs such as token economies (Paul & Lentz, 1977). Independent living skills training for the chronic mentally disabled (Wallace, Boone, Donahue, & Foy, 1985) and marital therapy (Wheeler, Christensen, & Jacobson, 2001; Wood & Jacobson, 1985).

Guidelines for systematic replication

The formulation of guidelines for conducting systematic replication is more difficult than for direct replication due to the variety of experimental efforts that comprise a systematic replication series. However, in the interest of providing some structure to future systematic replication, we outline the general procedures necessary for sound systematic replication in applied research. These procedures or guidelines fall into four categories.

1. Earlier we defined systematic replication in applied research as any attempt to replicate findings from a direct replication series, varying settings, behavior change agents, behavior disorders, or some combination thereof. Ideally, then, the systematic replication should begin with sound direct replication where the reliability of a procedure is established and the beginnings of client generality are ascertained. If results in the initial experiment and three to five or more replications are uniformly successful, then the important work of testing the effectiveness of the procedure in other settings with other therapists and so on can begin. If a series begins with a report of a single case (as it often does), then the first order of business is to initiate a direct replication series on this procedure, so that the search for exceptions can begin.

2. Investigators evaluating systematic replication should clearly note the differences among their clients, therapists, or settings from those in the original experiment. In a conservative systematic replication, one, or possibly two, variables differ from the original direct replication. If more than one or two variables differ, this indicates that the investigator is "gambling" somewhat (Sidman, 1960). That is, if the experiment succeeds, the series will take a large step forward in establishing generality of findings. If the experiment fails, the investigator cannot know which of the differing variables or combination of variables was responsible for the change and must go back and retrace his or her steps. Whether scientists take the gamble depends on the setting and their own inclinations; there is no guideline one could suggest here without also limiting the creativity of the scientific process. But it is important to be fully aware of previous efforts in the series and to list the number of ways in which the current experiment differs from past efforts, so that other investigators and clinicians can hypothesize along with the experimenter on which differences were important in the event of failure. In fact, most good scientists do this (e.g., Herbert et al., 1973).

3. Systematic replication is essentially a search for exceptions. If no exceptions are found as replications proceed, then wide generality of findings is established. However, the purpose of systematic replication is to define the conditions under which a technique will succeed or fail, and this means a search for exceptions or failures. Thus any experimental tactics that hinder the finding and reporting of exceptions are of less value than an experimental design that highlights failure. Of those experimental procedures typically found in a systematic replication series (e.g., see Table. 10.1), two fall into this category: the experimental analysis containing only one case and the group study.

As noted above, the report of a single-case, particularly when accompanied by an experimental analysis, can be a valuable addition to a series in that it describes another setting, behavior disorder, or other item where the procedure was successful. Reports of single cases also may lead to direct and systematic replication, as in the differential attention series. Unfortunately, however, failures in a single-case are seldom published in journals. Among the numerous successful reports of single-case studies contained in the differential attention series, very few reported a failure, although it is our guess that differential attention has failed on many occasions, and these failures simply have not been reported.

The group study suffers from the same limitation because failures are lost in the group average. Again, group studies can play an important role in systematic replication in that demonstration that a technique is successful with a given group, as opposed to individuals in the group, may serve an important function (see section 2.9). In the differential attention series, several investigators thought it important to demonstrate that the procedure could be effective in a classroom as a whole (e.g., Ward & Baker, 1968). These data contributed to generality of findings across several domains. The fact remains, however, that failures will not be detected (unless the whole experiment fails, in which case it would not be published), thus leading us no closer to the goal of defining the conditions in which a successful technique fails. In clinical replication, or *field testing*, described below, one has more flexibility in examining results from large groups of treated clients as long as it is possible to pinpoint individuals who succeed or fail.

4. Finally, the question arises: When is a systematic replication series over? For direct replication series, it was possible to make some tentative recommendations on a number of subjects, given experimental findings. With systematic replication, no such recommendations are possible. In applied research, we would have to agree with Sidman's (1960) conclusion concerning basic research that a series is never over, because scientists will always attempt to find exceptions to a given principle, as well they should. It may be safe to say that a series is over when no exception to a proven therapeutic principle can be found, but, as Sidman pointed out, this is entirely dependent on the complexity of the problem and the inductive reasoning of clinical researchers who will have to judge in the light of new and emerging knowledge which conditions could provide exceptions to old principles. Of course, series will eventually begin to "fade away," as with the differential attention series, when wide generality of applicability has been established.

Fortunately, practitioners do not have to wait for the end of a series to apply interim findings to their clients. In these series, knowledge is cumulative. A clinician may apply a procedure from an advanced series, such as differential attention, with more confidence than procedures from less advanced series (Barlow, 1974; Barlow, 2001). However, it is still possible through inspection of these data to utilize those new procedures with a degree of confidence dependent on the degree to which the experimental clients, therapists, and settings are similar to those facing the clinician. At the very least, this is a good beginning to the often discouraging and sometimes painful process of clinical trial and error.

10.4. CLINICAL REPLICATION

A somewhat different type of replication process occurs only in applied research. We termed this process in the first edition of this book *clinical replication* (Hersen & Barlow, 1976). Clinical replication is an advanced replication procedure in which a treatment program containing two or more distinct procedures is applied to a succession of clients with multiple behaviors or emotional problems that cluster together; in other words, the usual and customary types of multifaceted problems that present to practitioners such as conduct problems in children, depression, schizophrenia, or autism.

Direct replication was defined as the administration of a given procedure by the same investigator or group of investigators in a specific setting (e.g., hospital, clinic, classroom) on a series of clients homogeneous for a particular behavior disorder such as agoraphobia or compulsive hand washing. As this definition implies, one component of a treatment procedure is applied to one well-defined problem in succeeding clients. Similarly, systematic replication examines the effectiveness of this functional relationship across multiple settings, therapists, and (related) behaviors. Most often, direct and systematic replications are testing only one component of what eventually becomes a treatment program, as in the examples above, and therefore these replication series may not always have direct clinical relevance.

In constructing an effective treatment program, however, it is desirable that one develop and test procedures for one problem at a time, with the eventual goal of combining successful treatments for all coexisting problems. This is the technique-building strategy originally suggested by Bergin and Strupp (1972). For example, the insertion of differential attention, time-out, and other well-tested procedures into a "parenting" package is a good example of technique building resulting in a treatment ready for clinical replication.

Another name for clinical replication, then, could be field testing, because this is where clinicians and practitioners take newly developed treatments or newly modified treatments and apply them to the common, everyday problems encountered in their practice. While this process can be carried out by either full-time clinical investigators or scientist-practitioners (Barlow et al., 1984; Hayes et al., 1999), establishing the widest possible client and setting generality would require substantial participation by full-time practitioners. The job of these practitioners, then, would be to apply these treatments to large numbers of their clients while observing and recording successes and failures and analyzing through experimental strategies, where possible, the reasons for this individual variation. But even if practitioners are not inclined to analyze causes for failures in the application of a particular treatment package, full descriptions of these failures will be extremely important for those investigators who are in a position to carry on this search (Hayes et al., 1999).

Thus, while all facets of single-case experimental research are much closer to the procedures in clinical or applied practice than to other types of research methodology (see below), clinical replication in its most elementary form becomes almost identical with the activities of practitioners.

Definition of clinical replication

We would define clinical replication as the administration by the same investigator or practitioner of a treatment package containing two or more distinct treatment procedures. These procedures would be administered in a specific setting to a series of clients presenting similar combinations of multiple behavioral and emotional problems. Obviously, this type of replication process is advanced in that it should be the end result of a systematic, technique-building applied research effort, which should take years.

Of course, there are many clinical replication series in the literature describing the application of comprehensive treatments that did not benefit from careful technique-building strategies (or technique dismantling strategies). One good example is the Masters and Johnson series describing the treatment of sexual dysfunction. Because of this weakness, it was noted early on that this treatment approach did not necessarily have wide generality of effectiveness (Zilbergeld & Evans, 1980). And, because no technique-building strategy proceded the introduction of this treatment, we have no idea why.

More recently, Wilson (in press), following Hollan's 1999 analysis, has noted that cognitive therapy for depression, while clearly as effective as antidepressant medication even with severely depressed patients, contains a number of overlapping elements. These elements include the initial rationale for treatment, systematic self observation, behavioral activation, monitoring thoughts, challenging the accuracy of thoughts, exploring core underlining beliefs and relapse intervention. Most clinical trials have proceeded testing the full package of components comprising cognitive therapy. But Ilardi and Craighead (1994) pointed out that cognitive therapy for depression seems to produce much of its therapeutic benefit early in treatment before patients have experienced all of the components. Jacobson et al. (1996) also demonstrated that one component of cognitive therapy, behavioral activation, seems at least as effective as the full package (Dimidjian et al., 2006). Here again, a systematic replication series on varying components of the cognitive therapy package as part of a technique building enterprise might have put us further down the road to discovering the most efficient and effective treatment for depression. These shortcomings are not found in the following series.

Example: clinical replication with autistic children

One of the best examples of a clinical replication series is the work of Lovaas and his colleagues with very young autistic children (e.g., Lovaas, Berberich, Perloff, & Schaeffer, 1966; Lovaas, Schaeffer, & Simmons, 1965; Lovaas & Simmons, 1969). The diagnosis of autism fulfills the requirements of clinical replication in that it subsumes a number of behavioral or emotional problems and is a major clinical entity. DSM IV-TR lists three distinct broad areas of difficulties: impairment in social interaction, impairment in communication, and restricted repetitive and stereotyped patterns of behavior, interests and activities. Each broad category contains four specific symptom clusters. Step-by-step, Lovaas and colleagues developed and tested treatments for each of these behaviors, such as self-destructive behavior (Lovaas & Simmons, 1969), language acquisition (e.g., Lovaas et al., 1966), and social and self-help skills (Lovaas, Freitas, Nelson, & Whalen, 1967). These procedures were tested in separate direct replication series on the initial group of children. The treatment package constructed from these direct replication series was administered to subsequent children presenting a sufficient number of these behaviors to be labeled autistic.

Lovaas et al. (1973) initially presented the results and follow-up data from the initial clinical replication series for 13 children. Results were presented in terms of response of the group as a whole, as well as of individual improvement across the variety of behavioral and emotional problems. While these data are complex, they can be summarized as follows. All children demonstrated increases in appropriate behaviors and decreases in inappropriate behaviors. There were marked differences in the amount of improvement. At least one child was returned to a normal school setting, while several children improved very little and required continued institutionalization. In other words, each child improved, but the change was not clinically dramatic for several children.

Because clinical replication is similar to direct replication, it can be analyzed in a similar fashion, and conclusions can be made in two general areas. *First,* the treatment package can be effective for behaviors subsumed under the autistic syndrome. This conclusion is based on (1) the initial experimental analysis of each component of the treatment package in the original direct replication series (e.g., Lovaas & Simmons, 1969) and (2) the withdrawal and reintroduction of this whole package in A-B-A-B fashion in several children (Lovaas et al., 1973) with subsequent replications (Lovaas, 1987). *Second,* replication of this finding across all subjects indicates that the data are reliable and not due to idiosyncrasies in one child. It does not follow, however, that generality across children was established. As in example 3 in the section on direct replication, the results were clear and clinically significant for several children, but the results were also weak and clinically unimportant for at least one child. Thus the package had only limited generality across clients, and the task remained to pinpoint differences between children who improved and those who did not improve, to improve generality of findings.

As Lovaas et al. (1973) concluded:

> Finally a major focus of future research should attempt more functional descriptions of autistic children. As we have shown, the children responded in vastly different ways to the treatment we gave them. We paid scant attention to individual differences when we treated the first twenty children. In the future, we will assess such individual differences. (p. 163)

Taking cues from this initial clinical replication series, the investigators in this research group continued to refine their treatment package over the years, based on a long-term analysis of individual differences, and hypothesized reasons for failure or minimal success. Subsequent experimental analyses isolated some procedures and strategies that seem to improve the training program as a whole (e.g., Durand, 1990; Harris, Handleman, Kristoff, Bass, & Gordon, 1990; Koegel & Schreibman, 1982; Lovaas, 1987) and long term follow-up indicated these gains were maintained (McEachin, Smith, & Lovaas, 1993). Nevertheless, few of these children reached qualitatively normal status although predictors of extent of progress were identified in the series (Durand, 1999).

Guidelines for clinical replication are similar to those for direct replication when series are relatively small and contain four to six clients. A detailed discussion of series containing 20, 50, or even 100 clients is presented in Hayes et al. (1999).

10.5. BENCHMARKING

As noted at the beginning of the chapter, an effort very similar to clinical replication referred to as "benchmarking" has gained currency in recent years. The general purpose of a benchmarking trial is to treat clients in naturalistic treatment settings with a treatment program for a well defined disorder or problem, noting overall rates of success, as well of instances of failure or incomplete response. These results are then "benchmarked" to results from sophisticated clinical trials where patients are treated in more rigorously controlled setting (efficacy research) for the purposes of establishing generality of findings.

For example, a number of investigators have attempted to replicate the results obtained with cognitive behavioral treatments for panic disorder in controlled clinical trials (Barlow, Craske, Cerny, & Klosko, 1989; Barlow & Craske, 2000; Craske & Barlow, 2001). In the first of these studies, Wade, Treat, & Stuart (1998) found that unselected patients with panic disorder in a community mental health center achieved comparable gains to those in the clinical trial. One year later, these gains were maintained (Stuart, Treat, & Wade, 2000). Investigators from this same center extended this analysis to patients presenting with depression with similar outcomes (Merrill, Tolbert, & Wade, 2003). While others have reported on benchmarking studies for other disorders such as social phobia (e.g., Lincoln et al., 2003), noting general equivalence with published clinical trials. While the numbers are typically large in these reports, (e.g., $N = 192$, Merrill et al., 2003; $N = 217$, Lincoln et al., 2003) the reporting typically leaves something to be desired in terms of analyzing generalizability. Thus, results reported are usually limited to comparing effect sizes between the benchmarked group and research samples, looking at percent reaching an "improved" or "cured" status, and perhaps, examining predictors of response via regression analyses. For example, Merrill et al. (2003) found that lower pre-treatment severity, higher income, absence of axis II pathology, and a greater number of sessions predicted more favorable outcome, consistent with studies from research centers. A richer analysis of factors in individuals' cases or groups of cases associated with different degrees of response, as described above, that was "closer to the clinic" would provide clinicians with more information than an averaged response across large numbers of patients as represented by effect sizes or regression equations, valuable as those data are.

Of course, these efforts would be enhanced if investigators in these benchmarking trials engaged in more functional analysis of reasons for success and failure using standard functionally analytic single case procedures. Nevertheless, the process of intensive local observation in which clinicians hypothesize about reasons for lack of response and attempt mid-course corrections in therapeutic strategies contributes a significant amount of information if presented in sufficient detail as it does in any replication series. The presence of prior systematic replication series or dismantling strategies, of course, greatly assist clinicians in hypothesizing functionally active ingredients in treatments and why they might fail from time to time.

10.6. PRACTICE RESEARCH NETWORKS

In recent years a number of attempts have been made to increase communication and collaboration among clinical research facilities and clinical service settings. This type of effort should greatly enhance the production of clinical replication series. Perhaps the best example is found in practice research networks, such as the Pennsylvania Practice Research Network. This network has assembled an infrastructure that involves the collaboration of clinical researchers and full time practitioners expressly to examine the generalizeability and ability to disseminate newly developed treatments (e.g., Borkovec et al., 2001). Similarly, the Substance Abuse and Mental Health Services (SAMHSA) Administration established a National Child Traumatic Stress Network with funding of over $30,000,000 to develop and disseminate empirically supported interventions specifically focused on childhood trauma (SAMHSA, 2003). Because practitioners are fully incorporated into this network, and are funded to engage in clinical replication activities while keeping in close touch with research centers, this mechanism should prove to be productive.

Finally, the National Institute on Drug Abuse has funded a large scale effort to study dissemination of evidence based practice in the form of the Clinical Trial Network Initiative (NIDA, 2005). Once again, the purpose of this initiative is to evaluate promising new treatments as they are delivered on the front lines of care. With the advent of evidence based practice, state governments are also organizing similar networks of practitioners to collect outcome measures on empirically supported interventions (e.g., Chorpita et al., 2002).

Thus, the stage is set for a substantial leap forward in the collection of data from clinical replication series in the context of effectiveness or services research. But these data will only be valuable to the extent that the series analyze mechanisms of action of the treatment package and highlight the response of the individual examining, as far as possible, why certain individuals succeed and others fail. Only in this way will the full promise of our efforts to establish generality of findings be realized.

10.7. ADVANTAGES OF REPLICATION OF SINGLE-CASE EXPERIMENTS

In view of the reluctance of clinical researchers to carry out the large-scale replication studies required in traditional experimental design, one might be puzzled by the seeming enthusiasm with which investigators undertake replication efforts using single-case designs, as evidenced by the differential attention series and other less advanced series. A quick examination of Table 10.1 demonstrates that there is probably little or no savings in time or money when compared to the large-scale collaborative factorial designs. No fewer clients are involved and, in all likelihood, more applied researchers and settings are involved. Why, then, does this replication tactic succeed when Bergin and Strupp concluded that the alternative could not be implemented? In our view, there are four very important but rather simple reasons.

First, the effort is *decentralized*. Rather than in the type of large collaborative factorial study necessary to determine generality of findings at a cost of millions of dollars, the replication efforts are carried out in many settings such that funding, when available, is dispersed. This, of course, is more practical for government or other funding sources. Often these small studies involving three or four subjects are unfunded. Also, rather than administering a large collaborative study from a central location where all scientists or therapists are to carry out prescribed duties, each scientist administers his or her own replication effort based on his or her ideas and views of previous findings (see Hayes et al., 1999). What is lost here is some efficiency, since there is no guarantee that the next obvious step in the replication series will be carried out at the logical time. What is gained is the freedom and creativity of individual scientists to attack the problem in their own ways.

Second, replication efforts will continue because the professional contingencies are favorable to its success. The professional contingencies in this case are publications and the accompanying professional recognition. Initial efforts in a series experimentally demonstrating success of a technique on a single case are publishable. Direct replications are publishable. Systematic and clinical replications are publishable each time the procedure is successful in a different setting or with a behavioral problem. Finally, after a procedure has been proven effective, failures or exceptions to the success are publishable.

Third, the experimental analysis of the single-case is close to the clinic. As noted in chapter 1, this approach tends to merge the role of scientist and practitioner. Many an important series has started only after the clinician confronted an interesting case. Subsequently, measures were developed, and an experimental analysis of the treatment was performed (Mills et al., 1973). As a result, the data increase one's understanding of the problem, but the client also receives and benefits from treatment. If one plans to treat the client, it is an easy enough matter to develop measures and perform the necessary experimental analyses. Hayes et al. (1999) attempted to explore this potential in our full-time practitioners by demonstrating how they can incorporate these principles into their practices and thereby participate in the research process. This ability to work with ease within the clinical setting, more than any other fact, may ensure the future of meaningful replication efforts.

Finally, as noted above, the results of the series are cumulative, and each new replicative effort has some immediate payoff for the practicing clinician. As this is the ultimate goal of the applied researcher, it is far more satisfactory than participating in a multiyear collaborative study where knowledge or benefit to the clinician is a distant goal.

Nevertheless, the advancement of a replication series is a long and arduous road full of pitfalls and dead ends. In the face of the immediate demands on clinicians and behavior change agents to provide services to society, it is tempting to "grab the glimmer of hope" provided by treatments that prove successful in preliminary reports or case studies. That these hopes have been repeatedly dashed as therapeutic techniques and schools of therapy have come and gone supplies the most convincing evidence that the slow but inexorable process of the scientific method is the only way to meaningful advancement in our knowledge. Although we are a long way from the sophistication of the physical sciences, the single-case experimental design with adequate replication may provide us with the methodology necessary to overcome the complex problems of human behavior disorders.

HIAWATHA DESIGNS AN EXPERIMENT

MAURICE G. KENDALL

Hiawatha, mighty hunter,
He could shoot ten arrows upwards
Shoot them with such strength and swiftness
That the last had left the bowstring
Ere the first to earth descended.
This was commonly regarded
As a feat of skill and cunning.

One or two sarcastic spirits
Pointed out to him, however,
That it might be much more useful
If he sometimes hit the target.
Why not shoot a little straighter
And employ a smaller sample?

Hiawatha, who at college
Majored in applied statistics,
Consequently felt entitled
To instruct his fellow men on
Any subject whatsoever,
Waxed exceedingly indignant
Talked about the law of error,
Talked about truncated normals,
Talked of loss of information,
Talked about his lack of bias,
Pointed out that in the long run
Independent observations
Even though they missed the target
Had an average point of impact
Very near the spot he aimed at
(With the possible exception
Of a set of measure zero).

This, they said, was rather doubtful.
Anyway, it didn't matter
What resulted in the long run;
Either he must hit the target
Much more often than at present

(Originally published in *The American Statistician*, Dec. 1959, Vol. 13, No. 5. Reprinted by Permission).

343

Or himself would have to pay for
All the arrows that he wasted.
Hiawatha, in a temper,
Quoted parts of R. A. Fisher
Quoted Yates and quoted Finney
Quoted yards of Oscar Kempthorne
Quoted reams of Cox and Cochran
Quoted Anderson and Bancroft
Practically in extenso
Trying to impress upon them
That what actually mattered
Was to estimate the error.

One or two of them admitted
Such a thing might have its uses.
Still, they said, he might do better
If he shot a little straighter.

Hiawatha, to convince them,
Organized a shooting contest
Laid out in the proper manner
By experimental methods
Recommended in the textbooks
(Mainly used for tasting tea, but
Sometimes used in other cases)
Randomized his shooting order
In factorial arrangements
Used the theory of Galois
Fields of ideal polynomials,
Got a nicely balanced layout

And successfully confounded
Second-order interactions.

All the other tribal marksmen
Ignorant, benighted creatures,
Of experimental set-ups
Spent their time of preparation
Putting in a lot of practice
Merely shooting at a target.

Thus it happened in the contest
That their scores were most impressive
With one notable exception
This (I hate to have to say it)
Was the score of Hiawatha,
Who, as usual, shot his arrows
Shot them with great strength and swiftness
Managing to be unbiased
Not, however, with his salvo

Managing to hit the target.
There, they said to Hiawatha
That is what we all expected.

Hiawatha, nothing daunted,
Called for pen and called for paper
Did analyses of variance
Finally produced the figures
Showing, beyond peradventure,
Everybody else was biased
And the variance components
Did not differ from each other
Or from Hiawatha's
(This last point, one should acknowledge

Might have been much more convincing
If he hadn't been compelled to
Estimate his own component
From experimental plots in
Which the values all were missing.
Still, they didn't understand it
So they couldn't raise objections.
This is what so often happens
With analyses of variance.)

All the same, his fellow tribesmen
Ignorant, benighted heathens,
Took away his bow and arrows,
Said that though my Hiawatha
Was a brilliant statistician
He was useless as a bowman.
As for variance components,
Several of the more outspoken
Made primeval observations
Hurtful to the finer feelings
Even of a statistician.

In a corner of the forest
Dwells alone my Hiawatha
Permanently cogitating
On the normal law of error,
Wondering in idle moments
Whether an increased precision
Might perhaps be rather better,
Even at the risk of bias,
If thereby one, now and then, could
Register upon the target.

REFERENCES

Abel, G. G., Blanchard, E. B., Barlow, D. H., & Flanagan, B. (1975, December). *A Controlled Behavioral Treatment of a Sadistic Rapist.* Paper presented at the meeting of the Association for Advancement of Behavior Therapy, San Francisco.

Achenbach, T. M. (1991). *Manual for the Child Behavior Checklist.* Burlington, VT: University Associates in Psychiatry.

Agras, W. S. (1976). Behavior modification in the general hospital psychiatric unit. In H. Leitenberg (Ed.), *Handbook of Behavior Modification* (pp. 547–565). Englewood Cliffs, NJ: Prentice-Hall.

Agras, W. S., Barlow, D. H., Chapin, H. N., Abel, G. G., & Leitenberg, H. (1974). Behavior modification of anorexia nervosa. *Archives of General Psychiatry, 30,* 279–286.

Agras, W. S., Leitenberg, H., & Barlow, D. W. (1968). Social reinforcement in the modification of agoraphobia. *Archives of General Psychiatry, 19,* 423–427.

Agras, W. S., Leitenberg, H., Barlow, D. H., Curtis, N. A., Edwards, J. A., & Wright, D. E. (1971). Relaxation in systematic desensitization. *Archives of General Psychiatry, 25,* 511–514.

Agras, W. S., Leitenberg, H., Barlow, D. H., & Thomson, L. E. (1969). Instructions and reinforcement in the modification of neurotic behavior. *American Journal of Psychiatry, 125,* 1435–1439.

Akaike, H. (1974). A new look at the statistical model identification. *IEEE Trans. Automatic Control, AC-19,* 716–723.

Alford, G. S., Webster, J. S., & Sanders, S. H. (1980). Covert aversion of two interrelated deviant sexual practices: Obscene phone calling and exhibitionism. A single case analysis. *Behavior Therapy, 11,* 15–25.

Allen, K. E., & Harris, F. R. (1966). Elimination of a child's excessive scratching by training the mother in reinforcement procedures. *Behaviour Research and Therapy, 4,* 79–84.

Allen, K. E., Hart, B. M., Buell, J. S., Harris, F. R., & Wolf, M. M. (1964). Effects of social reinforcement on isolate behavior of a nursery school child. *Child Development, 35,* 511–518.

Allen, K. E., Henke, L. B., Harris, F. R., Baer, D. M., & Reynolds, N. J. (1967). Control of hyperactivity by social reinforcement of attending behavior. *Journal of Educational Psychology, 58,* 231–237.

Allen, K. D., & Evans, J. H. (2001). Exposure-based treatment to control excessive blood glucose monitoring. *Journal of Applied Behavior Analysis, 34* (4), 497–500.

Allen, K. D., & Shriver, M. D. (1997). Enhanced performance feedback to strengthen biofeedback treatment outcome with childhood migraine. *Headache: The Journal of Head and Face Pain, 37* (3), 169–173.

Allport, G. D. (1961). *Pattern and Growth in Personality.* New York: Holt, Rinehart and Winston.

Allport, G. D. (1962). The general and the unique in psychological science. *Journal of Personality, 30,* 405–422.

Altman, J. (1974). Observational study of behavior: Sampling methods. *Behaviour, 49,* 227–267.

Altman, K., Grahs, C., & Friman, P. C. (1982). Treatment of unobserved trichotillomania by attention-reflection and punishment of an apparent covariant. *Journal of Behavior Therapy and Experimental Psychiatry, 13,* 377–341.

American Psychiatric Association. (2000). *Diagnostic and Statistical Manual of Mental Disorders,* 4th ed: DSM-TR. Washington, DC: Author.

American Psychological Association. (1973). *Ethical Principles in the Conduct of Research with Human Participants.* Washington, DC: Author.

American Psychological Association. (2002). Criteria for evaluating treatment guidelines. *American Psychologist, 57,* 1052–1059.

Angold, A., Costello, E. J., & Erkanli, A. (1999). Comorbidity. *Journal of Child Psychology and Psychiatry, 40* (1), 57–87.

Antony, M. M., Orsillo, S. M., & Roemer, L. (2001). *Practitioner's Guide to Empirically Based Measures of Anxiety.* New York: Spring.

Ashem, R. (1963). The treatment of a disaster phobia by systematic desensitization. *Behaviour Research and Therapy, 1,* 81–84.

Austin, J., Alvero, A. M., & Olson, R. (1998). Prompting patron safety belt use at a restaurant. *Journal of Applied Behavior Analysis, 3,* 655–657.

Austin, J., Hackett, S., Gravina, N., & Lebbon, A. (2006). The effects of prompting and feedback on drivers' stopping at stop signs. *Journal of Applied Behavior Analysis, 39* (1), 117–121.

Ayllon, T., & Azrin, N. H. (1965). The measurement and reinforcement of behavior of psychotics. *Journal of the Experimental Analysis of Behavior, 8,* 357–383.

Ayllon, T., & Azrin, N. H. (1968). *The Token Economy: A Motivational System for Therapy and Rehabilitation.* New York: Appleton-Century-Crofts.

Bach, A. K., Barlow, D. H., & Wincze, J. P. (2004). The enhancing effects of manualized treatment for erectile dysfunction among men using sildenafil: A preliminary investigation. *Behavior Therapy, 35,* 55–73.

Baer, D. M., & Guess, D. (1971). Receptive training of adjectival inflections in mental retardates. *Journal of Applied Behavior Analysis, 4,* 129–139.

Baer, D. M., Wolf, M. M., & Risley, T. R. (1968). Some current dimensions of applied behavior analysis. *Journal of Applied Behavior Analysis, 1,* 91–97.

Bakeman, R., & Gottman, J. M. (1997). *Observing Interaction: An Introduction to Sequential Analysis* (2nd ed.). Cambridge, UK: Cambridge University Press.

Bandura, A. (1969). *Principles of Behavior Modification.* New York: Holt, Rinehart & Winston.

Barlow, D. H. (1980). Behavior therapy: The next decade. *Behavior Therapy, 11,* 315–328.

Barlow, D. H. (2001). *Clinical Handbook of Psychological Disorders* (3rd ed.) New York: Guilford Press.

Barlow, D. H. (2002) *Anxiety.* New York: Guilford Press.

Barlow, D. H. (2002). *Anxiety and its Disorders* (2nd ed.). New York: Guilford Press.

Barlow, D. H. (2004). Psychological treatments. *American Psychologist, 59* (9), 869–878.

Barlow, D. H., & Craske, M. G. (2000). *Mastery of Your Anxiety and Panic: Client Workbook for Anxiety and Panic* (3rd ed.). New York, New York: Oxford University Press.

Barlow, D. H., Craske, M. G., Cerny, J. A., & Klosko, J. S. (1989). Behavioral treatment of panic disorder. *Behavior Therapy, 20,* 261–282.

Barlow, D. H., Gorman, J. M., Shear, M. K., & Woods, S. W. (2000). Cognitive-behavioral therapy, imipramine, or their combination for panic disorder: A randomized controlled trial. *Journal of the American Medical Association, 283* (19), 2529–2536.

Barlow, D. H., & Hayes, S. C. (1979). Alternating treatments design: One strategy for comparing the effects of two treatments in a single subject. *Journal of Applied Behavior Analysis, 12,* 199–210.

Barlow, D. H., Hayes, S. C., & Nelson, R. O. (1983). *The Scientist-practitioner: Research and Accountability in Clinical and Educational Settings.* Elmsford, New York: Pergamon Press.

Barlow, D. H., & Hersen, M. (1973). Single-case experimental designs: Uses in applied clinical research. *Archives of General Psychiatry, 29,* 319–325.

Barlow, D. H., & Hersen, M. (1984). Single Case Experimental Designs: Strategies for Studying Behavior Change. New York: Pergamon Press.

Barlow, D. H., Leitenberg, H., & Agras, W. S. (1969). Experimental control of sexual deviation through manipulation of the noxious scene in covert sensitization. *Journal of Abnormal Psychology, 74,* 596–601.

Barlow, D. H., Mavissakalian, M., & Schofield, L. (1980). Patterns of desynchrony in agoraphobia: A preliminary report. *Behaviour Research and Therapy, 18,* 441–448.

Barnes, K. E., Wooton, M., & Wood, S. (1972). The public health nurse as an effective therapist-behavior modifier of preschool play behavior. *Community Mental Health Journal, 8*, 3–7.

Barron, F., & Leary, T. (1955). Changes in psychoneurotic patients with and without psychotherapy. *Journal of Consulting Psychology, 19*, 239–245.

Barton, E. S., Guess, D., Garcia, E., & Baer, D. M. (1970). Improvement of retardates' mealtime behaviors by timeout procedures using multiple baseline techniques. *Journal of Applied Behavior Analysis, 3*, 77–84.

Bauer, I. (2001). *Diaper free! The Gentle Wisdom of Natural Infant Hygiene.* Saltspring Island, B. C., Canada: Natural Wisdom Press.

Beasley, T. M., Allison, D. B., & Gorman, B. S. (1997). The potentially confounding effects of cyclicity: Identification, prevention, and control. In R. D. Franklin, D. B. Allison & B. S. Gorman (Eds.), *Design and Analysis of Single-case Research* (pp. 279–335). Mahwah, NJ: Lawrence Erlbaum Associates, Publishers.

Beck, A. T. (2005). The current state of cognitive therapy: A 40-year retrospective. *Archives of General Psychiatry, 62* (9), 953–959.

Beck, A. T., Rush, A. J., Shaw, B. J., & Emery, G. D. (1979). *Cognitive Therapy for Depression.* New York: Guilford Press.

Beck, A. T., Ward, C. H., Mendelson, M., Mock, J., & Erbaugh, J. (1961). An inventory for measuring depression. *Arch Gen Psychiatry, 4*, 561–571.

Bence, J. R. (1995). Analysis of short time series: Correcting for autocorrelation. *Ecology, 76* (2), 628–639.

Berk, L. B., & Friman, P. C. (1990). Epidemiological aspects of toilet training. *Clinical Pediatrics, 29*, 278–282.

Bergin, A. E. (1966). Some implications of psychotherapy research for therapeutic practice. *Journal of Abnormal Psychology, 71*, 235–246.

Bergin, A. E., & Lambert, M. J. (1978). The evaluation of therapeutic outcomes. In S. L. Garfield & A. E. Bergin (Eds.), *Handbook of Psychotherapy and Behavior Change. An Empirical Analysis* (2nd ed.). (pp. 139–191). New York: Wiley.

Bergin, A. E., & Strupp, H. H. (1970). New directions in psychotherapy research. *Journal of Abnormal Psychology, 76*, 13–26.

Bergin, A. E., & Strupp, H. H. (1972). *Changing Frontiers in the Science of Psychotherapy.* New York: Aldine.

Bijou, S. W., Peterson, R. F., Harris, F. R., Allen, K. E., & Johnston, M. S. (1969). Methodology for experimental studies of young children in natural settings. *Psychological Record, 19*, 177–210.

Birney, R. C., & Teevan, R. C. (Eds.). (1961). *Reinforcement.* Princeton, NJ: Van Nostrand.

Blake M. Lancaster, LeBlanc, L. A., Carr, J. E., Brenske, S., Peet, M. M., & Culver, S. J. (2004). Functional analysis and treatment of the bizarre speech of dually diagnosed adults. *Journal of Applied Behavior Analysis, 37*, 395–399.

Blanchard, E. B., Andrasik, F., Arena, J. G., Neff, D. F., Saunders, N. L., Jurish, S. E., Teders, S. J., & Rodichok, L. D. (1983). Psychophysiological responses as predictors of response to behavioral treatment of chronic headache. *Behavior Therapy, 14*, 357–374.

Blanchard, E. G., Theobold, D. E., Williamson, D. A., Silver, B. V., & Brown, D. A. (1978). *Archives of General Psychiatry, 35*, 581–588.

Blough, P. M. (1983). Local contrast in multiple schedules: The effect of stimulus discriminability. *Journal of the Experimental Analysis of Behavior, 39*, 427–437.

Bolger, H. (1965). The case study method. In B. B. Wolman (Ed.), *Handbook of Clinical Psychology* (pp. 28–39). New York: McGraw-Hill.

Borckardt, J. J., & Nash, M. R. (2002). How practitioners (and others) can make scientifically viable contributions to clinical-outcome research using the single-case time-series design. *International Journal of Clinical and Experimental Hypnosis, 50* (2), 114–148.

Boring, E. G. (1950). *A history of experimental psychology.* New York: Appleton-Century-Crofts.

Borkovec, T. D., Echemendia, R. J., Ragusea, S. A., & Ruiz, M. (2001). The Pennsylvania

Practice Research Network and future possibilities for clinically meaningful and scientifically rigorous psychotherapy effectiveness research. *Clinical Psychology: Science and Practice, 8,* 155–167.

Bornstein, M. R., Bellack, A. S., & Hersen, M. (1977). Social-skills training for unassertive children: A multiple-baseline analysis. *Journal of Applied Behavior Analysis, 10,* 183–195.

Bornstein, P. H., Sturm, C. A., Retzlaff, P. D., Kirby, K. L., & Chong, H. (1981). Paradoxical instruction in the treatment of encopresis and chronic constipation: An experimental analysis. *Journal of Behavior Therapy and Experimental Psychiatry, 12* (2), 167–170.

Boucke, L. (2002). *Infant Potty Training : A Gentle and Primeval Method Adapted to Modern Living.* White-Boucke Publishing: Lafayette, CO.

Bowdlear, C. M. (1955). *Dynamics of Idiopathic Epilepsy as Studied in One Case.* Unpublished doctoral dissertation, Case Western Reserve University, Cleveland, Ohio.

Box, G. E. P., & Cox, D. R. (1964). An analysis of transformations. *Journal of the Royal Statistical Society, B26,* 211–243.

Box, G. E. P., & Jenkins, G. M. (1970*). Time Series Analysis., Forecasting and Control.* San Francisco: Holden-Day.

Box, G. E. P., Jenkins, G. M., & Reinsel, G. C. (1994). *Time-Series Analysis: Forecasting and Control* (3rd ed.). New Jersey: Prentice-Hall.

Box, G. E. P., & Tiao, G. C. (1965). A change in level of non-stationary time series. *Biometrika, 52,* 181–192.

Bradley, J. (1968). *Distribution-free Statistical Tests.* Englewood Cliffs, NJ: Prentice-Hall.

Brady, J. P., & Lind, D. L. (1961). Experimental analysis of hysterical blindness. *Archives of General Psychiatry, 4,* 331–339.

Brawley, E. R., Harris, F. R., Allen, K. E., Fleming, R. S., & Peterson, R. F. (1969). Behavior modification of an autistic child. *Behavioral Science, 14,* 87–97.

Breuer, J., & Freud, S. (1957). *Studies on Hysteria.* New York: Basic Books.

Breuning, S. E., O'Neill, M. J., & Ferguson, D. G. (1980). Comparison of psychotropic drugs, response cost, and psychotropic drug plus response cost procedures for controlling institutionalized mentally retarded persons. *Applied Research in Mental Retardation, 1,* 253–268.

Brill, A. A. (1909). Selected papers on hysteria and other psychoneuroses: Sigmund Freud. *Nervous and Mental Disease Monograph Series, 4.*

Broden, M., Bruce, C., Mitchell, M. A., Carter, V., & Hall, R. V. (1970). Effects of teacher attention on attending behavior of two boys at adjacent desks. *Journal of Applied Behavior Analysis, 3,* 205–211.

Broden, M., Hall, R. V., Dunlap, A., & Clark, R. (1970). Effects of teacher attention and a token reinforcement system in a junior high school special education class. *Exceptional Children, 36,* 341–349.

Brown, G. K., Ten Have, T., Henriques, G. R., Xie, S. X., Hollander, J. E., & Beck, A. T. (2005). Cognitive therapy for the prevention of suicide attempts: A randomized controlled trial. *Jama, 294* (5), 563–570.

Browning, R. M. (1967). A same-subject design for simultaneous comparison of three reinforcement contingencies. *Behaviour Research and Therapy, 5,* 237–243.

Browning, R. M., & Stover, D. O. (1971). *Behavior Modification in Child Treatment. An Experimental and Clinical Approach.* Chicago: Aldine.

Brunswick, E. (1956). *Perception and the Representative Design of Psychological Experiments.* Berkeley: University of California Press.

Budd, K. S., Green, D. R., & Baer, D. M. (1976). An analysis of multiple misplaced parental social contingencies. *Journal of Applied Behavior Analysis, 9,* 459470.

Buell, J. S., Stoddard, P., Harris, F. R., & Baer, D. M. (1968). Collateral social development accompanying reinforcement of outdoor play in a preschool child. *Journal of Applied Behavior Analysis, 1,* 167–173.

Busk, P. L., & Marascuilo, L. A. (1988). Autocorrelation in single-subject research: A counterargument to the myth of no autocorrelation. *Behavioral Assessment, 10,* 229–242.

Buys, C. J. (1971). Effects of teacher reinforcement on classroom behaviors and attitudes. *Dissertation Abstracts International, 31*, 4884A1–4885A.

Byrd, M. R., Richards, D. F., Hove, G., & Friman, P. C. (2002). Treatment of early onset hair pulling as a simple habit. *Behavior Modification, 26*, 400–411.

Cacioppo, L. G., & Bernston, L. G. (Eds.) (2000). *Handbook of Psychophysiology*. New York: Cambridge University Press.

Campbell, D. T. (1969). Reforms as experiments. *American Psychologist, 24*, 40429.

Campbell, D. T., & Stanley, J. C. (1963). *Experimental and Quasi-experimental Designs for Research*. In D. T. Campbell & J. C. Stanley, *Handbook of Research on Teaching*. Chicago: Rand McNally.

Campbell, D. T., & Stanley, J. C. (1966). *Experimental and Quasi-experimental Designs for Research*. Chicago: Rand McNally.

Carlson, C. S., Arnold, C. R., Becker, W. C., & Madsen, C. H. (1968). The elimination of tantrum behavior of a child in an elementary classroom. *Behaviour Research and Therapy, 6*, 117–119.

Carr, E. (1977). The motivation of self injurious behavior: A review of some hypotheses. *Psychological Bulletin, 84*, 800–816.

Carr, J. E., & Bailey, J. S. (1996). A brief behavior therapy protocol for Tourette syndrome. *Journal of Behavior Therapy and Experimental Psychiatry, 27* (1), 33–40.

Caruso, M., & Kennedy, C. H. (2004). Effects of a reviewer-prompting strategy on timely manuscript reviews. *Journal of Applied Behavior Analysis, 37* (4), 523–526.

Cataldo, M. F., Bessman, C. A., Parker, L. A., Pearson, R. & Rogers, M. C. (1979). Behavioral assessment for pediatric intensive care units. *Journal of Applied Behavior Analysis, 12*, 83–97.

Chamberlain, P. (1980). Standardization of a parent report measure. Unpublished doctoral dissertation. University of Oregon.

Chamberlain, P., & Reid, J. B. (1987). Parent observation and report of child situations. *Behavioral Assessment, 9*, 97–109.

Chaplin, J. P., & Kraweic, T. S. (1960). *Systems and Theories of Psychology*. New York: Holt, Rinehart and Winston.

Chassan, J. B. (1960). Statistical inference and the single case in clinical design. *Psychiatry, 23*, 173–184.

Chassan, J. B. (1962). Probability processes in psychoanalytic psychiatry. In J. Scher (Ed.), *Theories of the Mind* (pp. 598–618). New York: Free Press of Glencoe.

Chassan, J. B. (1967). *Research Design in Clinical Psychology and Psychiatry*. New York: Appleton-Century-Crofts.

Chassan, J. B. (1979). *Research Design in Clinical Psychology and Psychiatry* (2nd ed.) New York: Irvington.

Choate, M. L., Pincus, D. B., Eyberg, S. M., & Barlow, D. H. (2005). Parent-Child Interaction Therapy for treatment of separation anxiety disorder in children: A pilot study. *Cognitive and Behavioral Practice, 12*, 126–135.

Chomsky, N. (1965). *Aspects of the Theory of Syntax*. Cambridge, MA: MIT Press.

Chorpita, B. F., Yim, L. M., Donkervoet, J. C., Arensdorf, A., Amundsen, M. J., & McGee, C., et al. (2002). Toward large-scale implementation of empirically supported treatments for children: A review and observations by the Hawaii Empirical Basis to Services Task Force. *Clinical Psychology: Science and Practice, 9*, 165–190.

Clayton, M., Helms, B., & Simpson, C. (2006). Active prompting to decrease cell phone use and increase seat belt use while driving. *Journal of Applied Behavior Analysis, 39* (3), 341–349.

Clever, S. L., Ford, D. E., Rubenstein, L. V., Rost, K. M., Meredith, L. S., & Sherbourne, C. D., et al. (2006). Primary care patients' involvement in decision-making is associated with improvement in depression. *Medical Care, 44* (5), 398–405.

Cohen, J. (1988). *Statistical Power Analysis for the Behavioral Sciences*, 2nd ed. New Jersey: Lawrence Erlbaum Associates.

Cohen, L. H. (1976). Clinicians' utilization of research findings. *JSAS Catalog of Selected Documents in Psychology, 6*, 116.

Cohen, L. H. (1979). The research readership and information source reliance of clinical psychologists. *Professional Psychology, 10*, 780–786.

Cohen, R. J., & Swerdlik, M. E. (2002). *Psychological Testing and Assessment* (5th ed). Boston: McGraw-Hill.

Conger, J. C. (1970). The treatment of encopresis by the management of social consequences. *Behavior Therapy, 1,* 386–390.

Conrin, J., Pennypacker, H. S., Johnston, J. M., & Rast, J. (1982). Differential reinforcement of other behaviors to treat chronic rumination of mental retardates. *Journal of Behavior Therapy and Experimental Psychiatry, 13,* 325–329.

Cook, T. D., & Campbell, D. T. (Eds.) (1979). *Quasi-experimentation: Design and Analysis Issues for Field Settings.* Chicago: Rand McNally.

Cormier, W. H. (1969). Effects of teacher random and contingent social reinforcement on the classroom behavior of adolescents. *Dissertation Abstracts International, 31,* 1615A–1616A.

Corsini, R. J., & Auerbach, A. J. (1996). *Concise Encyclopedia of Psychology* (2nd ed.). New York: John Wiley.

Corte, H. E., Wolf, M. M., & Locke, B. J. (1971). A comparison of procedures for eliminating self-injurious behavior of retarded adolescents. *Journal of Applied Behavior Analysis, 4,* 201–215.

Cossairt, A., Hall, R. V., & Hopkins, B. L. (1973). The effects of experimenters' instructions, feedback, and praise on teacher praise and student attending behavior. *Journal of Applied Behavior Analysis, 6,* 89–100.

Cote, C. A., Thompson, R. H., & McKerchar, P. M. (2005). The effects of antecedent interventions and extinction on toddlers' compliance during transitions. *Journal of Applied Behavior Analysis, 38* (2), 235–238.

Cox, B. S., Cox, A. B., & Cox, D. J. (2000). Motivating signage prompts safety belt use among drivers exiting senior communities. *Journal of Applied Behavior Analysis, 33* (4), 635–638.

Crabtree, B. F., Ray, S. C., Schmidt, P. M., O'Connor, P. J., & Schmidt, D. D. (1990). The individual over time: Time series applications in health care research. *Journal Clinical Epidemiology, 43* (3), 241–260.

Craske, M. G., & Barlow, D. H. (2001). Panic disorder and agoraphobia. In D. H. Barlow (Ed.), *Clinical Handbook of Psychological Disorders: A Step-by-step Treatment Manual* (3rd ed). New York: Guilford Press. pp. 1–59.

Critchfield, T., Haley, R., Sabo, B., Colbert, J., & Macropoulis, G. (2003). A half century of scalloping in the work habits of the United States Congress. *Journal of Applied Behavior Analysis, 36,* 465–487.

Crone, D. A., Homer, R. H., & Hawken, L. S. (2003). *Responding to Problem Behavior in Schools.* New York: Guilford Press.

Crosbie, J. (1987). The inability of the binomial test to control type-I error with single subject data. *Behavioral Assessment, 9,* 141–150.

Crosbie, J. (1993). Interrupted time-series analysis with brief single subject data, *Journal of Consulting and Clinical Psychology, 61,* 966–974.

Crosbie, J. (1995). Interrupted time-series analysis with short series: Why it is problematic; how it can be improved. In J. M. Gottman (Ed.), *The Analysis of Change* (pp. 361–395). Mahwah, NJ: Lawrence Erlbaum Associates, Inc.

Crowne, D. P., & Marlowe, D. (1960). A new scale of social desirability independent of psychopathology. *Journal of Consulting Psychology, 24,* 349–354.

Dallery, J., & Glenn, I. M. (2005). Effects of an Internet-based voucher reinforcement program for smoking abstinence: A feasibility study. *Journal of Applied Behavior Analysis, 38* (3), 349–357.

Davidson, P. O., & Costello, C. G. (1969). *N = 1: Experimental Studies of Single Cases.* New York: Van Nostrand Reinhold.

Davis, P. K., Young, A., Cherry, H., Dahman, D., & Rehfeldt, R. A. (2004). Increasing the happiness of individuals with profound multiple disabilities: replication and extension. *Journal of Applied Behavior Analysis, 37* (4), 531–534.

Davison, G. C. (1965). The training of undergraduates as social reinforcers for autistic children. In L. P. Ullmann & L. Krasner (Eds.), *Case Studies in Behavior Modification* (pp. 146–148). New York: Holt, Rinehart and Winston.

de Kinkelder, M., & Boelens, H. (1998). Habit-reversal treatment for children's stuttering: Assessment in three settings. *Journal of Behavior Therapy and Experimental Psychiatry, 29* (3), 261–265.

De La Paz, S. (1999). Self-regulated strategy instruction in regular education settings:

Improving outcomes for students with and without learning disabilities. *Learning Disabilities Research & Practice, 14* (2), 92–106.

DeProspero, A., & Cohen, S. (1979). Inconsistent visual analysis of intrasubject data. *Journal of Applied Behavior Analysis, 12,* 573–579.

Dimidjian, S., Hollon, S. D., Dobson, K. S., Schmaling, K. B., Kohlenberg, R. J., & Addis, M. E., et al. (2006). Randomized trial of behavioral activation, cognitive therapy, and antidepressant medication in the acute treatment of adults with major depression. *Journal of Consulting and Clinical Psychology, 74* (4), 658–670.

Dishion, T. J., McCord, J., & Poulin, F. (1999). When interventions harm. Peer groups and problem behavior. *American Psychologist, 54* (9), 755–764.

Doke, L. A., & Risley, I R. (1972). The organization of day-care environments: Required vs optional activities. *Journal of Applied Behavior Analysis, 5,* 405–420.

Dollard, J., Doob, L. W., Miller, N. E., Mowrer, O. H., & Sears, R. R. (1939). *Frustration and Aggression.* New Haven: Yale University Press.

Donny, E. C., Bigelow, G. E., & Walsh, S. L. (2006). Comparing the physiological and subjective effects of self-administered vs yoked cocaine in humans. *Psychopharmacology, 186* (4), 544–552.

Doss, A. J., & Weisz, J. R. (2006). Syndrome co-occurrence and treatment outcomes in youth mental health clinics. *Journal of Consulting and Clinical Psychology, 74* (3), 416–425.

Ducharme, J. M., & Worling, D. E. (1994). Behavioral momentum and stimulus fading in the acquisition and maintenance of child compliance in the home. *Journal of Applied Behavior Analysis, 27* (4), 639–647.

Dukes, W. F. (1965). N = 1. *Psychological Bulletin, 64,* 74–79.

duMas, F. M. (1955). Science and the single case. *Psychological Reports, 1,* 65–75.

Dunlap, K. (1932). *Habits: Their Making and Unmaking.* New York: Liveright.

Durand, M. V. (1990). *Severe Behavior Problems: A Functional Communication Training Approach.* New York, NY: Guilford Press, p. 183.

Durand, M. V. (1999). New directions in educational programming for students with autism. In D. Zager (Ed.), *Autism: Identification, Education, and Treatment* (2nd ed.) Hillsdale, NJ: Erlbaum.

Durbin, J. (1960). The fitting of time series models. *Review of the International Statistical Institute, 28,* 233–244.

Edgington, E. S. (1966). Statistical inference and nonrandom samples. *Psychological Bulletin, 66,* 485–487.

Edgington, E. S. (1967). Statistical inference from N = 1 experiments. *Journal of Psychology, 65,* 195–199.

Edgington, E. S. (1972). N = 1 experiments: Hypothesis testing. *Canadian Psychologist, 13,* 121–135.

Edgington, E. S. (1980). *Randomization tests.* New York: Marcel Dekker.

Edgington, E. S. (1982). Nonparametric tests for single-subject multiple schedule experiments. *Behavioral Assessment, 4,* 83–91.

Edgington, E. S. (1983). Response-guided experimentation. *Contemporary Psychology, 28,* 64–65.

Edgington, E. S. (1984). Statistics and single case analysis. In M. Hersen, R. M. Eisler, & P. M. Monti (Eds.). *Progress in Behavior Modification* (Vol. 16). New York: Academic Press.

Edgington, E. S. (1995). *Randomization Tests.* New York: M. Dekker.

Edwards, A. L. (1968). *Experimental Design in Psychological Research* (3rd ed.). New York: Holt, Rinehart and Winston.

Eisler, R. M., Hersen, M., & Agras, W. S. (1973). Effects of videotape and instructional feedback on nonverbal marital interaction: An analog study. *Behavior Therapy, 4,* 551–558.

Eisler, R. M., Miller, P. M., & Hersen, M. (1973). Components of assertive behavior. *Journal of Clinical Psychology, 29,* 295–299.

Ekman, P. (2003). *Emotions Revealed.* New York: Times Books.

Ellis, D. A., Templin, T., Naar-King, S., Frey, M. A., Cunningham, P. B., & Podolski, C. L., et al. (2007). Multisystemic therapy for adolescents with poorly controlled type I diabetes: Stability of treatment effects in a randomized controlled trial.

Journal of Consulting and Clinical Psychology, 75 (1), 168–174.

Ellis, D. P. (1968). The design of a social structure to control aggression. *Dissertation Abstracts, 29,* 672A.

Elkin, I., Shea, M. T., Watkins, J. T., Imber, S. D., Sotsky, S. M., Collins, J. F., et al. (1989). National Institute of Mental Health Treatment of Depression Collaborative Research Program. General effectiveness of treatments. *Archives of General Psychiatry, 46* (11), 971–982; discussion 983.

Elkin, T. E., Hersen, M., Eisler, R. M., & Williams, J. G. (1973). Modification of caloric intake in anorexia nervosa: An experimental analysis. *Psychological Reports, 32,* 75–78.

Emmelkamp, P. M. G. (1974). Self-observation versus flooding in the treatment of agoraphobia. *Behaviour Research and Therapy, 12,* 229–237.

Epstein, L. H., Beck, S. J., Figueroa, J., Farkas, G., Kazdin, A. E., Daneman, D., & Becker, D. (1981). The effects of targeting improvements in urine glucose on metabolic control in children with insulin dependent diabetes. *Journal of Applied Behavior Analysis, 14,* 365–375.

Epstein, L. H., & Hersen, M. (1974). Behavioral control of hysterical gagging. *Journal of Clinical Psychology, 30,* 102–104.

Epstein, L. H., Hersen, M., & Hemphill, D. P. (1974). Music feedback in the treatment of tension headache: An experimental case study. *Journal of Behavior Therapy and Experimental Psychiatry, 5,* 59–63.

Ervin, R. A., DuPaul, G. J., Kern, L., & Friman, P. C. (1998). Classroom-based functional assessment: A proactive approach to intervention selection for adolescents diagnosed with attention deficit/hyperactivity disorder. *Journal of Applied Behavior Analysis, 31,* 65–78.

Etzel, B. C., & Gerwitz, J. L. (1967). Experimental modifications of caretaker-maintained highrate operant crying in a 6- and 20-week-old infant (*Infans Tyrannotearus*): Extinction of crying with reinforcement of eye contact and smiling. *Journal of Experimental Child Psychology, 5,* 303–317.

Eysenck, H. J. (1952). The effects of psychotherapy: An evaluation. *Journal of Consulting Psychology, 16,* 319–324.

Eysenck, H. J. (1965). The effects of psychotherapy. *International Journal of Psychiatry, 1,* 97–178.

Facon, B., Beghin, M., & Riviere, V. (2007). The reinforcing effect of contingent attention on verbal perseverations of two children with severe visual impairment. *Journal of Behavior Therapy and Experimental Psychiatry, 38* (1), 23–28.

Ferron, J., & Onghena, P. (1996). The power of randomization tests for single-case phase designs. *Journal of Exp. Education, 64,* 231–239.

Finney, J. W., & Friman, P. C. (1988). The prevention of mental retardation. In D. C. Russo & J. H. Kedesdy (Eds.), *Behavioral Medicine with the Developmentally Disabled,* (173–200). New York: Plenum.

Finney, J. W., Russo, D. C., & Cataldo, M. F. (1982). Reducing pica in young children with lead poisoning. *Journal of Pediatric Psychology, 7,* 197–207.

Fisher, R. A. (1925). On the mathematical foundations of the theory of statistics. In Cambridge Phil. Society (Ed.), *Theory of statistical estimation* (Proceedings of the Cambridge Philosophical Society) England.

Fisher, W., Piazza, C. C., Bowman, L. G., Hagopian, L. P., Owens, J. C., & Slevin, I. (1992). A comparison of two approaches for identifying reinforcers for persons with severe and profound disabilities. *Journal of Applied Behavior Analysis, 25,* 491–498.

Foa, E. B. (1979). Failure in treating obsessive-compulsives. *Behaviour Research and Therapy, 17,* 169–175.

Foa, E. B., & Franklin, M. E. (2001). Obsessive-compulsive disorder. In D. H. Barlow (Ed.), *Clinical Handbook of Psychological Disorders: A Step-by-step Treatment Manual* (3rd ed.). New York: Guilford Press, pp. 209–263.

Foa, E. B., Grayson, J. B., Steketee, G. S., Doppelt, H. G., Turner, R. M., & Latimer, P. R. (1983). Success and failure in the behavioral treatment of obsessive compulsives. *Journal of Consulting and Clinical Psychology, 51*, 287–297.

Foa, E. B., Hembree, E. A., Cahill, S. P., Rauch, S. A., Riggs, D. S., & Feeny, N. C., et al. (2005). Randomized trial of prolonged exposure for posttraumatic stress disorder with and without cognitive restructuring: outcome at academic and community clinics. *Journal of Consulting and Clinical Psychology, 73* (5), 953–964.

Forehand, R., & Kotchick, B. A. (2002). Behavioral parent training: Current challenges and potential solutions. *Journal of Child and Family Studies, 11*, 377–384.

Forehand, R. L., & McMahon, R. J. (1981). *Helping the Noncompliant Child: A Clinician's Guide to Parent Training.* New York: Guilford Press.

Foster, S. L., & Cone, J. D., (1986). Design and use of direct observation procedures. In A. R. Ciminero, K. S., & Calhoun, & H. E. (Eds.), *Handbook of Behavioral Assessment* (pp. 253–324).

Frank, J. D. (1961). *Persuasion and healing.* Baltimore: Johns Hopkins University Press.

Frank, N. C., Spirito, A., Stark, L., & Owens-Stively, J. (1997). The use of scheduled awakenings to eliminate childhood sleepwalking. *Journal of Pediatric Psychology, 22* (3), 345–353.

Franklin, R. D., Allison, D. B., & Gorman, B. S. (Eds.). (1997). *Design and Analysis of Single-case Research.* Mahwah, NJ: Lawrence Erlbaum Associates.

Fredrikson; Wik, G., Fischer, H. K., & Andersson, J. (1995). Affective and attentive neural networks in humans: a PET study of Pavlovian conditioning. *Neurological Report, 7*, 97–101.

Freeman, K. (2006). Treating bedtime resistance with the bedtime pass: A systematic evaluation and component analysis with 3-year-olds. *Journal of Applied Behavior Analysis, 39*, 423–428.

Freud, S. (1933). Analysis of a phobia in a five-year-old boy. In *Collected papers (Vol. 3).* London: Hogarth Press.

Friman, P. C. (1988). Chronic thumb sucking: A threat to wellness in middle childhood. *Wellness Perspectives, 5*, 7–12.

Friman, P. C. (1990a). Concurrent habits: What would Linus do with his blanket if his thumb sucking were treated. *Archives of Pediatrics and Adolescent Medicine, 144*, 1316–1318.

Friman, P. C. (1990b). Nonaversive treatment of high rate disruption: Child and provider effects. *Exceptional Children, 57*, 64–69.

Friman, P. C. (1995). Nocturnal enuresis in the child. In R. Ferber, & M. H. Kryger (Eds.), *Principles and Practice of Sleep Medicine in the Child*, (pp. 107–114). Philadelphia: Saunders.

Friman, P. C. (1999). *Family Style Residential Care: Scientific Findings Demonstrating Multiple Benefits for Adolescents.* Boys Town, NE: Boys Town Press.

Friman, P. C. (2002). *The Psychopathological Interpretation of Common Child Behavior Problems: A Critique and Related Opportunity for Behavior Analysis.* Invited address at the 28th annual convention of the Association for Behavior Analysis, Toronto, Canada.

Friman, P. C. (2002). Treatment of early onset hair pulling (Trichotillomania) as a simple habit. *Behavior Modification, 26*, 400–411.

Friman, P. C. (2003). A biobehavioral bowel and toilet training treatment for functional encopresis. W. Odonohue, S. Hayes, & J. Fisher (Eds.), *Empirically Supported Techniques of Cognitive Behavior Therapy* (pp. 51–58). New York: Wiley.

Friman, P. C. (2004). Up with this I shall not put: 10 reasons why I disagree with Branch and Vollmer on 'behavior' used as a count noun. *The Behavior Analysts, 27*, 99–106.

Friman, P. C., Barone, V. J., & Christophersen, E. R. (1986). Aversive taste treatment of finger and thumb sucking. *Pediatrics, 78*, 174–176.

Friman, P. C., & Berk, L. B. (1990). On toilet training: A response to Furman. *Clinical Pediatrics, 29*, 546–547.

Friman, P. C., Finney, J. W., & Christophersen, E. R. (1984). Behavioral treatment of trichotillomania: An evaluative review. *Behavior Therapy, 15*, 249–266.

Friman, P. C., Finney, J. W., Glasscock, S. G., Weigel, J. W., & Christophersen, E. R. (1986). Testicular self-examination:

Validation of a training strategy for early cancer detection. *Journal of Applied Behavior Analysis, 19*, 87–92.

Friman, P. C., Finney, J. W., Rapoff, M. A., & Christophersen, E. R. (1985). Improving pediatric appointment keeping: Cost effectiveness and social validation of reminders and reduced response requirement. *Journal of Applied Behavior Analysis, 18*, 315–323.

Friman, P. C., Handwerk, M., Smith, G. L., Larzelere, R. E., Lucas, C. P., & Shaffer, D. M. (2000). External validity of conduct and oppositional defiant disorders determined by the NIMH Diagnostic Interview Schedule for Children. *Journal of Abnormal Child Psychology, 28*, 277–286.

Friman, P. C., Hayes, S. C., & Wilson, K. (1998). Why behavior analysts should study emotion: The example of anxiety. *Journal of Applied Behavior Analysis, 31*, 137–156.

Friman, P. C., Hoff, K. E., & Schnoes, C., Freeman, K., Woods, D., & Blum, N. (1999). The bedtime pass: An approach to bedtime crying and leaving the room. *Archives of Pediatrics and Adolescent Medicine, 153*, 1027–1029.

Friman, P. C., & Jones, K. M. (1998). Elimination disorders in children. In S. Watson & F. Gresham (Eds.), *Handbook of Child Behavior Therapy*, (239–260). New York: Plenum.

Friman, P. C., Jones, M., Smith, G., Daly, D., & Larzelere, R. (1997). Decreasing disruptive behavior by adolescents in residential placement by increasing their positive to negative interactional ratios. *Behavior Modification, 21*, 470–486.

Friman, P. C., & Leibowitz, J. M. (1990). An effective and acceptable treatment alternative for chronic thumb and finger sucking. *The Journal of Pediatric Psychology, 15*, 57–65.

Friman, P. C., McPherson, K. M., Warzak, W. J., & Evans, J. (1993). The influence of chronic thumb sucking on peer social acceptance in first-grade children. *Pediatrics, 91*, 784–786.

Friman, P. C., & Oliver-Hawkins, R. (2006). *Contributions of Establishing Operations to Antecedent Intervention: Clinical Implications of Establishing Operations.* In J. Luiselli (Ed.), *Antecedent Interventions: Recent Developments in Community-based Behavior Support* (pp. 31–52). Baltimore: Paul Brookes.

Friman, P. C., & Poling, A. (1995). Life does not have to be so hard: Basic findings and applied implications from research on response effort/force. *Journal of Applied Behavior Analysis, 28*, 583–590.

Friman, P. C., Wilson, K., & Hayes, S. C. (1998). Behavior analysis of private events is possible, progressive, and non-dualistic: A response to Lamal. *Journal of Applied Behavior Analysis, 31*, 707–708.

Galbicka, G., & Branch, M. (1981). Selective punishment of interresponse times. *Journal of the Experimental Analysis of Behavior, 35*, 311–322.

Galbicka, G., & Platt, J. R. (1984). Interresponse time punishment: A basis for shock maintained behavior. *Journal of the Experimental Analysis of Behavior, 41*, 291–308.

Gauthier, J., Bois Allaire, D., & Drolet, M. (1981). Evaluation of skin temperature biofeedback training at two different sites for migraine. *Journal of Behavioral Medicine, 4*, 407–419.

Garfield, S. L., & Bergin, A. E. (Eds.). (1978). *Handbook of psychotherapy and behavior change: An empirical analysis* (2nd ed.). New York: Wiley.

Gerin, W., Tobin, J. N., Schwartz, J. E., Chaplin, W., Rieckmann, N., & Davidson, K. W., (2007). The medication adherence and blood pressure control (ABC) trial: A multi-site randomized controlled trial in a hypertensive, multi-cultural, economically disadvantaged population. *Contemp Clin Trials, 28* (4), 459–471.

Glenn, I. M., & Dallery, J. (2007). Effects of internet-based voucher reinforcement and a transdermal nicotine patch on cigarette smoking. *Journal of Applied Behavior Analysis, 40* (1), 1–13.

Goldstein, H., Kaczmarek, L., Pennington, R., & Shafer, K. (1992). Peer-mediated intervention: attending to, commenting on, and acknowledging the behavior of preschoolers with autism. *Journal of Applied Behavior Analysis, 25* (2), 289–305.

Goodlet, G. R., Goodlet, M. M., & Dredge, M. (1970). Modification of disruptive behavior of two young children and follow-up one year later. *Journal of School Psychology, 8*, 60–63.

Goodwin, R. D., & Gotlib, I. H. (2004). Panic attacks and psychopathology among youth. *Acta Psychiatr Scand, 109* (3), 216–221.

Gorman, B. S., & Allison, D. B. (1997). Statistical alternatives for single-case designs. In R. D. Franklin, D. B. Allison & B. S. Gorman (Eds.), *Design and Analysis of Single-case Research* (pp. 159–214). Mahwah, NJ: Lawrence Erlbaum Associates.

Gottman, J. M. (1973). N-of-one and N-of-two research in psychotherapy. *Psychological Bulletin, 80* (2), 93–105.

Gottman, J. M. (1979). *Marital interaction: Experimental investigations.* New York: Academic Press.

Gottman, J. M. (1981). *Time-series Analysis: A Comprehensive Introduction for Social Scientists.* Cambridge: Cambridge University Press.

Gottman, J. M. (1994). *Why Marriages Succeed or Fail.* New York: Simon & Schuster.

Gottman, J. M., & Levenson, R. W. (1999). How stable is marital interaction over time? *Family Process. 38*, 159–165.

Gray, N. S., Brown, A. S., MacCulloch, M. J., Smith, J., & Snowden, R. J. (2005). An implicit test of the associations between children and sex in pedophiles. *Journal of Abnormal Psychology, 114* (2), 304–308.

Greene, R. (2001). *The Explosive Child: A New Approach for Understanding and Parenting Easily Frustrated, Chronically Inflexible Children.* New York: Harper.

Greenwald, A. G. (1976). Within-subjects designs: To use or not to use? *Psychological Bulletin, 83*, 314–320.

Greenwald, A. G., Banaji, M. R., Rudman, L. A., Farnham, S. D., Nosek, B. A., & Mellott, D. S. (2002). A unified theory of implicit attitudes, stereotypes, self-esteem, and self-concept. *Psychological Review. 109*, 3–25.

Greenwood, K. M., & Matyas, T. M. (1990). Problems with the application of interrupted time series analysis for brief single-subject data. *Behavioral Assessment, 12*, 355–370.

Hagopian, L. P., Bruzek, J. L., Bowman, L. G., & Jennett, H. K. (2007). Assessment and treatment of problem behavior

occasioned by interruption of free-operant behavior. *Journal of Applied Behavior Analysis, 40* (1), 89–103.

Hall, R. V., Axelrod, S., Tyler, L., Grief, E., Jones, F. C., & Robertson, R. (1972). Modification of behavior problems in the home with a parent as observer and experimenter. *Journal of Applied Behavior Analysis, 5*, 53–74.

Hall, R. V., & Broden, M. (1967). Behavior changes in brain-injured children through social reinforcement. *Journal of Experimental Child Psychology, 5*, 463–479.

Hall, R. V., Fox, R., Willard, D., Goldsmith, L., Emerson, M., Owen, M., Davis, F., & Porcia, E. (1971). The teacher as observer and experimenter in the modification of disputing and talking-out behaviors. *Journal of Applied Behavior Analysis, 4*, 141–149.

Hall, R. V., Lund, D., & Jackson, D. (1968). Effects of teacher attention on study behavior. *Journal of Applied Behavior Analysis, 1*, 1–12.

Hall, R. V., Panyan, M., Rabon, D., & Broden, M. (1968). Instructing beginning teachers in reinforcement procedures which improve classroom control. *Journal of Applied Behavior Analysis, 1*, 315–322.

Haney, C., Banks, C., & Zimbardo. P. (1973). Interpersonal dynamics in a simulated prison. *International Journal of Criminology and Penology, 1*, 69–97

Hanley, G. P., Iwata, B. A., & McCord, B. E. (2003). Functional analysis of problem behavior: A review. *Journal of Applied Behavior Analysis, 36*, 147–185.

Hantula, D. A. (2005). *The impact of JOBM: ISI Impact Factor Places the Journal of Organizational Behavior Management Third in Applied Psychology.* Paper presented at the 2005 Florida Association for Behavior Analysis in Sarasota, Florida.

Harbert, T. L., Barlow, D. H., Hersen, M., & Austin, J. B. (1974). Measurement and modification of incestuous behavior: A case study. *Psychological Reports, 34*, 79–86.

Harris, F. R., Johnston, M. K., Kelley, C. S., & Wolf, M. M. (1964). Effects of positive social reinforcement on regressed crawling of a nursery school child. *Journal of Educational Psychology, 5.5*, 35–41.

Harris, S., Handleman, J. S., Kristoff, B., Bass, L., & Gordon, R. (1990). Changes in language development among autistic and peer children in segregated and integrated preschool settings. *Journal of Autism and Developmental Disorders, 20*, 23–32.

Harrop, J. W., & Velicer, W. F. (1985). A comparison of alternative approaches to the analysis of interrupted time-series. *Multivariate Behavioral Research, 20*, 27–44.

Harrop, J. W., & Velicer, W. F. (1990). Computer programs for interrupted time series analysis: II. A quantitative evaluation. *Multivariate Behavioral Research, 25*, 233–248.

Hart, B. M., Allen, K. E., Buell, J. S., Harris, F. R., & Wolf, M. M. (1964). Effects of social reinforcement on operant crying. *Journal of Experimental Child Psychology, 1*, 145–153.

Hart, B. M., Reynolds, N. J., Baer, D. M., Brawley, E. R., & Harris, F. R. (1968). Effect of contingent social reinforcement on the cooperative play of a preschool child. *Journal of Applied Behavior Analysis, 1*, 73–76.

Hartmann, D. P. (1984). Assessment strategies. In D. H. Barlow and M. Hersen (Eds.), *Single Case Research Designs*. New York: Pergamon.

Hartmann, D. P., & Hall, R. V. (1976). The changing criterion design. *Journal of Applied Behavior Analysis, 9*, 527–532.

Harvey, M. T., May, M. E., & Kennedy, C. H. (2004). Nonconcurrent multiple baseline designs and the evaluation of educational systems. *Journal of Behavioral Education, 13* (4), 267–276.

Hasazi, J. E., & Hasazi, S. E. (1972). Effects of teacher attention on digit-reversal behavior in an elementary school child. *Journal of Applied Behavior Analysis, 5*, 157–162.

Hawkins, R. P. (1986). Selection of target behaviors. In R. O. Nelson & S. Hayes (Eds.), *The Conceptual Foundations of Behavioral Assessment* (pp. 329–385). New York: Guilford.

Haw, R. M., Dickinson, J. J., & Meissner, C. A. (2007). The phenomenology of carryover effects between show-up and line-up identification. *Memory, 15* (1), 117–127.

Hawkins, R. P., Peterson, R. F, Schweid, E., & Bijou, S. W. (1966). Behavior therapy in the home: Amelioration of problem parent-child relations with the parent in a therapeutic role. *Journal of Experimental Child Psychology, 4*, 99–107.

Hayes, S. C., Barlow, D. H., & Nelson-Gray, R. O. (1999). *The Scientist Practitioner: Research and Accountability in the Age of Managed care* (2nd ed.). Boston: Allyn & Bacon.

Hayes, S. C., Barnes-Holmes, D., & Roche, B. (2001). *Relational Frame Theory*. New York: Plenum.

Hayes, S. C., & Nelson, R. O. (1986). *Conceptual Foundations of Behavior Assessment*. New York: Guilford Press.

Hayes, S. C., Nelson, R. O., & Jarrett, R. B. (1986). Evaluating the quality of behavioral assessment. In R. O. Nelson & S. C. Hayes (Eds.), *Conceptual Foundations of Behavioral Assessment* (pp. 463–503).

Hayes, S. C., Strosahl, K. D., & Wilson, K. G. (1999). *Acceptance and Commitment Therapy: An Experiential Approach to Behavior Change*. New York: Guilford Press.

Haynes, S. N., & O'Brien, W. H. (2000). *Principles and Practice of Behavioral Assessment*. New York: Kluwer.

Heisenberg, W. (1999). *Physics and philosophy*. Amherst, NY: Prometheus Books.

Herbert, E. W., & Baer, D. M. (1972). Raining parents as behavior modifiers: Self-recording of contingent attention. *Journal of Applied Behavior Analysis, 5*, 139–149.

Herbert, E. W., Pinkston, E. M., Hayden, M. L., Sajwaj, I. E., Pinkston, S., Cordua, G., & Jackson, C. (1973). Adverse effects of differential parental attention. *Journal of Applied Behavior Analysis, 6*, 15–30.

Hersen, M. (1982). Single-case experimental designs. In A. S. Bellack, M. Hersen, & A. E. Kazdin (Eds.), *International Handbook of Behavior Modification and Therapy* (pp. 167–201). New York: Plenum.

Hersen, M., & Barlow, D. H. (1976). *Single-case Experimental Designs: Strategies for Studying Behavior Change*. New York: Pergamon Press.

Hersen, M., Eisler, R. M., & Miller, P. M. (1973). Development of assertive responses: Clinical, measurement, and research considerations. *Behaviour Research and Therapy, 11*, 505–522.

Hilgard, J. R. (1933). The effect of early and delayed practice on memory and motor performances studies by the method of co-twin control. *Genetic Psychology Monographs, 14,* 493–567.

Hinson, J. M., & Malone, J. C., Jr. (1980). Local contrast and maintained generalization. *Journal of the Experimental Analysis of Behavior, 34,* 263–272.

Hoch, P. H., & Zubin, J. (Eds.). (1964). *The Evaluation of Psychiatric Treatment.* New York: Grune & Stratton.

Hoff, K. E., Ervin, R. A., & Friman, P. C. (2005). Refining functional behavioral assessment: Analyzing the separate and combined effects of hypothesized controlling variables during ongoing classroom routines. *School Psychology Review, 34,* 45–57.

Hofmann, S. G., Newman, M. G., Ehlers, A., & Roth, W. T. (1995). Psychophysiological differences between subgroups of social phobia. *Journal of Abnormal Psychology, 104* (1), 224–231.

Holmes, D. S. (1966). The application of learning theory to the treatment of a school behavior problem: A case study. *Psychology in the School, 3,* 355–359.

Honig, W. K. (Ed.), (1966). *Operant Behavior: Areas of Research and Application.* New York: Appleton-Century-Crofts.

Horner, R. D., & Baer, D. M. (1978). Multiple-probe technique: A variation of the multiple baseline. *Journal of Applied Behavior Analysis, 11,* 189–196.

Houle, T. T., Remble, T. A., & Houle, T. A. (2005). The examination of headache activity using time-series research designs. *Headache, 45* (5), 438–444.

Houmanfar, R. & Johnson, R. (2003). Organizational implications of gossip and rumor. *Journal of Organizational Behavior Management, 23,* 117–138.

Huitema, B. E. (1985). Autocorrelation in behavioral analysis: A myth. *Behavioral Assessment, 7,* 107–118.

Huitema, B. E. (2005). Analysis of interrupted time-series experiments using ITSEE: A critique. *Understanding Statistics, 3* (1), 27–46.

Huybers, S., Van Houten, R., & Malenfant, J. E. (2004). Reducing conflicts between motor vehicles and pedestrians: The separate and combined effects of pavement markings and a sign prompt. *Journal of Applied Behavior Analysis, 37* (4), 445–456.

Hyman, R., & Berger, L. (1966). Discussion: In H. J. Eysenck (Ed.), *The Effects of Psychotherapy* (pp. 81–86). New York: International Science Press.

Ilardi, S. S., & Craighead, E. W. (1994). The role of nonspecific factors in cognitive-behavior therapy for depression. *Clinical Psychology: Science and Practice, 2,* 138–156.

Inglis, J. (1966). *The Scientific Study of Abnormal Behavior* Chicago: Aldine.

Ingvarsson, E. T., & Hanley, G. P. (2006). An evaluation of computer-based programmed instruction for promoting teachers' greetings of parents by name. *Journal of Applied Behavior Analysis, 39* (2), 203–214.

Iwata, B. A., Dorsey, M. F., Slifer, K. J., Bauman, K. E., & Richman, G. S. (1982). Toward a functional analysis of self-injury. *Analysis and Intervention in Developmental Disabilities, 2,* 3–20.

Jaccard, J., & Wan, C. K. (1993). Statistical analyses of temporal data with many observations: Issues for behavioral medicine data. *Annals Behavioral Medicine, 15* (1), 41–50.

Jacobson, N. S., Dobson, K. S., Truax, P. A., Addis, M. E., Koerner, K., & Gollan, J. K., et al. (1996). A component analysis of cognitive-behavioral treatment for depression. *Journal of Consulting and Clinical Psychology, 64* (2), 295–304.

Jayaratne, S., & Levy, R. L. (1979). *Empirical clinical practice.* New York: Columbia University Press.

Jordan, J., Singh, N. N., & Repp, A. C. (1989). An evaluation of gentle teaching and visual screening in the reduction of stereotype. *Journal of Applied Behavior Analysis, 22* (1), 9–22.

Johnson, B. M., Miltenberger, R. G., Egemo-Helm, K., Jostad, C. M., Flessner, C., & Gatheridge, B. (2005). Evaluation of behavioral skills training for teaching abduction-prevention skills to young children. *Journal of Applied Behavior Analysis, 38,* 67–78.

Johnson, T. M., Burgio, K. L., Redden, D. T., Wright, K. C., & Goode, P. S. (2005).

Effects of behavioral and drug therapy on nocturia in older incontinent women. *Journal of the American Geriatrics Society, 53*, 846–850.

Johnston, J. M. (1972). Punishment of human behavior. *American Psychologist, 27*, 1033–1054.

Johnston, J. M., & Pennypacker, H. S. (1981). *Strategies and Tactics of Human Behavioral Research.* Hillsdale, NJ: Erlbaum.

Johnston, J. M., & Pennypacker, H. S. (1993). *Strategies and Tactics of Behavioral Research.* Hillsdale, NJ: Lawrence Erlbaum.

Joint Commission on Mental Illness and Health (1961). *Action for Mental Health.* New York: Science Editions.

Jones, K. M., & Friman, P. C. (1999). Behavior assessment and treatment of insect phobia: A preliminary case study. *Journal of Applied Behavior Analysis, 32*, 95–98.

Jones, K. M., Swearer, S. M., & Friman, P. C. (1997). Relax and try this instead: Abbreviated habit-reversal for maladaptive oral self-biting. *Journal of Applied Behavior Analysis, 30*, 697–700.

Jones, R. R., Vaught, R. S., & Weinrott, M. R. (1977). Time-series analysis in operant research. *Journal of Applied Behavior Analysis, 10*, 151–167.

Jones, R. R., Weinrott, M., & Vaught, R. S. (1978). Effects of serial dependency on the agreement between visual and statistical inference. *Journal of Applied Behavioral Analysis, 11*, 277–283.

Jones, R. T., Kazdin, A. E., & Haney, J. L. (1981). Social validation and training of emergency fire safety skills for potential injury prevention and life saving. *Journal of Applied Behavior Analysis, 14*, 249–250.

Kahng, S., Boscoe, J. H., & Byrne, S. (2003). The use of an escape contingency and a token economy to increase food acceptance. *Journal of Applied Behavior Analysis, 36* (3), 349–353.

Kahng, S., & Iwata, B. A. (1998). Computerized systems for collecting real-time observational data. *Journal of Applied Behavior Analysis, 31*, 253–261.

Kahng, S., Iwata, B. A., & Lewin, A. B. (2002). Behavioral treatment of self-injury, 1964 to 2000. *American Journal of Mental Retardation, 107* (3), 212–221.

Kanfer, F. H., & Phillips, J. S. (1970). *Learning Foundations of Behavior Therapy.* New York: Wiley.

Kantorovich, N. V. (1928). An attempt of curing alcoholism by associated reflexes. *Novoye v Refleksologii i Fixiologii Nervnoy Sistemy, 3*, 436. Cited by Razran, G. H. S. (1934). Conditional withdrawal responses with shock as the conditioning stimulus in adult human subjects. *Psychological Bulletin, 31*, 111.

Kaplan, B. J., Crawford, S. G., Gardner, B., & Farrelly, G. (2002). Treatment of mood lability and explosive rage with minerals and vitamins: two case studies in children. *Journal of Child and Adolescent Psychopharmacology, 12* (3), 205–219.

Kay, S., Harchik, A. E., & Luiselli, J. K. (2006). Elimination of drooling by an adolescent student with autism attending public high school. *Journal of Positive Behavior Interventions, 8* (1), 24–28.

Kazdin, A. E. (1973). Methodological and assessment considerations in evaluating reinforcement programs in applied settings. *Journal of Applied Behavior Analysis, 6*, 517–531.

Kazdin, A. E. (1977). Assessing the clinical or applied significance of behavior change through social validation. *Behavior Modification, 1*, 427–453.

Kazdin, A. E. (1978). *History of Behavior Modification: Experimental Foundations of Contemporary Research.* Baltimore: University Park Press.

Kazdin, A. E. (1981). Drawing valid inferences from case studies. *Journal of Consulting and Clinical Psychology, 49* (2), 183–192.

Kazdin, A. E. (1982). *Single-case Research Designs: Methods for Clinical and Applied Settings.* New York: Oxford University Press.

Kazdin, A. E. (1984). Statistical analyses for single-case experimental designs. In D. H. Barlow & M. Hersen, *Single-case Experimental Designs: Strategies for Studying Behavior Change* (pp. 285–324). New York: Pergamon Press.

Kazdin, A. E. (1999). The meanings and measurement of clinical significance. *Journal of Consulting and Clinical Psychology, 67* (3), 332–339.

Kazdin, A. E. (2001). *Behavior Modification in Applied Settings* (6th ed.). Belmont, CA: Wadsworth/Thompson Learning.

Kazdin, A. E. (2000). *Psychotherapy for Children and Adolescents: Directions for Research and Practice.* New York: Oxford Univ. Press.

Kazdin, A. E. (2003b). *Research Design in Clinical Psychology* (4th ed.). Boston, MA: Allyn and Bacon.

Kazdin, A. E. (2005). *Parent Management Training: Treatment for Oppositional, Aggressive and Antisocial Behavior in Children and Adolescents.* New York: Oxford University Press.

Kazdin, A. E., & Bootzin, R. R. (1972). The token economy: An evaluative review. *Journal of Applied Behavior Analysis, 5,* 343–372.

Kazdin, A. E., & Kopel, S. A. (1975). On resolving ambiguities of the multiple-baseline design: Problems and recommendations. *Behavior Therapy, 6,* 601–608.

Kazdin, A. E., & Weisz, J. R. (Eds.). (2003). *Evidence-based Psychotherapies for Children and Adolescents.* New York: Guilford Press.

Kazdin, A. E., & Whitley, M. K. (2006). Comorbidity, case complexity, and effects of evidence-based treatment for children referred for disruptive behavior. *Journal of Consulting and Clinical Psychology, 74* (3), 455–467.

Kearney, C. A., & Silverman, W. K. (1990). Treatment of an adolescent with obsessive-compulsive disorder by alternating response prevention and cognitive therapy: An empirical analysis. *Journal of Behavior Therapy and Experimental Psychiatry, 21* (1), 39–47.

Kelley, M. E., Fisher, W. W., Lomas, J. E., & Sanders, R. Q. (2006). Some effects of stimulant medication on response allocation: A double-blind analysis. *Journal of Applied Behavior Analysis, 39* (2), 243–247.

Kelly, J. A. (1980). The simultaneous replication design: The use of a multiple baseline to establish experimental control in single group social skills treatment studies. *Journal of Behavior Therapy and Experimental Psychiatry, 11,* 203–207.

Kelly, J. A., Laughlin, C., Claiborne, M., & Patterson, J. T. (1979). A group procedure for teaching job interviewing skills to formerly hospitalized psychiatric patients. *Behavior Therapy, 10,* 299–310.

Kendall, P. C. (Ed.). (1999). Clinical significance [special section]. *Journal of Consulting and Clinical Psychology, 67,* 283–339.

Kendall, P. C., & Clarkin, J. F. (1992). Introduction to special section: Comorbidity and treatment implications. *Journal of Consulting and Clinical Psychology, 60* (6), 833–834.

Kernberg, O. F. (1973). Summary and conclusions of psychotherapy and psychoanalysis: Final report of the Menninger Foundation's psychotherapy research project. *International Journal of Psychiatry, 11,* 62–77.

Kessel, L., & Hyman, H. T. (1933). The value of psychoanalysis as a therapeutic procedure. *Journal of American Medical Association, 101,* 1612–1615.

Kessler, R. C., Chiu, W. T., Demler, O., Merikangas, K. R., & Walters, E. E. (2005). Prevalence, severity, and comorbidity of 12-month DSM-IV disorders in the National Comorbidity Survey Replication. *Archives of General Psychiatry, 62* (6), 617–627.

Kiesler, D. J. (1966). Some myths of psychotherapy research and the search for a paradigm. *Psychological Bulletin, 65,* 110–136.

Kiesler, D. J. (1971). Experimental designs in psychotherapy research. In A. E. Bergin & S. L. Garfield (Eds.), *Handbook of Psychotherapy and Behavior Change. An Empirical Analysis* (2nd ed.) (pp. 36–74). New York: Wiley.

Kirby, F. D., & Shields, F (1972). Modification of arithmetic response rate and attending behavior in a seventh-grade student. *Journal of Applied Behavior Analysis, 5,* 79–84.

Kirk, R. E. (1995). *Experimental Design: Procedures for the Behavioral Sciences.* New York: Brooks/Cole Publishing.

Knapp, T. J. (1983). Behavior analysts' visual appraisal of behavior change in graphic display. *Behavioral Assessment, 5,* 155–164.

Knight, R. P. (1941). Evaluation of the results of psychoanalytic therapy. *American Journal of Psychiatry, 98*, 434–466.

Koegel, R. L., & Schreibman, L. (1982). *How to teach autistic and other severely handicapped children.* Lawrence, KS: H & H Enterprises.

Koehler, M. J., & Levin, J. R. (2000). RegRand: Statistical software for the multiple baseline design. *Behavior Research Methods Instruments & Computers, 26*, 367–371.

Krasner, L. (1971). The operant approach in behavior therapy. In A. E. Bergin & S. L. Garfield (Eds.), *Handbook of psychotherapy and behavior change: An empirical analysis* (pp. 612–653). New York: Wiley.

Kratochwill, T. R. (Ed.) (1978). *Single-subject Research: Strategies for Evaluating Change.* New York: Academic Press.

Kryger, M. H., Roth, T., & Dement, W. C. (Eds.) (1994). *Principles and Practice of Sleep Medicine.* Philadelphia: W. B. Saunders.

Last, C. G., Barlow, D. H., & O'Brien, G. T. (1983). Comparison of two cognitive strategies in treatment of a patient with generalized anxiety disorder. *Psychological Reports, 53*, 19–26.

Laws, D. R., Brown, R. A., Epstein, J., & Hocking, N. (1971). Reduction of inappropriate social behavior in disturbed children by an untrained paraprofessional therapist. *Behavior Therapy, 2*, 519–533.

Lazarus, A. A. (1963). The results of behavior therapy in 126 cases of severe neurosis. *Behaviour Research and Therapy, 1*, 69–80.

Lazarus, A. A., & Davison, G. C. (1971). Clinical innovation in research and practice. In A. E. Bergin & S. L. Garfield (Eds.), *Handbook of Psychotherapy and Behavior Change: An Empirical Analysis* (pp. 196–213). New York: Wiley.

Leitenberg, H. (1973). The use of single-case methodology in psychotherapy research. *Journal of Abnormal Psychology, 82*, 87–101.

Leitenberg, H., Agras, W. S., Butz, R., & Wince, J. (1971). Relationship between heart rate and behavioral change during the treatment of phobias. *Journal of Abnormal Psychology, 78*, 59–68.

Leitenberg, H., Agras, W. S., Edwards, J. A., Thomson, L. E., & Wincze, J. P. (1970).

Practice as a psychotherapeutic variable: An experimental analysis within single cases. *Journal of Psychiatric Research, 7*, 215–225.

Leitenberg, H., Agras, W. S., Thomson, L. E., & Wright, D. E. (1968). Feedback in behavior modification: An experimental analysis of two phobic cases. *Journal of Applied Behavior Analysis, 1*, 131–137.

Lester, B. M., & Boukydis, C. F. Z. (Eds.) (1985). *Infant crying.* New York: Plenum.

Levine, M. D., Mazonson, P., & Bakow, H. (1980). Behavioral symptom substitution in children cured of encopresis. *American Journal of Diseases in Childhood, 134*, 663–667.

Lewin, K. (1933). Vectors, cognitive processes and Mr. Tolman's criticism. *Journal of General Psychology, 8*, 318–345.

Lewinsohn, P. M., Rohde, P., Seeley, J. R., Klein, D. N., & Gotlib, I. H. (2003). Psychosocial functioning of young adults who have experienced and recovered from major depressive disorder during adolescence. *J Abnorm Psychol, 112* (3), 353–363.

Liberman, R. P., Davis, J., Moon, W., & Moore, J. (1973). Research design for analyzing drugenvironment-behavior interactions. *Journal of Nervous and Mental Disease, 156*, 432–439.

Liberman, R. P., Neuchterlein, K. H., & Wallace, C. J. (1982). Social skills training in the nature of schizophrenia. In Curran, J. P. & Monti, P. M. (Eds.), *Social Skills Training* (pp. 1–56). New York: Guilford Press.

Lincoln, T. M., Winfried, R., Hahlweg, K., Frank, M., Witzleben, I. V., Schroeder, B., & Wolfgang, F. (2003). Effectiveness of an empirically supported treatment for social phobia in the field. *Behavior Research and Therapy, 41*, 1251–1269.

Lindsley, O. R. (1991). Precision teaching's unique legacy from B. F. Skinner. *Journal of Behavioral Education, 1*, 253–266.

Linehan, M. M. (1993). *Cognitive-behavioral Treatment of Borderline Personality Disorder.* New York: Guilford Press.

Ljung, G. M., & Box, G. E. P. (1978). On a measure of lack of fit in time series models. *Biometrika, 65*, 297–303.

Loening-Baucke, V. A., & Cruikshank, B. M. (1986). Abnormal defecation dynamics in chronically constipated children with encopresis. *The Journal of Pediatrics, 108,* 562–566.

Loening-Baucke, V. A., & Younoszai, M. K. (1984). Effect of treatment on rectal and sigmoid motility in chronically constipated children. *Pediatrics, 73,* 199–205.

Lohrmann, S., & Talerico, J. (2004). Anchor the boat: A classwide intervention to reduce problem behavior. *Journal of Positive Behavior Interventions, 6* (2), 113–120.

Lovaas, O. I. (1987) Behavioral treatment and normal educational and intellectual functioning in young autistic children. *Journal of Consulting and Clinical Psychology, 55,* 3–9.

Lovaas, O. I. (2003). *Teaching Individuals with Developmental Delays: Basic Intervention Techniques.* Autism: Pro-Ed, Inc.

Lovaas, O. I., Berberich, J. P., Perloff, B. F., & Schaeffer, B. (1966). Acquisition of imitative speech by schizophrenic children. *Science, 161,* 705–707.

Lovaas, O. I., Freitas, L., Nelson, K., & Whalen, C. (1967). The establishment of imitation and its use for the development of complex behavior in schizophrenic children. *Behaviour Research and Therapy, 5,* 171–18 1.

Lovaas, O. I., Koegel, R., Simmons, J. Q., & Long, J. D. (1973). Some generalization and follow-up measures on autistic children in behavior therapy. *Journal of Applied Behavior Analysis, 5,* 131–166.

Lovaas, O. I., Schaeffer, B., & Simons, J. Q. (1965). Experimental studies in childhood schizophrenia: Building social behaviors using electric shock. *Journal of Experimental Research in Personality, 1,* 99–109.

Lovaas, O. I., & Simmons, J. Q. (1969). Manipulation of self-destruction in three retarded children. *Journal of Applied Behavior Analysis, 2,* 143–157.

Luborsky, L. (1959). Psychotherapy. In P. R. Farnsworth & Q. McNemar (Ed.), *Annual Review of Psychology* (pp. 317–344). Palo Alto, CA: Annual Review.

Ludwig, T. D., Gray, T. W., & Rowell, A. (1998). Increasing recycling in academic buildings: A systematic replication. *Journal of Applied Behavior Analysis, 31* (4), 683–686.

Luiselli, J. K., Blew, P., Keane, J., Thibadeau, S., & Holzman, T. (2000). Pharmacotherapy for severe aggression in a child with autism: "open label" evaluation of multiple medications on response frequency and intensity of behavioral intervention. *Journal of Behavior Therapy and Experimental Psychiatry, 31* (3–4), 219–230.

Madsen, C. H., Becker, W. C., & Thomas, D. R. (1968). Rules, praise, and ignoring: Elements of elementary classroom control. *Journal of Applied Behavior Analysis, 1,* 139–150.

Malan, D. H. (1973). Therapeutic factors in analytically oriented brief psychotherapy. In R. H. Gosling (Ed.), *Support, Innovation and Autonomy* (pp. 187–205). London: Tavistock.

Malone, J. C., Jr. (1976). Local contrast and Pavlovian induction. *Journal of the Experimental Analysis of Behavior, 26,* 425–440.

Malott, J. M., Glasgow, R. E., O'Neill, H. K., & Klesges, R. C. (1984). Co-worker social support in a worksite smoking control program. *Journal of Applied Behavior Analysis, 17* (4), 485–495.

March, J., Silva, S., Petrycki, S., Curry, J., Wells, K., & Fairbank, J., et al. (2004). Fluoxetine, cognitive-behavioral therapy, and their combination for adolescents with depression: Treatment for Adolescents with Depression Study (TADS) randomized controlled trial. *Jama, 292* (7), 807–820.

Marks, I. M., & Mathews, A. M. (1979). Brief standard self-rating for phobic patients. *Behaviour Research and Therapy, 17* (3), 263–267.

Martell, C. R., Addis, M. E., & Jacobson, N. S. (2001). *Depression in context: Strategies for guided action.* New York: W. W. Norton.

Mash, E. J., & Terdal, L. G. (1997). *Assessment of Childhood Disorders.* New York: Guilford Press.

Masuda, A., Hayes, S. C., Sackett, C. F., & Twohig, M. P. (2004). Cognitive defusion and self-relevant negative thoughts: examining the impact of a ninety year old technique. *Behaviour Research and Therapy, 42* (4), 477–485.

Matching Alcoholism Treatments to Client Heterogeneity: Project MATCH post-treatment drinking outcomes. (1997). *Journal of Studies on Alcohol, 58* (1), 7–29.

Mathews, J. R., Friman, P. C., Barone, J. V., Ross, L. V., & Christophersen, E. R. (1987). Decreasing dangerous infant behavior through parent instruction. *Journal of Applied Behavior Analysis, 20,* 165–170.

Matyas, T. A., & Greenwood, K. M. (1990a). The effect of serial dependence on visual judgement in single-case charts: An addendum. *Occupational Therapy Journal of Research, 10,* 208–220.

Matyas, T. A., & Greenwood, K. M. (1990b). Visual analysis of single-case time-series: effects of variability, serial dependence, and magnitude of intervention effects. *Journal of Applied Behavior Analysis, 23,* 341–351.

Matyas, T. A., & Greenwood, K. M. (1991). Problems in the estimation of autocorrelation in brief time series and some implications for behavioral data. *Behavioral Assessment, 13,* 137–157.

McCallister, L. W., Stachowiak, J. G., Baer, D. M., & Conderman, L. (1969). The application of operant conditioning techniques in a secondary school classroom. *Journal of Applied Behavior Analysis, 2,* 277–285.

McCord, B. E., Iwata, B. A., Galensky, T. L., Ellingson, S. A., & Thomson, R. J. (2001). Functional analysis and treatment of problem behavior evoked by noise. *Journal of Applied Behavior Analysis, 34* (4), 447–462.

McDougall, D. (2005). The range-bound changing criterion design. *Behavioral Interventions, 20,* 129–137.

McDowall, D., McCleary, R., Meidinger, E. E., & Hay, R. A. (1980). Interrupted Time-Series Analysis. J. L. Sullivan & R. G. Niemi (Eds.). Sage University Papers. London: Sage Publications, Inc.

McEachin, J., J., Smith, T., & Lovaas, O. I. (1993). Long-term outcome for children with autism who received early intensive behavioral treatment. *Journal of Mental Retardation, 97,* 359–372.

McFall, R. M. (1970). Effects of self-monitoring on normal smoking behavior. *Journal of Consulting and Clinical Psychology, 35,* 135–142.

McKnight, S., McKean, J. W., & Huitema, B. E. (2000). A double bootstrap method to analyze linear models with autoregressive error terms. *Psychological Methods, 5,* 87–101.

McKnight, D. L., Nelson, R. O., Hayes, S. C., & Jarrett, R. B. (1984). Importance of treating individually assessed response classes in the amelioration of depression. *Behavior Therapy.*

McLean, A. P., & White, K. G. (1981). Undermatching and contrast within components of multiple schedules. *Journal of the Experimental Analysis of Behavior, 35,* 283–291.

McMahon, R., & Forehand, R. (2003). *Helping the Noncompliant Child* (2nd ed.). New York: Guilford Press.

Merrill, K. A., Tolbert, V. E., & Wade, W. A. (2003). Effectiveness of cognitive therapy for depression in a community mental health center: a benchmarking study. *Journal of Consulting Clinical Psychology, 71,* 404–409.

Metcalfe, M. (1956). Demonstration of a psychosomatic relationship. *British Journal of Medical Psychology, 29,* 63–66.

Meunier, P., Mollard, P., & Marechal, J. M. (1976). Physiopathy of the megarectum: The association of megarectum and encopresis. *Gut, 17,* 224–227.

Michael, J. (1974). Statistical inference for individual organism research: Mixed blessing or curse? *Journal of Applied Behavior Analysis, 7,* 647–653.

Miller, P. M. (1973). An experimental analysis of retention control training in the treatment of nocturnal enuresis in two institutionalized adolescents. *Behavior Therapy, 4,* 288–294.

Miller, D. L., & Kelley, M. L. (1994). The use of goal setting and contingency contracting for improving children's homework performance. *Journal of Applied Behavior Analysis, 27* (1), 73–84.

Millon, T., & Davis, R. D. (1996). *Disorders of Personality: DSM IV and Beyond.* New York: John Wiley.

Mills, H. L., Agras, W. S., Barlow, D. H., & Mills, J. R. (1973). Compulsive rituals treated by response prevention: An experimental analysis. *Archives of General Psychiatry, 28,* 524–51.

Miltenberger, R. G. (2001). *Behavior Modification* (2nd ed.). Belmont, CA: Wadsworth.

Miltenberger, R. G., Flessner, C., Gatheridge, B., Johnson, B., Satterlund, M., & Egemo, K. (2004). Evaluation of behavioral skills training to prevent gun play in children. *Journal of Applied Behavior Analysis, 37,* 513–516.

Miltenberger, R. G., Fuqua, R. W., & McKinley, T. (1985). Habit reversal with motor tics: Replication and component analysis. *Behavior Therapy, 16,* 39–50.

Miltenberger, R. G., Gatheridge, B. J., Satterlund, M., Egemo-Helm, K. R., Johnson, B. M., & Jostad, C., et al. (2005). Teaching safety skills to children to prevent gun play: An evaluation of in situ training. *Journal of Applied Behavior Analysis, 38* (3), 395–398.

Miltenberger, R. G., Rapp, J. T. & Long, E. S. (1999). A low-tech method for conducting real-time recording. *Journal of Applied Behavior Analysis, 32,* 119–120.

Minkin, N., Braukmann, C. J., Minkin, B. L., Timbers, G. D., Timbers, B. J., Fixsen, D. L., Phillips, E. L., & Wolf, M. M. (1976). The social validation and training of conversational skills. *Journal of Applied Behavior Analysis, 9,* 127–140.

Moher, D., Schulz, K. F., & Altman, D. G. (2001) The CONSORT statement for revised recommendations for improving the quality of reports of parallel-group randomized trials. *Lancet, 357* (9263), 1191–1194.

Moore, B. A, Fruzetti, A. E., & Friman, P. C. (2007). Brief report: Evaluating the bedtime pass program for child resistance to bedtime: A randomized controlled trial. *Journal of Pediatric Psychology, 32,* 283–287.

Moore, K. J., Osgood, W., Larzelere, R. E., & Chamberlain, P. (1994). Use of pooled time series in the study of naturally occurring clinical events and problem behavior in a foster care setting. *Journal of Clinical and Consulting Psychology, 62,* 718–728.

Moras, K., Telfer, L. A., & Barlow, D. H. (1993). Efficacy and specific effects data on new treatments: A case study strategy with mixed anxiety-depression. *Journal of Consulting and Clinical Psychology, 61* (3), 412–420.

Munford, F. R., & Liberman, R. P. (1978). Differential attention in the treatment of operant cough. *Journal of Behavioral Medicine, 1,* 280–289.

Nathan, P. E., & Gorman, J. M. (Eds.) (2002). *Treatments that Work* (2nd ed.). New York: Oxford University Press.

National Institute on Drug Abuse. (2005). Clinical trials network. Retrieved December, 16, 2005, from NIDA Web site: www.nida.nih.gov/ctn.

National Institute of Mental Health. (1980). *Behavior Therapies in the Treatment of Anxiety Disorders: Recommendations for Strategies in Treatment Assessment Research. (Final report of NIMH conference #RFP NIMH ER-79–003).* Unpublished manuscript.

Neef, N. A. (1994). Editors note for the special issue on functional analysis approaches to behavioral assessment and treatment. *Journal of Applied Behavior Analysis, 27,* 196.

Neef, N. A., McCord, B. E., & Ferreri, S. J. (2006). Effects of guided notes versus completed notes during lectures on college students' quiz performance. *Journal of Applied Behavior Analysis, 39* (1), 123–130.

Nelson, B. K. (1998). Statistical methodology: V. Time series analysis using autoregressive integrated moving average (ARIMA) models. *Academy Emergency Medicine, 5* (7), 739–744.

Nelson, R., & Hayes, S. C. (1986). The nature of behavioral assessment. In R. O. Nelson & S. C. Hayes (Eds.), *Conceptual Foundations of Behavioral Assessment* (pp. 3–41). New York: Guilford Press.

Nelson, J. R., Roberts, M. L., & Smith, D. J. (1998) *Conducting Functional Behavior Assessments: A Practical Guide.* Longmont, CO: Sopris West.

Nock, M. K. (2002). A multiple-baseline evaluation of the treatment of food phobia in a young boy. *Journal of Behavior Therapy and Experimental Psychiatry, 33* (3–4), 217–225.

Nock, M. K., & Banaji, M. R. (2007). Assessment of self-injurious thoughts using a behavioral test. *American Journal of Psychiatry, 164* (5), 820–823.

Nock, M. K., Goldman, J. L., Wang, Y., & Albano, A. M. (2004). From science to practice: The flexible use of evidence-based treatments in clinical settings. *Journal of the American Academy of Child and Adolescent Psychiatry, 43* (6), 777–780.

Nock, M. K., Janis, I. B., & Wedig, M. M. (2008). Research design. In A. M. Nezu & M. Nezu (Eds.), *Evidence-based Outcome Research: A Practical Guide to Conducting Randomized Controlled Trials for Psychosocial Interventions.* pp. 201–208. New York: Oxford University Press.

Nock, M. K., & Kurtz, S. M. S. (2005). Direct behavioral observation in school settings: Bringing science to practice. *Cognitive and Behavioral Practice, 12,* 359–370.

Nock, M. K., Michel, B. D., & Photos, V. (2007). Single-case research designs. In D. McKay (Ed.), *Handbook of Research Methods in Abnormal and Clinical Psychology.* pp. 337–350. Thousand Oaks, CA: Sage Publications.

Nock, M. K., & Prinstein, M. J. (2004). A functional approach to the assessment of self-mutilative behavior. *Journal of Consulting and Clinical Psychology, 72,* 885–890.

Nock, M. K., & Prinstein, M. J. (2005). Contextual features and behavioral functions of self-mutilation. *Journal of Abnormal Psychology, 144,* 140–146.

Nordquist, V. M. (1971). The modification of a child's enuresis: Some response-response relationships. *Journal of Applied Behavior Analysis, 4,* 241–247.

Northup, J., Fusilier, I., Swanson, V., Huete, J., Bruce, T., & Freeland, J., et al. (1999). Further analysis of the separate and interactive effects of methylphenidate and common classroom contingencies. *Journal of Applied Behavior Analysis, 32* (1), 35–50.

Nugent, W. R. (1996). Integrating single-case and group-comparison designs for evaluation research. *Journal of Applied Behavioral Science, 32,* 209–226.

O'Brien, F., Azrin, N. H., & Henson, K. (1969). Increased communication of chronic mental patients by reinforcement and by response priming. *Journal of Applied Behavior Analysis, 2,* 23–29.

O'Brien, F., Bugle, C., & Azrin, N. H. (1972). Training and maintaining a retarded child's proper eating. *Journal of Applied Behavior Analysis, 5,* 67–72.

O'Donohue, W., Plaud, J. J., & Hecker, J. E. (1992). The possible function of positive reinforcement in home-bound agoraphobia: A case study. *Journal of Behavior Therapy and Experimental Psychiatry, 23* (4), 303–312.

O'Leary, K. D., & Becker, W. C. (1967). Behavior modification of an adjustment class: A token reinforcement program. *Exceptional Children, 9,* 637–642.

O'Leary, K. D., Becker, W. C., Evans, M. B., & Saudargas, R. A. (1969). A token reinforcement program in a public school: A replication and systematic analysis. *Journal of Applied Behavior Analysis, 2,* 3–13.

Ollendick, T. H., Shapiro, E. S., & Barrett, R. P. (1981). Reducing stereotypic behaviors: An analysis of treatment procedures utilizing an alternating treatments design. *Behavior Therapy, 12,* 570–577.

Onghena, P. & Egington, E. S. (2005). Customization of pain treatments: Single-case design and analysis. *Clinical Journal of Pain, 21,* 56 – 68.

Onghena, P. & Van Damme, G. (1994). SCRT 1.1: Single case randomization tests. *Behavior Research Methods, Instruments, & Computers, 32,* 369.

Orne, M. T. (1962). On the social psychology of the psychological experiment: With particular reference to demand characteristics and their implications. *American Psychologist, 17,* 776–783.

Pace, G. M., Ivancic, M. T., Edwards, G. L., Iwata, B. A., & Page, T. J. (1985). Assessment of stimulus preference and reinforcer value with profoundly retarded individuals. *Journal of Applied Behavior Analysis, 18,* 249–255.

Parsonson, B. S., & Baer, D. M. (1992). The visual analysis of data, and current research in the stimuli controlling it. In: T. R. Kratochwill & J. R. Levin (Eds.), *Single-case Research Design and Analysis: New Directions for Psychology and Education.* Hillsdale, NJ: Erlbaum, pp. 15–40.

Paul, G. L. (1967). Strategy of outcome research in psychotherapy. *Journal of Consulting Psychology, 31,* 104–118.

Paul, G. L. (1969). Behavior modification research: Design and tactics. In C. M. Franks (Ed.), *Behavior therapy: Appraisal and Status* (pp. 29–62). New York: McGraw-Hill.

Pavlov, I. P. (1927). *Conditioned Reflexes.* New York: Dover.

Pavlov, I. P. (1928). *Lectures on Conditioned Reflexes.* (W. H. Gantt, Trans.) New York: International.

Pedhauzer, E. J. (1997). *Multiple Regression in Behavioral Research.* New York: Harcourt Brace College Publishers.

Phillips, E. L., Phillips, E. A., Fixsen, D. L., & Wolf, M. M. (1974). *The Teaching Family Handbook.* Lawrence, KS: University of Kansas.

Photos, V. I., Michel, B. D., & Nock, M. K. (2008). Single-case research designs. In M. Hersen, A. M. Gross, *Handbook of Clinical Psychology, Volume 1: Adults* (pp. 224–245). Hoboken, NJ: John Wiley & Sons.

Piazza, C. C., Fisher, W. W., Brown, K. A., Shore, B. A., Patel, M. R., Katz, R. M., Sevin, B. M., Gulotta, C. S., & Blakely-Smith, A. (2003). Functional analysis of inappropriate mealtime behaviors. *Journal of Applied Behavior Analysis, 36,* 187–204.

Pinkston, E. M., Reese, N. M., LeBlanc, J. M., & Baer, D. M. (1973). Independent control of a preschool child's aggression and peer interaction by contingent teacher attention. *Journal of Applied Behavior Analysis, 6,* 115–124.

Porritt, M., Burt, A., & Poling, A. (2006). Increasing fiction writers' productivity through an internet-based intervention. *Journal of Applied Behavior Analysis, 39* (3), 393–397.

Porterfield, J., Blunden, R., & Blewitt, E. (1980). Improving environments for profoundly handicapped adults: Using prompts and social attention to maintain high group engagement. *Behavior Modification, 4,* 225–241.

Powell, J., & Hake, D. F (1971). Positive vs. negative reinforcement: A direct comparison of effects on a complex human response. *Psychological Record, 21,* 191–205.

Powell, J., Martindale, A., & Kulp, S. (1975). An evaluation of time-sample measures of behavior. *Journal of Applied Behavior Analysis, 8,* 463–469.

Powers, E., & Witmer, H. (1951). *An Experiment in the Prevention of Delinquency.* New York: Columbia University Press.

Rachlin, H. (1973). Contrast and matching. *Psychological Review, 80,* 297–308.

Rachman, S. J., & Hodgson, R. J. (1980). *Obsessions and Compulsions.* Englewood Cliffs, NJ: Prentice-Hall.

Ramp, E., Ulrich, R., & Dulaney, S. (1971). Delayed timeout as a procedure for reducing disruptive classroom behavior: A case study. *Journal of Applied Behavior Analysis, 4,* 235–239.

Rapp, J. T., Miltenberger, R. G., Galensky, T. L., Ellingson, S. A., & Long, E. S. (1999). A functional analysis of hair pulling. *Journal of Applied Behavior Analysis, 32,* 329–337.

Rassau, A., & Arco, L. (2003). Effects of chat-based on-line cognitive behavior therapy on study related behavior and anxiety. *Behavioural and Cognitive Psychotherapy, 31,* 377–381.

Raudenbush, S. W., & Byk, A. S. (2002). *Hierarchial Linear Models: Applications and Data Analysis Methods* (2nd ed.). Newbury Park, CA: Sage.

Rehfeldt, R. A., & Chambers, M. R. (2003). Functional analysis and treatment of verbal perseverations displayed by an adult with autism. *Journal of Applied Behavior Analysis, 36,* 259–262.

Repp, A. C., & Horner, R. H. (1999). *Functional Analysis of Problem Behavior.* Belmont, CA: Wadsworth.

Reyes, J. R., Vollmer, T. R., Sloman, K. N., Hall, A., Reed, R., & Jansen, G., et al. (2006). Assessment of deviant arousal in adult male sex offenders with developmental disabilities. *Journal of Applied Behavior Analysis, 39* (2), 173–188.

Revusky, S. H. (1967). Some statistical treatments compatible with individual organism methodology. *Journal of the Experimental Analysis of Behavior, 10,* 319–330.

Reynolds, G. S. (1968). *A Primer of Operant Conditioning.* Glenview, IL: Scott, Foresman.

Reynolds, N. J., & Risley, T. R. (1968). The role of social and material reinforcers in increasing talking of a disadvantaged preschool child. *Journal of Applied Behavior Analysis, 1,* 253–262.

Rhodes, P. (2003). Behavioral and family systems interventions in developmental disability: Towards a contemporary and integrative approach. *Journal of Intellectual and Developmental Disability 28* (1), 51–64.

Rimland, B., & Edelson, S. M. (1995). Brief report: A Pilot study of auditory integration training in autism. *Journal of Autism and Development Disorders, 25* (1), 61–70.

Risley, T. R., & Wolf, M. M. (1972). Strategies for analyzing behavioral change over time. In J. Nesselroade & H. Reese (Eds.), *Life-span Developmental Psychology. Methodological Issues* (pp. 175–183). New York: Academic Press.

Roberts, M. W., Hatzenbuehler, L. C., & Bean, A. W. (1981). The effects of differential attention and timeout on child noncompliance. *Behavior Therapy, 12,* 93–99.

Roberts, M. C., & Ilardi, S. S. (2005). *Handbook of Research Methods in Clinical Psychology,* Oxford: Blackwell.

Rogers, C. R., Gendlin, E. T., Kiesler, D. J., & Truax, C. B. (1967). *The Therapeutic Relationship and its Impact. A Study of Psychotherapy with Schizophrenics.* Madison: University of Wisconsin Press.

Rosemond, J. (2005). Infant toilet training reinforces wrong notion. *Kansas.com: The Whichita Eagle.* Retrieved October 27, 2005 from http://www.kansas.com/mld/kansas/living/13003705.htm.

Rosenzweig, S. (1951). Idiodynamics in personality therapy with special reference to projective methods. *Psychological Review, 58,* 213–223.

Rounsaville, B. J., Carroll, K. M., & Onken, L. S. (2001). A stage model of behavioral therapies research: Getting started and moving on from stage 1. *Clin Psychol Sci Pract 8,* 133–142.

Rubenstein, E. A., & Parloff, M. B. (1959). Research problems in psychotherapy. In E. A. Rubenstein & M. B. Parloff (Eds.), *Research in psychotherapy,* (Vol. 1) (pp. 276–293). Washington, DC: American Psychological Association.

Ruckstuhl, S., & Friman, P. C. (2002). *Evaluating the Vibrating Urine Alarm: A study*

of Effectiveness, Social Validity, and Path to Continence. Paper presented at the 36th annual convention of the Association for Advancement of Behavior Therapy, Reno, NV.

Rusch, F. R., & Kazdin, A. E. (1981). Toward a methodology of withdrawal designs for the assessment of response maintenance. *Journal of Applied Behavior Analysis, 14,* 131–140.

Russo, D. C., & Koegel, R. L. (1977). A method for integrating an autistic child into a normal public school classroom. *Journal of Applied Behavior Analysis, 10,* 579–590.

Ryle, G. (1949). *The Concept of Mind.* Chicago: University of Chicago Press.

Sajwaj, T. E., & Dillon, A. (1977). Complexities of an "elementary" behavior modification procedure: Differential adult attention used for children's behavior disorders. In B. C. Etzel, J. M. LeBlanc, & D. M. Baer (Eds.), *New Developments in Behavioral Research: Theory, Methods and Application* (pp. 303–315). Hillsdale, NJ: Erlbaum.

Sajwaj, T. E., & Hedges, D. (1971). Functions of parental attention in an oppositional retarded boy. In *Proceedings of the 79th Annual Convention of the American Psychological Association* (pp. 697–698). Washington, DC: American Psychological Association.

Sajwaj, T. E., Twardosz, S., & Burke, M. (1972). Side effects of extinction procedures in a remedial preschool. *Journal of Applied Behavior Analysis, 5,* 163–175.

Sattler, J. M. (2002). *Assessment of children: Behavioral and clinical applications.* San Diego: Jerome M. Sattler.

Saunders, R. R., McEntee, J. E., & Saunders, M. D. (2005). Interaction of reinforcement schedules, a behavioral prosthesis, and work-related behavior in adults with mental retardation. *Journal of Applied Behavior Analysis, 38* (2), 163–176.

Savoy, C., & Beitel, P. (1996). Mental imagery for basketball. *International Journal of Sport Psychology, 27* (4), 454–462.

Schermerhor, J. R. (2004). *Organizational behavior assessment.* New York: John Wiley.

Schindele, R. (1981). Methodological problems in rehabilitation research. *International*

Journal of Rehabilitation Research, 4, 233–248.

Schumaker, J., & Sherman, J. A. (1970). Training generative verb usage by imitation and reinforcement procedure. *Journal of Applied Behavior Analysis, 3,* 273–287.

Schutte, R. C., & Hopkins, B. L. (1970). The effects of teacher attention following instructions in a kindergarten class. *Journal of Applied Behavior Analysis, 3,* 117–122.

Schwartz, M. S., & Andrasik, F. (Eds.) (2003). *Biofeedback: A Practitioners Guide* (3rd edition). New York: Guilford Press.

Schwarz, G. (1978). Estimating the dimension of a model. *Annals of Statistics, 6,* 461–464.

Segal, Z. V., Williams, J. M. G., & Teasdale, J. D. (2002). *Mindfulness-based Cognitive Therapy for Depression: A New Approach to Preventing Relapse.* New York: Guilford Press.

Shadish, W. R., Cook, T. D., & Campbell, D. T. (2001). *Experimental and Quasi-experimental Designs for Generalized Causal Inference.* Boston: Houghton Mifflin Company.

Shapiro, D. A., & Shapiro, D. (1983). Comparative therapy outcome research: Methodological implications of meta-analysis. *Journal of Consulting and Clinical Psychology, 51,* 42–53.

Shapiro, E. S., Kazdin, A. E., & McGonigle, J. J. (1982). Multiple-treatment interference in the simultaneous- or alternating-treatments design. *Behavioral Assessment, 4,* 105–115.

Shapiro, M. B. (1961). The single case in fundamental clinical psychological research. *British Journal of Medical Psychology, 34,* 255–263.

Shapiro, M. B. (1966). The single case in clinical-psychological research. *Journal of General Psychology, 74,* 3–23.

Shapiro, M. B. (1970). Intensive assessment of the single case: An inductive-deductive approach. In P. Mittler (Ed.), *Psychological Assessment of Mental and Physical Handicaps.* London: Methuen.

Shapiro, M. B., & Ravenette, A. T. (1959). A preliminary experiment of paranoid delusions. *Journal of Mental Science, 105,* 295–312.

Sheldrick, R. C., Kendall, P. C., & Heimberg, R. G. (2001). The clinical significance of treatments: A comparison of three treatments for conduct disordered children. *Clinical Psychology: Science and Practice, 8* (4), 418–430.

Shontz, F. C. (1965). *Research Methods in Personality.* New York: Appleton-Century-Crofts.

Shumway, R. H., & Stoffer, D. S. (2000). *Time series analysis and its applications.* New York: Springer.

Sideridis, G. D., & Greenwood, C. R. (1997). Is human behavior autocorrelated? An empirical analysis. *Journal of Behavioral Education, 7* (3), 273–293.

Sidman, M. (1960). *Tactics of Scientific Research: Evaluating Experimental Data in Psychology.* New York: Basic Books.

Sierra, V., Quera, V., & Solanas, A. (2000). Autocorrelation effect on type I error rate of Rvusky's R_n tests: A Monte Carlo study. *Psicologica, 21,* 91–114.

Singh, N. N., Dawson, J. H., & Gergory, P. R. (1980). Suppression of chronic hyperventilation using response contingent aromatic ammonia. *Behavior Therapy, 11,* 561–566.

Singh, N. N., Landrum, T. J., Ellis, C. R., & Donatelli, L. S. (1993). Effects of thioridazine and visual screening on stereotype and social behavior in individuals with mental retardation. *Research in Developmental Disabilities, 14* (3), 163–177.

Skiba, E. A., Pettigrew, E., & Alden, S. E. (1971). A behavioral approach to the control of thumbsucking in the classroom. *Journal of Applied Behavior Analysis, 4,* 121–125.

Skinner, B. F. (1938). *The Behavior of Organisms.* New York: Appleton-Century-Crofts.

Skinner, B. F. (1953). *Science and Human Behavior.* New York: Macmillan.

Skinner, B. F. (1966a). Invited address to the Pavlovian Society of America, Boston.

Skinner, B. F. (1966b). Operant behavior. In W. K. Honig (Ed.), *Operant Behavior: Areas of Research and Application* (pp. 12–32). New York: Appleton-Century-Crofts.

Sloane, H. N., Johnston, M. K., & Bijou, S. W. (1967). Successive modification of aggressive behavior and aggressive fantasy play by management of contingencies.

Journal of Child Psychology and Psychiatry, 8, 217–226.

Smeets, P. M. (1970). Withdrawal of social reinforcers as a means of controlling rumination and regurgitation in a profoundly retarded person. *Raining School Bulletin, 67,* 158–163.

Smeets, P. M., Lancioni, G. E., Ball, T. S., & Oliva, D. S. (1985). Shaping self-initiated toileting in infants. *Journal of Applied Behavior Analysis, 18,* 303–308

Smith, M. L., & Glass, G. V. (1977). Meta-analysis of psychotherapy outcome studies. *American Psychologist, 32,* 752–760.

Soenksen, D., & Alper, S. (2006). Teaching a young child to appropriately gain attention of peers using a social story intervention. *Focus on Autism and other Developmental Disabilities, 21* (1), 36–44.

Sowers, J., Rusch, F R., Connis, R. T., & Cummings, L. T. (1980). Teaching mentally retarded adults to time-manage in a vocational setting. *Journal of Applied Behavior Analysis, 13,* 119–128.

Steketee, G. & Barlow, D. H. (2002). Obsessive-compulsive disorder. In D. H. Barlow (Ed.), *Anxiety and its Disorders* (2nd ed.). New York: Guilford Press.

Stilson, D. W. (1966). *Probability and Statistics in Psychological Research and Theory.* San Francisco: Holden-Day.

Stone, A. A, Broderick, J. E., Schwartz, J. E., Shiffman, S., Litcher-Kelly, L., & Calvanese, P. (2003). Intensive momentary reporting of pain with an electronic diary: Reactivity, compliance, and patient satisfaction. *Pain, 104* (1–2), 343–51.

Stricker, G., & Trierweiler, S. (1995). The local clinical scientist: A bridge between science and practice. *American Psychologist, 50,* 995–1002.

Striefel, S., Bryan, K. S., & Aikens, D. A. (1974). Transfer of stimulus control from motor to verbal stimuli. *Journal of Applied Behavior Analysis, 7,* 123–135.

Striefel, S., & Wetherby, B. (1973). Instruction following behavior of a retarded child and its controlling stimuli. *Journal of Applied Behavior Analysis, 6,* 663–670.

Strupp, H. H., & Hadley, S. W. (1979). Specific vs. nonspecific factors in psychotherapy. *Archives of General Psychiatry, 36,* 1125–1137.

Strupp, H. H., & Luborsky, L. (Eds.) (1962). *Research in Psychotherapy (Vol. 2).* Washington, DC: American Psychological Association.

Substance Abuse and Mental Health Administration (2003). SAMHSA agency overview. Retrieved January 9, 2004, from www.samsha.gov/about/about.html.

Suen, H. K. (1988). Agreement, reliability accuracy, and validity: Toward a clarification. *Behavior Assessment, 10,* 343–366.

Suen, H. K., Ary, D., & Covalt, W. C. (1990). A decision tree approach to selecting an appropriate observational reliability index. *Journal of Psychopathology and Behavioral Assessment, 12,* 359–363.

Tarbox, R., Williams, L., & Friman, P. C. (2004). Extended diaper wearing: Effects on continence in and out of the diaper. *Journal of Applied Behavior Analysis, 37,* 97–101.

Taylor, T. E., & Lupker, S. J. (2007). Sequential effects in time perception. *Psychonomic Bulletin & Review, 14* (1), 70–74.

Thomas, D. R., Becker, W. C., & Armstrong, M. (1968). Production and elimination of disruptive classroom behavior by systematically varying teachers' behavior. *Journal of Applied Behavior Analysis, 1,* 35–45.

Thomas, D. R., Nielsen, T. J., Kuypers, D. S., & Becker, W. C. (1968). Social reinforcement and remedial instruction in the elimination of a classroom behavior problem. *Journal of Special Education, 2,* 291–305.

Thomas, J. D., & Adams, M. A. (1971). Problems in teacher use of selected behaviour modification techniques in the classroom. *New Zealand Journal of Educational Studies, 6,* 151–165.

Thomas, J. L., Howe, J., Gaudet, A., & Brantley, P. J. (2001). Behavioral treatment of chronic psychogenic polydipsia with hyponatremia: A unique case of polydipsia in a primary care patient with intractable hiccups. *Journal of Behavior Therapy and Experimental Psychiatry, 32,* 241–250.

Thorne, F. C. (1947). The clinical method in science. *American Psychologist, 2,* 161–166.

Tiger, J. H., Hanley, G. P., & Heal, N. A. (2006). The effectiveness of and preschoolers' preferences for variations of multiple-schedule arrangements. *Journal of Applied Behavior Analysis, 39* (4), 475–488.

Todman, J., & Dugard, P. (1999). Accessible randomization tests for single-case and small-n experimental designs in AAC research. *Augment Alternative Communication, 15*, 69–82.

Toothaker, L. E., Banz, M., Noble, C., Camp, J., & Davis, D. (1983). N = 1 designs: The failure of ANOVA-based tests. *Journal of Educational Statistics, 8*, 289–309.

Truax, C. B. (1966). Reinforcement and non-reinforcement in Rogerian psychotherapy *Journal of Abnormal Psychology, 71*, 1–9.

Truax, C. B., & Carkhuff, R. R. (1965). Experimental manipulation of therapeutic conditions. *Journal of Consulting Psychology, 29*, 119–124.

Tsay, R. S. (2002). Time series and forecasting: Brief history and future research. In A. E. Raftery, M. A. Tanner, & M. T. Wells (Eds.), *Statistics in the 21st Century.* New York: Chapman & Hall/CRC.

Turner, S. M., Hersen, M., Bellack, A. S., Andrasik, F., & Capparell, H. V. (1980). Behavioral and pharmacological treatment of obsessive-compulsive disorders. *Journal of Nervous & Mental Disease, 168*, 651–657.

Twardosz, S., & Sajwaj, T. E. (1972). Multiple effects of a procedure to increase sitting in a hyperactive, retarded boy. *Journal of Applied Behavior Analysis, 5*, 73–78.

Ullmann, L. P., & Krasner, L. (Eds.) (1965). *Case Studies in Behavior Modification.* New York: Holt, Rinehart and Winston.

Ulman, J. D., & Sulzer-Azaroff, B. (1975). Multielement baseline design in educational research. In E. Ramp & G. Semb (Eds.), *Behavior Analysis: Areas of Research and Application* (pp. 377–391). Englewood Cliffs, NJ: Prentice-Hall.

Underwood, B. J. (1957). *Psychological Research.* New York: Appleton-Century-Crofts.

Van Hasselt, V. B., & Hersen, M. (1981). Applications of single-case designs to research with visually impaired individuals. *Journal of Visual Impairment and Blindness, 75*, 359–362.

Van Hasselt, V. B., Hersen, M., Kazdin, A. E., Simon, J., & Mastantuono, A. K. (1983). Social skills training for blind adolescents. *Journal of Visual Impairment and Blindness, 7.5*, 199–203.

Varni, J. W., Russo, D. C., & Cataldo, M. F. (1978). Assessment and modification of delusional speech in an 11-year-old child: A comparative analysis of behavior therapy and stimulant drug effects. *Journal of Behavior Therapy and Experimental Psychiatry, 9*, 377–380.

Veenstra, M. (1971). Behavior modification in the home with the mother as the experimenter: The effect of differential reinforcement on sibling negative response rates. *Child Development, 42*, 2079–2083.

Velicer, W. F., & Harrop, J. W. (1983). The reliability and accuracy of the time-series model identification. *Evaluation Review, 7*, 551–560.

Wade, W. A., Treat, T. A., & Stuart, G. L. (1998). Transporting an empirically supported treatment for panic disorder to a service clinic setting: A benchmarking strategy. *Journal of Consulting and Clinical Psychology, 66*, 231–239.

Wahler, R. G. (1968, April). *Behavior Therapy for Oppositional Children: Love is not Enough.* Paper presented at the meeting of the Eastern Psychological Association, Washington, DC.

Wahler, R. G. (1969). Oppositional children: A quest for parental reinforcement control. *Journal of Applied Behavior Analysis, 2*, 159–170.

Wahler, R. G. (1969). Setting generality: Some specific and general effects of child behavior therapy. *Journal of Applied Behavior Analysis, 2*, 239–246.

Wahler, R. G., Berland, R. M., & Coe, T. D. (1979). Generalization processes in child behavior change. In B. B. Lahey & A. E. Kazdin (Eds.), *Advances in clinical child psychology* (pp. 36–72). New York: Plenum.

Wahler, R. G., & Pollio, H. R. (1968). Behavior and insight: A case study in behavior therapy. *Journal of Experimental Research in Personality, 3*, 45–56.

Wahler, R. G., Sperling, K. A., Thomas, M. R., Teeter, N. C., & Luper, H. L. (1970). Modification of childhood stuttering: Some response-response relationships.

Journal of Experimental Child Psychology, 9, 411–428.

Wahler, R. G., Winkel, G. H., Peterson, R. F., & Morrison, D. C. (1965). Mothers as behavior therapists for their own children. *Behaviour Research and Therapy,* 3, 113–124.

Waite, W. W., & Osborne, J. G. (1972). Sustained behavioral contrast in children. *Journal of the Experimental Analysis of Behavior,* 18, 113–117.

Walker, H. M., & Buckely, N. K. (1968). The use of positive reinforcement in conditioning attending behavior. *Journal of Applied Behavior Analysis,* 1, 245–250.

Walker, H. M., & Lev, J. (1953). *Statistical Inference.* New York: Holt, Rinehart and Winston.

Wallace, C. J., Boone, S. E., Donahue, C. P., & Foy, D. W. (1985). The chronically mentally disabled: Independent living skills training. In D. H. Barlow (Ed.), *Clinical Handbook of Psychological Disorders: A Step-by-step Treatment Manual* (1st ed.), New York: Guilford Press. pp. 462–501.

Wallace, C. J., & Elder, J. P. (1980). Statistics to evaluate measurement accuracy and treatment effects in single subject research designs. In M. Hersen, R. M. Eisler, & P. M. Monti (Eds.), *Progress in Behavior Modification,* (Vol. 10, pp. 40–82). New York: Academic Press.

Wallenstein, M. B., & Nock, M. K. (2007). Physical exercise for the treatment of non-suicidal self-injury: Evidence from a single-case study. *American Journal of Psychiatry,* 164, 350–351.

Ward, M. H., & Baker, B. L. (1968). Reinforcement therapy in the classroom. *Journal of Applied Behavior Analysis,* 1, 323–328.

Warnes, E., & Allen, K. D. (2005). Biofeedback treatment of paradoxical vocal fold motion and respiratory distress in an adolescent girl. *Journal of Applied Behavior Analysis,* 38 (4), 529–532.

Watson, J. B., & Rayner, R. (1920). Conditioned emotional reactions. *Journal of Experimental Psychology,* 3, 1–14.

Watson, P. J., & Workman, E. A. (1981). The non-concurrent multiple baseline across-individuals design: An extension of the traditional multiple baseline design.

Journal of Behavior Therapy and Experimental Psychiatry, 12, 257–259.

Watson, T. S., Allen, S. J., & Allen, K. D. (1993). Ventricular fold dysphonia: Application of biofeedback technology to a rare voice disorder. *Behavior Therapy,* 24, 439–446.

Watson, T. S., & Sterling, H. E. (1998). Brief functional analysis and treatment of a vocal tic. *Journal of Applied Behavior Analysis,* 31, 471–474.

Wearn, J. T., & Sturgis, C. C. (1919). Studies on epinephrine: I. Effects on injection of epinephrine in soldiers with "irritable fear". *Archives of Internal Medicine,* 24, 247–268

Weiss, B., Caron, A., Ball, S., Tapp, J., Johnson, M., & Weisz, J. R. (2005). Iatrogenic effects of group treatment for antisocial youths. *Journal of Consulting and Clinical Psychology,* 73 (6), 1036–1044.

Wenzl, T. G., Schneider, S., Scheele, F., Silny, J., Heimann, G., & Skopnik, H. (2003). Effects of thickened feeding on gastroesophageal reflux in infants: A placebo-controlled crossover study using intraluminal impedance. *Pediatrics, 111* (4 Pt 1), 355–359.

West, S. G., & Hepworth, J. T. (1991). Statistical issues in the study of temporal data: Daily experiences. *Journal of Personality, 59* (3), 609–661.

Wheeler, J. G., Christensen, A., Jacobson, A., & Neil, S. (2001). Couple Distress. In D. H. Barlow (Ed.), *Clinical Handbook of Psychological Disorders: A Step-by-step Treatment Manual* (3rd ed.). New York: Guilford Press, pp. 609–630.

White, O. R. (1971). A glossary of behavioral terminology. Champaign, IL: Research Press.

Wilder, D. A., Chen, L., Atwell, J., Pritchard, J., & Weinstein, P. (2006). Brief functional analysis and treatment of tantrums associated with transitions in preschool children. *Journal of Applied Behavior Analysis,* 39 (1), 103–107.

Wilkinson, L., & the APA Task Force on Statistical Inference. (1999). Statistical methods in psychology journals: Guidelines and explanations. *American Psychologist, 54,* 594–604.

Williams, C. D. (1959). Case report: The elimination of tantrum behavior by extinction procedures. *Journal of Abnormal and Social Psychology, 59*, 269.

Williams, E. A., & Gottman, J. M. (1999). *A user's Guide to the Gottman-Williams Time-series Analysis Computer Programs for Social Scientists.* New York: Cambridge University Press.

Wilson, G. T., & Rachman, S. J. (1983). Meta-analysis and the evaluation of psychotherapy outcome limitations and liabilities. *Journal of Consulting and Clinical Psychology, 51*, 54–64.

Wilson, T. G. (in press). Manual-based treatment: Evolution and evaluation.

Wincze, J. P. (1982). Assessment of sexual disorders. *Behavioral Assessment, 4*, 257–271.

Wincze, J. P., & Lange, J. D. (1981). Assessment of sexual behavior. In D. H. Barlow (Ed.), *Behavioral Assessment of Adult Disorders* (pp. 301–329). New York: Guilford Press.

Wincze, J. P., Leitenberg, H., & Agras, W. S. (1972). The effects of token reinforcement and feedback on the delusional verbal behavior of chronic paranoid schizophrenics. *Journal of Applied Behavior Analysis, 5*, 247–262.

Wolf, M. M. (1978). Social validity: The case for subjective measurement or how applied behavior analysis is finding its heart. *Journal of Applied Behavioral Analysis, 11*, 203–215.

Wolpe, J. (1958). *Psychotherapy by Reciprocal Inhibition.* Stanford: Stanford University Press.

Wolpe, J. (1976). *Theme and variations: A Behavior Therapy Casebook.* Elmsford, New York: Pergamon Press.

Wood, L. F., & Jacobson, N. S. (1985). Marital distress. In D. H. Barlow (Ed.), *Clinical Handbook of Psychological Disorders: A Step-by-step Treatment Manual* (1st ed.), New York: Guilford Press, pp. 344–416.

Woodard, C., Groden, J., Goodwin, M., & Bodfish, J. (2007). A placebo double-blind pilot study of dextromethorphan for problematic behaviors in children with autism. *Autism, 11* (1), 29–41.

Woods, D. W., Watson, T. S., Wolfe, E., Twohig, M. P., & Friman, P. C. (2001). Analyzing the influence of tic-related talk on vocal and motor tics in children with Tourette's syndrome. *Journal of Applied Behavior Analysis, 34*, 353–356.

Wright, J., Clayton, J., & Edgar, C. L. (1970). Behavior modification with low-level mental retardates. *Psychological Record, 20*, 465471.

Yates, A. J. (1970). *Behavior Therapy.* New York: Wiley.

Yaffee, R., & McGee, M. (2000). *Introduction to Time Series Analysis and Forecasting: With Applications of SAS and SPSS.* San Diego: Academic Press.

Yawkey, I. D. (1971). Conditioning independent work behavior in reading with seven-year-old children in a regular early childhood classroom. *Child Study Journal, 2*, 23–34.

Yule G. (1927). On a method of investigating periodicities in disturbed series, with special reference to wolfer's sunspot numbers. *Philos Trans Roy Soc, A226*: 267–298.

Zeilberger, J., Sampen, S. E., & Sloane, H. N. (1968). Modification of a child's problem behaviors in the home with the mother as therapist. *Journal of Applied Behavior Analysis, 1*, 47–53.

Zilbergeld, B., & Evans, M. B. (1980). The inadequacy of Masters and Johnson. *Psychology Today, 14*, 28–43.

Zimbardo, P. (2007). *The Lucifer effect: Understanding How Good People Turn Evil.* New York: Random House.

Zimmerman, E. H., & Zimmerman, J. (1962). The alteration of behavior in a special classroom situation. *Journal of the Experimental Analysis of Behavior, 5*, 59–60.

SUBJECT INDEX

NAME INDEX